MACROECONOMICS

ADVANCED MACROECONOMICS
Beyond IS/LM

Derek Leslie
Senior Lecturer in Economics
Manchester University

McGRAW-HILL BOOK COMPANY

London · New York · St Louis · San Francisco · Auckland · Bogotá · Caracas
Hamburg · Lisbon · Madrid · Mexico · Milan · Montreal · New Delhi · Panama
Paris · San Juan · São Paulo · Singapore · Sydney · Tokyo · Toronto

Published by
McGRAW-HILL Book Company Europe
SHOPPENHANGERS ROAD, MAIDENHEAD, BERKSHIRE, SL6 2QL, ENGLAND
Telephone 0628 23432
Fax 0628 770224

British Library Cataloguing in Publication Data
Leslie, Derek
 Advanced Macroeconomics: Beyond IS/LM
 I. Title
 339

 ISBN 0-07-707724-5

Library of Congress Cataloging-in-Publication Data
Leslie, Derek
  Advanced macroeconomics: Beyond IS/LM/Derek Leslie.
    p.   cm.
  Includes bibliographical references and index.
  ISBN 0-07-707724-5
  1. Macroeconomics.   I. Title.
 HB172.5.L47   1993
339--dc20

1234 CUP 9543

Typeset by P&R Typesetters Ltd, Salisbury, Wilts. (UK)
and printed and bound in Great Britain at the University Press, Cambridge.

For
Annie, Declan, Ben, Jonathan, Oswald and Zachary

CONTENTS

PREFACE

One of the greatest pleasures of writing a text such as this comes from the large number of colleagues who are prepared to give up their valuable time to read one's humble efforts. Among those I have to acknowledge for their considerable help are Mike Artis, Chris Birchenhall, David Blackaby, Robin Bladen-Hovell, Mark Clayton, Kenneth Clark, Bill Farebrother, Paul Madden, William Peters, Helena Scott (who also typed a considerable portion of the manuscript—I did the equations!), Ian Steedman, Akira Takamusa, Nick Weaver, and finally George Zis who took it upon himself to read the whole manuscript and to redraft the text at many points. To all of these, many thanks—and apologies if not every suggestion was followed up. I alone am responsible for what remains. Thanks also to Brendan Lambon, for encouraging this project, and to Lavinia Porter and Alex Whyte, for their dedicated work in honing my manuscript into the finished product.

Last, but not least, I must acknowledge the distinguished exemplar of rational expectations, Thomas Sargent of the University of Wisconsin. Much of the material for this book, particularly Chapters 1, 3 and 4, is derived from his work. Indeed, when I was given the task of lecturing third-year macroeconomics at Manchester University, the course quickly became a case of trying to understand Sargent. In many ways, this book is the result of my clumsy efforts to understand just a very small part of what he has written and teach it to undergraduates. If this book stimulates readers to explore further, I shall be well satisfied.

Finally, some words on chapter structure and how to approach the book. To make the book easier to read, there are no footnotes. Secondly, I have avoided, as much as possible, citing references in the text. The book is intended to instruct students how to *do* economics rather than be a survey of a large number of articles. At the end of each chapter I give a selected and limited bibliography, indicating where the chapter material is derived from. My intention is to explain the issues to the readers and to express my own opinions where I think it is appropriate, rather than to say who said what and when.

No doubt, some might find the book hard going in places; no one claims that to acquire, hopefully worthwhile, knowledge is always easy. My advice is not to simply 'read' the book but to keep a pencil and paper at one's side and carefully work through the equations as one reads. I have deliberately left it to the reader to deduce some of the steps, but rest assured these manipulations are not enormous, just sufficient to stretch the alert readers and keep them on their toes! The process of becoming a professional economist must involve 'sweating the action' somewhat and not just passively absorbing information without ever putting pen or pencil to paper. To this end, each chapter contains some suggested essay topics and a set of exercises. Answers to the exercises are given at the end of the text.

INTRODUCTION

This book is intended as suitable for an advanced third-year undergraduate or introductory graduate course. The typical student should have completed a second-level course in macroeconomics and have confronted some of the variants of the IS/LM framework, introducing the open economy, wealth effects, the government financing constraint and so on. The task of this introduction is to explain why it is both useful and interesting to explore 'beyond' the IS/LM model.

A central feature of this book is the issue of time. Economic agents have a memory of the past, are aware of the present and can conceive of the future. Because outcomes such as the level of output, the inflation rate, the exchange rate and so on are the results of purposeful actions by economic agents, it should be obvious that the most general macroeconomics should be based on these three elements of time. A proper economics should, therefore, start with the presumption that the current value of an economic variable is driven by past events, present happenings and what it is believed might happen in the future. One should then build down, if it can be justified that one or more of the three elements of time can be excluded from explaining a particular economic process.

The central problem with the IS/LM approach is that it starts with one element of time—current values driven by current events—and then tries to build up. The IS/LM model then resembles a stretched and endlessly modified version of an aircraft, which never does its job properly because it can never overcome the link with its basic design flaw. A classic example of this was the attempt in the late sixties and early seventies to attach the permanent income hypothesis—a dynamic, forward-looking concept—to the IS/LM model. The whole exercise, though technically admirable, proved to be somewhat fruitless and has quietly been forgotten.

There is a dilemma when trying to teach an introductory economics course. To make the material accessible, it is necessary to simplify. The standard method is to make economics timeless and then to add to this later; though, in fact, most students never develop beyond the simplistic timeless mode of thought. This structure has a tendency to brainwash all of us, who in modelling economic processes are predisposed towards retracing their upbringing. 'Let's formulate this as a static equilibrium model and now let's add bits here and bits there.' The IS/LM model as a pedagogical device suffers because of its static straitjacket. Agents have no memory and rudimentary ideas about the future. Although the IS/LM will remain the 'core' macroeconomic paradigm, useful for many purposes, there are alternative ways of looking at macroeconomic problems which give a less dominant role for the IS/LM core model.

This book tries to encourage students to think dynamically from the outset. When government policy is mentioned, it is not just current policy that matters but beliefs about the whole future path of that policy that count. The past record of how well governments have kept to their promises also enters the picture because this will, in part, drive future beliefs. The standard textbook IS/LM model is not well adapted to conceptualizing these questions, let alone answering them.

It is the rational expectations revolution that provides the great technological breakthrough and it is increasingly becoming a standard pedagogical device supplementing other paradigms. Rational expectations enable us to take an eclectic view of time and to take account of its three dimensions—the past, the present and the future—directly. There are undoubtedly considerable objections to the rational expectations hypothesis and it is an open question whether agents always *do* form their expectations in this way, if at all. Many economists brought up in the traditional liturgy of Keynesian macroeconomics might listen somewhat enviously to those New Classical evangelicals enjoying themselves preaching the new creed of rational expectations, but who cannot quite as yet bring themselves to knock on the door and join in the song. The task is to communicate to the reader in an accessible way what some of these ideas are all about.

The idea behind rational expectations is disarmingly simple, though one should not be deceived by this because, when explored more deeply, the mathematical complexities are considerable (Chapter 4 should make this clear!). Consider the simplest possible economic model:

$$Y_t = \alpha + gX_t. \tag{1}$$

The actual value of Y at time t is determined by a constant α plus g times the actual value of X at time t. Now in many economic problems we are often interested in the forecast or the expectation of Y_t. For example, stock prices are driven by the expectation of future dividends. Money wage inflation is driven by the expectation of future inflation. The demand for real cash balances also depends on the expected inflation rate. Indeed, macroeconomics could almost be defined as the study of expectations.

Denote a forecast of Y_t as $_{t-1}Y_t$. (This means the forecast of Y_t made at time $t-1$.) Now $_{t-1}Y_t$ is any old forecast of Y_t. Rational expectations is the claim that this forecast is made in a particular way. The method is so direct and so obvious that it is surprising that the idea has only recently been explored and exploited.

Denote the rational expectations forecast as $E_{t-1}Y_t$, to distinguish it from $_{t-1}Y_t$. The rational expectations forecast is the prediction of the economic model that determines Y_t. Thus:

$$E_{t-1}Y_t = \alpha + gE_{t-1}X_t. \tag{2}$$

The forecast of Y_t is simply α plus g times the forecast of X_t, based on the information available at time $t - 1$. That's all there is to it, but it is really quite amazing the radical consequences for macroeconomics if the hypothesis is acceptable. Economic models are required to do double duty; if there is a theory for the *value* of an economic variable, it must also encompass a theory for the *forecast* of that variable, which is simply the prediction of the theory contingent on the available information set at the time the forecast is made.

Rational expectations are, therefore, just a consistency requirement in economic modelling—indeed, one of the earliest writers on the subject, Sir Alan Walters, dubbed the idea 'consistent expectations'. In many ways it is a pity that the Walters' nomenclature 'consistent expectations' did not stick, since it is rather more neutral than the term 'rational'. Rational, in everyday parlance, has the meaning of sensible, with the connotation that any other mode of thinking is, *ipso facto*, somewhat inferior. However, in its economic usage, rational expectations are only rational with respect to a *particular* economic model. The actual model itself could, by common consent, be completely daft yet the expectations mechanism still rational. Thus Y_t could refer to the inflation rate and X_t to the number of fleas on a parson's nose. The rational expectations forecast is simply the consistency requirement that the expected inflation rate is related to the expected number of fleas on a parson's nose. Rational expectations are only as good as the model they are derived from, although believers in rational expectations would argue that 'poor' models, through a process of ruthless Darwinian selection, would soon be discarded.

The rational expectations forecast error is obviously:

$$Y_t - E_{t-1}Y_t = g[X_t - E_{t-1}X_t]. \tag{3}$$

The forecast error need not always be zero and, in general, will not be. There is no reason why X_t and $E_{t-1}X_t$ should be the same. Perfect foresight is a special case of rational expectations in which there are never any forecast errors, that is when $E_{t-1}Y_t = Y_t$ always. For example, let Eq. (1) be modified to:

$$Y_t = \alpha + gX_{t-1}. \tag{4}$$

In this case the rational expectations forecast of Y_t would exhibit perfect foresight with respect to the model, since the forecast $E_{t-1}Y_t$ would be Eq. (4) once again. $E_{t-1}X_{t-1}$ obviously equals X_{t-1} in this case.

Rational expectations are not the only way of modelling expectations and could hardly be so, because the idea only began to filter through the profession from about the early 1970s. Prior to that, expectations were commonly modelled extrapolatively, though some imaginative empirical work used direct evidence gleaned by actually asking people their opinions. An extrapolative predictor has the property that the forecast $_{t-1}Y_t$ is based on past values of the actual behaviour of Y_t. Denoting the extrapolative forecast as Y_t^*, then:

$$Y_t^* = a_1 Y_{t-1} + a_2 Y_{t-2} + a_3 Y_{t-3} + \cdots \tag{5}$$

where the a_1, a_2, etc., represent appropriate weights. A frequently used scheme is a special case of Eq. (5) known as first-order adaptive expectations:

$$Y_t^* = (1 - \lambda)(Y_{t-1} + \lambda Y_{t-2} + \lambda^2 Y_{t-3} + \cdots) \tag{6}$$

which is characterized by a single parameter λ ($O \le \lambda \le 1$) in the above geometrically declining way. Both Eq. (5) and its special case Eq. (6) are *ad hoc* and have little theoretical basis. The fact that such schemes are *ad hoc* does not necessarily make them wrong. It may be that simple rules-of-thumb are preferred even though they are known to give poor answers in some situations. Most of us do not aspire to be perfect drivers, but merely to drive well enough to avoid catastrophe on most journeys.

Rational expectations are appealing because they are inherently logical. They are particularly appealing to economic theorists, who are ideologically hostile to the idea of individual behaviour not being based on systematic optimizing behaviour. Voltaire said that if God did not exist it would have been necessary to invent him. With rational expectations, it might be said that even if they could be definitively shown not to exist, economists would nevertheless continue to assume they held.

With rational expectations it is a case of 'putting one's money where one's mouth is'. If the model is supposed to be true, then one should have the courage of one's convictions and use the model for forecasts as well. A further argument in their favour emphasized in this book is that big issues can be directly tackled, where past values and future expectations of exogenous variables appear in an entirely natural way. For example, it is not such a large step from Eq. (1) to a model of the type:

$$Y_t = \alpha + b_1 Y_{t-1} + b_2 E_t Y_{t+1} + a X_t. \tag{7}$$

This is a second-order difference equation in Y_t, since it involves both a lagged value Y_{t-1} and the rational expectations forecast $E_t Y_{t+1}$. (Note that in this case the forecast of interest is based on information at time t and it is useful to adopt the nomenclature of associating a time subscript with E to denote this. The model context should make clear the point from which available information is to be dated.) The solution to such problems is explored more deeply in Chapter 4, but the following intuition is helpful for the argument to be made here. Since expectations are held to be rational in Eq. (7), if an expression for $E_t Y_{t+1}$ was written down, this would involve both $E_t Y_{t+2}$ and the forcing variable $E_t X_{t+1}$. By a process of continuous forward iteration, it is clear that Y_t would, in part, be determined by all future expected values of the forcing variable. Similarly, an expression for Y_{t-1} would involve Y_{t-2} and X_{t-1}. A process of infinite regress would, therefore, involve all past values of X_t. One representation consistent with Eq. (7) then turns out to be:

$$Y_t = \alpha_0 + a_1 \sum_{i=0}^{\infty} \lambda_1^i X_{t-i} + a_2 \sum_{i=1}^{\infty} \lambda_2^i E_t X_{t+i} \tag{8}$$

where α_0, a_1, a_2, λ_1 and λ_2 are parameters of the problem.

Equation (8) precisely articulates the idea of an economic variable being driven by the present, past history and expected future history of the forcing variable. (X could also represent a vector of such variables.) It is about the most general view possible and introspection supports the view that this is how many economic variables are actually determined. Introductory static macroeconomics is just the special case Eq. (1) version of Eq. (8). 'Traditional' dynamics is just the backward-looking representation which sets $\lambda_2 = 0$. Many rational expectations models are also special cases of Eq. (8) in which the umbilical cord to the past is completely slashed with λ_1 set equal to zero; the solutions in these cases are purely forward-looking. It may be that representations similar to Eq. (8) are derivable from models that do not mention the assumption of rational expectations, but the point is that rational expectations give an immediate leap into a rich and fascinating dynamic structure.

Perhaps the most telling argument in favour of studying rational expectations is the one based on the idea of what must happen when history comes to an end, when all arguments have been settled and there is complete unanimity of view as to how the economy works. History comes to an end when everything of importance is known to everyone. In this case, rational expectations are bound to win because of their irrefutable basis in logic, and any other way of forming expectations would be seen to be an inferior forecasting device.

Unlike a pure science, economics has a peculiar and unique property—namely, the fact that theorists and agents interact. Suppose a pure scientist is trying to explain why a particular natural phenomenon occurs. That person develops a theory and will, undoubtedly, expend some time and effort championing that theory and explaining why it is superior to others on offer. Economists try to explain behaviour in exactly the same way, and because economics affects everyone the proselytizing role is often very public and acrimonious, but it is actually no different from other sciences. The crucial difference is that, unlike natural phenomena, the behaviour of agents which the theorist tries to explain can be modified (and often is) by a knowledge of the theories on offer.

The proselytizing role of economists can thus 'contaminate' the very behaviour that they seek to explain. For example, the last 25 years can be regarded as the story of the eclipse of simple Keynesianism by Monetarism. City experts, television pundits and other important opinion-formers now pay close attention to monetary indicators and many base their decisions upon what these monetary indicators say. 'M3 up more than target, stock market falls', was a familiar headline of the early 1980s. Behaviour is modified not because agents know how the world works but because they have been persuaded that particular variables have a peculiar and significant influence.

Now, with the New Classical brand of Monetarism, it turns out that the influential Friedmanite brand of 'traditional' Monetarism was wrong after all. The proselytizing role of economists begins all over again. In explaining the past, it then becomes (or rather, it should become) difficult for rational expectationalists to maintain that agents always acted according to the now correct present model on offer. If that was so, why is so much time spent showing the incorrectness of other paradigms? Once it is recognized that, in economics, behaviour and professional economists who write about the subject are not independent of each other, the philosophical complexities are enormous, not least the question of expectation formation based on the knowledge of an economic model.

The end of history is the optimistic (or perhaps rather depressing) view that one day all these theoretical battles will have been settled and for every human action there will be a relevant theory, correct and agreed upon in every detail. Suppose at the end of history it turns out that agents form their expectations according to first-order adaptive expectations. Before the end of history such a strategy might have been perfectly sensible. After all, in the 1960s agents were told that that is how they actually *did* form their expectations, by large numbers of highly respected economists. It might also have been sensible as a risk-averting strategy. Observing the extreme disagreement among theorists, an agent would conclude that, although adaptive expectations are certainly wrong, in using them one was probably less likely to be wrong than if one had chosen rationality and the wrong model. At the end of history, agents who hold adaptive expectations are now open to persuasion into a different way of thinking. If they are consistent optimizers, rational expectations must triumph because any other method will lead to inferior forecasts with the probability of systematic errors. Agents would be better off with the rational forecast and will be persuaded to act accordingly. The only reasonable argument against using rational forecasts would be that the expense of computing them outweighed the losses from an inaccurate yet easily computed rule of thumb.

However, the relevant question is not how people will eventually form their expectations, but how they act now. The present state of the revolution may be the first tentative steps towards the beginning of the end of history, but there is still a long way to go. If expectations are formed in a suboptimal, extrapolative way, then that is how they should be modelled. The world cannot be re-invented because we do not happen to like the one we presently live in. Many eminent economists simply do not accept the hypothesis of rational expectations and this scepticism commands a degree of cross-party support. Robert Solow and Milton Friedman, both Nobel laureates, probably do not agree on most things, but they both do not accept the rational expectations hypothesis.

The defence of paying close attention to rational expectations is therefore three-fold. First, as a means to an end, enabling us to reach the dynamic heart of macroeconomics and forcing us to confront issues that are known to be important but which other modelling frameworks cannot readily accommodate. Secondly, rational expectations, unlike other promising ideas, will not disappear. It is the way the world must eventually end up. Finally, some of the implications of rational expectations are just too interesting and unusual to ignore.

Another argument is to withdraw from the battlefield somewhat and simply claim that rational expectations is prescriptive rather than descriptive. It shows how a rational agent would behave, where rational here means consistent with a set of assumptions about optimizing behaviour. The appropriate analogy is with the expected utility maximization hypothesis (discussed in Chapter 6, incidentally), which again is a description of rational behaviour rather than actual behaviour. There is considerable accumulated evidence suggesting that agents do not in fact behave in ways consistent with expected utility maximization, yet this has in no way diminished the popularity of the framework, not least among those who exhibit the most hostility towards rational expectations. We are describing 'ideal types' and not necessarily reality, whatever that is.

Much of the literature on rational expectations is obscure, highly technical and somewhat inaccessible even to highly trained professional economists. There is a danger of becoming so absorbed in the detail, viewing it as a technocratic mathematical puzzle, that one loses out on the broader picture. The aim of this book is to try to indicate some of the technicalities, but without losing sight of the wood for the trees. Not every problem is reducible to an economic dimension and much of the rational expectations literature of the New Classical variety has a more or less open political agenda. Thus, even if one is persuaded by the New Classical arguments, this still does not mean accepting the policy advice that follows from such arguments. The benefits may be marginal compared to the cost of a loss of fundamental freedoms which are intrinsically 'good'. Another of the book's themes is that we should cease the illusion that 'proper' economics must be purely scientific, composed only of 'is' statements and no 'ought' statements and with little or no interface with the political dimension. Hopefully, readers will become more aware of what the issues are and be able to make up their own minds or suspend judgement and research further.

PLAN OF THE BOOK

Chapter 1 is mainly about budget deficits and the government financing constraint. The purpose here is to make the reader think in a dynamic way from the outset. It is the whole expected future history of government finances that is important and not just how any current deficit is financed. This leads to a discussion of the National Debt and the arguments in favour of indexation if credible inflation promises are to be made. It strongly signals the themes that will recur in subsequent chapters. The analytical framework is adapted to discuss some issues in personal debt finance. It is shown that the government financing constraint and the 'personal' financing constraint raise very similar issues, in particular how inflation can introduce somewhat artificial distortions into both.

Chapter 2 raises the issue of whether there is an optimal size to the government or state sector. Does too large a government kill the goose that pays the bills, namely the private sector? The purpose of this is to reinforce the lesson that to think dynamically is a good way of viewing macroeconomic problems. The argument is that there can be no optimal size in competitive growing economies and that the more successful the economy the greater the growth rate of government activity in GNP. This is a fascinating topic in its own right. The chapter stresses the point that worthwhile macroeconomics need not concern itself with the rational expectations hypothesis.

Chapter 3 considers a New Classical rational expectations theory of the price level. This represents a natural extension of the material in Chapter 1. Here the richness of the New Classical version of Monetarism is explored and how current inflation is driven by the whole future expected path of monetary policy, not just by the current policy stance. Thus the question of how an apparently tight monetary policy can be inflationary is explored. The policy prescriptions of New Classical and traditional Monetarism are assessed and the critical point of difference as to how agents are presumed to form their expectations, namely rational versus extrapolative forecasts, is emphasized.

Chapter 4 is a key chapter, which explores the mathematical and methodological underpinnings of the rational expectations method. This shows that it really is not quite as simple as it sounds! It uses the solution techniques described by Sargent and contains some of the most difficult material. It can be avoided at first pass without too much loss of continuity. However, if readers are to be really aware of what is at stake and want to be able to handle more complex models with greater confidence, Chapter 4 is essential.

Chapter 5 discusses business cycle theory and explores the key differences between the equilibrium approach of the New Classicals and the disequilibrium paradigm. As well as the Lucas equilibrium monetary business cycle, one important development—namely, the real business cycle, which retains the equilibrium idea—is also described in this chapter.

Chapter 6 breaks away from rational expectations to review a necessary piece of bookwork for studying economies where there is uncertainty about outcomes, which is, after all, bound to be the typical case. The key device to handle uncertainty is the idea of expected utility maximization and the theoretical basis for this is described. Several examples are explored and the method applied in later chapters. A good understanding of this general tool for problem solving is essential for any macroeconomist claiming to be well trained. All too often the idea is applied with only the vaguest idea of what is involved.

Chapter 7 reviews some implications of the New Classical agenda. The first is the 'rules versus discretion' and 'time inconsistency' arguments which have profound implications for how macroeconomic policy should be conducted. Secondly, the deservedly famous Lucas Critique of policy evaluation is reviewed, which also has profound implications for many aspects of empirical economics and associated policy advice. Finally, two examples of 'random walks' are given. The prediction that many economic time series will follow a random walk seems to arise in many instances in models using rational expectations.

Chapter 8 explores some New Keynesian themes with an emphasis on the labour market. New Keynesians throw some institutional grit into the smoothly running machinery of the neoclassical economy and this often leads to a reassessment of some of the stronger New Classical prescriptions. There is not one universal New Keynesian paradigm and the chapter explores a variety of ideas such as Insider–Outsider theory, implicit contracts and efficiency wages.

Chapter 9, the final chapter, draws some of the arguments together, arguing that so-called 'scientific' economics cannot be separated from some fundamental political questions. The book throws up the issue of the limits to be placed on democratically elected governments in the conduct of economic policy. Should there be a legal requirement for a balanced budget? Should monetary policy be under the control of an independent central bank? These are two such questions which typically are asked. It is not just rational expectationalists who regard the specification of the economic 'rules of the game', within which individuals are free to pursue their own interests, as being the proper subject-matter of economics. The radical 'constitutionalists' confront the issue of what makes a society democratic and challenge the reasonable layman's view that it has something to do with 'one person one vote'. It is simply ridiculous for economists to pretend a certain 'scientific' lofty detachment from these normative issues. Some claim that modern technical economics has become a futile, sterile exercise, and the view that economic problems can be resolved if only suitably advanced mathematical tools were available is regarded as a form of madness. This view is assessed.

READING

There are a large number of expository texts on rational expectations, emphasizing the philosophical basis of the idea. By far the best, in my view, is Hoover (1988), a book which I highly recommend. Two examples of attempted dynamic IS/LM are by Laidler (1968 and 1973), but I do not recommend these unless readers simply want an exercise to improve their technical proficiency. Having said that, Laidler is just about the best expositor of traditional Monetarism and is highly critical of rational expectations. Laidler (1982) is a very accessible and thorough account of the issues, which has obviously influenced this introduction. Readers who feel that they have not got the required proficiency in IS/LM are recommended the concise and excellent text of Artis (1984). If you want to know all about extrapolative predictors and how to apply them in a very imaginative way, without the penny dropping about rational expectations, try Flemming (1976). Disequilibrium macroeconomics, which comprises a vast literature and is the official opposition to the New Classical equilibrium paradigm, is best described in Malinvaud (1977). A more polemical piece is Malinvaud (1984). Lucas (1987) forcefully repudiates the ideas there put forward. The invention of rational expectations is generally ascribed to Muth (1961), though it must be said that he probably did not fully comprehend the significance of his idea. Walters (1971) can lay some claim to being an independent discoverer, where he calls it 'consistent expectations'—arguably the better name—but which will never now come into common parlance. Finally, Solow's attitude to the New Classical agenda can be gleaned from Klamer (1984), which is hugely entertaining and excellent bedtime reading. Finally, if you want to know more about Keynes' life and his stockmarket adventures, try Skidelsky (1983), which is, again, highly entertaining.

The last resort of a competitive economy is the bailiff, the ultimate sanction of the planned economy is the hangman.

F.A. Hayek

BUDGET DEFICITS: NATIONAL AND PRIVATE DEBT

This chapter aims to teach good dynamic modes of thought at the outset. It will consider how the government finances a budget deficit or accommodates a budget surplus. The important point to be emphasized is that it is the whole expected future history of deficits which is crucial when it comes to making an assessment of government policy. The deficit in any particular year is not of such great significance, except insofar as it provides information about expected future behaviour.

In March 1991 the nominal value of the UK's National Debt (including foreign currency debt) stood at £163 448 million, or 28.9 per cent of GDP. Evidently, the government has found it useful to finance part of its expenditures by borrowing in the past. As of March 1991, the UK's National Debt to income ratio was historically low; at the end of the Second World War it stood at nearly three times GNP. Part of the purpose of this chapter will be to explain this dramatic fall in debt level, despite the fact that the UK ran large budget deficits more often than not.

Table 1-1 shows the Financial Deficit of the UK government from 1963, where the negative figures in certain years indicate a financial surplus. Column (3) expresses these numbers in a more meaningful way as a percentage of GNP, measured at factor cost. As can be seen, the sums involved are considerable, with a turnaround of 9.7 per cent of GNP between the largest deficit and surplus figures. Studying budget deficits affords considerable insight into how the economy operates and this will be our concern in what follows.

Column (2) shows the Financial Deficit, which is the excess of public sector current and capital expenditure over receipts. This is the figure which is most closely allied to the concepts to be developed later in this chapter and is not quite the same thing as the Public Sector Borrowing Requirement (PSBR), which is the figure most widely quoted. Latterly, the PSBR has been christened the PSDR, or Public Sector Debt Repayment, as the economy has most unusually (by historical standards) run into a financial surplus. From 1991, it has moved into deficit once more (estimated at £7.9 billion) and is predicted to remain as

Table 1-1 UK Financial Deficits

(1) Year	(2) Financial Deficit (£m)	(3) (2) as % of GNP	(4) PSBR (£m)	(5) (4) as % of GNP
1963	813	3.0	834	3.0
1964	928	3.1	980	3.2
1965	780	2.4	1 170	3.6
1966	835	2.5	949	2.8
1967	1 435	4.0	1 844	5.2
1968	915	2.4	1 252	3.2
1969	− 502	− 1.2	− 534	− 1.3
1970	− 685	− 1.5	− 51	− 0.1
1971	325	0.6	1 320	2.6
1972	1 585	2.8	1 950	3.4
1973	2 767	4.1	4 093	6.0
1974	4 737	6.1	6 451	8.4
1975	7 604	7.9	10 161	10.6
1976	8 453	7.4	8 899	7.8
1977	6 076	4.7	5 419	4.1
1978	8 421	5.6	8 340	5.5
1979	8 692	5.0	12 551	7.1
1980	10 443	5.2	11 786	5.9
1981	7 880	3.6	10 507	4.8
1982	7 759	3.2	4 868	2.0
1983	10 456	3.9	11 574	4.3
1984	13 183	4.6	10 300	3.6
1985	10 155	3.3	7 445	2.4
1986	7 746	2.3	2 499	0.7
1987	4 255	1.2	− 1 434	− 0.3
1988	− 7 176	− 1.8	− 11 858	− 2.9
1989	− 6 636	− 1.5	− 9 276	− 2.1
1990	− 317	0.0	− 2 136	− 0.4

Source: *Economic Trends Annual Supplement 1992.*

such for some time. In January 1991 the authorities were obliged to sell gilt-edged stock for the first time since October 1988. The PSBR is shown for comparative purposes in column (4) of Table 1-1. It differs from the Financial Deficit in two main ways. First, privatization receipts are counted as reducing the PSBR. Privatization receipts represent the proceeds of *asset* swaps, and since they are strictly speaking not *recurrent* items it is perhaps more correct to think of them as a way of financing a deficit rather than of reducing the deficit itself. In recent years, privatization receipts have been considerable and account for the large difference between the PSBR and the Financial Deficit. Secondly, net overseas purchases of government debt and a fall in reserves are also counted as reducing the PSBR.

However, the purpose of this chapter is not to become embroiled in accounting technicalities. The basic idea of expenditure exceeding current tax receipts is simple enough and this is measured by the Financial Deficit. Government expenditure includes interest payments on the National Debt. For example, in 1990 the government paid out £18 544 million in debt interest, or 3.8 per cent of GNP at factor cost. The Financial Deficit, therefore, includes interest payments on debt. The Financial Deficit is crucial to answering the question whether or not the government can run a credible anti-inflation policy. The importance of words like 'credibility' and 'reputation' will be explained; but they would be impossible to introduce in a meaningful way were a static framework to be adopted as a framework for analysis.

The object of this chapter, as well as explaining many useful concepts, is to put forward the following argument. Since 1945 all elected governments have promised to reduce inflation. In general, these promises (whether or not for the most laudable of reasons) have been reneged upon. As a consequence of this fact, the government of the day (whether Labour or Conservative) has acquired a poor reputation and policy announcements of large inflation reductions are simply not believed by financial markets or the public. It then becomes extremely difficult and expensive to deliver low inflation, compared to the case when the low-inflation target is believed. Given the expense and high costs, the government usually opts to deliver the (high) rates of inflation the people have been expecting anyway.

The government could, however, avoid many of these high costs by financing any budget deficit with index-linked debt. (An index-linked bond is simply a financial instrument promising to pay a real rate of interest with automatic compensation for inflation.) With index-linked debt, low inflation would be cheaper in terms of the taxes that must be raised to finance repayment, compared to the alternative of selling debt offering a sufficiently high nominal yield for the public to be prepared to purchase it, given their own views as to what the inflation rate is likely to be. Indeed, a really credible strategy would be for the government to offer to buy out the existing National Debt at market prices and re-issue an equivalent value of index-linked debt. This would be cheaper still.

With index-linked debt, the real resource costs in terms of the real taxes that must be raised to pay the interest and principal on debt are independent of the inflation rate. With non-index-linked debt this real resource cost increases to the extent that the delivered rate of inflation (which the government announces is to be low) differs from the expected rate of inflation (which the public expects to be high). If the government actually delivers what it promises, index-linking avoids these high real costs. The public are much more likely to believe the index-linked strategy and therefore to adjust their inflation expectations downwards. The strategy is, therefore, much more likely to be successful. That, in a nutshell, is the argument. The purpose is not to engage in some mindless and irritating political axe-grinding for its own sake, but rather to work through the logical consequences of thinking about the macroeconomy in a particular way. Not all economists accept that the fiscal-monetary nexus of the government is the fundamental source of inflation and they would look elsewhere—at the labour market, for example—for its source and propagation mechanism.

The view of inflation considered here, and to be extended in Chapter 3, is much more subtle than simplistic notions of blaming it all on selfish trade unions or the vagaries of the exchange rate markets. Although subtle, the ideas are not very complicated or difficult to understand when properly unravelled. Even if the reader concludes that indexation is just far too dangerous a strategy, the concepts in what follows are essential knowledge for any macroeconomist. The ideas can also be easily generalized to apply to important issues in personal debt finance, and this is done at the end of the chapter.

1-1 REAL VERSUS NOMINAL INTEREST RATES

Because consideration is to be given to an economy where there is inflation and because agents are likely to be uncertain about future inflation, it is important to distinguish the *real* rate of interest from the *nominal* rate and the *actual* and *expected* rates of interest. Suppose at time $t - 1$ an asset of nominal value $P_{t-1}V_{t-1}$ is purchased. For example, $P_{t-1}V_{t-1}$ could represent £10 000 worth of shares in British Petroleum. P_{t-1} is the price level prevailing at time $t - 1$ and V_{t-1} represents that real basket of goods that is equivalent to £10 000 worth of British Petroleum shares. (Note that P_{t-1} is *not* the share price and V_{t-1} is *not* the number of shares in British Petroleum.) If there existed a single commodity world then V_{t-1} would just be the number of units of that commodity—bushels of corn, or whatever. It is not proposed to become embroiled in complex index number problems here, nor is it necessary. V_{t-1} is simply the number of units of some standard consumption basket.

Now, after one year the shares are sold. An amount $P_t V_t$ (including any dividend payments) is received. The nominal rate of return is clearly given by

$$r = \frac{P_t V_t - P_{t-1} V_{t-1}}{P_{t-1} V_{t-1}}. \tag{1-1}$$

However, investors are not really concerned about the nominal return. $P_t V_t$ could exceed $P_{t-1}V_{t-1}$, yet V_t be much less than V_{t-1} because of high inflation. The real rate of return is

$$\rho = \frac{V_t - V_{t-1}}{V_{t-1}}. \tag{1-2}$$

The nominal and real rates are therefore linked according to

$$1 + r = \frac{(1 + \rho)P_t}{P_{t-1}} = (1 + \rho)(1 + \pi) \tag{1-3}$$

where π, the inflation rate, is $(P_t - P_{t-1})/P_{t-1}$.

Now let us apply these ideas to an individual or institution who might consider lending to the government. In reality, a large part of government borrowing from the public is in the form of gilt-edged securities (bonds) with varying years to maturity, though there are other important forms such as National Savings, which are rather akin to building society accounts. The maturities could range from three-month Treasury Bills to bonds with an infinite life having no date of maturity. The issues involved can all be seen, however, by considering a 'prototype' bond which has exactly a one-year maturity. After one year all the interest and the principal must be redeemed by the government. Later, the implications of selling long-term debt are considered.

Let $P_{t-1}Z_{t-1}$ be the nominal value of the bonds sold by the government to the public. As before, Z_{t-1} represents the real basket of goods to which this purchase is equivalent. Unlike an equity investment, where the sale price of the asset is uncertain, depending on the stock market valuation on a particular day, the bond is a financial instrument that will offer a fixed nominal repayment, which includes interest and principal. Call this known amount $P_t^\varepsilon Z_t^\varepsilon$, where P_t^ε is the expected price level at time t and Z_t^ε the expected real commodity basket. The nominal rate of return is, therefore,

$$r = \frac{P_t^\varepsilon Z_t^\varepsilon - P_{t-1}Z_{t-1}}{P_{t-1}Z_{t-1}}. \tag{1-4}$$

What determines $P_t^\varepsilon Z_t^\varepsilon$ and hence r (the nominal rate of return that has to be offered to persuade the investor to purchase)? We can assume that the investor wants a real rate of return and wants to be compensated for the anticipated inflation that might occur over the period. The *ex ante* or expected real rate of return is, therefore,

$$\rho^\varepsilon = \frac{(Z_t^\varepsilon - Z_{t-1})}{Z_{t-1}}. \tag{1-5}$$

Hence,

$$1 + r = \frac{(1 + \rho^\varepsilon)P_t^\varepsilon}{P_{t-1}} = (1 + \rho^\varepsilon)(1 + \pi^\varepsilon) \tag{1-6}$$

where π^ε is the expected inflation rate $= (P_t^\varepsilon - P_{t-1})/P_{t-1}$. As ρ^ε is the baseline real return that investors seek, then nominal yields must adjust to accommodate expected inflation as shown by Eq. (1-6).

However, because inflation is uncertain, there is no guarantee that the investor will receive the *ex ante* real rate ρ^ε. To the extent that the realized price level P_t differs from P_t^ε, then ρ^ε and ρ—the realized real return—also differ. The contracted-for nominal payment is the same in any event, so the following relationship holds:

$$P_t^\varepsilon Z_t^\varepsilon = P_t Z_t. \tag{1-7}$$

Z_t^ε is the basket of goods the investor expected and Z_t is the basket actually received. The realized real rate of return is

$$\rho = \frac{Z_t - Z_{t-1}}{Z_{t-1}} \tag{1-8}$$

and hence

$$1 + r = \frac{(1 + \rho)P_t}{P_{t-1}} = (1 + \rho)(1 + \pi) \tag{1-9}$$

where $\pi = (P_t - P_{t-1})/P_{t-1}$ is the realized inflation rate.

Noting that $1 + \rho^\varepsilon = (Z_t^\varepsilon/Z_t)(Z_t/Z_{t-1})$, then from Eqs (1-7) and (1-8) comes the obvious connection between ρ and ρ^ε:

$$1 + \rho = \frac{(1 + \rho^\varepsilon)P_t^\varepsilon}{P_t}. \tag{1-10}$$

If the investor makes a lucky guess and P_t turns out to be less than P_t^ε, obviously a surprisingly high real return is made; and contrariwise if the inflation rate is higher than expected.

A special case is that of an index-linked bond. The UK has recently begun to issue this type of financial instrument in a limited way and in March 1991, and although a steadily increasing proportion of total debt, index-linked bonds accounted for 11.9 per cent of the nominal outstanding amount of the National Debt. An index-linked bond automatically compensates for inflation and guarantees the investor a fixed real return. Indexation takes the 'guessing' pain out of inflation. Denote the guaranteed real rate on the index-linked bond as ρ^i. The question is, will $\rho^i = \rho^\varepsilon$? A one-period index-linked bond is clearly of a different *quality* compared to a non-indexed bond. In the case of the latter, the real rate of return is risky with $E\{\rho\} = \rho^\varepsilon$, where E is the expectational operator. (If you are unsure of what E is, the appendix to Chapter 3 has some more information, or refer to any introductory statistics text.) Although, on average, the realized real rate will be the expected real rate, investors must accept some degree of risk. Now, it is often assumed that investors dislike risk and are prepared to pay a premium to reduce it. If this is so, it might be expected that $\rho^i < \rho^\varepsilon$ since the government can still persuade investors to purchase index-linked stock by offering a lower real rate. The issues involved concerning risk premia are, however, extremely complicated and it does not always follow that an asset with a large variance of real returns will command a risk premium compared to less risky assets. Chapter 6 introduces some of the issues involved when investors have to choose among risky assets.

The simple points made here do not really require us to become involved in such advanced issues at this stage, and in a world of perfect foresight ρ^i and ρ^ε would be the same, since as far as their risk quality is concerned the index-linked bond and the non-index-linked bond would be perfect substitutes. In what follows, since it is hardly critical, it will be assumed that there is a common (expected) real rate for all financial instruments with $\rho^i = \rho^\varepsilon$.

A final preliminary is to distinguish carefully between the nominal value of a bond and its market value. The two, in general, need not be the same. At certain times the market value of the National Debt has exceeded its nominal value and at other times has been far below it. For example, in 1980 the market to nominal value ratio of the National Debt stood at 0.81, yet by 1988 this had increased to 1.13. For long-dated maturities, there can be particularly wide variations in this ratio. The reason for this should become clear.

All gilt-edged securities are traded in organized markets—indeed, the daily prices of a broad range of government securities are quoted in the City pages of the press. Any gilt-edged security is a claim to certain payments in the future and as such has a value. The market price of a bond is precisely that; it is the price that can be obtained in the market for that financial instrument on a particular day. The difference between the nominal and market price can be seen in the following way for the one-period bond. Suppose bonds of nominal value $P_{t-1}Z_{t-1}$ are sold on the basis of an expected price level P_t^ε. From Eq. (1-6),

$$\frac{P_t Z_t}{P_{t-1}Z_{t-1}} = \frac{(1 + \rho^\varepsilon)P_t^\varepsilon}{P_{t-1}} \tag{1-11}$$

or

$$P_{t-1}Z_{t-1} = \frac{[P_t Z_t/(1 + \rho^\varepsilon)]P_{t-1}}{P_t^\varepsilon}. \tag{1-12}$$

Viewed in this way, $P_t Z_t$, P_{t-1} and $1 + \rho^\varepsilon$ are parametric and what sustains the nominal price $P_{t-1}Z_{t-1}$ is P_t^ε. If this changes, then so must $P_{t-1}Z_{t-1}$.

Suppose that, immediately after the bonds have been sold in the belief of P_t^ε, expectations about the future price level change to $P_t'^\varepsilon$. Clearly, the market price of the bonds will now change, since investors will still want the same expected real rate of interest. This will be given by

$$P_{t-1}Z'_{t-1} = \frac{[P_t Z_t/(1 + \rho^\varepsilon)]P_{t-1}}{P'^\varepsilon_t}. \qquad (1\text{-}13)$$

The ratio of the nominal to market price of the bonds will simply be

$$\frac{P_{t-1}Z_{t-1}}{P_{t-1}Z'_{t-1}} = \frac{P'^\varepsilon_t}{P^\varepsilon_t}. \qquad (1\text{-}14)$$

If $P'^\varepsilon_t > P^\varepsilon_t$, the original investor will, with the benefit of hindsight, regret the investment; and contrariwise if $P'^\varepsilon_t < P^\varepsilon_t$.

Thus, market and nominal prices differ to the extent that expectations about inflation change from the time for which the bond was contracted. For bonds of short maturity, these differences are likely to be small, hence the market to nominal value is likely to be close to 1. For long-dated bonds, the differences can be substantial and Sec. 1-8 will further clarify the issue. Figure 1-1 gives some interesting information on the issue. It plots the market/nominal value of gilt-edged stocks for three types of bond from 1973 to 1991. They are 'Shorts', bonds of 5 years' maturity or less; 'Mediums', with 5 to 15 years' maturity; and finally 'Longs', which are those over 15 years and undated. As expected, the variations are most substantial for 'Longs'. It also illustrates the fact that there can be substantial differences in the valuation of the National Debt by the market as opposed to its nominal value.

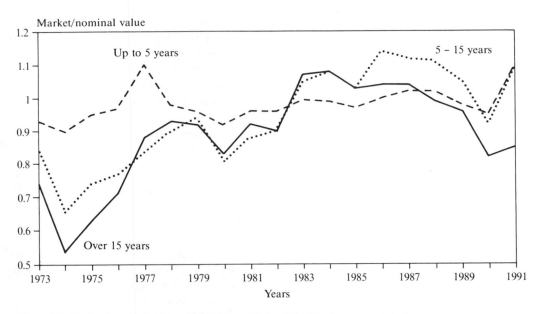

Figure 1-1 Market/nominal value ratio of fully-paid dated British Government stocks
Source: Bank of England Quarterly Bulletin

PROBLEM

1-1 P_{t-1} is 100. The price level expected in the next period is 110. Investors seek a real rate of return of 2 per cent. Government bonds are sold in units of £1 and mature after one period.

(*a*) What is the expected inflation rate?
(*b*) If investors are to be persuaded to buy bonds at £1, at what price must the government offer to redeem the bonds when they mature?
(*c*) Suppose *immediately* after the bonds have been sold at £1, the expected inflation rate changes to 5 per cent. What will happen to the market price of the bonds?
(*d*) Does it now pay bondholders to sell or keep the bonds? What factors might influence this choice?

1-2 THE GOVERNMENT FINANCING CONSTRAINT

The government financing constraint can be expressed in several equivalent ways and the preparatory work of the previous section will prove useful in showing these equivalences. As before, it is assumed that all debt is in the form of non-index-linked one-period bonds. Later, other types of financial instrument will be considered, such as index-linked and undated bonds.

In nominal terms, the financing constraint can be expressed as:

$$P_t G_t - P_t T_t + (1 + r)P_{t-1}B_{t-1} = P_t B_t + M_t - M_{t-1} \tag{1-15}$$

where

$P_t G_t$ = nominal government expenditure at time t. G_t is obviously real expenditure
$P_t T_t$ = nominal tax receipts; T_t are real tax receipts
$P_t G_t - P_t T_t$ = nominal budget deficit or the surplus if this happens to be negative; it *excludes* interest payments on the National Debt and therefore differs from the Financial Deficit figures of Table 1-1 which *include* interest payments
r = nominal interest rate payable on the National Debt between time $t - 1$ and t
$P_{t-1}B_{t-1}$ = nominal value of the National Debt contracted for at time $t - 1$; B_{t-1} is the real value of the debt
$P_t B_t$ = nominal value of the National Debt contracted for at time t
$M_t - M_{t-1}$ = change in the amount of high-powered money issued between t and $t - 1$

The financing constraint is easily interpreted. The current deficit $P_t G_t - P_t T_t$ must be financed and, in addition, the whole of the National Debt (since it is a one-period bond) matures. Thus an additional amount $(1 + r)P_{t-1}B_{t-1}$ must be financed, which represents the principal $P_{t-1}B_{t-1}$ plus the interest payments $rP_{t-1}B_{t-1}$. This total is the exact analogue of $P_t Z_t$ in the previous section.

The right-hand side of Eq. (1-15) shows how these amounts can be financed. First, new debt could be sold at a cost of $P_t B_t$. Alternatively, it could be financed by borrowing from the Central Bank—that is, by resorting to the printing press and issuing high-powered money of amount $M_t - M_{t-1}$. It might seem that printing money to finance any deficit is an archetypal 'free lunch'. In fact this is not so, and it will be shown later how this can be just as much a tax on the public as $P_t T_t$.

There is nothing mysterious about the financing constraint, despite the fact that in some expositions it appears as a dark, arcane science designed to scare off the unwary. What applies to individuals applies equally well to governments. Individuals can only pay off old debts as well as spend more than is earned, by finding someone willing to lend to them. The only option denied to individuals, apart from the criminal classes, is the ability to print money to pay the bills.

The financing constraint can be expressed in real terms by dividing Eq. (1-15) by P_t on both sides. Thus:

$$G_t - T_t + (1 + \rho)B_{t-1} = B_t + \frac{(M_t - M_{t-1})}{P_t}. \tag{1-16}$$

Notice that ρ is the realized real rate of interest, where Eq. (1-9) has been used to substitute out r. An alternative expression for Eq. (1-15) or Eq. (1-16), which is useful for some purposes, is

$$G_t - T_t + (1 + \rho^\varepsilon)\left(\frac{P_t^\varepsilon}{P_t}\right)B_{t-1} = B_t + \frac{(M_t - M_{t-1})}{P_t}. \tag{1-17}$$

This expresses the financing constraint in terms of the *ex ante* real rate and uses Eq. (1-10) to derive it. There should be absolutely no confusion between expressions (1-15), (1-16) and (1-17). They are equivalent ways of expressing exactly the same thing.

Finally, the special case of debt financed by the issue of index-linked bonds is considered. In this case $\rho^\varepsilon = \rho$ and Eq. (1-16) becomes

$$G_t - T_t + (1 + \rho^\varepsilon)B_{t-1} = B_t + \frac{(M_t - M_{t-1})}{P_t}. \tag{1-18}$$

This is just the same as the case when agents guess the one-period inflation rate correctly with $\rho^\varepsilon = \rho$. This is hardly surprising, since indexation means removing the guesswork about expected inflation.

PROBLEM

1-2 You are given the following information:

(i) $P_t G_t - P_t T_t = £1$ billion
(ii) $P_{t-1} B_{t-1} = £10$ billion
(iii) $P_{t-1} = 1$
(iv) $r_{t-1} = 12.2$ per cent
(v) $\rho^\varepsilon_{t-1} = 2$ per cent.

Government bonds have a one-year maturity.

(a) What was the expected inflation rate between t and $t - 1$?
(b) If the inflation forecast turned out to have been correct, what will be the real value of bonds sold at t, assuming no monetization of the deficit is permitted?
(c) What must have been the difference between the actual and expected inflation rates if the real value of bonds B_t equals the real value of debt, B_{t-1}, outstanding at $t - 1$?
(d) What would B_t be if the delivered inflation rate between t and $t - 1$ was zero?

1-3 PERMANENT BUDGET DEFICITS

The first question to be posed is whether the government can permanently run any size of deficit through borrowing from the public without having recourse to the printing press or raising extra taxes to pay off the debt. Obviously, such a thing would be possible if there were no upper limit to the capacity of the public to absorb debt. This is akin to the case of a lady who permanently spends more than she earns. An accommodating bank manager might simply lend this individual sufficient funds to pay off old debts and finance further current fiscal excess. If the bank manager is willing to roll over debt continuously in this way, then the lady can effectively evade the intertemporal budget constraint and die happy with, perhaps, a codicil to her will asking for a whip-round from the bank's shareholders to meet the funeral expenses.

Can the government play the same game with the public? Yes, if there is no upper limit to the public's capacity to absorb debt; so it must be supposed that such an upper limit does exist. For example, if borrowing is restricted to its own citizens, the government could not borrow more than National Income in any one period, though one would guess that the upper limit to borrowing would be reached well before this, even if some foreign borrowing was permitted. Let $b_t = B_t/Y_t$ be the debt to income ratio, where Y_t is real GNP. It is assumed that $b_t \leq \bar{b}$, where $\bar{b}$ represents the upper limit. In the UK, $\bar{b}$ appears to be quite large. As has been seen, b_t was almost 3 at the end of the war and it was by no means clear that this represented an upper limit. With the historically low debt to income ratio of the early 1990s, it is also clear that the authorities could borrow huge amounts—at least temporarily.

To fix these thoughts, suppose that agents have perfect foresight, or that the interest payments on debt are index-linked. Consequently, versions (1-15) or (1-18) of the government's financing constraint are appropriate. Afterwards the complexities involved when agents do make errors in their inflation forecasts will be considered. Inflation does have consequences for the National Debt and there are two aspects to this. First, perfectly anticipated inflation will have some consequences and, secondly, 'surprise' or unanticipated inflation will have other consequences. A logical strategy in trying to understand the problems is to rule out by construction the latter difficulty of 'surprise' inflation in the first instance.

A useful point of reference is the so-called 'tight' fiscal and 'tight' monetary regime. In this regime, printing money is eschewed and $M_t = M_{t-1}$ always. The authorities also aim to raise sufficient taxes to balance the budget—excluding payments on the National Debt. Given this regime, from Eqs (1-18) and (1-15) the following equivalent statements must be true:

$$B_t = (1 + \rho^\varepsilon)B_{t-1} \tag{1-19}$$

$$P_t B_t = (1 + r)P_{t-1}B_{t-1}. \tag{1-20}$$

The authorities simply roll over the National Debt. From Eq. (1-19) it follows that the growth in real debt, which is $(B_t - B_{t-1})/B_{t-1}$, is equal to the real interest rate, ρ^ε and, from Eq. (1-20), that the growth rate of nominal debt, which is $(P_t B_t - P_{t-1}B_{t-1})/P_{t-1}B_{t-1}$ is equal to the nominal interest rate, r. Can this fiscal regime be maintained indefinitely— in other words, is it credible? The answer is 'No' if the real growth of output lies below the real rate of interest or, equivalently, if the nominal growth in output lies below the nominal interest rate. If this does not hold, then eventually the $\bar{b}$ constraint must be reached and the authorities will eventually be obliged to monetize fiscal deficits.

Thus a preliminary conclusion is that the fiscal and monetary regimes are inextricably linked. A fiscal deficit is not a free-choice variable to be financed by borrowing or monetization. In the short run, this might be true, but in the long run there are important constraints on the extent to which deficits can be financed by borrowing. A naive objection to this is that it does not apply when interest rates exceed the growth in output—though in recent years, in both the USA and the UK, real rates of interest have exceeded real growth rates. The point of the analysis is that by choosing a particular reference point, it was possible to make the constraints on borrowing clear. There must always be some limit to the fiscal regime, which would lead to the $\bar{b}$ constraint being reached.

This discussion emphasizes the doctrine of Ricardian equivalence. Expenditure financed by borrowing is just deferred taxation; eventually the bills have to be paid. On this level, the government is no different from an individual. If less is earned than spent in one period, more must be earned than is spent in future periods to pay off the debts plus the accrued interest. For a government this means raising extra taxes in future years to pay off present borrowing plus interest. Monetization, as will shortly be seen, is just another way of raising taxes from the public.

The doctrine of Ricardian equivalence is easily seen in a two-period model. Let disposable income in both periods be $Y_t - T_t$ and $Y_{t+1} - T_{t+1}$ respectively. The individual formulates a consumption plan C_t and C_{t+1} on the basis of this budget constraint. This says that the present value of consumption, which is $C_t + C_{t+1}/(1 + \rho^\varepsilon)$, cannot exceed the present value of receipts, which is $(Y_t - T_t) + (Y_{t+1} - T_{t+1})/(1 + \rho^\varepsilon)$. Now let the government reduce current taxes by borrowing D. Disposable income this period rises to $Y_t - T_t + D$. Should the individual alter the original consumption plan, say by spending more this period? Apparently not, because the individual must pay an extra amount in taxes next period of $D(1 + \rho^\varepsilon)$. The 'new' consumption plan is chosen on the basis of the modified budget constraint, which says that the present value of consumption cannot exceed $(Y_t - T_t + D) + [Y_{t+1} - T_{t+1} - D(1 + \rho^\varepsilon)]/(1 + \rho^\varepsilon)$. But this is easily seen to reduce to the original budget constraint once more. Hence the doctrine—the original consumption plan is independent of the tax/borrowing regime adopted by the government.

On this view, government bonds do not represent net wealth, because the smart public who own them realize that offsetting this apparent wealth is an equivalent amount of deferred taxation, whose present value is bound to be the market value of the outstanding stock of bonds. Ricardian equivalence challenges the notion that a government can make society wealthier just by borrowing and the alternative canard that borrowing destroys 'capital' and makes society poorer. As always in economic theory, there are sophisticated arguments to counter the natural common sense and intuition of this idea, and not everyone accepts that Ricardian equivalence is true in all circumstances. However, given the sound basis in logic of the doctrine, it seems reasonable to start discussion on government finances by assuming Ricardian equivalence holds rather than the contrary.

A non-credible fiscal regime is one where, although current deficits are not being monetized, they must eventually be so because the $\bar{b}$ constraint will be hit. What are the current consequences of this non-credible fiscal regime? If the underlying inflation rate is a monetary phenomenon, then a preliminary conclusion is that a non-credible fiscal regime is bound to lead to inflation in the future as the monetary base is expanded. Chapter 3 leads to a considerable and fundamental modification of this preliminary view. There the stakes are upped by the assumption that expectations are formed rationally, in addition to inflation being taken as a monetary phenomenon. The conclusion from this is that the expectation of future monetization will have *current* inflationary consequences. Thus a currently tight monetary policy could, at the same time, be inflationary—a view far removed from traditional Monetarism.

In a famous article entitled, 'Some unpleasant monetarist arithmetic', Sargent and Wallace upped the stakes even more by arguing that in some circumstances a tight monetary regime now could have worse current inflation consequences than if the fiscal deficit were monetized immediately. These issues are explored in Chapter 3, but the present discussion is essential preparation for future analysis. The analysis of Chapter 3 goes beyond traditional monetarist ideas.

PROBLEMS

1-3 You are given the following information:

(i)   The expected and actual inflation rates are always the same.
(ii) The real rate of interest is 2 per cent.
(iii) The real rate of output growth is 1 per cent.
(iv) The current debt to output ratio B_t/Y_t is 1.
(v)   The maximum obtainable value of B_t/Y_t is 3.

Given a tight fiscal and monetary regime after how many years will the borrowing constraint be hit?

1-4 You are given the following information about an individual's disposable income:

(i) $Y_t - T_t = 1000$.
(ii) $Y_{t+1} - T_{t+1} = 1020$.
(iii) The real rate of interest is 2 per cent and there is no inflation.
(iv) Consumption in period t is 900.

(*a*) What will consumption in period $t + 1$ be? (Assume the individual lives for just two periods.)
(*b*) The government increases taxes by 500 units in the first period with an offsetting reduction in the next. What will the revised consumption plan be?
(*c*) Are there any problems with the revised consumption plan?

1-4 THE COSTS OF SERVICING THE NATIONAL DEBT

The National Debt is the nation's equivalent of an individual's bank overdraft. It shows the liability side of the balance sheet. Just as an individual with debts might typically have assets such as a house or whatever to offset these liabilities, so a nation will have assets to offset the National Debt. A proper picture of the nation's wealth should show the complete balance sheet, assets as well as liabilities. That such a view is sensible is thrown into sharp relief by the process of privatization. National assets—the 'family silver', in the famous phrase of the former Prime Minister Harold Macmillan—are sold off. At a stroke, the National Debt is reduced. It appears as if the nation's indebtedness has diminished. Of course, nothing real has actually happened; there has just been a transfer of ownership from the public to the private sector, with offsetting changes on both sides of the balance sheet, leaving aside the argument put forward by some, namely that such assets are valued too little on the asset side and offered to the public at bargain prices.

Any individual, with or without offsetting assets, knows that running an overdraft is an expensive business. Just to service the liability side of the balance sheet, by maintaining the real value of the debt through meeting interest payments, involves considerable expense. It is, therefore, interesting to produce an estimate of the tax burden of the National Debt. Figure 1-2 shows the National Debt to National Income ratio from 1963 to 1991. This is the nominal debt to income ratio and is not quite the same as the market value of the debt to income ratio. However, both show the same dramatic decline. To show the cost of servicing debt, the high figure of debt to income of 3 is compared to the low figure of 0.25. The calculation is therefore a rough comparison of 1945 with 1990.

Suppose the government seeks to maintain the real value of its debt by raising sufficient extra taxation to keep $B_t = B_{t-1}$ for all t. In simple terms, it is keeping the bank manager happy by not letting its debts grow. From Eq. (1-16), setting $M_t = M_{t-1}$ and $B_t = B_{t-1}$ and dividing by Y_t, gives

$$\frac{G_t - T_t}{Y_t} = \frac{-\rho B_t}{Y_t}. \tag{1-21}$$

Comparing a B_t/Y_t of 3 with a value of 0.25, the extra taxes required to be raised as a proportion of output are therefore $\rho(3 - 0.25)$. Assuming a real rate of interest of 2 per

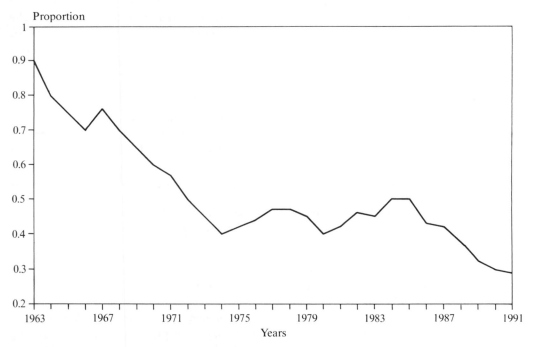

Figure 1-2 National Debt as a proportion of GDP
Source: Bank of England Quarterly Bulletin

cent, this is approximately 5.5 per cent of GNP. This is a considerable amount of extra taxation and gives some indication of the burden of high debt levels. The additional burden placed on future taxpayers by borrowing money today instead of raising taxes can be considerable.

Of course, Ricardian equivalence teaches us that such calculations are a slight chimera. In reality, the government is simply transferring money from the left-hand pocket (taxpayers) to the right-hand pocket (bondholders). And the public should have seen through the veil of debt-finance, so that their behaviour should not have been affected in any way by the government having chosen debt-finance as opposed to tax-finance. From another point of view, however, the picture may not look quite so harmless, especially for people who are not bondholders and for whom Ricardian equivalence is just a textbook *curiosum*. Those who live for today may not have adjusted their consumption downwards in previous years in anticipation of future tax payments.

It might also be claimed that borrowing from abroad, instead of from domestic residents, imposes more of a tax burden on future generations. The argument here would be that extra tax revenues would be remitted to foreigners instead of simply being transferred back to domestic residents. Strictly interpreted, those espousing the doctrine of Ricardian equivalence would argue that the source of debt finance is irrelevant. If the government borrows from abroad today, domestic residents should save an equivalent amount today in anticipation of future tax liabilities to be remitted abroad—perhaps they might defer their consumption by themselves purchasing foreign National Debt. However, to the extent that domestic residents do not defer current consumption, foreign borrowing does impose an additional burden on the future. What the issue boils down to once again is that there is only a burden if Ricardian equivalence does not hold. In reality, the proportion of the UK's National Debt that is held in foreign hands is quite small. In 1991 it accounted for just 13.9 per cent of the National Debt.

PROBLEM

1-5 Assume that the current debt to output ratio is 3, whereas in the base year it was 1. The government has maintained a tight monetary policy throughout, but has permitted a steady growth in real debt $(B_t - B_{t-1})/B_{t-1}$ of 5 per cent per year from the base year. The real rate of interest is 2 per cent.

(a) Calculate the budget deficit as a proportion of output in the base and current years. What is the intuition for the result obtained?
(b) Calculate the growth in debt allowable in the current year if the budget deficit as a proportion of output in the current year is to be the same as the base year.

1-5 SEIGNIORAGE AND INFLATION TAXES

An interesting exercise is to consider an alternative financing regime. Instead of borrowing, suppose that the deficit is financed by printing money. The picture of such an extreme regime helps clarify the notion of seigniorage and inflation taxes charged against real money balances held by the public. Printing money to pay for a deficit appears to be a soft option.

Raising taxes is unpopular and unpleasant. Borrowing, as has been seen, is just deferred taxation, which is equally unpleasant. Unfortunately, printing money is a tax like any other, but one which is 'hidden away' and not directly discernible.

As before, the discussion assumes perfect foresight and consequently there is no surprise inflation. Inflation taxes need have nothing to do with inflation surprises—agents losing out because the actual inflation rate turns out to be higher than expected. Assuming perfect foresight serves to emphasize this point. Consider first a case of pure seigniorage with the government raising tax revenue by expanding the monetary base with no inflationary consequences. The government is financing at least a part of its deficit by printing money; the question is, in what way is this a tax? To show how it is a tax, let the demand for real money balances be given by

$$\frac{M_t}{P_t} = A + bY_t - c\rho. \tag{1-22}$$

The demand for real money balances, M_t/P_t, is a linear function of real output and a declining function of the real interest rate. More usually, the demand for real balances is made a function of the nominal interest rate, but because an assumption of zero inflation has been made, the demand for real balances in this instance can be related to the real interest rate ρ (also $= \rho^\varepsilon$ because of perfect foresight). The linear representation is chosen not because of any particular belief that this is the true functional form, but for pedagogical purposes. As long as Eq. (1-22) is a reasonable description of the truth, it will do.

Now suppose there is a growing level of real output, which could arise from population growth or increases in productivity. With no monetary expansion to accommodate the implied increase in demand for real money balances, the price level would have to fall, given a constant real rate of interest. The authorities now have an opportunity to extract seigniorage by supplying this extra demand for real balances through expansion of the monetary base.

To illustrate this, let $Y_t = Y_{t-1}(1 + g)$, hence real output grows at a rate g. Let the authorities expand the monetary base at a sufficient rate to maintain a constant price level P_t. The following must therefore be true:

$$\frac{M_t}{P_t} = A + bY_{t-1}(1 + g) - c\rho \tag{1-23}$$

$$\frac{M_{t-1}}{P_t} = A + bY_{t-1} - c\rho. \tag{1-24}$$

Hence:

$$\frac{M_t - M_{t-1}}{P_t} = bgY_{t-1}. \tag{1-25}$$

The left-hand side represents the seigniorage levied from expanding the monetary base. The right-hand side shows the maximum amount that can be extracted without any inflation penalty. Clearly, this amount depends on the precise functional form of the demand for real balances. Friedman, for example, has advocated an x per cent rule, where x is the underlying growth rate in demand for real money balances. If x equals the growth of real income, this reflects a belief that the growth of demand for real money balances is proportional to real income growth in a long-run equilibrium.

What is the intuition behind the idea that the seigniorage is a tax just like any other? On one level, it represents a convenient windfall for the authorities because they are the monopoly suppliers of currency which they produce at near zero cost and they are simply exploiting a growing demand from the public. It is, however, a tax in the following manner. The public, whether from new entrants or productivity growth, demands larger real balances. To accumulate these additional real balances it is necessary to defer some consumption. This deferred consumption—increased saving—will be permanent to the extent that the growth in real balances is permanent. It is this that the authorities exploit, with the deferred consumption spending power being transferred to the authorities. What appears to be additional saving by the public is, in fact, a tax.

Now consider the case of an inflation tax on real money balances. To fix thoughts, assume that real output is constant, thus no seigniorage can be extracted from this source. There is perfect foresight and the seigniorage extracted from steady-state inflation rates is derived. This assumption avoids the particular problems of what happens in the *transition* from one steady-state inflation rate to another steady-state rate. Suppose the steady-state inflation rate is $(P_t - P_{t-1})/P_{t-1} = \pi$. This is sustained by expanding the monetary base at a rate equal to π. Thus the authorities fuel the inflation, validating the given rate π by this monetary expansion.

As before, the authorities are levying an amount of real seigniorage equal to $(M_t - M_{t-1})/P_t$ from this expansion. To see how this is a tax on real balances, the intuition is quite straightforward. The demand for real money balances is now:

$$\frac{M_t}{P_t} = A + bY_t - cr \tag{1-26}$$

where r is the nominal interest rate which embodies the inflation rate ($= \rho + \pi + \rho\pi$ from Eq. (1-3)). The public will therefore seek to maintain the real value of their money balances. Note, however, that Eq. (1-26) says that this constant real value *declines* with higher values of π. This, as will shortly be seen, puts an upper limit on the amount of seigniorage that can be extracted. To maintain their real balances, the public must accumulate nominal money holdings since their value is being eroded by the inflation. Thus the public must defer some consumption just to maintain the real value of their money balances, something they would not have to do if there was no inflation. This is the essence of the inflation tax. Since the authorities are the monopoly suppliers of high-powered money, this deferred consumption is transferred to the government. As before, what appears to be saving is in reality a tax.

For the value of real balances to be unaltered requires $(M_t - M_{t-1})/M_{t-1} = \pi$, therefore $M_{t-1} = M_t/(1 + \pi)$. The real inflation tax $Z_t = (M_t - M_{t-1})/P_t$ can be written as

$$Z_t = \frac{[\pi/(1 + \pi)]M_t}{P_t}. \tag{1-27}$$

It may be helpful to think of this as being approximately equal to the inflation rate times the level of real money balances. Equation (1-27) is the accurate expression for the period-by-period analysis adopted here. It would reduce to $\pi M_t/P_t$ in the limit for continuous compounding.

There is an upper limit to the steady-state real seigniorage extractable from an inflation tax. The intuition is as follows. Note from Eq. (1-26) that M_t/P_t falls as π increases. Thus, from Eq. (1-27), there are two countervailing forces: a rise in π tends to increase the inflation tax, but the fall in M_t/P_t tends to reduce it. The maximum value of the seigniorage is easily calculated. Equation (1-26) can be written as

$$\frac{M_t}{P_t} = A_0 - e\pi \tag{1-28}$$

where $A_0 = A + bY_t - c\rho$ and is considered as constant for the purpose of this argument; and $e = c(1 + \rho)$ is also a parameter.

Differentiating Eq. (1-27), the maximum inflation tax occurs when $dZ_t/d\pi = 0$. It is easy to verify that the required second-order condition holds.

$$\frac{dZ_t}{d\pi} = \frac{M_t/P_t}{1 + \pi} - e\pi = 0 \tag{1-29}$$

which uses the fact that $d(M_t/P_t)/d\pi = -e$ from Eq. (1-28). Substituting out M_t/P_t from Eq. (1-28), the steady inflation rate which extracts the maximum inflation tax must satisfy

$$A_0 = e\pi(2 + \pi). \tag{1-30}$$

Again, in the limiting case where the inflation tax is just $\pi M_t/P_t$, expression (1-30) would reduce to $\pi = A_0/2e$.

The 'revenues' extracted from this source have actually been quite small, less than 0.3 of 1 per cent of GNP per annum in the 1980s in the UK. In other countries the amounts extracted have been considerably higher. The reason is not the UK's superior inflation performance, but rather because the monetary base is smaller relative to GNP in the UK. Countries with underdeveloped financial institutions have a high demand for cash, which gives greater opportunities for seigniorage. In Greece, for example, the average size of the inflation tax has been estimated as 2.9 per cent of GNP in the 1980s. Financial repression, whereby the authorities maintain artificially low interest rates, is also another important source of hidden taxation.

PROBLEM

1-6 The demand for real balances is given by $M_t/P_t = A(Y_t)^\delta(\rho + \pi)^\Phi$, where Y_t is real output, ρ is the real interest rate and π is the inflation rate. A, δ and Φ are parameters.

(a) If output grows at the rate g, what rate of money growth gives the maximum non-inflationary seigniorage?
(b) What value of δ would make this monetary growth rate $= g$?
(c) Given that $g = 0$ and $\Phi = -1$, what inflation rate gives the highest real inflation tax?
(d) Calculate the inflation rate giving the highest real inflation tax for any value of Φ less than -1.

1-6 INFLATION AND THE NATIONAL DEBT

It is frequently claimed that, 'Inflation erodes the value of the National Debt.' The issues involved are quite complicated, so it is as well to approach the argument in stages. Basically, the aim here is to explain the apparent paradox between Table 1-1, where the government appears to be running a large Financial Deficit and Fig. 1-2, where the value of the debt appears to decline—indeed quite considerably. As before, the assumption of perfect foresight is retained as a useful preliminary. Unfortunately, there are several specious arguments surrounding the whole issue of budget deficits and the National Debt; the initial assumption of no inflation surprises helps to disentangle the genuine from the false arguments.

The first and most obvious point is that the Financial Deficit includes nominal interest payments on the National Debt. Thus, suppose there was a zero Financial Deficit, implying that $P_t G_t - P_t T_t + r P_{t-1} B_{t-1} = 0$, then from Eq. (1-15) it follows that, with $M_t = M_{t-1}$:

$$P_t B_t = P_{t-1} B_{t-1}. \tag{1-31}$$

The nominal value of the National Debt would remain constant. Clearly, with moderate rates of inflation the debt to income ratio would quickly be eroded. This gets to the heart of the question 'When is a budget deficit really a budget deficit?' If the real value of debt is being eroded, then the authorities must be running a financial surplus, even though ostensibly there appears to be a budget deficit. It must be stressed that the argument is well-founded when there is perfectly anticipated inflation—in other circumstances, it could be entirely specious.

A balanced budget might more properly be regarded as a situation where the real value of the National Debt remains unchanged. From Eq. (1-16) this can immediately be seen to be the case where the real Financial Deficit $G_t - T_t + \rho B_{t-1} = 0$. With inflation the authorities would issue some new nominal debt to keep the outstanding real value constant. With a zero real Financial Deficit as shown above, the relationship between the nominal deficit and the inflation rate is calculated as

$$P_t G_t - P_t T_t + r P_{t-1} B_{t-1} = \pi P_{t-1} B_{t-1} \tag{1-32}$$

where we have used the fact that $\rho = (r - \pi)/(1 + \pi)$ and $P_t = P_{t-1}(1 + \pi)$. The l.h.s. is the nominal Financial Deficit and is increasing with π; it is the relationship that must hold if the real value of the National Debt is to remain constant. It is an alternative and arguably better definition of what must hold for budget balance. It implies nominal Financial Deficits when there is inflation. Notice that it has nothing to do with 'surprise' inflation, which has, at this stage, been assumed away.

Is inflation a tax on the real value of the National Debt in the same way as it is a tax on real balances? Remembering the present assumption of perfect foresight, we can see that the claim that there is an inflation tax is false. Certainly, inflation erodes the real value of the nominal debt held by the public, but they are automatically compensated for this erosion by a nominal interest rate which incorporates the erosion in value caused by inflation. The definition of budget balance to be a zero *nominal* Financial Deficit always is, as we have seen, somewhat arbitrary. The real budget deficit varies with the inflation rate and this causes the erosion of real National Debt. Surprise inflation, on the other hand, might be regarded as giving rise to an inflation tax, as will be seen later. Anticipated inflation cannot be so regarded.

Another reason why the National Debt has a degree of independence from the Financial Deficit is because of open market operations. The National Debt, perhaps somewhat arbitrarily, is defined as the interest-bearing liabilities of the Central Bank held in private hands. Specifically, non-interest-bearing liabilities, cash or high-powered money, is not counted as part of the National Debt. Suppose the authorities, over and above any funding requirement to meet a budget deficit, engage in an open-market operation by selling securities and removing cash from the system. The Financial Deficit is said to be 'overfunded' in this situation. Clearly, this open-market operation leads to an increase in the size of the National Debt to the extent that the deficit is overfunded. The first Thatcher government in its early years, from 1979 onwards, engaged in overfunding of the Financial Deficit, as it attempted—vainly as it turned out—to stay within the strict monetary targets laid down by the Medium Term Financial Strategy. Part of the increase in debt around that period, observable in Fig. 1-2, must be accounted for by these open-market operations.

Finally, recall the subject of privatization receipts alluded to earlier. A large Financial Deficit can be and was 'funded' by selling off public assets, with a corresponding 'reduction' in the National Debt. The set of PSBR figures of Table 1-1, since it takes these factors into account, is therefore a better guide to the amount of any Financial Deficit that must be financed by the issue of new debt or high-powered money.

PROBLEM

1-7 Real output is constant, with debt financed by a one-period bond. The annual inflation rate is 10 per cent and the real rate of interest is 2 per cent. The monetary base is being expanded at 10 per cent per year and all these values are expected to remain unchanged. The fiscal stance is such as to maintain the nominal value of outstanding debt.

(*a*) Calculate the number of years after which the debt to output ratio is at least one half its current value.

(*b*) What does the fiscal stance imply about the real budget deficit, $G_t - T_t$?

1-7 LONG-TERM DEBT FINANCE

So far, the story has been told using the convenient device of the one-period bond. In fact, this is sufficient to illustrate virtually all of the underlying issues; nevertheless, it is an extremely useful exercise to consider the finance of deficits through the issue of long-term debt instruments. This forces us to confront additional concerns. First, what exactly is meant by the expected inflation rate? With the one-period bond the only concern was inflation over one future period. With a long-term bond, the concern must be with the inflation rate over many future periods and not just one period, as was the case with the one-period bond. Thus there could be a short-term expected inflation rate and a longer term expected inflation rate. The two need not be the same and thinking carefully about long-dated maturities enables us to be more precise about this. Secondly, the price of long-term maturities will be more sensitive to changes in the expected rate of inflation— but again, which expected rate of inflation: the long-term or the short-term rate? As always, we start by keeping things as simple as possible. Perfect foresight is assumed and, secondly, the inflation rate π is constant over all future periods. Both of these simplifications will be dropped later.

The extreme opposite to the one-period bond is the infinitely dated perpetuity. An infinitely dated maturity is one that has no defined redemption date. Thus the bond is simply a promise to pay a fixed nominal sum once per period for ever. Most government debt instruments lie between these two extremes of the infinitely dated maturity and the one-period maturity. In the UK infinitely dated financial instruments actually exist—'war loan' is one such example; 'consols' are another; and their market value is quoted daily in the financial press. To fix these thoughts, the value of an index-linked perpetuity will be compared with the value of a non-index-linked perpetuity. The index-linked perpetuity to be considered is a promise to pay a real consumption basket once per period for ever. Let the real payment, measured in consumption units, be D per period. Clearly, such a financial instrument is a valuable possession. What price will this instrument command in the market?

For arithmetic convenience, assume that the first payment D occurs at the end of the period. The market value is the present value of all the future receipts. These are:

$$PV = \frac{D}{1+\rho} + \frac{D}{(1+\rho)^2} + \cdots. \tag{1-33}$$

This sums to D/ρ. Because of index-linking the realized and the *ex ante* real rates are the same and the price could equally well be written as D/ρ^ε. The price of the index-linked bond must adjust to ensure a period-by-period real return of ρ. This price is D/ρ. Note that this is the real price of the bond defined in consumption units. The price at current values would obviously be $P_t D/\rho$ and would therefore increase in *nominal* terms if there was inflation. Our concern will focus on the real price (defined in consumption units) and not on the nominal price, since it is the former quantity that tells us whether or not debts are being paid off in real terms.

Now move one period forward. The value value of the bond will remain at D/ρ. Consequently, if the authorities raise sufficient taxes to pay for the coupon D in every period, the real value of index-linked debt will remain unchanged—this is the equivalent to the case of rolling over the National Debt, with its value neither increasing nor decreasing in real terms. The important point to be demonstrated is that raising taxes to pay off the coupon on non-indexed debt does *not* leave its real value unchanged.

A non-indexed perpetuity is the promise to pay the fixed nominal sum $P_t D$ once per period for ever. The real coupon payments will therefore be $DP_t/P_{t+1}, DP_t/P_{t+2}, \ldots$. The present value of these payments is therefore:

$$PV = \frac{DP_t/P_{t+1}}{1+\rho} + \frac{DP_t/P_{t+2}}{(1+\rho)^2} + \cdots. \tag{1-34}$$

This can be written as:

$$PV = \frac{D}{(1+\rho)(1+\pi)} + \frac{D}{(1+\rho)^2(1+\pi)^2} + \cdots \tag{1-35}$$

noting that $P_t/P_{t+1} = 1/(1+\pi)$ and $P_t/P_{t+2} = 1/(1+\pi)^2$, etc., and where π is the assumed constant rate of inflation. As before, with perfect foresight $\rho = \rho^\varepsilon$. Since $(1+\rho)(1+\pi) = 1 + r$, with the non-indexed coupon, payments are simply discounted at the nominal, rather than the real, rate of interest. The present value of Eq. (1-35) is $D/(\rho + \pi + \rho\pi)$, which is the price the coupon will command to guarantee a real rate of ρ. This is the real price—the current market price would be $P_t D/(\rho + \pi + \rho\pi)$. In a world of perfect foresight the index-linked and non-index-linked coupons would be perfect substitutes at the price ratio of $\rho/(\rho + \pi + \rho\pi)$. Obviously with a positive rate of inflation π, the index-linked coupon would command a higher price in the market.

Now consider the value of the non-indexed coupon one period ahead. This will be $(P_{t+1}/P_{t+2})D/(\rho + \pi + \rho\pi)$. The *real* value of the non-index-linked coupon declines if there is a positive rate of inflation. It declines by a factor $1/(1 + \pi)$ every period. Thus, if the government financed a deficit by issuing non-index-linked debt and raised sufficient taxes to meet the nominal coupon, it would effectively be paying off some of its *real* debt when there was inflation. It would not merely be rolling over the real value of the debt.

This is precisely analogous to the one-period case considered in the last section, though the argument is not as obvious as it was there. Inflation erodes the value of the National Debt on the long-dated maturity in just the same way as on the short-dated maturity, because to raise taxes to meet the *nominal* coupon means running an effective budget surplus in the sense that real debts decline. To make this absolutely clear, suppose there is a real budget deficit of Z. Financing it by the issue of index-linked debt would require $Z\rho/D$ units to be sold. To meet the coupon payments would require the levy of $Z\rho$ additional taxes in every period. Consequently, if $G_t - T_t = -Z\rho$, the real value of the outstanding debt would remain the same in every subsequent period.

Now suppose Z is financed through sales of non-index-linked debt. This requires the sale of $Z(\rho + \pi + \rho\pi)/D$ units. Suppose sufficient taxes are raised to meet the first coupon payment DP_t/P_{t+1}. This requires an amount $Z(\rho + \pi + \rho\pi)/(1 + \pi)$ in additional taxes. As long as π is positive this exceeds $Z\rho$. Inflation erodes the value of the National Debt here, not because it is a tax, but rather because the authorities are raising taxes in addition to the rate required to maintain the real value of debt. The arbitrary decision to call a budget 'balanced' if the nominal coupon payments are met out of taxation is seen to be somewhat absurd, since it automatically implies higher real tax payments with higher inflation rates. The issue is of some importance, because Keynesians argue for less fiscal stringency at times of high unemployment. Fiscal conservatives might falsely claim fiscal prolificacy by pointing up to the actual nominal deficit when, in reality, there is no deficit properly defined.

The problem is rather akin to the front-loading problem in personal debt finance. With borrowers obliged to reduce the nominal values of their debts, this implies a higher real burden at the beginning of the repayment period with higher rates of inflation. There is a correspondingly lower burden at the end. Inflation causes an arbitrary shifting of the burden to the front end. However, the problem should be recognized for what it is. It is not an inevitable consequence of inflation, rather a conscious choice to react to inflation in an arbitrary way. Section 1-10 examines what is, in effect, the equivalent issue in personal debt finance.

PROBLEMS

1-8 With constant inflation of π and a constant real rate of interest of ρ, what happens to the nominal value of a non-indexed perpetuity through time?

1-9 Assuming a constant real interest and inflation rate once more, how does the relative price of the index-linked and non-indexed perpetuities vary through time?

1-8 INFLATION SURPRISES AND THE NATIONAL DEBT

We now have enough understanding to abandon the artifice of perfectly anticipated inflation. When debt is contracted for in nominal terms and without index-linking, a positive inflation surprise *de facto* results in the authorities reneging on part of their real debt obligations. When debt is contracted for in nominal terms, surprise high inflation is good for debtors and bad for creditors; and contrariwise with surprise low inflation. Inflation surprises, by reducing the real taxes that must be raised to pay off debts, can be regarded as an inflation tax charged against the National Debt. It is *unanticipated* inflation that results in this tax and not anticipated inflation, as the discussion in the previous section has made clear.

With debt financed through one-period bonds, the revenue-raising properties of inflation surprises are best seen through Eq. (1-16) or (1-17). With a positive inflation surprise, $P_t > P_t^\varepsilon$, the realized rate of return falls, and with a sufficiently high surprise the realized return could even be negative. By delivering a higher rate of inflation than that expected, the government need raise less real taxes to pay off its debts. To the extent that bondholders anticipate the change in the realized real rate as inflation forecasts are revised, the market value of the bond will fall. Equation (1-14) is an example of such a calculation with the one-period bond. The sums of money involved can be considerable, because changes in the expected rate of inflation can result in large changes in the market value of long-dated bonds. This will be illustrated with reference to the infinitely dated nominal coupon considered previously.

With a long-dated maturity, unlike the one-period bond, it is now necessary to take a view of the expected inflation rate over all future periods, not just one period ahead. Careful consideration must be given to the concepts of the short-term and long-term inflation rates. With perfect foresight no longer being the case, the value of the bond can be calculated as

$$PV = \frac{D(P_t/P_{t+1}^\varepsilon)}{1 + \rho^\varepsilon} + \frac{D(P_t/P_{t+2}^\varepsilon)}{(1 + \rho^\varepsilon)^2} + \cdots \tag{1-36}$$

$$PV = \frac{D}{(1 + \rho^\varepsilon)(1 + \pi_1^\varepsilon)} + \frac{D}{(1 + \rho^\varepsilon)^2(1 + \pi_1^\varepsilon)(1 + \pi_2^\varepsilon)} + \cdots \tag{1-37}$$

where π_j^ε is the expected inflation rate, based on current information, between $t + j$ and $t + j - 1$. There is no need for these period-by-period expected inflation rates to be the same—it is perfectly reasonable for agents to believe that inflation will be higher in the short term but decline in the longer term, or any other pattern.

Because there is uncertainty, the non-index-linked coupon no longer guarantees a real rate of return, unlike the index-linked coupon whose value, described by Eq. (1-33), is independent of any inflation rate. The differing risk characteristics mean that the two financial instruments are no longer perfect substitutes and the expected real rate of return ρ^ε of the non-index-linked bond may now differ from the real rate of the index-linked coupon. The following calculation effectively ignores these complications and assumes a constant ρ^ε, independent of changing risk characteristics. It describes the basic forces by which inflation affects bond prices, without claiming to be a complete theory.

Suppose that agents naively believe the authorities' typical pronouncement about high inflation rates, namely that they are a mere 'blip' and will quickly disappear. To be precise, let $\pi_1^\varepsilon > 0$ and $\pi_j^\varepsilon = 0$ for all $j > 1$. The bond price is easily calculated as $D/(1 + \pi_1^\varepsilon)\rho^\varepsilon$. If, by contrast, the 'blip' was believed to be permanent, with $\pi_j^\varepsilon = \pi_1^\varepsilon$ for all j, then the bond price falls to $D/[\pi_1^\varepsilon + \rho^\varepsilon(1 + \pi_1^\varepsilon)]$. These large differences in price strongly indicate that when the expected inflation rate is considered, the time period over which it holds is crucial to the valuation.

A simple trick, however, serves to cut across the problem of period-by-period varying of expected inflation rates. Equation (1-37) gives the bond price based on expected future 'lumpy' inflation rates π_j^ε. Now imagine a *constant* expected inflation rate that would give the bond the same present value as Eq. (1-37). If π_L^ε is the constant expected rate with the required property then the bond price is $D/(\pi_L^\varepsilon + \rho^\varepsilon(1 + \pi_L^\varepsilon))$, with the equivalent *PV* given by Eq. (1-36) or (1-37). It seems reasonable to interpret π_L^ε as the long-term expected inflation rate—it is the average of the future lumpy rates defined in a particular way, based on the value agents would place on equivalent bonds. The idea is analogous to the concept of permanent income. Permanent income is that *constant* expected future income flow with the same present value as expected future lumpy receipts.

A change in π_L^ε can exert considerable leverage on the market price of non-index-linked debt. If the bond was sold on the basis of a long-term expected inflation rate of 2 per cent and a real return of 1 per cent, the bond price would be (in consumption units)

$$\frac{D}{\pi_L^\varepsilon + \rho^\varepsilon(1 + \pi_L^\varepsilon)} = \frac{D}{0.02 + 0.01 + 0.0002} = \frac{D}{0.0302}.$$

If the expected long-term rate of inflation rose to 4 per cent, the bond price would almost halve to $D/0.0504$. By contrast, note that the price of index-linked debt is bound to remain constant at D/ρ. The near halving in value of the non-index-linked bond simply reflects the size of the amount of debt-reneging by the authorities. In the example, the present value of the future real tax burden is almost halved by the doubling of the expected long-term inflation rate.

Consequently, if the authorities renege on their promises and deliver higher than anticipated inflation rates, this can lead to considerable erosion of the National Debt. Figure 1-1 illustrated this, showing the ratio of market to nominal value of bonds of differing maturity. Notice that, as expected, it is long-dated maturities which show the greatest variation. Figure 1-1 is easily explained. The 1970s were a time of historically high inflation rates in the UK. Thus the low ratios of that time reflect the fact that debt was sold in earlier years when the expected rate of inflation was relatively low. These rates were then revised upwards, with a corresponding fall in market values. The 1980s represented a time of lower inflation and a strong commitment to lower inflation. New debt had been contracted for on the basis of much higher expected inflation rates and these rates were revised *downwards* as lower inflation rates were delivered. The ratio increased as a result and was above 1 for several years. In the late 1980s, this index fell as inflationary pressures took off once again.

It is important to remember that a ratio of 1 does not necessarily imply low yields on gilt-edged stock; merely that the current guess about future inflation roughly coincides with the expected future rate at the time the debt was sold. All in all, market prices would seem the most sensible way to measure the National Debt, since it represents the current value of expected future tax liabilities required to pay off the debt. Indeed, the nominal value may not even reflect the actual price at which the stock was sold! For example, gilt-edged stock is often sold below par value, yet it is the par value that is entered as the nominal value of the stock. For some stocks the difference between market and nominal values is rather glaring; for example 'war loan' in 1992 was given a nominal value about three times its market value.

Previously, it was shown how perfectly anticipated inflation could erode the real value of the National Debt. With high anticipated inflation, a nominal Financial Deficit was consistent with budget balance in the sense of maintaining the real value of the National Debt. Surprise inflation, by contrast, gives an entirely *specious* argument for claiming that a budget deficit is not really a budget deficit. Suppose the government runs a fiscally irresponsible regime, incurring huge deficits. This causes a large upward revision in the expected inflation rate, thus eroding the real value of the National Debt. The false claim is then made that because the real value of the debt has been eroded, the budget deficit was not really a deficit after all and there is a case for even higher deficits in the future.

The authorities are simply paying off their debts here through deceit—effectively reneging on their obligations. Consequently, care must be taken when simply valuing the National Debt year by year as a measure of fiscal stance, because debt erosion through anticipated inflation is bound to be confused with debt erosion through unanticipated inflation.

PROBLEM

1-10 The expected real rate of interest is ρ^ε. The expected inflation rate is believed to follow the following pattern: $1 + \pi_t^\varepsilon = (1 + \pi_{t-1}^\varepsilon)(1 + g)$ for all $t > 0$ and g is a parameter. Calculate the long-run expected inflation rate.

1-9 THE CASE FOR INDEXATION OF DEBT

On one level, it appears to be a good idea to renege on debt obligations by continually delivering higher than expected inflation. The problem with this strategy is that the government acquires a poor reputation and its policy promises then cease to be believed. Because they are not believed, the most benign policy course for the government to adopt is actually to do what the public is expecting all along, because to do what had been originally promised might produce an even worse outcome. Poor reputations can thus lead to very inferior economic results. Chapter 7 pursues this theme in more detail. Part of the problem can easily be seen at this stage and it is the theme developed by Sargent in his critique of the initial failure of the 1979 Thatcher government's economic policy.

The government, when elected, promised to deliver a very low rate of inflation. As can be seen from Table 1-1, the government also had to fund huge budget deficits. These were financed by borrowing—indeed, the deficits were *over-funded* in an attempt to meet monetary targets. The government, therefore, sold large quantities of debt which had long dates of maturity. However, because of the poor reputation of the government reneging on previous promises to deliver low inflation, the debt could only be sold by offering extremely high nominal yields (around 13 per cent). With historical real rates of 2 per cent, this simply reflected the market's refusal to believe that the promised low rate of inflation would actually be delivered.

Here's the rub. Suppose the government actually kept to its promise and delivered zero inflation. (In fact it never did, so the markets were more accurate in their guesses than the government.) Obviously, that would mean an unexpectedly high realized real yield. An infinitely dated coupon sold at price $D/[\rho^\varepsilon + \pi_L^\varepsilon + \rho^\varepsilon\pi_L^\varepsilon]$ represents the present value of the real tax receipts which the market expects will have to be levied in the future. If the government *delivers* zero inflation, the present value of the real tax receipts that would in fact have to be levied becomes D/ρ^ε—which is simply the price the bond would command if there were zero inflation. Clearly, then, to deliver these surprisingly high yields would impose a huge extra burden of taxes to be levied in the future. Sargent pronounced the whole thing to be literally incredible. In reality, the government had little incentive to deliver its promised rate of inflation and it would arguably have been immoral to deliver such a low rate of inflation, since it would have meant an arbitrary redistribution of wealth from taxpayers to fortunate bondholders.

Thus, saving money in the past by reneging on inflation promises becomes a two-edged sword. To reclaim a good reputation in the future requires paying higher than expected real yields. Restoring one's good name becomes an expensive business! Can the government, which has a poor reputation, deliver zero inflation and yet avoid having to pay the above real costs? Is there any way of avoiding the two-edged sword? Yes, there is. The strategy would be for the government to finance deficits by selling index-linked debt. That offers a less costly method of restoring a diminished reputation.

With index-linked stock, the present value of future taxes to fund a real deficit Z will be exactly Z. An index-linked stock has a value which is independent of the expected inflation rate. If, by contrast, Z is covered by issuing non-indexed stock on the basis of an expected long-term rate of inflation π_L^ε, then it takes little thought to realize that the real tax burden of the non-indexed method of finance will lie above Z, to the extent that the *delivered* rate of inflation lies below π_L^ε.

The credibility of an anti-inflation policy could be further enhanced by buying out non-indexed stock already issued and replacing it with an equivalent market value of index-linked stock. The market value of the National Debt depends on the levels of future expected inflation—for example, in 1980 the market to nominal value index stood at 0.8. By 1988, when the Conservative government's anti-inflation credibility, though far from perfect, had peaked, this ratio stood at 1.2. Buying out the National Debt in 1980 could have saved a huge amount in future real taxation, instead of giving bondholders surprisingly large real rates of return. A further point is that index-linked stock offers a guaranteed real return, whereas the real return for non-index-linked stock is risky. Indexation is cheaper to the extent that the authorities could exploit the associated risk premium.

The standard objection to indexation is that taking the pain out of inflation—effectively restoring the economy to work in real terms as would occur in an environment of zero inflation—makes high inflation more likely. This argument is extremely dubious and it has been demonstrated that indexation is cheaper for governments with poor reputations. Indexation, especially if the public were correctly educated as to its purpose, would restore the authorities' reputation and make an anti-inflation strategy more likely to be successful. Of course, it would be a dangerous strategy to index debt and then to adopt highly inflationary policies. Indexation on its own cannot solve the problem of inflation. It could form a small but vital part of an anti-inflation strategy.

PROBLEM

1-11 The long-term expected inflation rate is 10 per cent and the real rate of interest is 2 per cent. A budget deficit of £1 billion is to be financed either by the issue of an indexed perpetuity or a non-indexed perpetuity. Calculate the tax implications for either strategy for:

(*a*) a delivered long-run inflation rate of 0 per cent;
(*b*) a delivered long-run rate of 20 per cent.

1-10 THE MORTGAGE LOBBY

The discussion of the government financing constraint helps to clarify certain issues in personal debt finance. All that is required is to move from the macro level of the government to the micro level of the individual. As before, arbitrary and flawed institutional arrangements regarding interest rates can cause inflation to lead to somewhat anomalous outcomes. The first of these concerns the so-called 'mortgage lobby', which is a broad and powerful coalition arguing for low nominal interest rates, because of the burden high nominal rates put on hard-pressed home-owners. The mortgage lobby is listened to carefully by politicians, since to offend it is to risk the votes of millions of home-owners.

The flawed institutional arrangement is the following. High inflation means higher nominal interest rates. Because debt is paid off in *nominal* and not in *real* terms, this places an undue burden on mortgage payers, which would not occur with a more sensible set of arrangements. The mortgage lobby presses for cuts in nominal rates, bolstered by some choice pictures of middle-class families being thrown onto the streets as the bailiffs reclaim the property. The pressure for premature cuts in interest rates becomes irresistible, which is ultimately self-defeating because it fuels the inflation. The result is high average inflation and the absurdity of the young burdened with ruinously high mortgage payments when, with small children, they can least afford them. Older home-owners, by contrast, have a barely noticeable mortgage at a time when they can most afford large payments. These undesirable consequences of inflation are not really necessary. As will be seen, the argument almost exactly replicates the argument favouring the indexation of public debt. Since the largest financial decision made by most people is to borrow money to purchase a house, these issues should be of direct personal concern to younger readers!

Mortgages, in the UK at least, come mainly in the form of a variable interest loan. The individual must make monthly repayments over a fixed number of years until the loan is eventually paid off. The monthly repayments move up and down in line with market interest rates. The repayment in a typical month can be described in the following way, similar to the government financing constraint:

$$P_t R_t = (1 + r)P_{t-1}B_{t-1} - P_t B_t. \tag{1-38}$$

$P_t R_t$ is the nominal amount of the monthly repayment and R_t is the real payment. $P_{t-1}B_{t-1}$ is the outstanding nominal amount of the loan and r is the nominal interest rate charged between t and $t-1$. This rate need not be fixed and would typically vary over the lifetime of the mortgage. To see why Eq. (1-38) is an exact description of the repayment scheme, suppose the mortgagee was obliged to pay off the whole of the outstanding amount plus interest in one period. This would amount to $(1 + r)P_{t-1}B_{t-1}$. However (conceptually) the mortgagee can contract to borrow an amount $P_t B_t$ to be repaid in subsequent periods. The 'new' amount borrowed reduces the amount that must be repaid this month.

Now consider two contrasting repayment regimes. Regime (1) says $B_t = aB_{t-1}$ where $a < 1$. The mortgagee's repayments must be such that the *real* value of the outstanding debt declines each month. Regime (2) has $P_t B_t = aP_{t-1} B_{t-1}$, where $a < 1$. Here, by contrast, the mortgagee's repayments must be such that the *nominal* value of the loan declines each month. The latter scheme is the typical one; most building societies insist that the outstanding balance declines in nominal terms. Suppose the individual's nominal income is $P_t Y_t$. Under regime (1) the repayment-to-income ratio R_t/Y_t—the fraction of one's salary paid out on the mortgage—is easily derived as

$$\frac{R_t}{Y_t} = \frac{(1 + \rho - a)B_{t-1}}{Y_t}. \tag{1-39}$$

The important point to note is that R_t/Y_t is independent of the rate of inflation. This conclusion has to be tempered somewhat to the extent that there are inflation surprises, which will lead to a varying ρ, which is the *realized* real rate of interest. This factor is not likely to be large because r is highly responsive to the actual inflation rate. Under this regime inflation does not impose an additional burden on the mortgagee and the debt is still being paid off in real terms. Notice also that the R_t/Y_t ratio declines, given that B_{t-1} must be falling and Y_t is increasing.

Now consider regime (2). The repayment-to-income ratio is easily evaluated as

$$\frac{R_t}{Y_t} = \frac{[1 + \rho - a/(1 + \pi)]B_{t-1}}{Y_t} \tag{1-40}$$

For a given value of B_{t-1}, the R_t/Y_t is higher under regime (2) for positive values of π. Furthermore, this burden is increasing with π. Regime (2) leads to the well-known front-loading problem and is entirely equivalent to the case of a government running a Financial Deficit so as to maintain a constant nominal value of debt rather than a constant real value of debt. There it was seen that high inflation required an arbitrary real budget surplus for a zero nominal Financial Deficit. Here inflation loads the burden of debt to the front end of the repayment period in exactly the same way. Given higher initial real payments, naturally enough the burden of debt declines most rapidly for regime (2). Notice, however, that it is not inflation *per se* that causes this redistribution of repayments, but rather the arbitrary choice of a scheme requiring debts to be repaid in nominal terms.

The effect of inflation on R_t/Y_t is quite severe, with an elasticity close to 1. Thus a doubling of the inflation rate would roughly double the required repayment. Letting $Z_t = R_t/Y_t$, the elasticity of repayments with respect to inflation is then

$$\frac{[dZ_t/d\pi]\pi}{Z_t} = \frac{a\pi}{[(1 + \rho)(1 + \pi) - a][1 + \pi]}. \tag{1-41}$$

With a value for a of approximately 1, this elasticity is less than 1, but nevertheless close to 1 for reasonable parameter values.

With a steady inflation rate, young couples with the heaviest financial commitments are obliged to pay most at precisely the wrong time. Of course, after several years of struggle, mortgage payments become a trivial burden because front-loading implies a corresponding lower burden as the mortgage progresses. Long-time house-owners boast about their good fortune and 'cheap' houses, often forgetting earlier struggles. New entrants, mortgaged to the hilt, struggle to cope. A two-class society of home-owner is thereby created which is socially divisive. All these problems are exacerbated by rises in the inflation rate, as Eq. (1-40) shows. Young couples take out the maximum R_t/Y_t they can afford, only to find a large increase in their monthly repayments as the inflation rate worsens, leading to severe financial hardship.

Raising interest rates in response to inflation is logical and appropriate. Regime (1), which works in real terms—effectively the equivalent to indexation in bond finance—should cause little or no pain to mortgagees. It is regime (2) that creates the mortgage lobby clamouring for premature reductions in nominal interest rates. Understandably, politicians find this pressure hard to resist, with the result that monetary policy often becomes a case of too little too late and a worse than average inflation performance. Regime (1) takes a more relaxed attitude to debt. With high inflation, nominal debt is allowed to rise even though debt is being paid off in real terms.

The front-loading problem is perhaps the most important one, but there are other aspects of the housing market deserving of mention. Foremost are two important tax concessions. First, the interest on a mortgage up to a fixed value (currently £30 000 in 1991) is tax-deductible. Secondly, in selling one's home one is exempt from capital gains tax, unlike most other assets. The problem with tax concessions such as these is that, far from making house purchase cheaper, the tax benefits simply become capitalized. With cheaper mortgages, purchasers are able to afford a higher gross monthly payment. With a fixed housing stock and scarcity of land for new houses, the concession drives up house prices, making them more expensive than they would otherwise be. The capital gains concession reinforces the view of housing not just as a place to live but also as a form of saving. People tend to over-invest in housing, purchasing the highest-priced property they can afford rather than the property best suited to their housing needs. Once granted, such concessions become extremely difficult to remove. The effect of their removal would be to make existing householders face a once-only capital loss on their houses. Over the years, the tax concessions have been gradually eroded as the tax-deductible amount has not been increased in line with inflation and in 1991 relief was restricted to the standard rate of tax only. This gradualist approach is probably sensible.

This discussion illustrates the general principle that an 'old policy is often a good policy'. This is the principle that if we were able to design an ideal system afresh, all anomalies would be removed from the outset, but that does not imply that it is sensible or desirable to move immediately to the 'ideal' system, given that a less than ideal system is actually in place. For example, it was argued that regime (1), with $B_t = aB_{t-1}$, had some advantages, but, with high positive inflation, a move to this system would mean a drop in average mortgage repayments. An undesirable consequence of the change would be to drive up house prices once more. Thus it is no longer clear that a move to regime (1) would be desirable. What one could say is that if regime (1) were the existing system it would definitely be undesirable to move to regime (2).

The discussion highlights a general theme about rational expectations, which will be emphasized in later chapters. However, one does not necessarily have to believe in rational expectations to accept the following point. Believers in rational expectations argue that *surprises* are undesirable. Agents base their decisions on a particular policy regime, which the government has assured them will not be reneged upon. To face agents with a sudden, unexpected change in regime can have extremely high real costs. If someone makes a house purchase decision on the basis of a promise of a tax concession, it is clearly unfair and costly to renege on that promise.

The principle can be expressed in the following way. Suppose a new policy regime is to come into force and there is a choice between regime X and regime Z. At the outset, the government determines that regime X is the most desirable. They announce that this regime is the chosen one and that this is the policy they will stick to. Agents' decisions are therefore based to a large extent on the assumption that regime X will remain in force for the foreseeable future. Now somewhere along the line it is realized that regime Z would have been the most desirable policy to have followed at the outset. It does not follow that an immediate switch to regime Z is now desirable. Regime Z now, given agents' beliefs that regime X was in fact to prevail, is not the same as the unconditional regime Z. This simple insight is often overlooked, yet it is actually rather important. Some argue that policy certainty is critical to economic success—a notion which sits uncomfortably with the ballot box where it is accepted that policy regimes, through the will of the people, can be and are reneged upon. However, some people do not accept the commonly held view that democracy should always mean 'one person one vote'. This theme is developed further in Chapter 9.

It is often claimed that 'you can never go wrong by investing in property'. Certainly, as can be seen from Table 1-2, for anyone who invested in housing in the early 1970s or the mid-1980s, house purchase seemed like a one-way bet. Not only was the nominal value of their mortgage being eroded, but also their asset was appreciating much faster than general prices. Many engaged on a cycle of round-tripping, selling their house at an enormous tax-free profit and using the proceeds as a deposit on the next, more expensive house. Clearly, those years represented a South Sea Bubble with the naive belief that the cycle was bound to continue for ever and that any price for a house would prove to be cheap in the very near future. Chapter 4 will examine a rational expectations rationale for such bubbles.

The housing market can be perverse, creating the illusion that the way to wealth creation is to invest in housing. From an individual point of view this has frequently proved true, but from the social viewpoint it is not clear a society can be made more wealthy by playing games of musical chairs with the existing housing stock. Just as it had in 1974,

Table 1-2 UK ratio of house prices to average prices (1970 = 100)

Year	Price ratio	Year	Price ratio	Year	Price ratio
1970	100	1977	115	1984	137
1971	106	1978	127	1985	141
1972	129	1979	144	1986	160
1973	161	1980	146	1987	180
1974	147	1981	134	1988	216
1975	130	1982	126	1989	238
1976	121	1983	133	1990	236

Source: *Economic Trends Annual Supplement 1992.*

the speculative bubble in housing ended once again in the middle of 1990—the figures in Table 1-2 do not fully reflect the dramatic decline in house prices in the latter part of that year. Many who purchased houses around that time were badly caught out. They are burdened with exceptionally high nominal rates on mortgages and their collateral asset has declined in value. That's the joy of capitalism! Losing money is more a case of bad luck combined with a smidgen of greed, than of bad judgement. Only wimps squeal.

PROBLEM

1-12 An individual borrows £80 000 to purchase a house at a nominal interest rate of 10 per cent. The loan must be fully repaid at the end of 20 years and there is to be a fixed annual nominal repayment over the life of the loan.

(*a*) Calculate the fixed annual repayment.
(*b*) Design and comment upon alternative repayment schemes.

1-11 TAXATION OF INTEREST INCOME

The previous discussion has highlighted how inflation, through specific institutional arrangements, can cause unintended distortions. Because nominal interest receivable is treated as taxable income, yet another arbitrary distortion is introduced. High inflation leads to higher nominal interest rates. As a consequence, the authorities receive a higher *real* tax take. This is a rather different effect from inflation taxes, discussed earlier, and the two ideas should not be confused. To see the precise nature of the distortion, the nominal after-tax yield on an asset is given by

$$\frac{(1-t)(P_t B_t - P_{t-1} B_{t-1})}{P_{t-1} B_{t-1}} \equiv \frac{P_t B_t^* - P_{t-1} B_{t-1}}{P_{t-1} B_{t-1}} \tag{1-42}$$

where t is the tax rate and B_t^* is defined to be the real after-tax value of the asset. Solving for B_t^* gives:

$$B_t^* = (1-t)B_t + \frac{t B_{t-1}}{1+\pi}. \tag{1-43}$$

The after-tax real rate of return $\rho^* = (B_t^* - B_{t-1})/B_{t-1}$ is, therefore, related to the pre-tax or gross real rate of return $\rho^g = (B_t - B_{t-1})/(B_{t-1})$ as follows:

$$\rho^* = (1-t)\rho^g - \frac{t\pi}{1+\pi}. \tag{1-44}$$

This shows that for any given gross real rate of return ρ^g, the after-tax real rate of return declines with π. To give some idea of the size, suppose $\rho^g = 5$ per cent and $t = 0.25$. Then an inflation rate of 17.6 per cent would be sufficient to reduce ρ^* to zero.

Alternatively, lenders, if they demand a fixed after-tax real return, will ensure an increase in the gross real rate to compensate for the distortion introduced by inflation. Either way, it can be seen that inflation induces an entirely arbitrary effect. If one believes in conspiracy theories, inflation offers governments yet another easy way to raise real tax revenues without having to change tax parameters. As before, the way to avoid this distortion is to index-link interest payments so that tax is payable only on the real rate of return. Since zero inflation, at present, appears to be an unobtainable ideal, a fairer deal for savers would be to set ρ^* to equal $(1 - t)\rho^g$, independent of the rate of inflation at all times.

PROBLEM

1-13 The relationship between the nominal gross interest and the real gross interest rate is given by $(1 + r) = (1 + \rho)(1 + \pi)$. A tax system is designed so that the net real interest rate $\rho(1 - t)$ is to be independent of the inflation rate. How must t_0, the tax rate on nominal interest, respond to the inflation rate?

1-12 SUMMARY

This chapter has covered a lot of ground and laid essential foundations for what is to follow. Foundations are sometimes less interesting than the structures they support, so bear with it if the appetite is not fully whetted as yet! The key point is that by thinking carefully about the government financing constraint we can move away from the static straitjacket of IS/LM to a richer dynamic structure. It was shown that what constitutes a budget deficit in an environment of inflation is somewhat complicated. As an aid to understanding, the close conceptual relationship between the government financing constraint and the personal financing constraint was emphasized, though the latter analogy should not be pushed too far.

ESSAY TOPICS

1-1 What is meant by the term 'a balanced budget'?
1-2 Was the policy, whether intended or not, of reduction in the National Debt since the Second World War a mistaken one?
1-3 What makes an economic policy credible?
1-4 Does debt financing of current government consumption necessarily reduce the wealth of the nation?
1-5 Put the arguments for and against the indexation of debt instruments.

READING

This chapter is largely inspired by Chapters 1 and 2 of Sargent (1986), which includes the article 'Some unpleasant monetarist arithmetic'. Useful supplementary material is taken from Chapter 4 of Hoover (1988). Much useful information about the National Debt is to be found in the *Bank of England Quarterly Bulletin*. As proprietors of the debt, they publish an annual update in the November issue. Chapters 9, 10 and 12 of Morris (1985) also have a lot of useful descriptive material. The issue of risk premia and similar items are covered by the Capital Asset Pricing Model, for which Chapter 10 of Blanchard and Fischer (1989) provides a most readable introduction. The government financing constraint and its importance for macroeconomics was 'discovered' by Christ (1968). Blinder and Solow (1973) later exploited the idea, though it must be said that this article is something of a red herring in the history of macroeconomics. The classic article on Ricardian equivalence, expounding the idea that bonds are just deferred taxation and not wealth, is by Barro (1974). Chapter 7 of Hoover (1988) is, however, much more readable. The welfare costs of inflation taxes are described in Bailey (1956) and Foster (1976). The figures quoted on the size of the inflation tax is from Sachinides (1991). Finally, for a discussion of public debt from a 'constitutional contractarian' viewpoint see Chapters 17 and 18 of Buchanan (1986). Buchanan believes deficit financing should be made illegal.

2

IS THERE AN OPTIMAL SIZE FOR THE GOVERNMENT SECTOR?

The previous chapter was about the *difference* between government expenditure and tax receipts, where the focus of attention was on how these differences could be financed and the consequences of the financing regime. The present chapter explores a rather different question: what is the appropriate *level* of government expenditure? Most, barring some extreme libertarians and anarchists, would agree a need for some minimal claim by the state on current economic resources, since only a centrally organized government can provide the necessary authority to enforce the moral order. In the absence of such power a state of Hobbesian anarchy would prevail where 'Life is poor, brutish and shorte.' In short, the *Wealth of Nations* derives from this fundamental role of the state and is not independent of it. But is there or should there be a limit to the maximum claim of the state on currently available resources?

There is a view that if the public sector becomes too large and bloated it will smother and eventually kill off the private sector. It is taxes levied on the private sector which finance state expenditures, and, if this burden becomes too great, the private sector will lose any incentive to be productive and grow. A vicious circle of national decline then ensues, with the public sector carcinogenically consuming the private sector. Certainly, this was a view widely held by the ascendant New Right in the Conservative party when they were elected in Britain in May 1979. They were pledged to reverse the trend of the state claiming a progressively larger share of national output. This chapter aims to put forward some cogent arguments to place the issues in some kind of perspective.

Chapter 1 showed that it is a good idea to think about problems in a dynamic way and the present chapter re-emphasizes this important lesson. Thus a fruitful approach is to think about what might happen to the level of government expenditure through time, rather than its absolute level at a particular point of time, which ignores the dynamic forces. The dynamic picture is ultimately more revealing and, indeed, such an approach is the only sensible way of studying the problem.

Figure 2-1 shows the ratio of the total current expenditure of both central government and local authorities to GNP in the UK from 1948 to 1990. This peaked at 42.3 per cent in 1982. The figures exclude expenditure on capital items, which would have added a further 2.6 per cent of GNP in 1982. Broadly, there has been a long-term tendency for the proportion of expenditure to increase, though the rather dramatic fall since 1982 should be noted (upon which further comment will be made). The Conservatives can claim to have reduced the size of the government sector. Note also that the figures exclude the market activity of publicly owned corporations such as British Rail or the Post Office, so the post-1982 decline cannot be explained by the policy of widespread privatization of such activities.

As all readers know—or ought to know—government expenditure consists of two broad categories. The first category consists of expenditure on goods and services; all those state activities with which everyone is familiar: health care, the armed forces, social services, police, teachers, dustbin collection and so on. The second category, which is roughly the same size as the former, consists of transfer payments. These items are not about productive activity and hence do not contribute to GNP. These consist of items such as social security benefits, child benefits, the state pension and interest on the National Debt.

This chapter is all about the forces that drive the first category of expenditure. The level of transfer payments will be determined by three broad factors. First, there are demographic factors such as the numbers over retirement age and specifically economic factors such as the numbers unemployed. Secondly, there are the levels of benefits to be paid. For example, linking benefit levels to just the rate of inflation will, *ceteris paribus*, reduce the proportionate burden as living standards rise. Historically, benefit levels since

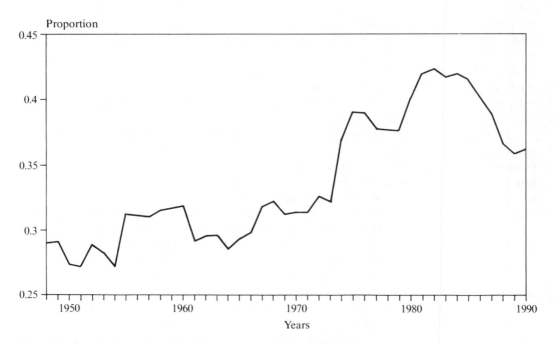

Figure 2-1 Government current expenditure as a proportion of GNP
Source: Central Statistical Office

1945 have risen by more than the rate of inflation, though in the 1980s benefits were generally only index-linked to inflation. Thus, governments have generally operated a relative rather than an absolute poverty standard. The third factor is the generosity with which the system is operated. For example, the numbers in receipt of long-term sickness benefit, or invalidity pension as it is now known, increased by 552 000 (excluding those over 65) from 1971 to 1989, figures which cannot simply be explained away by demographic factors since every age category, both male and female, has shown a sizeable increase. Obviously, there has not been a dramatic decline in the nation's health over this relatively short period and such figures can only be explained by a system being operated more benignly with regard to the question of what qualifies as long-term disability.

Figure 2-2 focuses on the main topic of concern. Expenditure on goods and services as a proportion of GNP is shown on the left-hand scale. Again, this shows the same long-term increase, peaking at 22 per cent of GNP in 1981. As before, there is a decline after this time, but this decline is much less pronounced (less than 2 per cent) compared to the fall in total current expenditure (including transfer payments). Government final consumption can itself be split into two roughly equal categories. First, the government will make purchases directly from the private sector. These range from items such as military equipment down to chalk for school blackboards. The second broad category consists of wages and salaries of state employees—doctors, teachers, police, military, social workers, civil servants, tax collectors and so on. The proportion of expenditure on this category is shown on the right-hand scale of Fig. 2-2. It is wages and salaries which show the greatest long-term increase in terms of the proportion of GNP being claimed in 1990 (about a 50 per cent increase). As before, there has been a small decline since 1981. However,

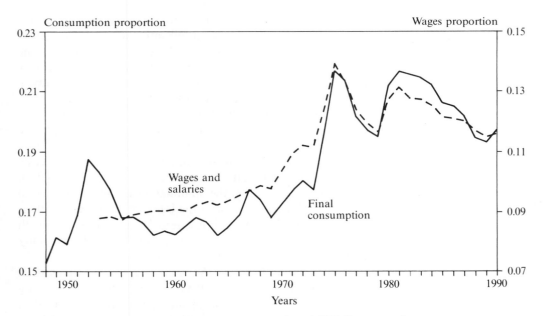

Figure 2-2 Government current expenditure as a proportion of GNP (by category)
Source: Central Statistical Office

some caution is required here because of the government policy of 'contracting out' to the private sector a lot of activities previously undertaken by public sector employees. For example, hospital cleaning contracts, refuse collection and so on, are now frequently carried out by the private sector. What previously appeared as wages and salaries now becomes a direct purchase from the private sector. It all goes to show that taking figures at face value should only be done with a lot of care!

Nevertheless, it is fair to conclude that government economic activity has become increasingly important and the fastest-growing category has been the wage and salary bill of public sector employees. (Note once more that Fig. 2-2 excludes employees in public corporations.) The task of this chapter is to explain the forces which make this so and to explain why it will be very difficult for any government to resist such forces, despite periods of temporary success.

It is the general increase in expenditure, with consequent rises in the tax burden, which is a cause of general alarm in the body politic. There always seem to be excellent claims for more public expenditure, yet if these claims are not resisted the feeling is that the public sector will eventually emasculate the private sector. Those who see a strong connection between personal freedom and the free enterprise system regard such growth as anathema. Expenditure, from this viewpoint, should be a matter of individual and not collective choice insofar as it is possible. It certainly formed a large part of the Conservative political agenda when they were elected in 1979.

The question to be posed is whether the growth in the state sector's role in the economy is pathological or whether it represents something else. Is it simply the unpleasant manifestation of a profligate centre, inefficient and unwilling to resist the overblown claims of sectional interest groups—the health lobby, the law-and-order brigade, the education lobby, *et al.*? The theme of this chapter is that such growth is not necessarily pathological; it is precisely what would be expected in a healthy, growing and successful economy. This argument should not be misunderstood, since it is easy to fall into the trap of asserting that *any* growth in state expenditure is acceptable; and as the chapter proceeds some discussion of pathological aspects will be included. Many of the activities currently undertaken by the state could actually be taken over by the private sector, leaving just a very small state sector. The point of this chapter is not to adjudicate on whether such changes are desirable, but rather to show that such activities would tend to grow as a proportion of GNP, whether or not they were undertaken by the state or by the private sector.

The growth in the public sector is inextricably linked with another great modern issue in macroeconomics, the question of de-industrialization. Concomitant with the growth in the public sector has been a dramatic decline in the manufacturing and production industries' share of GNP. Although the 'disease' is worse in the UK than in other countries, such declines have been a general feature of most wealthy countries as well as a growth in the state sector. De-industrialization and the growth in the public sector are virtually Siamese twins and it is the same forces that drive both phenomena.

Figure 2-3 illustrates de-industrialization. It shows the value share of manufacturing as a proportion of GNP from 1948 to 1990. Note that it is the *value* of manufacturing output in any particular year expressed as a proportion of the current value of GNP in that particular year. The value share can change for two reasons. First, the relative price of manufactured goods could change and, secondly, the quantity could change. It must

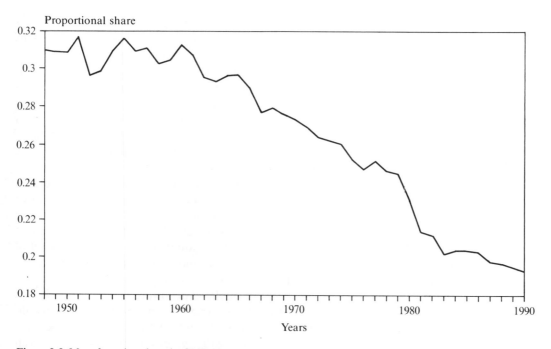

Figure 2-3 Manufacturing share in GNP 1948–1990
Source: Central Statistical Office

not be confused with the real output share, which attempts to abstract from changes in relative prices. This issue will be *critical* to the ensuing arguments.

A second, very minor, point is that manufacturing is a subset, albeit the largest proportion by far, of production industries. De-industrialization really refers to the whole of the production sector; however, what is true for manufacturing is also largely true for the production sector, with the notable exception of North Sea Oil and Gas exploitation. Another, even more minor, point is that the denominator in all the figures is GNP at market prices. The choice is dictated by the fact that this is the most widely quoted figure, but there are reasons for preferring a factor cost measure. However, the broad tendencies would not be changed one iota by changing the GNP measure. The complement of the decline in the production sector is, relative to this, a growing and successful service sector. The reason why de-industrialization and a growing public sector are basically the same topic is because the public sector is almost exclusively engaged in the business of providing services.

Services can be split into two categories. First, there are marketed services, which are almost exclusively provided by the private sector. Secondly, there are non-marketed services, which are effectively the exclusive preserve of central government and local authorities. Individuals are not charged personally when they receive non-marketed services. If I have an operation on the National Health I am not personally liable for the cost of the operation. I do not pay to have a crime investigated or to be visited by a social worker and so on. Such items are financed through taxation levied on all.

Marketed services, by contrast, are paid for as they are received. I am charged for each restaurant meal, theatre ticket, package holiday and so on. When the plumber mends my burst pipe, I am liable for the bill. The more I buy, the more I am charged. Thus, unlike non-marketed services, there is a well-defined price for each unit. There is, however, a shadow or implicit price for non-marketed services. The fact that non-marketed services are not charged for directly does not make them 'free'. In essence, there is not much difference between non-marketed and marketed services. Many non-marketed services could easily be transferred to the private sector and much of what is provided by the state in the UK is marketed activity in many other countries. Health care in Germany, higher education in the USA, toll roads in France, are three among numerous possible examples.

There is a problem about the extent of provision of state-organized non-marketed services, because their level of provision is not directly subject to the rigours of the price mechanism. If, because of rising costs, the price of a privately provided service should rise excessively, demand will fall and provision decline to reflect that fact. There is a direct market test which relates the cost of the service to the amount of provision. The level of provision of non-marketed services is based on political judgement, with the ballot box the final sanction. Ultimately it depends on how much voters are prepared to pay in taxes. Many claim that this is not an effective check on public expenditure.

Is the provision of health care, to give just one example, the same as that which would arise in a privately run, charged-for system? If hospitals and doctors had to compete for business might this not lead to large efficiency gains, with high cost providers being driven out of business? In reality, government ministers decide the appropriate level of provision, bearing in mind all those 'political' factors which are thought to be important. It is argued that such a process, because ministers do not like to be seen as mean and penny-pinching, leads to over-provision. Furthermore, the actual resources deployed are not used in the most efficient manner. The health reforms introduced in 1991 have tried to introduce explicit prices, without actually charging the patients, into the Health Service in an attempt to create a 'market' within the state-provided sector. This has excited considerable controversy and it must be said that the level of debate on the issues is shockingly low—but let that pass, it is not central to the main theme, which concerns the growth of services in general. The appropriate split between the market and non-market is a separate question altogether.

The method adopted in this chapter poses the question: what must be the consequences through time if consumers' tastes are such that they demand a certain level of services, both marketed and non-marketed? Given a chosen split between the marketed and non-marketed sectors, the consequences for the growth of the public sector can then be derived. There can be no grounds for complaining with this methodology. What people spend on *marketed* services is there for all to see and, although you and I might disapprove of other people's tastes, if that's how others choose to spend their money then so be it. With *non-marketed* services one is free to argue that the ratio compared to the market is too large or too small. One can easily work out the consequences for the public sector of changing the ratio through time. For example, one strongly held view is that the ratio of government final consumption should remain constant or even decline as a proportion of GNP. One can then trace the argument backwards to find out what this really imposes on the consumption pattern of the country's citizens. It is up to readers to say whether they find it acceptable or would prefer something else. It is by such stratagems that respectable economists maintain their dubious reputations for impartiality!

The remainder of the chapter is structured in the following way. Section 2-1 puts forward the argument in an intuitive way. Section 2-2 then assembles some interesting empirical evidence of direct relevance and Sec. 2-3 puts forward a simple model to rationalize the facts. The mathematics involved in Sec. 2-3 is very elementary, yet it describes something that is important and really worth knowing something about. Of the many thousands of economic models that are on offer, very few are actually useful beyond providing theorists with a means of advancing their careers. The unbalanced growth model of Sec. 2-3 has many classic virtues. It is simple to comprehend and does describe something that actually happens out there in the world. The chapter will conclude with a brief discussion of how the open economy impinges upon the processes described in what follows.

2-1 AN OVERVIEW

The argument is based on three critical assumptions that will be supported by empirical evidence in the next section. The assumptions are:

1. Labour markets, *in the long run*, behave competitively. Wage rates for the same type of labour cannot permanently become out of line.
2. Productivity growth in production industries is faster than in the service sector.
3. As living standards rise, consumers wish to maintain a roughly constant proportion between the real volume of services and the quantity of manufactured goods consumed.

Consider each of these assumptions in turn, starting with proposition 1. Nowadays, it is fashionable theoretical practice to view labour markets as not behaving competitively, and Chapter 8 will consider several variants of this theme. For short-term analysis this may be a very fruitful approach, but over the broad sweep of years—several decades are considered here—to assume that the competitive paradigm holds is far more accurate than any existing alternative and is amply justified by empirical evidence. At any point in time there may be substantial divergences from the competitive outcome, but the point is that these divergences cannot and do not increase for ever. Wage rates, under the force of competition, cannot become increasingly out of line. Thus the claim that labour markets are competitive is here meant to be the *weaker* one, that the growth in real wages over long periods of time will be the same for comparable types of labour. The stronger claim, that the *level* of real wage should be the same, is not really necessary to the argument.

I often play a game with my students to check if they really understand how competitive capitalist economies really work, by posing the following question. Suppose there are two firms, A and B, employing roughly comparable types of labour. Now suppose firm A secures a large productivity increase, whereas firm B secures none. The question is this. Should firm B workers be entitled to a real wage increase if firm A workers are rewarded with a real wage rise? The average response rate to this question, of which I have kept a careful record over the years, is 83 per cent against any wage increase for firm B workers. In fact, 83 per cent have got the wrong answer. Rest assured, however, that the majority of trained economists would respond in the same way and, at a guess, 95 per cent of those politicians who pronounce themselves in favour of unfettered competition and free enterprise. It simply proves the general proposition that fanatics do not always understand precisely what it is they are so enthusiastic about.

The reason why firm B workers must receive a wage increase is the iron law of competition. Workers in both firms are comparable and firm B must eventually pay a comparable wage, otherwise it will be unable to recruit labour. In the short run it may perhaps get away with a low wage rise because firm B workers are temporarily locked in and there are high transaction costs associated with changing jobs. In the long term, however, employers must pay the 'going rate' and firm B cannot forever insist that its workers earn less. The *reductio ad absurdum* would be when firm A regularly secured higher productivity increases than firm B. According to the proposition that wage increases should only go to those who have productivity increases, earnings differentials between firm A and firm B would permanently widen.

Given that firm B must pay the going rate to retain and recruit labour, then its unit labour costs must rise faster than in firm A. (Unit labour costs are simply the labour costs associated with producing one unit of output.) If firm B wants to retain its profit margin, maintaining a fixed mark-up on unit labour costs, then the price at which firm B must sell its output must rise faster than firm A's price. Thus, in the long term, firm B must raise its prices faster than firm A. If the public are not prepared to purchase the higher priced products of firm B—and if the products of both firms are comparable they certainly will not be—then firm B will simply go out of business. The proposition that workers will be permanently prepared, or even should be prepared, to work for less than the 'going rate' to ensure the survival of enterprises is a fundamental canard about how competitive systems work. (Academic salaries seem to be the one clear exception to this general rule!) Competition is not about ethics, it is about survival.

Firm A and firm B could employ comparable labour types but produce quite different outputs. Then firm B could quite happily survive despite rising unit labour costs, providing the public are prepared to pay the higher price relative to firm A. Not only could this happen, it is what does happen among the low-productivity growth enterprises which survive. Neither need firm A nor firm B necessarily employ directly comparable labour types for the above propositions to hold. For example, A might employ mainly manual type labour whereas B might employ white collar professionals. With differing productivity growth, unless the benefits are shared between both groups of workers, an ever-widening differential would arise between manual and white collar workers. In the short run, some variation might be expected, but in the long run there will be a far greater variation in the productivity growth between industries than the growth rates in real wages across industries.

This all shows how careful one must be when discussing the real wage. The real wage can be defined in two very different ways. First, there is the product real wage, whereby money wages are deflated by the price of the firm's output. Textbook microeconomic theory says marginal physical product should equal the product real wage. Secondly, there is the consumption real wage where the deflator is the consumer price index. The consumption real wage is of most immediate concern to employees because it represents the consumption basket that money wages can buy. Therefore, the product real wage drives labour demand and the consumption real wage drives labour supply. The discussion shows that much smaller variation should be observed in the growth rate of the *consumption* real wage across industries compared to *product* real wage growth across industries. Productivity growth and product real wage growth should be positively correlated, whereas no such correlation need be observed for productivity growth and the consumption real wage. Many people seem to believe that the choice of deflator for the real wage is an unimportant issue, but our discussion shows that it is crucial.

The foregoing is a broadly accurate picture of what actually happens in real economies. Naturally enough, there are several complications that will add interesting detail and blur the sharp picture that has been drawn. To give one example: a firm could secure productivity increases by employing higher quality labour, say, by moving towards a more skilled labour force. In this case, a correlation between the *average* real (consumption) wage growth and productivity growth would be expected. The real wage growth simply reflects an increase in the proportion of the higher paid, higher quality labour within the firm. Despite such short-run complications, it remains true that the broad canvas that has been painted is an accurate description.

The discussion now leads nicely into the second of the two propositions, for which, again, there is overwhelming empirical evidence. The very nature of the service sector is such that the opportunities for productivity enhancements are bound to be limited compared to the production sector. The classic example is that of an orchestra attempting to secure a large pay increase for its players by agreeing to play Beethoven's fifth symphony in five minutes! That is not to say that there are no possibilities for productivity enhancements in the service sector. For example, in health care the length of time spent in hospital for standard operations such as an appendix removal has been greatly reduced. In banking, the use of automated cash dispensers is a recent and important productivity innovation. In retailing, the move to supermarkets and self-service petrol stations are longer-standing productivity enhancements that have proved widely popular with consumers.

But overall the opportunities are bound to be smaller compared to the production sector. At the end of the day, the teachers with their chalk and slate have not changed since the age of Socrates. Indeed, it is the very fact that many services are labour intensive that makes them attractive to consumers. The well-off prefer to dine in restaurants with a large number of waiters to enhance their enjoyment of the experience. The wealthier demand a better haircut, which basically involves the barber—or as he or she is now re-christened, the 'hairstylist'—taking more time over each head of hair.

Combine this second proposition with the first and there are the beginnings of a promising theory. Think of firm B as the service sector and firm A as the production sector. To compete in the labour market, the service sector must pay the 'going rate'. Unit labour costs must therefore be rising more quickly in the service sector and this applies equally well to the non-marketed government sector. The real consumption wage of government employees is bound to rise. The same quantity of government services must inevitably become more expensive in successful capitalist economies. Indeed, the more successful a country is in terms of a higher differential growth rate between both sectors, the faster will be the rise in costs for government services relative to the private sector.

This provides a neat resolution of the perennial paradox of the government claiming to spend more on services, yet the public complaining about the diminution in quality of those same services. With rising unit labour costs, total *real* expenditure can easily rise while, at the same time, the physical volume of services is declining. In reality, it is very difficult for any government to limit, except in the short run, the growth in public expenditure, except by transferring what were previously state responsibilities into the private sector. The Conservatives tried from 1979, but in the General Election of 1992 effectively admitted failure with a large increase in state expenditure expected.

Now consider proposition 3 to derive the complete picture. With consumers wanting to maintain a constant proportion between their consumption of services and produced goods, de-industrialization must be inevitable. If no employment shifted from manufacturing to the service sector then, with differential productivity growth, output of services would decline relative to manufacturing, which contradicts the initial assumption. Consumer tastes are king, driving the whole picture, given propositions 1 and 2. If the industrial structure is to respond to individual tastes—and it seems eminently reasonable that it should—then de-industrialization should be welcomed and not resisted. Far from being a sign of economic failure, a growing service sector (of which state-provided services form an important component) and a declining manufacturing base can be testimony to economic success.

Two points of qualification need to be made at this juncture. First, domestic consumer demand has been implicitly identified with domestic output. Open economy aspects obviously temper this somewhat. A thriving manufacturing base could still be maintained with a declining domestic demand for manufactures, providing there was an increasing export market for manufactures. Japan is an excellent example of this phenomenon. In the UK the share of exported manufactures has also declined, exacerbating any underlying tendency to de-industrialize. Again, this need not be a sign of failure, a point to which we will return in the last part of this chapter.

The idea that there is no need for any concern about the figures revealed in Fig. 2-3 would be a premature conclusion. Some decline in manufacturing may be healthy, but the very steep decline observed in the UK may have had pathological aspects. For example, manufacturing employment fell by over 10 per cent in just one year in 1981–82 and the essence of the de-industrialization thesis is that this labour surplus would have been absorbed by an expanding and buoyant service sector. This did not happen; after 1979 service sector employment hardly increased at all, with a huge rise in unemployment as the result.

Returning to the main theme: in a society composed of markets and with freedom of choice, a country's industrial structure largely mirrors consumers' tastes. (The open economy is one important wedge preventing an exact correspondence.) If tastes were such that consumers demanded an increasing proportion of manufactures, then de-industrialization would be severely reduced or even reversed. In less affluent countries it appears that people do want the 'basics' of life. In such societies agriculture plays a dominant role, with a small manufacturing base and a minimal role for services apart from domestic servants. The production sector is bound to appear highly successful in the early stages of development as tastes and increasing wealth drive a huge increase in demand for its products. However, as economies mature, so tastes change and de-industrialization is the inevitable result. Notice also that as economies mature and the service sector becomes more dominant, the underlying growth rate must slow down. It is the transitional economies, such as South Korea, Hong Kong, Taiwan and Singapore, which show the fastest growth rates.

Marketed services must become more expensive relative to manufactured goods, a feature particularly noticeable to those people approaching an advanced age, who can recall less wealthy times. It is not that inflation makes theatre tickets, haircuts, plumbers, electricians and so on *seem* more expensive than they once were; they *are* more expensive. Why then does the service sector not only survive but prosper? Basically, there are two countervailing forces at work. The first is the price effect, which, excepting the highly unusual Giffen good case, would tend to make individuals buy less services. The second is the income effect. Overall, as is entirely possible, there must be a strong positive income effect which dominates the price effect, thus maintaining the buoyant demand for services.

The following is a consequence of the rise in the price of services. If consumers seek to maintain a constant output share, then expenditure shares (in current prices) will rise in favour of services, for the simple reason that the unit price of the latter must rise relative to the former. What applies to the marketed sector applies equally well to the non-marketed sector. To maintain a constant volume share of non-marketed to marketed services requires increased state expenditure, as a proportion of total national expenditure.

Herein lies the heart of this chapter's thesis. There is no absolute level of government expenditure which is optimal. In a growing economy, with the state providing a fixed range of services, government expenditure must increase as a proportion of GNP if people wish to maintain a constant proportion of non-marketed services in the economy. This produces an almost irresistible pressure for the share of government expenditure as a proportion of GNP to grow and, at the time of writing (early 1992) it appears that the Conservative government, despite temporary successes, must once again bow to the incoming tide. This need not be a source of alarm. Even if the government reduced the range of services it provided to arbitrarily reduce its budget, those privatized services would also start to claim an increased proportion of GNP.

Does a growing government sector imply the triumph of state socialism over the private sector? One response might be to accept the force of the foregoing arguments, yet regard a small government sector as so fundamental to freedom that one is simply not prepared to let it grow. One solution is the privatization route, but that clearly has its limits. However, concern that the government sector will inevitably dominate the private sector is misplaced. It demonstrates the naivety of projecting trends and that formal modelling of processes is a good idea before jumping to premature conclusions. The classic example of spurious projection is that of horse-drawn traffic in London. At turn of the century rates of growth, London would now be covered in 50 feet of dung. As long as there is a sufficiently large private service sector with the same smaller opportunity for productivity enhancements as the non-marketed sector, then this will place a limit on the dominance of the government sector. Reports of the imminent collapse of the capitalist system are therefore somewhat exaggerated. Stripping away transfer payments, Fig. 2-2 shows there is still quite some way to go. The theoretical model will make these limits clear.

One popular target is for nominal government expenditure to be a constant proportion of nominal GNP. People imbued with static modes of thought become obsessed with numbers that do not change! A useful way of viewing the question is to work backwards and see what this must imply about output shares, given the first two assumptions of the unbalanced growth model. Since unit costs rise exactly as before, this implies a fall in the share of non-marketed services relative to the private sector. Now, it may be that the state has become too large and bloated, but people should be aware of what the constant expenditure share requirement means.

We now move on to explore some empirical evidence. The next section does not rely on sophisticated econometrics to make its points. That is not to say that sophisticated econometric technique is an unessential part of the economist's armoury. Far more important is an overall understanding and an intuitive feel for data. Eyeballing data is very useful in this respect and one can learn a lot from it, and the next section does precisely that. The problem with much modern econometrics is that its practitioners have no intuitive feel for the data they are investigating. Some, indeed, seem to regard this as a virtue. Great kudos is attached to advanced econometrics in undergraduate degrees. The problem is that undergraduates do absolutely stupid things which, if they sat back and thought out the commonsense approach to the problem, they would not do. *Understanding* is not taught as it once was, because technique claims an increasing proportion of a fixed teaching budget. Undergraduates do what they are taught to do, which often involves the mindless quotation of a large number of test statistics as if that was the beginning and end of knowledge. A classic example of modern econometric practice as a form of 'madness maddened' was a seminar in which the speaker—a lecturer at a well-regarded British university—produced a paper consisting entirely of various diagnostic tests, but absolutely no results. 'They weren't of primary interest', was his reply when asked what he was trying to do.

Good econometric technique, reinforced with the ballast of a clear understanding of data, is an unstoppable combination which few possess. Intuitive feel is far more important than good technique, which divorced from the rest is a complete disaster. Unfortunately, the *zeitgeist* of the profession seems to attach overwhelming importance to technique at the expense of understanding. Thus endeth the sermon!

PROBLEMS

2-1 In an economy pensions are financed by a proportionate tax $z(t)$ on earned income. The numbers of pensioners are given by $P = [1 - b^t]\delta N$, where P = pensioners, N = total population, b is a constant $(0 < b < 1)$ and $\delta \leq 1$. Earned income is given by $(N - P)Y_0[1 + g]^t$, where Y_0 is a constant and g is a growth rate. Living standards for pensioners are set at a fraction $\gamma \leq 1$ of the take-home pay of non-pensioners. Calculate the value of $z(t)$ through time. Comment on your results for particular parameter values. Is the system described always feasible?

2-2 The current cost of a standard hip replacement operation is £6000. The price of a standard fridge is £200.

(*a*) Calculate the opportunity cost of a hip replacement operation in terms of standard fridges.

(*b*) Making clear your assumptions, calculate the opportunity cost of a hip replacement operation in terms of standard fridges 20 years hence. Does your result imply an inevitable increasing excess demand for this type of operation?

2-2 SOME EMPIRICAL EVIDENCE

The most telling statistic documenting the extent of the UK's de-industrialization is to examine numbers employed and the proportion of total employment in manufacturing and production industries. Numbers employed are the 'headline' figure, but it does exaggerate the industrial decline compared to the output figures because of the higher productivity growth in the manufacturing and production sectors.

Figure 2-4 shows the absolute numbers employed in manufacturing from 1948 and in production industries from 1970. The numbers of general government employees, including local authorities, is shown from 1957. It confirms the dramatic decline in the manufacturing base; the manual worker is no longer the typical employee he or she once was. The UK peaked as a manufacturing nation in 1956, with numbers growing up until then. The decline becomes most noticeable after 1968, with the most dramatic falls occurring after 1979. Employment in production industries shows the same dramatic falls as in manufacturing.

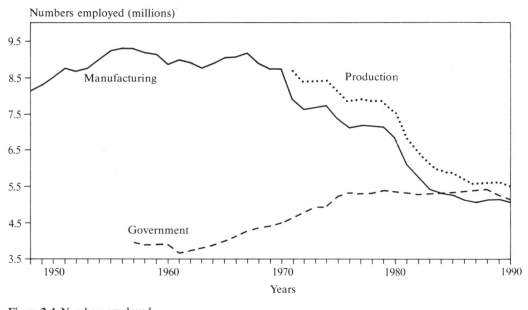

Figure 2-4 Numbers employed
Source: Central Statistical Office

Production industries is a somewhat more comprehensive group than manufacturing, including in addition energy products such as electricity, coal and petroleum product extraction. Clearly, there is bound to be a grey area between what is truly a service-type industry and what is a manufacturing-type industry. However, the figures are so striking that the fact of industrial decline simply cannot be disputed. Figure 2.4 also shows the rise of the state sector with a steady increase in the numbers employed. The level of provision of non-marketed services has steadily increased. Note, however, the sudden stop in government sector employment growth after 1979. In a sense, prior to 1979 the labour surplus from manufacturing was absorbed by increased state employment. After this date the dole queues simply lengthened.

As has been mentioned, about half of government consumption consists of purchases from the private sector and this presumably reaps the benefits of lower prices, relative to services, for manufactured goods in the same way as the private consumer. Really, the theory of Sec. 2-1 refers to the growth in the provision of non-marketed services, so it is the wage and salary bill and numbers employed that are most directly relevant. Some purchases from the private sector will, however, consist of private services and not just final goods and the Conservative government philosophy of the 1980s was for these to increase.

Absolute numbers tell one story, but it is really the proportions employed that are the most important statistics. It is possible for the absolute numbers employed to increase and still mask considerable industrial decline because of a large increase in the workforce. In the UK, the employed workforce (that is excluding those unemployed) had grown by 3 million to 26.9 million by 1990. Consequently, Fig. 2-4 underestimates the extent of the UK's de-industrialization. Figure 2-5 shows employment shares (as a proportion of the

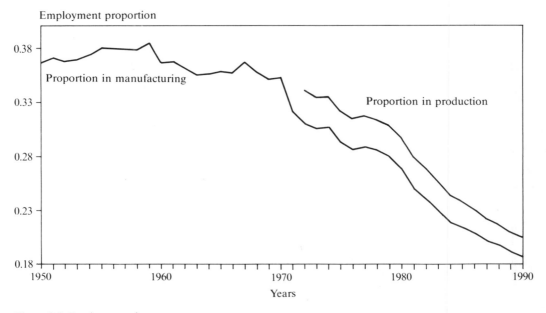

Employment proportion

Figure 2-5 Employment shares
Source: Central Statistical Office

employed labour force). It confirms the decline, with 1960 now the peak proportion. The steady rise in the proportion of government employees is shown in Fig. 2-6 and actually exceeds the proportion in manufacturing for the first time in 1984. Note also the decline in the proportion of government employees from 1984.

Just as the government has engaged in a policy of contracting out services to the private sector, a similar process has occurred within the manufacturing sector. Many manufacturing plants now contract out activities that were previously carried out in-house. Two examples are cleaning and catering contracts. This warns us once again not to take figures at face value since the above process arbitrarily increases service sector employment and decreases manufacturing employment, as shown in the statistics. Thus the extent of the de-industrialization is exaggerated. It is difficult to get accurate information as to the extent of the above type of process, though Inman has suggested that up to 30 per cent of service employment growth could come from this source.

Figure 2-7 gives information on differential productivity growth. It shows output per person since 1960 for the manufacturing sector and the whole economy, starting from a common base. It provides conclusive evidence for the assumption of differential productivity growth. Note that the figures underestimate the difference between the manufacturing and service sectors, because the whole economy *includes* the faster productivity growth manufacturing sector. Table 2-1 gives a much more detailed breakdown for individual industries over the period 1948–68 (later data are unavailable). Column (2) shows the average productivity growth over the 21-year period. Column (3) shows the average growth in the product real wage, that is, the money wage deflated using implicit price deflators for each particular industry. Column (4) shows the average growth in the consumption real wage, where money wages have been deflated by a cost of living index.

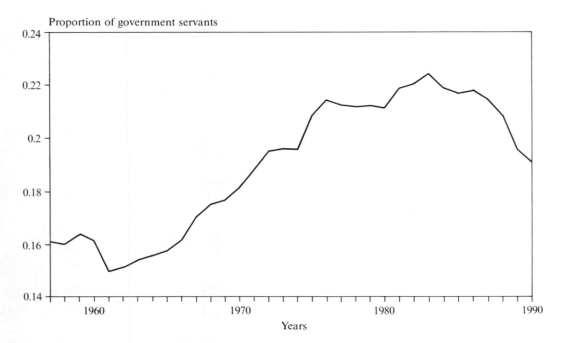

Figure 2-6 Employment shares (public sector)
Source: Central Statistical Office

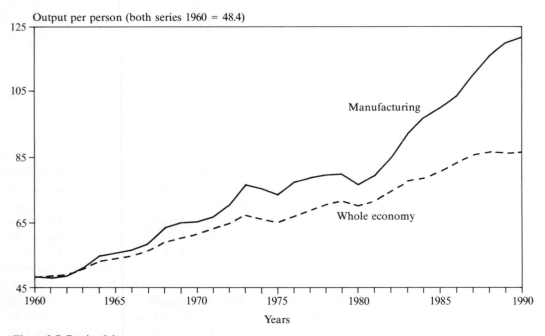

Figure 2-7 Productivity
Source: Central Statistical Office

Table 2-1 Industry growth rates 1948–68 (annual average rates of growth)

(1) Industry	(2) Productivity growth (%)	(3) Product real wage growth (%)	(4) Consumption real wage growth (%)
Agriculture	6.18	5.41	2.13
Mining	3.42	1.65	1.73
Food	1.27	2.94	2.65
Drink and tobacco	2.53	3.65	4.12
Mineral oil refining	6.33	6.01	3.64
Chemicals	4.82	5.52	3.01
Iron and steel	2.11	2.75	2.61
Non-ferrous metals	1.54	1.48	1.95
Engineering	2.48	3.13	2.73
Shipbuilding	1.02	1.74	2.28
Vehicles	4.47	4.66	2.66
Aircraft	2.16	2.73	3.18
Vehicles n.e.s.	1.38	2.87	2.05
Metals n.e.s.	0.76	1.14	2.38
Textiles	2.79	4.24	2.39
Clothing	2.64	2.63	1.43
Building materials	2.89	2.60	1.37
Pottery and glass	3.35	4.08	3.64
Timber	2.36	2.51	2.01
Printing	2.89	3.70	2.74
Rubber	3.03	3.42	3.48
Manufacturing n.e.s.	2.85	4.04	3.28
Construction	1.69	1.34	2.43
Gas	1.05	0.23	2.90
Electricity	5.65	3.48	3.20
Water	0.52	0.97	2.29
Transport	2.42	2.33	2.73

Source: Leslie (1987).
Note: n.e.s. = not elsewhere specified.

These data are entirely consistent with the story of the previous section. The consumption real wage shows the least variation compared to productivity growth and the product real wage growth. Real wage growth has a coefficient of variation of 25.8 per cent. (The coefficient of variation is just the ratio of the standard deviation to the mean of a distribution and is a useful summary measure of the spread of any set of data.) By contrast, productivity growth has a coefficient of variation of 56.7 per cent and the product real wage 48.0 per cent. Finally, as expected, there is a strong correlation between productivity growth and the product real wage. The correlation coefficient is a highly significant 0.82. By contrast, there is a much smaller and insignificant correlation between productivity growth and the consumption real wage of 0.27. All this supports the idea of competitive labour markets in the long term, bearing in mind the early important distinction between being competitive in terms of wage growth rates rather than being competitive in terms of levels. Those industries with the highest productivity growth show the smallest growth in prices. Growth in the consumption real wage is much more uniform across industries.

Figure 2-8 provides a useful aggregate summary to confirm the above points. It plots unit labour costs for manufacturing and the whole economy from 1950. The competitive thesis is that unit labour costs should rise fastest in the service sector that has the slowest productivity growth. Again the figures amply confirm this, with unit labour costs rising fastest for the whole economy. It looks as if unit labour costs have been growing at the same rate in both sectors over the first part of the period, but in fact this is not so. The scaling of the graph simply makes it difficult to pick out the faster growth in manufacturing in the initial years. Note once again that it underestimates the situation in the service sector, because the whole economy includes the manufacturing sector.

Finally, Fig. 2-9 gives some information on consumer tastes. The top line shows the proportion spent on private marketed services at constant prices (excluding rents, rates and water charges). As can be seen, there is a tendency for an increased proportion to be spent on services towards the end of the period. The assumption of a constant proportion is therefore a conservative one, and is generally true throughout most of the period considered. It is these consumer tastes that drive the whole system. The bottom line of Fig. 2-9 shows expenditure shares in current prices. It confirms the rising price of services relative to other goods. The nominal expenditure share shows a systematic upward trend.

With this solid preparation, we are now in a position to explore the simple formalities of the unbalanced growth model.

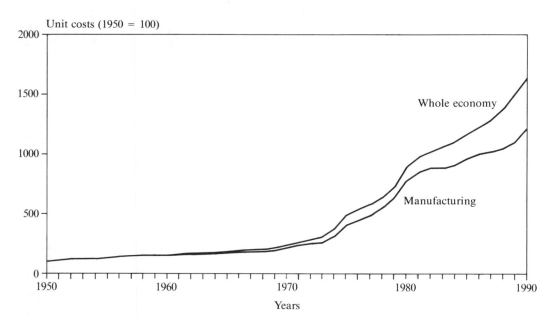

Figure 2-8 Unit labour costs
Source: Central Statistical Office

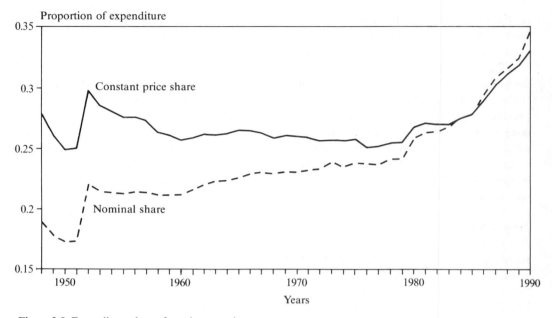

Figure 2-9 Expenditure shares for private services
Source: Central Statistical Office

PROBLEMS

2-3 (For non-UK based students.) Replicate, insofar as it is possible, the data found in Figs 2-1 to 2-9 for your own country. Are your findings consistent with the themes developed in this chapter?
2-4 (For UK-based students.) Update the information found in Figs 2-1 to 2-9. Does the latest information require any modification of the themes developed in this chapter?

2-3 THE UNBALANCED GROWTH MODEL

The economy is composed of three sectors. The first is the private marketed service sector. Output is

$$Y_{mt} = e^{\alpha t} L_{mt} \tag{2-1}$$

where Y_{mt} = output at time t, L_{mt} = employment and α = rate of productivity growth. Since the units of measurement Y_{mt} are arbitrary, these are chosen to give a unit scale factor with respect to the production function.

The second sector is non-marketed government services. Their output is described by

$$Y_{gt} = e^{\alpha t} L_{gt}. \tag{2-2}$$

Units of measurement are again normalized to give a unit scaling factor and productivity growth is assumed to occur at the same rate in both the marketed and non-marketed service sectors. Differences in productivity growth could be allowed for without changing the central thrust of the story beyond complicating the arithmetic. The provision of non-marketed services is financed through taxation. Finally, there is the output of the production sector, given by

$$Y_{pt} = e^{\gamma t} L_{pt}. \tag{2-3}$$

Central to the whole theory is the assumption of differential productivity growth, thus $\gamma > \alpha$.

The next set of assumptions concerns consumer tastes. First, a fixed proportion of non-marketed to marketed service output is assumed. Thus:

$$\frac{Y_{gt}}{Y_{mt}} = A_1 \tag{2-4}$$

where A_1 is a constant. This is a useful benchmark. Alternative regimes could easily be explored. Secondly, consumers are assumed to maintain a constant proportion between marketed services and manufactured goods. Thus:

$$\frac{Y_{mt}}{Y_{pt}} = A_2 \tag{2-5}$$

where A_2 is a constant. Note that this implies that $(Y_{mt} + Y_{gt})/Y_{pt} = A_1 A_2 + A_2 = A_0$. Expenditure is assumed to mirror this production pattern. Open economy aspects might alter this somewhat—a country could, for example, export manufactures in return for services and raw materials. However, it would require an ever-increasing surplus in manufactures for the basic findings of this model to be changed.

Finally comes the assumption of perfect competition in the labour market. The money wage rate in all three sectors is assumed to grow at the same rate δ. Thus:

$$W_{gt} = b_1 W_{mt} = b_2 W_{pt} = W_0 e^{\delta t} \tag{2-6}$$

where W_0 is the base money wage rate. Like α and γ, δ is completely parametric to the problem. This makes it absolutely clear that the model in no way explains the absolute rate of inflation in the economy—a point that is often a source of confusion. What the model explains is the growth in *relative* prices, not *absolute* prices. The value of δ is immaterial to answering the former question and consequently this model is logically disconnected from the material of the next chapter, which is all about the inflation rate. The parameters b_1 and b_2 are there to reflect differences in average labour quality across sectors or even some distortion in the competitive wage level. The common growth rate assumption therefore implies that wage rates cannot become increasingly out of line, although there may be distortion in absolute terms at any point in time.

These three simple assumptions are sufficient to generate considerable insights into how economies actually operate and help rationalize the empirical evidence of the previous section. The first proposition concerns employment shares, emphasizing the success of services over production. The employment share of services (marketed plus non-marketed) is $L_s/(L_s + L_p)$ where $L_s = L_g + L_m$. (The t subscripts are now dropped without loss of clarity.) Noting that

$$\frac{L_s}{L_s + L_p} = \frac{1}{1 + (L_p/L_s)} = \frac{1}{[1 + Y_p e^{(\alpha - \gamma)t}/(Y_m + Y_g)]} \tag{2-7}$$

then:

$$\frac{L_s}{L_s + L_p} = \frac{1}{1 + A_0^{-1} e^{(\alpha - \gamma)t}}. \tag{2-8}$$

Since $\gamma > \alpha$ then $A_0^{-1} e^{(\alpha - \gamma)t} \to 0$ as $t \to \infty$. Thus the share of employment in services must increase as the economy grows. By construction, there is a constant ratio of government to private services, and with an equal productivity growth, employment must grow at a uniform rate in both these sectors.

The next proposition concerns average productivity growth and, as it is so obvious, no formal mathematics is required. As the economy matures, employment becomes more dominant in the service sector. Thus productivity growth must decline and in the limit equal α. Now consider unit labour costs. Unit labour costs in each sector are

$$\frac{W_m L_m}{Y_m} = B_m e^{(\delta - \alpha)t} \tag{2-9}$$

$$\frac{W_g L_g}{Y_g} = B_g e^{(\delta - \alpha)t} \tag{2-10}$$

$$\frac{W_p L_p}{Y_p} = B_p e^{(\delta - \gamma)t} \tag{2-11}$$

where B_m, B_g and B_p are all easily derived constants. Because $\alpha < \gamma$, unit labour costs rise most rapidly in the non-marketed and marketed service sectors. Notice that a sufficiently high δ implies that the absolute unit labour costs will be rising in all sectors. However, as has been repeatedly emphasized, *relative* costs and not *absolute* costs are of major concern. Unbalanced growth in competitive economies necessarily implies that all services—not just the supposedly inefficient government sector—become more expensive. There is nothing perverse or sinister about this.

This is brought into sharp focus by considering the growth in relative prices of marketed services and its exact counterpart, the growth in taxation required to finance a fixed ratio of non-marketed services. Suppose that the price of marketed service output is a fixed mark-up on unit labour costs:

$$P_m = (1 + \pi_m) B_m e^{(\delta - \alpha)t} \tag{2-12}$$

where π_m is the profit mark-up. The price of services grows at the rate $\delta - \alpha$. For manufactured goods:

$$P_p = (1 + \pi_p) B_p e^{(\delta - \gamma)t}. \tag{2-13}$$

Providing γ is large enough, the absolute price of manufactured goods could even decline. Computers are the classic example of a product which, because of rapid technical advance, have declined in absolute price despite, on average, high rates of general price inflation. The relative growth in the price ratio P_m / P_p is therefore $\gamma - \alpha$, which means the relative price rises because $\gamma > \alpha$. Notice also how this growth in relative prices is independent of δ. It also implies that if individuals wish to maintain a fixed quantity proportion of marketed services to manufactures, then an increasing proportion of their after-tax expenditure will be devoted to marketed services. Empirical evidence of the previous section amply supports this contention.

Non-marketed services are no different from this general proposition. If Eq. (2-4) is to remain true, then the proportion of GNP raised in taxes must also increase. The net cost of producing Y_g units of government services is the net cost of government salaries:

$$[1 - z(t)]B_g e^{(\delta - \alpha)t} Y_g \qquad (2\text{-}14)$$

where $z(t)$ is the average rate of tax paid by government employees. These expenditures are financed by levying taxes on the private sector. For convenience, assume a common $z(t)$ across all sectors, including private sector profits. Thus:

$$[1 - z(t)]B_g e^{(\delta - \alpha)t} Y_g = z(t)(P_m Y_m + P_p Y_p) \qquad (2\text{-}15)$$

or

$$z(t) = \frac{B_g e^{(\delta - \alpha)t} Y_g}{P_m Y_m + P_p Y_p + B_g e^{(\delta - \alpha)t} Y_g} \qquad (2\text{-}16)$$

$$\Rightarrow \quad z(t) = \frac{B_g e^{(\delta - \alpha)t}}{P_m Y_m / Y_g + P_p Y_p / Y_g + B_g e^{(\delta - \alpha)t}}. \qquad (2\text{-}17)$$

Note that Y_m / Y_g and Y_p / Y_g are constants, P_m grows at the rate $\delta - \alpha$ (see Eq. (2-12)) and P_p grows at the rate $\delta - \gamma$ (see Eq. (2-13)). Now divide through by $B_g e^{(\delta - \alpha)t}$:

$$z(t) = \frac{1}{K_m + K_p e^{(\alpha - \gamma)t} + 1} \qquad (2\text{-}18)$$

where K_m and K_p are again easily derived constants. Noting that $K_p e^{(\alpha - \gamma)t} \to 0$ as $t \to \infty$, it follows that $z(t)$ must increase through time. Note, however, that the doomsday scenario of $z(t)$ converging to 1 does not in fact happen. It converges to $1/(1 + K_m) < 1$. The reason is that private marketed services with their equally low productivity growth put a brake on the rate of growth of government services, given that a fixed ratio of marketed to non-marketed services is required.

The problem with non-marketed services is that they do not directly reflect individual tastes. There is no P_m for non-marketed services; the size of the non-marketed sector is reflected in $z(t)$ and the electorate only have a marginal opportunity to influence this amount through the ballot box. This is the heart of the famous thesis of Robert Bacon and Walter Eltis in their book entitled *Britain's Economic Problem: Too Few Producers*, which was first published in 1976. As the title suggests, they argued that much of the UK's de-industrialization was pathological and that the growth of the public sector was overdone—at the expense of the market sector.

According to Bacon and Eltis, the ultimate sanction of the ballot box after 1945 was not a sufficient restraint to stop politicians spending an ever-increasing fraction of national income on non-marketed services. The resulting increases in $z(t)$ were felt by workers in the form of a lower growth in real take-home pay, which was necessarily below the underlying real growth rate of the economy. Politicians would argue that workers should feel no relative deprivation because the social wage, which includes the value of government services as well as take-home pay, was rising faster because of the increased provision of non-marketed services. Bacon and Eltis argued that this was not true. The share $z(t)$, claimed by the government, was in excess of what the average individual would have chosen to spend, had such services been marketed. They simply did not perceive the social benefits of lower retention ratios—the ratio of take-home to gross pay.

A vicious circle of decline then ensued. Workers pressed for higher real wage claims in order to satisfy what they perceived to be a reasonable expectation of take-home pay. It was the veritable quest for a quart out of a pint pot. Such claims could never be met. Damaging wage inflation was one possible consequence, though not everyone shares this belief as a cause of inflation, as Chapter 3 will demonstrate. There was, however, one more insidious effect which was rather more deleterious. Recall Eqs (2-12) and (2-13), where a fixed profit mark-up in the private marketed services and manufactured goods was assumed. In fact, over the period up to the 1979 election, the share of value added going to profits consistently declined. For example, for industries in Table 2-1 the profit rate declined by 2.2 per cent per annum over the period. Part of the workers' real wage claims was being met by an increasing share of output going to wages. This was what was most damaging to the private sector, because lack of profitability damaged enterprise and initiative. Firms were reluctant to take anything other than a narrow, short-term view in decision making, and this was killing the private sector.

The Bacon and Eltis thesis was extremely influential, and part of the political agenda of the 1979 Conservative government was to reverse what they regarded as this unhealthy process which was considered to be a major contributing factor to Britain's economic decline. The data of Sec. 2-2 show some of this attempted reversal, but there were others, in particular a dramatic recovery of profitability in the private sector. Comparing 1980–85 with 1974–79, real profits increased on average by 35.7 per cent over the period and real dividend payments by 21.3 per cent. The share of profits in national income improved by 27.0 per cent and the share of dividends by 12.4 per cent. Despite this freeing of the private sector from the shackles of the state, Britain's underlying economic performance does not seem to have improved in the dramatic way that the Bacon and Eltis thesis might have predicted. Perhaps business is not totally convinced that such changes are permanent. One simply has to accept that in a democratic system an alternative government can be elected which has a positive attitude to public expenditure and will not be reluctant to increase it. The Labour party has the same basic visceral hostility towards free enterprise that exists among the Conservatives towards the state sector. Perhaps it is the British people's ambivalent attitude to capitalism itself which accounts for the country's poor economic performance.

Brief mention should be made of the open-economy aspects of de-industrialization. From Sec. 2-2 it is clear that the most rapid period of de-industrialization occurred after 1978. This was the time when the UK was receiving the maximum benefit from North Sea Oil and Gas production and the claim is that this discovery would further exacerbate the process of de-industrialization. The phenomenon has the generic title of 'Dutch Disease', because Holland was the first country to exploit North Sea Gas assets.

Figure 2-10 shows oil and gas production in the UK from 1976 to 1989 in volume terms. The crucial point to note about this massive gift from the Gods is its potential effect on the exchange rate. Prior to North Sea Oil, Britain was obliged to import the vast majority of its oil-based energy requirements. These imports had to be paid for and this was achieved by the export of finished manufactured goods. Thus, Britain could be viewed

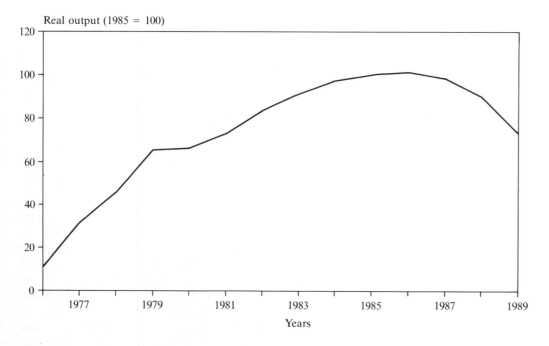

Figure 2-10 Oil and gas production
Source: Central Statistical Office

as the 'workshop of the world', paying for its lack of natural energy resources, coal excepted, through its manufacturing prowess. With North Sea Oil that necessity changed—indeed, the UK became a net exporter of oil.

How should an economy react to such circumstances? Given the constraint on the balance of payments, namely that we cannot permanently run a surplus or deficit, clearly something has to go. The response would be further de-industrialization, since there is now less 'need' for manufactured exports. The mechanism that achieves this is the exchange rate, which would appreciate in response to the favourable flow of North Sea Oil revenues. Thus manufacturing exports would become less competitive and export volumes fall, reinforcing any tendency for de-industrialization. The benefits of North Sea Oil, therefore, accrue in part to residents, by imports being cheaper than they otherwise would be, meaning a rise in the consumption real wage. Secondly, because the main beneficiary is the government through oil tax revenues, everyone benefits because taxes are lower than they would otherwise be. However, without doubt, the manufacturing sector faces additional problems as a result of the resource discovery. To that extent there are *disproportionate* gains, but overall the gains are bound to be positive.

Thus, the correct response to a natural resource discovery such as North Sea Oil would be de-industrialization. The labour shake-out should have been redeployed into the service sector as rising real income should have stimulated demand in that sector. In fact, this latter effect did not happen; the de-industrialization occurred, but not enough labour was absorbed by the service sector—hence, the term 'Dutch Disease'.

Two further points are worthy of mention. Because the exchange rate is driven by speculation rather than by flows of foreign exchange coming from trade, the exchange rate effects can be spectacularly large and often appear illogical and irrational. Indeed, in a world of rational expectations, it is perfectly plausible for the exchange rate to appreciate on the *discovery* of the resource before it is actually exploited. Rational agents, realizing that the rate is bound to go up in the future, will immediately take positions which ensure that the rate is bid up today, in the same way as a stock price will be bid up today in the expectation of higher profits tomorrow. If there are frictions in other markets, then this type of process can cause 'Dutch Disease'. Furthermore, it was claimed that the pound acquired a premium status at that time because high oil prices and the UK's new large reserves made it more attractive relative to other currencies. This further exacerbated the 'Dutch Disease'.

A second point is that the benefits of North Sea Oil production are strictly temporary. Consequently, once the oil runs out a reverse process of re-industrialization would be required. Obviously a process of de-industrialization and re-industrialization involves huge transaction costs and is structurally damaging. A less damaging strategy has been suggested which would have involved less de-industrialization at the outset. Instead of spending the revenues as they arrive, the strategy would be to invest the revenues abroad. Thus the stock of wealth as represented by the North Sea Oil deposits is converted into a permanent income flow. The capital invested abroad would cause a smaller appreciation of the exchange rate because a current account surplus would be required to finance the capital outflow. There would have been less severe de-industrialization as a result. When the oil runs out, the resultant repatriation of profits from foreign investments would mean no need for post-oil re-industrialization. The Labour party has proposed using oil revenues to invest in the domestic manufacturing base. Such a strategy seems misconceived, since it identifies a natural consequence of an oil discovery as being inherently pathological. There is no point in investing in the manufacture of products that no one would want to buy. However, the idea of not blowing a windfall all at once seems to be sensible.

PROBLEMS

2-5 Derive explicit values for the constants K_m and K_p in Eq. (2-18). Hence determine explicitly what the tax rate $z(t)$ converges to.

2-6 Suppose the government's objective is to maintain a constant value for $z(t)$ through time. Furthermore, suppose that the ratio of government to marketed services remains constant at $Y_{gt}/Y_{mt} = A_1$. What does this imply about the behaviour of $A(t)$ through time, where $A(t) = Y_{gt}/Y_{pt}$ is the ratio of government services to manufactured output?

2-4 SUMMARY

This chapter has posed a very practical question about the appropriate proportion of economic activity to be undertaken by the government. Like many questions in macroeconomics, it is one about which many have strong opinions but rather less knowledge. It dominates political debate—indeed, it was the defining issue of the 1992 UK General Election. The unbalanced growth model demonstrates the power of modelling and that thinking abstractly about economic processes, using just three simple assumptions about behaviour, generates useful insights about the issues. De-industrialization was also shown to be part of the same overall question. Once again, the main lesson is that a dynamic mode of thought is a better analytical framework.

ESSAY TOPICS

2-1 Is there an optimal size for the government?

2-2 'The correct response to a natural resource discovery is to invest the proceeds abroad, not to prop up flagging domestic industries.' Discuss.

2-3 Is growth in real take-home pay a good way of measuring the change in living standards?

2-4 'The growth in the public sector and de-industrialization are inextricably linked phenomena.' Discuss.

2-5 'De-industrialization is a sign of a healthy economy, not evidence of a pathological malfunction.' Discuss.

READING

For a philosophical view of the ethical limits to the size of the state by one of the great political economists, try Chapter 15 of Buchanan (1986). The unbalanced growth model of Section 2-3 is largely based on Baumol (1967), which is a classic but little-read article. In fact, the ideas of this chapter largely pre-date Baumol and are very much a feature of the distinctive style of economics found in Cambridge, England. Many of the ideas on de-industrialization can be found in the book by Salter (1960), which is yet another classic by a brilliant economist who died at a tragically early age. These themes were pursued by Kaldor (1966) in his famous Cambridge Inaugural lecture which led to a tax called Selective Employment Tax, which effectively made labour costs cheaper in manufacturing. The idea was to re-invigorate the British economy through the 'engine of growth', manufacturing. The tax was abandoned when the Conservatives were elected in 1970. The only certain positive thing to come out of it was the eventual ennoblement of Kaldor. A recent and comprehensive study, again from two Cambridge economists, is Rowthorn and Wells (1987). Inman (1985) discusses the question of manufacturing contracting out tasks to the service sector and likely sizes. On the important issue of real wage deflators, see Geary and Kennan (1982). Bacon and Eltis (1976) is the classic reference articulating the despair of Britain's post-war malaise, though the argument is presented much more succinctly in Eltis (1979). Open-economy aspects, particularly the effects of a natural resource discovery, are to be found in Forsyth and Kay (1980). This does tend to labour the point somewhat and a much simpler reference is in Chapter 23 of Winters (1985). A much more complex analysis under the full rational expectations technology is Eastwood and Venables (1982). Finally, the data from Table 2-1 are taken from Leslie (1987), which has an extensive discussion of various aggregation problems and the importance of value added and gross output measures. Johnston and Timbrell (1973) provide some evidence on real wage claims in the face of declining retention ratios.

A NEW CLASSICAL THEORY OF INFLATION

This chapter has several purposes. First, it carries forward the theme of the previous two chapters that thinking of problems in a dynamic way from the outset makes for a much more interesting and fruitful macroeconomics. Because a very specific model of the inflation process is considered in this chapter, the dynamics are much more explicit, in contrast to the previous discussion. However, rest assured that the actual model considered is very simple—a statement explicitly designed to demoralize poets who might find it tricky going! Technicalities are consigned to the next chapter.

A second purpose is to introduce the idea of rational expectations in a specific model. Whether for better or for worse, the concept of rational expectations has revolutionized macroeconomics and no modern treatment can comfortably ignore its existence. A large part of current research effort is conducted within this framework and it is appropriate to know a little about what is being done by economists at the present time. However, even if rational expectations are currently fashionable as a research topic, this does not necessarily make rational expectations the correct approach. As of now, it can claim to be a promising idea on which the jury is still deliberating. Economic theory is littered with promising ideas!

A third purpose is to discuss one of the great problems of most advanced economies, namely the persistent tendency for moderate rates of inflation. In the UK, the Conservatives were elected on an avowedly anti-inflation ticket in 1979 and with a distinctive monetarist creed as the method of control. Thirteen years on the phenomenon still persists. Is Monetarism an incorrect analysis of the problem? This chapter reviews a New Classical monetarist approach and its relevance to the early Thatcher years. It aims to make clear the difference between this approach and the 'traditional' Monetarism of Friedman, Brunner and the Chicago school of the 1950s and 1960s. This latter approach still has many advocates.

The chapter is structured in the following way. Section 3-1 introduces the model and is a logical extension of the material in Chapter 1. Rational expectations will be introduced into the framework in a natural way without particularly querying the notion. Indeed, so natural is the move to rational expectations that most readers would not notice what was being done unless it was specifically flagged. It is not, however, quite as innocent and innocuous as it appears at first blush. The next chapter aims to go behind it all and explore more deeply what exactly is involved.

Section 3-2 compares this version of Monetarism with the traditional variety and the contrasting policy prescriptions. Before commencing, heed this warning: it is very important not to confuse the ideas of rational expectations and Monetarism. The two are very definitely *not* the same thing. Rational expectations is the claim that agents form their expectations in a particular way, whereas Monetarism is a claim about the proximate cause of inflation and a basis for some strong policy prescriptions. It just so happens that many practitioners of the rational expectations method also believe that inflation is everywhere and always a monetary phenomenon—hence the confusion. It is perfectly possible to believe in rational expectations yet reject most if not all of the tenets of Monetarism; there is, indeed, a distinctive school of New Keynesians who routinely use the assumption of rational expectations but yet provide an interesting contrast to pure New Classical doctrines and some of these ideas will be explored later in the book. It is also perfectly possible to believe that inflation is a monetary phenomenon and yet reject the rational expectations hypothesis.

3-1 A NEW CLASSICAL THEORY OF INFLATION

The New Classical theory consists of two elements. First, it is considered that inflation is a monetary phenomenon and, secondly, that expectations are formed rationally. Traditional monetarists accept the first proposition but not the second. It is not the purpose of this chapter to adjudicate on the merits or otherwise of monetarist doctrines. Suffice it to say that if the next two propositions are rejected then the subsequent analysis is vitiated, even if the notion of rational expectations is acceptable. The essential elements of Monetarism are that there exists a stable demand function for real money balances and that the money supply formation process is, in the final analysis, under the control of the authorities. The exception to this latter proposition would be the case of an economy operating under fixed exchange rates. Balance of payments surpluses or deficits, in the absence of sterilization, would have monetary consequences outside of the direct control of the authorities. For traditional monetarists a stable money demand and control of the growth of the money supply are sufficient for control of inflation and this explains their general hostility to fixed exchange rates where this essential degree of freedom is lost.

For the purposes of this chapter, the reader need not be overconcerned about the monetary consequences of different exchange rate regimes. It will be assumed that broad money aggregates are ultimately determined by the size of the monetary base, of which the government is the monopoly supplier. If the government is determined enough it can restrict the size of the money supply, or its rate of growth, by acting on the monetary base through open-market operations. It may be that the 'money multipliers' connecting the monetary base to some broad money aggregate such as M3, M4, etc., vary in the short term. Monetarists would not deny this. The claim is that all money aggregates can be controlled by sufficiently determined open-market operations. Day-to-day control over the money supply may be practically impossible given present institutional arrangements; but, in the long term, the authorities can and do determine the money supply. They have the last say.

People are often confused over what a stable demand function for money really means. Stable does not imply being a simple function of one or two variables, though early studies suggested this might be so. The money demand function could be exceedingly complicated, yet stable. Secondly, it does not imply the naive assertion that there is an obvious and simple correlation between the inflation rate and monetary growth. The present analysis should make the latter misconception particularly clear.

Furthermore, most traditional monetarists would believe that the demand for money can and does shift, for them the key proposition is *predictability*. For example, at Christmas there is always a strong demand for cash—obviously there has been a shift in demand for a key monetary aggregate if this is the case. The authorities, quite sensibly, accommodate this seasonal demand to avoid a seasonal crisis in interest rates. The fact of this seasonal 'instability' is neither here nor there, providing the demand for money remains predictable, just as the fact that the authorities respond to seasonal demands for cash has absolutely no bearing on the issue of the exogeneity of money supply.

With these preliminaries having been made, the demand for real money balances is given by

$$\frac{M_t}{P_t} = \alpha'_1 - \frac{\alpha_2(_tP_{t+1} - P_t)}{P_t} \tag{3-1}$$

where M_t is the money supply at time t; $_tP_{t+1}$ is the expectation of the price level at time $t + 1$, formed at time t (we are not yet committed to $_tP_{t+1}$ being a rational expectation); P_t is the price level at time t; and α'_1 and α_2 are positive constants.

Equation (3-1) is a simple, stable demand function for real money balances. It is made simple in order to focus on the main object of concern, namely the process of price level formulation and hence the inflation rate. The demand for real money balances is assumed to be a negative function of the expected inflation rate $(_tP_{t+1} - P_t)/P_t$. Obviously, other variables would enter into any realistic money demand function—for example, real output and the real interest rate are obvious omissions. However, for the purposes of this argument these two variables can be considered constant and subsumed into α'_1. Equation (3-1) is a suitably parsimonious representation that allows the basic argument to proceed. The next equation simply rearranges Eq. (3-1) to make it explicit that what is being considered is a theory of the price level:

$$P_t = \frac{M_t}{\alpha_1} + \left(\frac{\alpha_2}{\alpha_1}\right) {_tP_{t+1}} \tag{3-2}$$

where $\alpha_1 = \alpha'_1 + \alpha_2 > \alpha_2$, hence $\alpha_2/\alpha_1 < 1$.

The fundamental problem to be solved is the determination of $_tP_{t+1}$. The approach of traditional Monetarism is to argue that this expectation is largely formed extrapolatively; its value is driven mainly by agents' experience of previous inflation rates. For example, one frequently invoked scheme is first-order adaptive expectations:

$$[P^*_{t+1} - P^*_t] = [1 - \lambda][P_t - P^*_t], \quad 0 \le \lambda \le 1 \tag{3-3}$$

where P^*_{t+1} has been written instead of $_tP_{t+1}$ to designate that the expectation is hypothesized to be driven by the scheme shown by Eq. (3-3). Equation (3-3) simply says that agents revise their expectations by a fraction of the forecast error $P_t - P_t^*$. Special cases would be $\lambda = 1$, where there is complete myopia, with agents never revising their expectations, and $\lambda = 0$ would be the case when $P_{t+1}^* = P_t$. Incidentally, do not be concerned that inflation and the price level are being used virtually interchangeably in the exposition; equations such as (3-2), which is an assertion about the price level, are easily transformed into assertions about the rate of inflation, as will shortly be seen. Simplifying Eq. (3-3) gives:

$$P_{t+1}^* = [1 - \lambda]P_t + \lambda P_t^*. \tag{3-4}$$

Now:

$$P_t^* = [1 - \lambda]P_{t-1} + \lambda P_{t-1}^*. \tag{3-5}$$

Substituting into Eq. (3-4) gives

$$P_{t+1}^* = [1 - \lambda][P_t + \lambda P_{t-1}] + \lambda^2 P_{t-1}^*. \tag{3-6}$$

Repeated lagging and substitution therefore leads to

$$P_{t+1}^* = [1 - \lambda] \sum_{i=0}^{\infty} \lambda^i P_{t-i}. \tag{3-7}$$

Substituting into Eq. (3-2) gives the following theory of the price level:

$$P_t = \frac{M_t}{\alpha_1} + \left[\frac{\alpha_2}{\alpha_1}\right][1 - \lambda] \sum_{i=0}^{\infty} \lambda^i P_{t-i}. \tag{3-8}$$

Notice how this is entirely backward-looking. The price level—and the rate of inflation—is determined by the *current* monetary stance M_t and the weighted sum of previously observed prices, with geometrically declining weights of size λ. Any other extrapolative predictor would give an equation of the same generic type as Eq. (3-8).

Rational expectations takes an entirely different route, which leads to a result *far* removed from any of the implications of Eq. (3-8). First, move Eq. (3-2) one period forward and write out the equation for P_{t+1}. This is

$$P_{t+1} = \frac{M_{t+1}}{\alpha_1} + \left(\frac{\alpha_2}{\alpha_1}\right)_{t+1} P_{t+2}. \tag{3-9}$$

Now rational expectations is the claim that agents' forecasts will be coterminous with the model's predictions. Thus, if Eq. (3-2) is true, then the forecast of P_{t+1} should simply be the expectation of equation (Eq. (3-9)) based on all the information available at time t. Taking expectations of Eq. (3-9), therefore, gives

$$E_t P_{t+1} = \frac{E_t M_{t+1}}{\alpha_1} + \left(\frac{\alpha_2}{\alpha_1}\right) E_t P_{t+2} \tag{3-10}$$

where $E_t P_{t+1}$ is now the rational expectations forecast of P_{t+1}. This is given, *inter alia*, by the forecast of the monetary stance at time $t + 1$, based on the information available at time t. Notice it is the forecast $E_t M_{t+1}$ and not the actual value M_{t+1} one period hence. The rational expectations approach in no way claims that agents have perfect foresight, only that they use the available model and that they do the best they can, given the available information. Notice also that the model directs what is the *relevant* information to use; in this case only the money supply is relevant because, according to the model, nothing else affects the price level.

$E_t P_{t+1}$ also depends on $E_t P_{t+2}$, the forecast of the price level at time $t + 2$, based on information at time t. Since $_t P_{t+1}$ is formed rationally, so must $_t P_{t+2}$. The best current guess of what this should be is $E_t P_{t+2}$. Substitute what has been achieved so far into Eq. (3-2):

$$P_t = \frac{M_t}{\alpha_1} + \left[\frac{\alpha_2}{\alpha_1}\right]\left[\frac{E_t M_{t+1}}{\alpha_1} + \left(\frac{\alpha_2}{\alpha_1}\right) E_t P_{t+2}\right].$$ (3-11)

It looks as if not much progress has been made since all that Eq. (3-11) seems to do is to push the expected price level one period forward. In fact, the theory is nearly complete, because analogously with the extrapolative predictor, we can simply engage in a process of successive forward iteration to derive:

$$P_t = \frac{M_t}{\alpha_1} + \left[\frac{1}{\alpha_1}\right] \sum_{j=1}^{\infty} \left(\frac{\alpha_2}{\alpha_1}\right)^j E_t M_{t+j}.$$ (3-12)

The reasoning undertaken to derive Eq. (3-12) seems straightforward and uncontroversial. Chapter 4 will explore these underpinnings in much more detail, so Eq. (3-12) will be taken at face value here. Readers who do not wish to explore the logic of Eq. (3-12) more deeply can quite happily ignore Chapter 4 altogether. What in fact has been done to derive Eq. (3-12) is to solve a first-order difference equation in a particular way. Structurally Eq. (3-2), combined with the assumption of rational expectations, is being treated as a first-order difference equation in the expectation $E_t P_{t+j}$ running from time t to the infinite future. $E_t M_{t+j}$ is a typical value for the exogenous forcing variable which drives the system. It is, to stress the point once again, a *forecast* value not an *actual* value.

Those familiar with first-order difference equations will know the distinction between a general and a particular solution. Difference equations have a multiplicity of possible solutions unless a specific starting value is designated to pin down the solution to a specific, particular path. Equation (3-2) is no exception to this and Eq. (3-12) is in fact a particular solution of Eq. (3-2). It is important to realize that there are a whole set of other solutions like Eq. (3-12) which are consistent with Eq. (3-2). However, rational expectations would claim that Eq. (3-12) has some very desirable properties which would effectively rule out other solutions. Other solutions, although consistent with Eq. (3-2), would be ruled out on the grounds that agents would not plausibly form their expectations on that basis. For this reason, Eq. (3-12) is often known as the 'fundamentals' solution to distinguish it from the others. The purpose of this digression has been to show that it is not quite as simple as it might at first appear, and the whole area is beset with controversy, which Chapter 4 will explore. It is possible, therefore, to reject the 'fundamentals' solution as embodied in Eq. (3-12).

There are several important comments to be made about Eq. (3-12). It will form the basis of a New Classical theory of the price level, since it captures all the essential elements that typify that approach. Notice also that it is almost essential for α_2/α_1 to be <1. For P_t to be defined requires the right-hand sequence in Eq. (3-12) to converge. This would be most unlikely if $\alpha_2/\alpha_1 > 1$, though not impossible, as Chapter 4 will show.

Notice how Eq. (3-12) completely severs the umbilical cord with the past. The price level today, according to the equation, depends not just on the current monetary stance

M_t, but on the whole expected future path of monetary policy. This is what makes the rational expectations approach so interesting and novel. There surely has to be something in the idea. Behaviour is determined not only by what the government is currently doing but also by our beliefs about what its future policy actions will be. The static IS/LM model can hardly begin to capture that richness. The rational expectations approach leads rapidly to an interesting and fruitful way of viewing the economy. This is a dynamic picture. Equation (3-12) says that current policy has some influence on current events, but the true picture is that it is the whole expected future course of policy (in this case, monetary policy) which drives the *current* price level.

The second point to grasp is the extreme contrast between traditional Monetarism as exemplified by Eq. (3-8) and New Classical Monetarism exemplified by Eq. (3-12). These extreme differences are entirely founded on different views as to how agents form their expectations. It is, therefore, not the case that monetarists are divided over some trivial point of detail; the difference is large and fundamental. Equation (3-8) is entirely backward-looking and the future is entirely absent. Equation (3-12) is entirely forward-looking and the past is entirely absent. Not surprisingly, the policy prescriptions are rather different as well.

Which approach has the better claim? Rational expectationalists would point to the illogicality of Eq. (3-3) if the price level is, in fact, determined by Eq. (3-2). Equation (3-2) asserts that the money supply determines the price level, yet Eq. (3-3) *denies* any role for the money supply in determining people's expectations. Traditionalists point out that economic modelling is not always a question of internal consistency but a question of how agents *do* form their expectations. It is impossible to provide any definite adjudication at this stage; arguments will be deployed at various points as the chapter proceeds.

Clearly, the foregoing may be a case of 'protesting too much'—making over-sharp distinctions between two camps, which in reality do not exist. Most traditionalists would probably not deny a role for future expectations of government policy, just as (sensible) New Classicals would be foolish to deny a role for history in shaping present outcomes. Procrustean distinctions—turning up the contrast knob, so to speak—are nevertheless very useful to clarify the basic points. The sharp contrast in views arises from a modelling framework which is the simplest possible, namely a dynamic theory based around a first-order difference equation. With first-order difference equations, there are two choices. Either solve backwards and forget the future, or solve forwards and forget the past. Higher order difference equations offer the choice of a more eclectic viewpoint. Chapter 4 should make this clear.

Although Friedman rejects the New Classical variant of Monetarism, there is, in fact a close affinity between the theory of the price level as embodied in Eq. (3-12) and Friedman's own permanent income hypothesis. The permanent income hypothesis maintains that

$$C_t = kY_t^p \tag{3-13}$$

where C_t is current consumption and Y_t^p is permanent income. This is contrasted with the absolute income hypothesis which claims that current consumption is determined by current income:

$$C_t = kY_t \tag{3-14}$$

where Y_t is current income.

Just as in Eq. (3-12), permanent income is a forward-looking concept and can be defined in the following way. Wealth is given by the present value of future expected income receipts. Thus:

$$W_t = \frac{Y_t}{1+r} + \frac{E_t Y_{t+1}}{(1+r)^2} + \cdots + \frac{E_t Y_{t+j}}{(1+r)^{j+1}} + \cdots \qquad (3\text{-}15)$$

where $E_t Y_{t+j}$ are expected future receipts for j periods hence, and r is the subjective discount rate. Permanent income is the useful construct defined as the *constant* income stream which has the same present value as the 'lumpy' future receipts given by Eq. (3-15):

$$W_t = \frac{Y_t^p}{1+r} + \frac{Y_t^p}{(1+r)^2} + \cdots \qquad (3\text{-}16)$$

The right-hand side is a geometric series which sums to Y_t^p/r. Thus permanent income is just the return on subjective wealth $Y_t^p = rW_t$.

This suggests that permanent money would be an equally useful construct. Define permanent money as that constant value of the money supply which generates the same P_t as in Eq. (3-12):

$$P_t = \left[\frac{1}{\alpha_1}\right] \sum_{j=0}^{\infty} \left(\frac{\alpha_2}{\alpha_1}\right)^j M_t^p \qquad (3\text{-}17)$$

where M_t^p is permanent money. Just like Eq. (3-16), Eq. (3-17) is a geometric series which sums to $M_t^p/(\alpha_1 - \alpha_2)$. Thus the present New Classical theory of the price level can be succinctly summarized as

$$P_t = aM_t^p \qquad (3\text{-}18)$$

where $a = 1/(\alpha_1 - \alpha_2)$.

A more general statement of Eq. (3-18) would be to allow the parameter a to vary with the level of real income and the real interest rate—easily derived if we introduced these variables at the outset into Eq. (3-1). Thus:

$$P_t = a(Y_t, \rho)M_t^p. \qquad (3\text{-}19)$$

For fixed Y_t and ρ, Eq. (3-19) reduces to Eq. (3-18). This contrasts with the familiar *LM* schedule of the usual textbook model:

$$P_t = a(Y_t, \rho)M_t. \qquad (3\text{-}20)$$

Thus Eq. (3-20) asserts that the current price level is driven by the current money supply—just as the absolute income hypothesis makes current income drive current consumption. The New Classical theory asserts that the current price level is driven by permanent money, just as current consumption is driven by permanent income in the permanent income hypothesis. Permanent money is a useful summary measure of the whole expected future path of monetary policy, in exactly the same way as permanent income is a summary measure of expected future income receipts.

The current inflation rate is obviously derived as

$$\frac{P_{t+1} - P_t}{P_t} = \frac{M_{t+1}^p - M_t^p}{M_t^p}. \qquad (3\text{-}21)$$

Thus there need be no simple correlation between the current inflation rate and *current* monetary policy, rather it is driven by changes in the permanent money supply. (Incidentally, traditional Monetarism also makes no claim for a contemporaneous correlation.)

The New Classical approach therefore leads to many fascinating predictions. For example, there could at present be a very tight and restrictive monetary policy, but nevertheless high rates of inflation could still be observed as long as *permanent* money, as embodied in Eq. (3-21), was growing. Similarly, a currently profligate monetary policy need not be inflationary, provided that permanent money is not growing.

The present framework carries forward a major theme of the rational expectations approach, which now has the advantage of being explicitly modelled. The theme is the idea that it is the *credibility* of policy which makes it effective, just as much as the policy itself. Credibility is embodied in Eq. (3-21). Permanent money is determined in large part by the *expectations* of future monetary policy, not the actual or *ex post* policy. A tight monetary policy will not be deflationary if it is not credible. Lack of credibility is simply the general belief that, despite current strictness, the government will inevitably loosen restrictions in the future. This belief is reflected in the fact that agents do not revise their views as to the behaviour of permanent policy.

This simply re-echoes the theme of Chapter 1, namely that governments with poor reputations will find it difficult to make policies work because they will simply not be believed. Thus, although at a formal level the past is completely disconnected from the New Classical theory of the price level, it does in fact appear indirectly. Past behaviour of the government is bound to affect the way agents will view any current policy change. Thus, in Germany the Bundesbank has a high reputation based on previous inflation performance. Only small adjustments in policy would be required to alter agents' perceptions about the behaviour of permanent money. In the UK, because of a poor reputation, it requires draconian and employment-damaging policy changes to drive inflation out of the system when it appears.

To illustrate this, imagine a government with perfect credibility which has all its policy pronouncements believed. Assume also perfect foresight so that actual and expected inflation rates are the same. What agents believe will happen is actually delivered. This simplification is not central to the point to be made and removes one layer of complication. Suppose, in such a situation, the government announces that the money supply will grow at a rate of g for ever. The following calculations are based on a constant real output, but a steady rate growth in output could easily be incorporated. From Eq. (3-12), we can write:

$$P_{t+1} = \frac{M_{t+1}}{\alpha_1} + \left[\frac{1}{\alpha_1}\right] \sum_{j=1}^{\infty} \left(\frac{\alpha_2}{\alpha_1}\right)^j E_{t+1} M_{t+j+1}. \tag{3-22}$$

Now since $E_{t+1} M_{t+j+1} = M_{t+j}(1 + g)$ for all $j \geq 0$, reflecting agents' underlying beliefs, then:

$$P_{t+1} = \left[\frac{1}{\alpha_1}\right] \sum_{j=0}^{\infty} \left(\frac{\alpha_2}{\alpha_1}\right)^j M_{t+j}(1 + g) = aM_t^{\text{p}}(1 + g). \tag{3-23}$$

Hence,

$$\frac{P_{t+1} - P_t}{P_t} = g. \tag{3-24}$$

Here there is a perfect correlation between current inflation and current monetary growth, but notice the strong assumptions required to achieve it. If the government announced g to be zero, inflation would immediately fall to zero. The government trades on its good reputation—but it had better deliver what it promises because reputations are quickly tarnished.

By contrast, suppose agents believe that the government's new-found monetarist purity is a strictly temporary affair despite all its announcements of piety and future probity. To be specific, let the belief be $M_{t+1} = M_t$ (currently strict) but $M_{t+j+1} = M_{t+j}(1 + g)$ for $j \geq 1$ thereafter. Thus, agents believe monetary policy will be currently strict but will be somewhat profligate thereafter. This generates some inflation now. To see this note that

$$P_t = \left\{\frac{1}{\alpha_1}\right\}\left\{M_t + \left(\frac{\alpha_2}{\alpha_1}\right) \sum_{j=0}^{\infty} \left[\left(\frac{\alpha_2}{\alpha_1}\right)(1 + g)\right]^j M_t\right\} \tag{3-25}$$

and

$$P_{t+1} = \left[\frac{1}{\alpha_1}\right] \sum_{j=0}^{\infty} \left[\left(\frac{\alpha_2}{\alpha_1}\right)(1 + g)\right]^j M_t \tag{3-26}$$

and the current inflation rate is easily derived to be

$$\frac{P_{t+1} - P_t}{P_t} = \frac{(\alpha_2/\alpha_1)g}{1 - (\alpha_2/\alpha_1)g} > 0. \tag{3-27}$$

How strict would current monetary policy have to be to deliver zero inflation, if at time $t + 1$ agents believed that monetary growth would continue at g? Thus M_{t+1} is no longer $= M_t$ and we calculate a value of M_{t+1} in relation to M_t which would make $P_{t+1} = P_t$. (Here M_t is being treated as given and current policy as operating on M_{t+1}.) This turns out to be $M_{t+1} = M_t[\alpha_1 - \alpha_2(1 + g)]/(\alpha_1 - \alpha_2)$. This is less than M_t and represents a stricter monetary stance and increasingly so with higher values of g. Thus governments with poor reputations can deliver low inflation immediately, but this does require a much more severe monetary stance, with all the inherent recessionary dangers. Chapter 5 will explore the theme that monetary *surprises*, in particular those in which the delivered monetary stance is much stricter than the expected monetary stance, result in recession. It can be seen that when a government has a poor reputation and wants to eradicate inflation, the possibility of severe monetary surprises and high unemployment is much greater.

The intuition is not hard to see. Consider a union trying to negotiate a year-long contract with an employer as of mid-1990. The government urges wage restraint as 'excessive' claims cause unemployment. Now this analysis is correct if, indeed, the government does deliver its low-inflation promise. However, based on recent experience, the union is correct in not taking this promise seriously. The wage claim is not an excessive real wage claim seen in this light. If the government delivers what it promises, the result is a large negative inflation surprise. The union has with benefit of hindsight negotiated too high a real wage and unemployment will be the unintended result. It is, however, disingenuous of the government to blame the labour market for excessive wage claims when the government's inflation record is the source of the confusion.

In common with all rational expectations models—except when there is perfect foresight—agents will make forecast errors, but they will not make systematic forecast errors. This does not mean that forecast errors are necessarily small. Forecasts are only as good as the information set available at the time the forecast is made, and if information is scarce and of poor quality, then forecast errors could be large. The claim is simply that any such errors will not be systematic—on average the inflation forecast will be correct. To see this, note that the expected price level is given by

$$E_t P_{t+1} = E_t a M_{t+1}^p.$$ (3-28)

The forecast error is therefore

$$P_{t+1} - E_t P_{t+1} = a(M_{t+1}^p - E_t M_{t+1}^p).$$ (3-29)

Now take expectations at time t:

$$E_t a(M_{t+1}^p - E_t M_{t+1}^p) = a E_t M_{t+1}^p - a E_t M_{t+1}^p = 0.$$ (3-30)

(For those unfamiliar with the properties of the expectational operator E, it is explained in a short mathematical appendix at the end of this chapter.) Intuition confirms the above trivial mathematical mechanics. Suppose M_{t+1}^p was to be systematically larger than its expectation $E_t M_{t+1}^p$. This is quite simply a contradiction, because agents would immediately revise their expectation $E_t M_{t+1}^p$ to take account of this and eliminate any such systematic bias.

Remember that, unless there is a very fortuitous set of circumstances, systematic errors will be made if Eq. (3-12) is the incorrect theory of the price level. If P_t is driven by some alternative process, then systematic errors will, in general, be made, even though rational forecasts are being taken from the now incorrect model. Rational expectationalists would then argue that agents would quickly realize this and *reject* the incorrect model and seek out a better one that did not make these systematic errors. The problem with this line of reasoning is that it is often difficult in practice to distinguish a sequence of systematic errors from a sequence of unsystematic errors which just happen to be of the same sign. There is always a finite probability of the latter, even though errors are random. Theorists are extremely reluctant to give up conflicting models and there are always powerful arguments for not doing so!

Extrapolative predictors do not, except in special circumstances, have the property of non-systematic forecast errors and this is one strong reason why rational expectationalists argue that their approach is superior. A simple example using the first-order adaptive scheme described by Eq. (3-3) is sufficient to make the point here. Suppose the actual price level over a period of five years is the sequence shown in the second column of Table 3-1. Let:

$$[P_{t+1}^* - P_t^*] = \tfrac{1}{2}[P_t - P_t^*]$$ (3-31)

and furthermore suppose that $P_1^* = P_1 = 100$. It is easy to verify that the expected price level generated by Eq. (3-31) will be the sequence shown in the third column of Table 3-1. Notice how the forecast systematically underpredicts, the reason being that the first-order scheme given by Eq. (3-31) fails to pick up the increase in the inflation rate. Now it is always possible to improve the forecasting performance by adopting a more complicated higher-order extrapolative process, but the point is that as soon as there is a systematic change in the inflation rate, so must there be a change in the form of extrapolative predictor

Table 3-1

Year no.	Price level	Expected price level
1	100	100
2	105	100
3	120	102.5
4	140	111.3
5	180	125.7

in order for it not to make systematic errors. A model which becomes an infinitely collapsible meccano set can hardly claim to be a model at all.

PROBLEMS

3-1 From Eq. (3-8) derive an expression for P_t in terms of the current and lagged values of M_t alone. (*Note*: The easiest way to approach this is to use the lag operator technology of Chapter 4. Look ahead to this if unsure.)

3-2 Consider the model:

$$\ln P_t = \sum_{j=0}^{\infty} b^j \ln M_{t+j}$$

where $\ln P_t$ is the log of the price level and M_{t+j} is the money supply at $t + j$. Perfect foresight is assumed and the inflation rate is $\ln P_{t+1} - \ln P_t$. The government announces in advance two strategies for financing a budget deficit. *Case* 1: The deficit is monetized at once with $M_{t+1} - M_t = $ budget deficit and $M_{t+j} = M_{t+1}$ thereafter for all $j \geq 2$. *Case* 2: A tight monetary policy operates with the issue of a one-period bond at a nominal rate of interest r to finance the deficit. This debt is then monetized with $M_{t+2} - M_t = (1 + r)$ times the budget deficit and $M_{t+j} = M_{t+2}$ thereafter, for $j \geq 3$. Calculate the critical value of r above which bond financing would lead to a higher *current* inflation rate compared to the *immediate* monetization of Case 1.

3-2 IMPLICATIONS: RADICALISM VERSUS GRADUALISM

Sargent has applied the foregoing theory to speculate on the initial failure of the 1979 Conservative government's inflation performance. When elected, the government introduced an extremely tight monetary policy. At the time there was considerable debate as to whether or not monetary policy was tight, because of the apparent failure to control pre-specified monetary aggregates. Hindsight now shows that monetary policy was, in fact, extremely restrictive. The usual money aggregates masked the degree of tightness somewhat because of the relaxation of some important banking regulations that occurred at the same time.

The paradox to be resolved is the following. After the election the British economy moved quickly into a deep and severe recession. Table 3-2 gives some salutary figures in this respect. Of the 23 countries listed, none moved faster into a recession than the UK, whether in absolute or percentage terms. Now the usual analysis would suggest that this would have a strong deflationary impact. Yet the inflation rate actually accelerated at this

Table 3-2 Comparative unemployment experience, 1979–1981

Country	Absolute unemployment rise (%)	Rank	Percentage unemployment rise (%)	Rank
UK	5.1	1	96.2	1
Spain	4.2	2	53.4	4
Netherlands	4.1	3	78.4	3
Denmark	3.1	4	50.8	5
Belgium	2.7	5	32.1	7
Italy	1.7	6	9.1	13
Germany	1.7	7	44.7	6
USA	1.7	8	29.3	8
New Zealand	1.6	9	80.0	2
France	1.4	10	23.7	10
Korea	0.7	11	18.4	12
Sweden	0.4	12	26.6	9
Austria	0.4	13	20.0	11
Japan	0.1	14	4.8	14
Canada	0.1	15	1.4	15
Norway	0.0	16	0.0	16
Portugal	0.0	17	0.0	16
Iceland	−0.1	18	−20.0	21
Switzerland	−0.2	19	−50.0	23
Australia	−0.2	20	−3.4	18
Singapore	−0.5	21	−14.7	19
Hong Kong	−0.7	22	−20.6	22
Finland	−0.9	23	−15.0	20

Source: International Labour Office, *Yearbook of Statistics*.

time. The year-on-year inflation rate rose from 10.6 per cent in the second quarter of 1979 to 21.6 per cent in the second quarter of 1980. This exaggerates the acceleration somewhat because VAT was raised from 8 per cent to 15 per cent and there was a further direct impact on the price index because of the oil shock. Furthermore, there were large price increases in nationalized industry prices, which had been artificially restrained in earlier years. Against this, there was a strong appreciation of sterling which served to make the underlying inflation rate appear lower than it was. Even with all these effects stripped away, there was still a sizeable acceleration in the inflation rate, before the inflation rate eventually began to decline.

This is what Sargent sought to explain and his analysis is just a logical extension of Chapter 1, Eq. (1-15), with the added ingredient of rational expectations described here. Recall the essential features of that time. There was a tight monetary policy, but huge fiscal deficits. These were financed by borrowing at exceptionally high nominal interest rates, reinforcing the view that the government was not really serious about its inflation promises. Consequently, agents formed the view that the deficits would be monetized some time in the future and this view led to high current inflation—despite the severe recession. At that time, the government was unpopular and it was unclear that it would win the next general election. This further reinforced the expectation of future profligacy. Thus the economy ended up with the worst of both worlds. There was a surprisingly strict monetary policy which caused the severe downturn. Because the whole policy regime lacked any credibility, it failed to control inflation promptly. It was not a failure of Monetarism, rather a failure of the government to comprehend properly the logical consequences of its own poor reputation.

To see precisely how the expectation of future monetary laxity can cause inflation now, suppose agents believe that at time t the money supply will remain constant for T further periods and at that point there is believed to be a one-off monetization of ΔM, with no money supply growth after that date. Figure 3-1 illustrates the hypothetical monetary path and, as before, the calculations assume perfect foresight. The current price level is given by

$$P_t = \left[\frac{1}{\alpha_1}\right][M_t + bM_t + \cdots + b^T M_t + b^{T+1}(M_t + \Delta M) + \cdots] \tag{3-32}$$

where $b = \alpha_2/\alpha_1$. Noting that Eq. (3-32) can be considered as the sum of two geometric series, one for M_t starting at M_t and one for ΔM starting at $\Delta M b^{T+1}$, then P_t is

$$P_t = \frac{M_t + \Delta M b^{T+1}}{\alpha_1(1-b)}. \tag{3-33}$$

Analogously, P_{t+1} is

$$P_{t+1} = \frac{M_t + \Delta M b^T}{\alpha_1(1-b)}. \tag{3-34}$$

Hence the inflation rate is

$$\frac{P_{t+1} - P_t}{P_t} = \frac{\Delta M(b^T - b^{T+1})}{M_t + \Delta M b^{T+1}}. \tag{3-35}$$

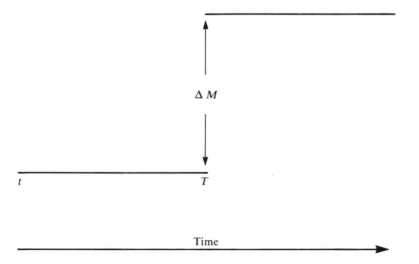

Figure 3-1 Future monetization

This is positive because $b^T > b^{T+1}$. Dividing the top and bottom of Eq. (3-34) by b^{T+1} gives

$$\frac{P_{t+1} - P_t}{P_t} = \frac{\Delta M(1/b - 1)}{M_t/b^{T+1} + \Delta M} \tag{3-36}$$

since $b^{T+1} \to 0$ as $T \to \infty$, this means that as the doomsday monetization looms closer with T declining, the inflation rate must be increasing. The pattern is shown in Fig. 3-2, with inflation coming to an abrupt halt at $t + T$. A currently strict monetary policy is associated with increasing inflation in this instance.

So far, the examples have been constructed quite carefully in order to avoid one particular problem which must now be confronted. The examples have assumed that agents have always held the belief about the expected future path of policy. Some modification is necessary to confront the case of a change in people's beliefs. The point can be seen immediately from Eq. (3-1). Suppose there is a sudden change in $_tP_{t+1}$, in particular let this rise. The demand for real balances will now instantly fall and, unless there is an immediate accommodating monetary contraction, the price level is bound to jump immediately, to maintain the validity of Eq. (3-1).

The recognition of such a process has a long history and should not be thought of as something unique to the rational expectations concept. Any change in $_tP_{t+1}$ will require an immediate jump in P_t, unless there is some monetary accommodation. Friedman, for example, has maintained that the expectation of inflation—whatever the source of that expectation—will in itself tend to be a self-fulfilling prophecy. From Eq. (3-1), it can be seen that this leads to an immediate rise in the prise level, hence Friedman's point. With

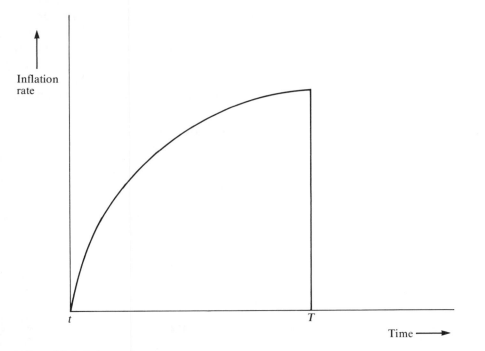

Figure 3-2 Inflation path

rational expectations, however, expectations can change rapidly and dramatically. This contrasts with the traditional extrapolative view of expectations, which cannot change as dramatically because such expectations will have momentum or persistence built into them. Consequently, sudden jumps in the price level from one old equilibrium path to another new equilibrium path are often a feature of the solutions to rational expectations models. Indeed, such variables are often referred to as 'jump' variables.

Figure 3-3 illustrates a change in policy belief. In the old regime agents believe that M_t will remain constant for ever. The new regime simply replicates Fig. 3-1 and we previously explored the behaviour of the inflation rate under this regime. Expectations therefore change instantly at time t. Under the old belief:

$$P_t^o = \frac{M_t}{\alpha_1(1 - b)}. \tag{3-37}$$

Under the new belief:

$$P_t^n = \frac{M_t + \Delta M b^T}{\alpha_1(1 - b)}. \tag{3-38}$$

There is thus an immediate jump in the price by an amount $(1/\alpha_1)\Delta M b^T/(1 - b)$ as the regimes are switched. The price level therefore follows the path as shown in Fig. 3-4.

There is a qualitative difference between the inflation path of Eq. (3-36)—shown in Fig. 3-2, and as the line from P_t^n onwards in Fig. 3-4, but note that Fig. 3-2 shows the inflation rate path whereas Fig. 3-4 shows the price level path—and the jump from P_t^o to P_t^n. The inflation path of Eq. (3-36) takes place in 'real time', whereas the jump does not take place over any finite time period—it occurs instantaneously. Inflation, whatever else it is, is a 'real time' phenomenon, so this particular property is hard to justify as being a literal description of actual inflation processes. Individual prices certainly 'jump' but we never observe an equiproportionate 'jump' in all prices at a single point in time.

This is a convenient moment to emphasize one property of New Classical Monetarism. This is the claim that all inflations, whether of a moderate degree or severe hyper-inflations,

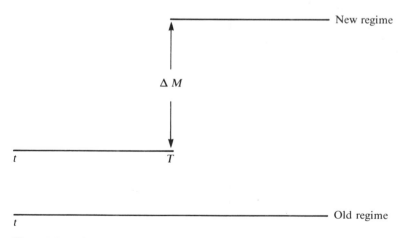

Figure 3-3 Regime change

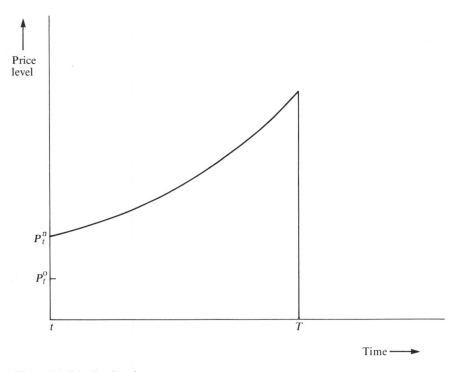

P_t^n

Figure 3-4 Price level path

can be stopped suddenly without much loss of output or rise in unemployment. It is certainly a radical idea and contrasts strongly with the policy prescription of gradualism advocated by traditional Monetarism.

Why is this so? The answer is that current inflation is basically driven by the expectation of future policy as embodied in the 'permanent monetary policy' construction of Eq. (3-18). These expectations exist entirely in the mind and, in principle, if the government can successfully convince its people that it will follow a new policy regime whereby there will be no excessive monetary growth now and for always, inflation can and will stop suddenly. The requirement for little or no output loss is that the government delivers exactly what it promises and that these promises are believed. Notice, in the context of Chapter 1, that this means it must convince the people that budget deficits will not be monetized either now or in the future. People must believe that any deficit will eventually be paid off by the government raising sufficient extra taxes to pay off borrowings and accrued interest.

This is why New Classicals attach such importance to institutions that lend credibility to government policy pronouncements. For example, they would advocate a legally binding requirement for a balanced budget except for certain capital items and national emergencies such as war. After all, local councils, Liverpool included, are legally required to balance their books, so why should central government play to a different set of rules? Another frequently advocated institutional change would be a legally independent Bank of England, so that monetary policy would be free from day-to-day political interference. Such ideas, although possibly inflation-reducing, may be succinctly described as taking the democracy out of economic policy-making. They are policy changes of the greatest significance and not something that should be subscribed to without considerable thought. We return to this theme again in Chapters 7 and 9.

For Sargent, sudden changes in policy regime, where the regime changes have little or no credibility, are self-defeating and damaging. Economic policy, as practised in the UK after 1979, unfairly blackened all variants of Monetarism as the only sensible way of conducting macroeconomic policy. It was labelled 'Monetarism' but bore little or no relation to the New Classical creed. Sudden changes in policy regime that have credibility and commitment behind them can lead to dramatic changes in inflation performance with small, if any, short-term output reductions. Sargent quotes evidence of four European inter-war hyper-inflations that were abruptly halted in precisely the way that the New Classical theory predicts.

One objection to the Sargent thesis is the observation that hyper-inflations are qualitatively different animals from the moderate inflations that characterize post-Second World War western economies. The former can be stopped suddenly because, when a currency collapses completely, the population is amenable to a fresh start and is prepared to undertake the radical changes in behaviour required. With moderate rates of inflation, institutional arrangements do not collapse in the same way, hence reform and rapid reductions are impossible. Sargent's counter to this was to examine the case of France in the mid-1920s where a modest inflation rate was abruptly halted, the so-called Poincaré miracle.

Notice another feature of abrupt halts to hyper-inflation, to which Sargent draws attention. Sudden downward changes in inflation can be accompanied by a huge expansion in the monetary base. Thus the authorities can exact considerable seigniorage from this source. Equations (3-37) and (3-38) are the key to this apparently counter-intuitive paradox. With a hyper-inflation, the demand for real money balances is almost nothing—indeed, in the German hyper-inflation, the demand for real balances was calculated to be less than one US dollar. A sudden change in regime and the belief that inflation would end, would have led to a huge expansion in the demand for real money balances. As can be seen from Eqs (3-37) and (3-38), unless there was an increase in the money supply to accommodate this expansion, a one-off fall in the price level would have been required.

Traditional Monetarism, in strong contrast, is a counsel of moderation and caution. Gradualism is the watchword of the traditional school. Inflation, according to Friedman, takes a long time to become endemic in economic systems and it would be surprising if it did not take a long time to eliminate it. The inflation process has momentum and persistence behind it, which makes it difficult and undesirable to stop quickly. Mental pictures of the two contrasting schools are useful. For New Classicals, inflation is like a large puffed-up balloon, which looks impressive but which can be pricked with a single needle. For traditionalists, inflation is like an extremely heavy flywheel, which took enormous energy to set in motion, but which, once moving, is extremely difficult to stop. To stop it, the brake should be applied gently. Throwing a spoke into the wheel to stop it quickly could cause the whole mechanism to disintegrate.

Why does inflation have momentum for the traditionalists? The answer is that for them, agents form their expectations extrapolatively. The expected inflation rate is largely determined by the past history of actual inflation performance. If this is so, then no policy change today, no matter how credible, can change people's expectations immediately.

Literally interpreted, extrapolative predictors mean that at any particular point in time the expected level of inflation is exogenous, because history, being history, cannot be changed except in science fiction. The only way to reduce the expectation of inflation is therefore to deliver lower actual rates of inflation, which then, via the extrapolative process, feeds into agents' expectations. For traditionalists it is performance not promises that really matters.

Given agents' expectations, if the authorities delivered zero inflation by a draconian monetary squeeze, this would imply a large inflation surprise—the difference between the expected inflation rate and the actual inflation rate. The large surprise will result in a severe and unnecessary recession, which a gradual policy of inflation reduction would have avoided. In a nutshell, traditionalists believe that large inflation reductions inevitably mean large negative inflation surprises, whereas New Classicals claim there need not be any such surprise. Consequently, traditional monetarists do not deny that inflations can be stopped quickly if the authorities are determined enough. Rather, their claim is that such a strategy is misconceived, because it would involve an enormous and unnecessary output cost.

The contrasting viewpoint can be illustrated with the help of Fig. 3-5. It shows the trade-off between the inflation rate and the level of unemployment. The expectations-augmented Phillips curve holds that

$$\dot{P}_t = f(U) + \dot{P}_t^* \tag{3-39}$$

where $\dot{P}_t$ is the actual inflation rate, $\dot{P}_t^*$ is the expected inflation rate, and $f(U)$ is the unemployment trade-off. (Most readers should be familiar with the Phillips curve idea. The inflation–unemployment trade-off is dealt with thoroughly in Chapter 5. Rational expectations leads to a trade-off similar to Eq. (3-39), but the theoretical underpinnings are very different from the traditional Phillips curve trade-off.)

Figure 3-5 shows the trade-off for two expected inflation rates. In the first case $\dot{P}_t^*$ is zero and is shown as the lower of the two lines. The second is for a high $\dot{P}_t^*$ and is just a vertical displacement of the lower line by this value of $\dot{P}_t^*$. The point U^* is the natural or equilibrium level of unemployment which is consistent with zero or steady rates of inflation. Suppose the initial position is at X with high inflation and high expected inflation. Under the traditional view, $\dot{P}_t^*$ (high) is invariant to any current policy change; thus the economy can only trade-off along the $\dot{P}_t^*$ (high) line. For sure, inflation could be stopped suddenly by moving to point Z. This requires a very large negative inflation surprise and, consequently, an extremely large rise in unemployment, far beyond the natural rate U^*.

Traditionalists would favour a gradual policy with the P_t^* (high) line gradually descending downwards towards the zero line—the so-called soft landing—as lower delivered inflation snuffs out expectations of future inflation. Traditionalists would not deny that there is an element of rationality in expectation formation. Thus policy announcements of strict future monetary targets and inflation targets would form an important part of an anti-inflation strategy; indeed, they formed part of the post-1979 strategy. However, such pronouncements only have a marginal influence in reducing the underlying momentum in inflationary expectations.

The New Classicals claim that the $\dot{P}_t^*$ (high) line is not immutable in the short run; it is simply an epiphenomenon. Since $\dot{P}_t^*$ is driven only by current policy and expected future policy it can, in principle, be changed to any value whatsoever, depending on

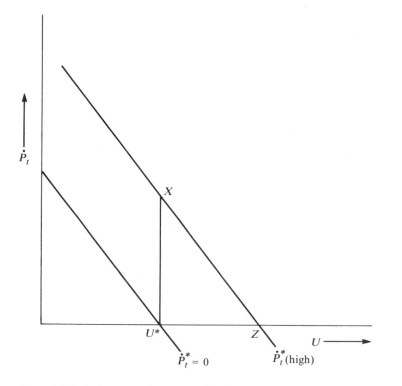

Figure 3-5 Inflation–unemployment trade-off

underlying beliefs about the policy regime. Thus New Classicals claim that it is possible to move directly from X to U^* and achieve zero inflation instantaneously and with no deleterious output reductions. The short run and the long run simply coalesce.

Figure 3-5 also illustrates the problems of the traditional view in explaining why large increases in unemployment were accompanied by increasing inflation. Presumably, and it would be highly implausible to claim otherwise, the post-1979 recession pushed unemployment well above the natural rate U^*. Given this, the gradualist view would have to predict *some reduction*—albeit possibly small—in the inflation rate. This did not happen.

There are, however, some weaknesses in the New Classical view. Equation (3-12) is hardly relevant if people *in fact* operate with finite and probably quite short time-horizons. How many of us have any strong views on what monetary policy is likely to be in five years time? If this is true, then Eq. (3-12), although formally correct, is the solution to a somewhat artificial problem. Another problem with Eq. (3-12) as an explanation of the UK's inflation performance is that current inflation is ultimately driven by the belief of future monetization of budget deficits. Yet the post-1945 history of the UK has been one where the National Debt has been systematically eroded, as Chapter 1 made clear. Furthermore, although inflation reduced after 1981 it did not disappear and it began to accelerate again in the late 1980s despite record budget surpluses and even more rapid erosion of the National Debt.

The foregoing illustrates a difficulty of using forward-looking models to explain current events. Since it is a hypothetical future which drives the present, it is always possible to rationalize any current event by invoking some expected future event as an explanation. If one is not careful, such reasoning can become utterly vacuous, since there is nothing tangible to test the theory against and it can never be proved wrong. It is rather like the share tipster who advises clients to buy a stock which the next day becomes valueless. Explanations that the tip was a good one based on the information available at the time about the future prospects of the company may be correct, but they are not much comfort to the unfortunate people who have lost all their money. This does not mean rational expectations should be dismissed, but it does indicate that testing of such models is bound to be extremely difficult. Chapter 7 will illustrate another such difficulty, first discovered by a famous exemplar of rational expectations and known as the Lucas Critique. The fact that such models involve more elusive concepts and are more difficult to test does not, *ipso facto*, make them wrong.

The New Classical thesis is that any inflation can be stopped suddenly. The fact that it may be possible does not necessarily make it a wise policy. Presumably governments with good reputations will have a good inflation performance, so the question of stopping an inflation suddenly in this instance need hardly arise. Poor inflation performance is most likely associated with poor reputations and it is not immediately clear that a radical policy is appropriate in this instance. Laidler makes this point most forcefully. It may be that agents hold rational expectations. Their expectations are unlikely to change no matter what government policy is announced because the government lacks any credibility. Thus, in fact, agents behave as if they hold extrapolative expectations and the case for gradualism is reinforced. The case of a poor inflation performance associated with a good reputation is effectively a contradiction in terms—what government promises to deliver high inflation and then sticks to its promise? Thus any anti-inflation strategy should be predicated on the assumption that policy is unlikely to be believed. Credibility must first be earned by *delivered* performance.

A second argument in favour of gradualism is to ask what advantage there is to a rapid reduction in the inflation rate as opposed to a gradual reduction. It is generally agreed that the welfare losses from an inflation which is perfectly anticipated are much smaller than the welfare losses arising from discrepancies between the actual and expected inflation rates. Thus the welfare loss from an inflation rate of 15 per cent which was perfectly anticipated may be considerably *lower* than a zero inflation rate when a 15 per cent rate was expected. Now, under rational expectations, a policy of gradual reductions is just as possible as one of rapid reductions. Given poor reputations, sudden reductions are more likely to deliver large inflation forecast errors, with highly damaging consequences. Gradual reductions, by definition, cannot do so. Governments should surely restore tarnished reputations slowly rather than quickly.

On the whole, it must be said that the New Classical economics rather resembles a classic feature of the American psychological make-up in this one respect. This is the doctrine of the 'quick fix' like the diet that promises you will lose 14 pounds in 14 days. It is the American dream once more; instant success is readily available and obtainable with sufficient energy and application. European culture takes a more sedate view, with a strong belief in moderation in all things. Milton Friedman, though an articulate spokesman on behalf of the ideals of that most excellent country, is at heart a European.

PROBLEMS

3-3 Model:

$$\dot{P}_t = 0.4 - 0.04U^{-1} + \dot{P}_t^*$$

where $\dot{P}_t$ is the inflation rate, $\dot{P}_t^*$ is the expected inflation rate, and U is the rate of unemployment. Expectations are formed extrapolatively according to $\dot{P}_t^* = \dot{P}_{t-1}$.

(a) Calculate the natural rate of unemployment.
(b) Suppose $\dot{P}_t = \dot{P}_t^* = 20$ per cent per annum. What would unemployment be if inflation were stopped suddenly?
(c) Suppose a gradualist strategy were adopted of reducing inflation by equal amounts to zero over 5 years. Compare the unemployment costs to the sudden reduction strategy.

3-4 Layard *et al.* (1991) have suggested that 'hysteresis' is an important factor in the inflation process. Hysteresis is the idea that the *change* in the unemployment rate, as well as its level, influences the inflation rate. The Phillips curve relationship can be described as

$$\Delta^2 P = -a(U_t - U^*) - b\,\Delta U$$

where $\Delta^2 P$ is the change in the inflation rate, U^* is the natural rate and $\Delta U = U_t - U_{t-1}$ is the change in unemployment. If the initial unemployment rate is U_0, show that there is a path for unemployment to adjust to U^* which gives a constant level of inflation ($\Delta^2 P = 0$).

3-3 SUMMARY

This chapter has shown that thinking dynamically reaps a rich harvest indeed. It introduced a rational expectations theory of the price level, which, when solved, involved the whole future path of policy. This gives a whole new way of thinking about the effects of government policy and several of the implications were explained. Government policy cannot be described by the inert mechanical rules of the static IS/LM model. Everyone knows that the promises made by that apocryphal used car salesman are different from those made by one's maiden aunt. Government policy intentions are no different in this respect and the rational expectations approach gives a ready-to-hand analytical framework for grappling with immensely difficult issues.

APPENDIX

The expectational operator

Suppose X is a random variable taking the values $X_1, \ldots, X_n$ with probabilities $p_1, \ldots, p_n$ respectively. The expected value of X is defined to be

$$E\{X\} = \sum_{i=1}^{n} p_i X_i. \tag{A3-1}$$

The above is true by definition, but can be thought of as the average outcome if there was a large number of drawings of the random variable X. The reader can easily verify that the E operator has the following properties:

1. $E\{aX\} = aE\{X\}$. Thus a new random variable taking the values aX_1, $aX_2, \ldots, aX_n$ with probabilities $p_1, \ldots, p_n$ would have an expected value of a times the expected value of the original random variable X.
2. $E\{aX + aY\} = aE\{X\} + bE\{Y\}$.

But note the following properties:

3. $E\{X/Y\} \neq E\{X\}/E\{Y\}$.
4. $E\{XY\} \neq E\{X\}E\{Y\}$; this would be true if X and Y were independent random variables.

Now apply these ideas to Eq. (3-12). M_{t+j} is not known to the agent at time t (except in the special case of perfect foresight). Thus M_{t+j} might be thought of as a random variable taking the values M^1_{t+j}, $M^2_{t+j}, \ldots, M^n_{t+j}$ with probabilities $p_1, \ldots, p_n$, where these probabilities are assigned on the basis of information available at time t.

Thus,

$$E_t M_{t+j} = \sum_{i=1}^{n} p_i M^i_{t+j}. \tag{A3-2}$$

Notice that Eq. (3-12) consists of a whole sequence of such random variables, one for each j, all of which have an expected value like Eq. (A3-2). Notice also that the expectation is dated because the forecast is based on information at time t. In general, $E_t M_{t+j} \neq E_{t+1} M_{t+j}$. Why not? Because $E_{t+1} M_{t+j}$ is made one period forward, the agent is more than likely, in the light of new information, to form a new distribution about the values of M_{t+j} and their associated probabilities. Thus it is important to date the time at which the expectation is made, because it is a contingent forecast, based on the available information at that time. For example, $E_t M_{t+j}$ could have been based on the assumption of a Conservative administration. Suppose the Labour party subsequently won the election. It is now more than likely that $E_{t+1} M_{t+j}$ would be greatly revised. Readers should be clear that although, in general, $E_t M_{t+j} \neq E_{t+1} M_{t+j}$, under rational expectations $E_t\{E_{t+1} M_{t+j}\} = E_t M_{t+j}$; today's 'best guess' of tomorrow's 'best guess' is just today's 'best guess'.

Now let us long-handedly derive the result, succinctly arrived at via Eq. (3-30). Equation (3-22) is:

$$P_{t+1} = \frac{M_{t+1}}{\alpha_1} + \left[\frac{1}{\alpha_1}\right] \sum_{j=1}^{\infty} \left(\frac{\alpha_2}{\alpha_1}\right)^j E_{t+1} M_{t+j+1}. \tag{A3-3}$$

Now consider $E_t P_{t+1}$—that is, the forecast of P_{t+1} based on information available at time t. Clearly the expectation of $E_{t+1} M_{t+j}$ cannot be applied because E_{t+1} refers to the information set at $t+1$. It is clear that

$$E_t P_{t+1} = \left[\frac{1}{\alpha_1}\right] \sum_{j=0}^{\infty} \left(\frac{\alpha_2}{\alpha_1}\right)^j E_t M_{t+j+1}. \tag{A3-4}$$

The forecast error is therefore, remembering property 2:

$$P_{t+1} - E_t P_{t+1} = \frac{M_{t+1} - E_{t+1}M_{t+1}}{\alpha_1} + \left[\frac{1}{\alpha_1}\right] \sum_{j=1}^{\infty} \left(\frac{\alpha_2}{\alpha_1}\right)^j [E_{t+1}M_{t+j+1} - E_t M_{t+j+1}]. \quad \text{(A3-5)}$$

The terms in square brackets will be a white noise process. This result follows when forecasts are the same as the model's predictions. Rational expectations make precisely this assumption. The price level is actually modelled as a random variable. The forecast error is just the realization minus the expected value. It is true for any random variable X that $E\{X - E\{X\}\} = 0$. Consequently, the expectation of the forecast error must be zero under the assumption of rational expectations. Notice that the claim of non-systematic errors is simply $E\{X - E\{X\}\} = 0$. It could be that $X - E\{X\}$ is extremely large without contradicting the conclusion of no systematic errors.

ESSAY TOPICS

3-1 Assess the rival claims that price expectations are formed (*a*) extrapolatively, (*b*) rationally.
3-2 Assess the claim that the current price level is determined by the expected future path of monetary policy.
3-3 Are budget deficits inflationary?
3-4 Should inflation be stopped suddenly or gradually?
3-5 If inflation is not 'everywhere and always a monetary phenomenon' (Friedman), does this have damaging consequences for the rational expectations hypothesis?

READING

This chapter is largely based on Sargent (1986). Unlike much of Sargent's work, which is extremely difficult, this reference is fairly accessible. The discussion of the hyper-inflations is particularly interesting and well worth reading. Supplementary material is from Hoover (1988). A distinguished exemplar of traditionalist Monetarism is Laidler (1982), all of which is worth reading. For a staunchly anti-monetarist view try Kaldor (1986). The interchange between Kaldor (1970) and Brunner (1971) (the latter reference less often read by Cambridge undergraduates!) is also useful. Brunner, in my view, won the debate hands down. A discussion of extrapolative predictors is to be found in Flemming (1976) and for a history of the problems of monetary control in the early Thatcher years and the famous 'Goodhart's law', try Goodhart (1984). For the received view on the relationship between the monetary base and other monetary aggregates read Bain (1980). Laidler (1985) is also a useful reference on conventional Monetarism. Friedman (1957) is the classic reference for the permanent income hypothesis, where, interestingly enough, he rejects the now common approach of modelling permanent income as a perpetuity. There are many places to read about the expectations-augmented Phillips curve. Two sources are Friedman (1975) and Friedman (1968). The former is a particularly readable account by someone whose writing is always characterized by admirable clarity. The latter reference is particularly interesting because it shows Friedman's amazing intuition and foresight. This article was written well before the high inflations of the 1970s. Yet he accurately predicted the demise of the traditional non-expectations-augmented Phillips curve. New Classicals read carefully what Friedman writes because he is usually right, although, in their view, for the wrong reasons. The fact that the New Classical theory is consistent with the post-1979 events does not necessarily make it correct, because there are other paradigms which could equally well be consistent with the facts. Leslie (1990) tells an alternative story within the contrasting disequilibrium or temporary equilibrium framework.

THE MATHEMATICS OF RATIONAL EXPECTATIONS

(*Note*: Some of the material in this chapter is difficult and may be comfortably avoided at first reading.)

The first three chapters have emphasized that placing economic questions in a dynamic context is both useful and interesting. Static modelling causes static thinking! The major effort of this chapter will be to understand forward-looking rational expectations models, of which Chapter 3 provided an extensive example. Just precisely what is involved in the method of forward iteration described by Eq. (3-12) of Chapter 3? This chapter aims to give a good understanding of the process as well as explaining more complicated systems expressed either in discrete or continuous time. Hopefully, by the end the reader should not only be able to solve some fairly complex systems, but also understand why the solutions work.

When a problem is studied in some depth, there is a tendency for the economics to be dominated by the mathematics. Mathematical economics should be precisely what it says it is, namely mathematics in the service of economics and not the other way round. Although this chapter contains some fairly advanced material, it lacks the formal rigour of pure mathematics. It is written with the express aim of emphasizing the economic dimension of why models are solved in a particular way. Indeed, the claim is that rational expectations models cannot be solved without a knowledge of the economic context in which they are set. This contrasts with the view that any model is soluble once certain qualitative information about parameter values is known, independent of any economic context.

When discussing dynamic systems, there are basically two choices: either one can work in discrete terms, with time split into discrete blocks, $t - 1$, t, $t + 1$, and so on; or one can work in continuous time. In the latter case, time derivatives are used to indicate dynamic behaviour. Difference equations are the appropriate mathematical tool for models formulated in discrete time, whereas differential equations are the appropriate tool for continuous time models. At this level, the adoption of either difference or differential equations will not make a great deal of difference to the conclusions reached. In other contexts the choice is far from being cosmetic or a matter of convenience.

Some rational expectations models are formulated in discrete time and others in continuous time. For example, Eq. (3-1) of Chapter 3 could easily be reformulated in continuous time, and the latter part of this chapter will look at a continuous time analogue of this discrete case. Not surprisingly, models formulated in discrete systems have many properties that are also found, analogously, in those same models when formulated continuously. The rules that govern solutions in discrete models of rational expectations are virtually the same when they are formulated in continuous time. Thus a good understanding of one approach necessarily assists towards an understanding of the other. One attractive feature of differential equations is that solutions can often be neatly summarized in graphical form, called phase diagrams.

The major effort of this chapter will be devoted to difference equations. In the interest of completeness, there will still be quite a lot of material on differential equations and there should be enough clues from the discussion of difference equations to make it unnecessary to reiterate arguments justifying particular solution methods. Rather, the task will be to emphasize the close connections between both approaches. On the way we shall examine two famous rational expectations models, one a discrete time model and the other a continuous time model. The first is the overlapping wage contracts model which presents a challenge to some of the conclusions of the pure New Classical thesis of the previous chapter. The continuous time example is the exchange rate overshooting model, which tries to cast light on why floating exchange rates exhibit exaggerated fluctuations. In fact, both these models have a common core idea, namely that there are imperfections and rigidities in the goods market. This type of modelling framework often goes under the generic title of New Keynesian and offers an interesting counterpoint to New Classical themes.

4-1 SOLVING BY DIRECT ITERATION

The first thing to do is to forget all about rational expectations for the present and focus entirely on the solution of a difference equation. The simplest possible case is the linear first-order equation:

$$Y_t = a + \lambda Y_{t-1} \tag{4-1}$$

where a and λ are both parameters. Now Eq. (4-1) could equally be written as

$$Y_{t-1} = -\frac{a}{\lambda} + \frac{Y_t}{\lambda} \tag{4-2}$$

or, moving one period forward,

$$Y_t = -\frac{a}{\lambda} + \frac{Y_{t+1}}{\lambda}. \tag{4-3}$$

These equations are exactly the same thing, even though Eq. (4-1) looks backwards and Eqs (4-2) and (4-3) look forwards. Absolutely no significance about how to solve a difference equation can therefore be attached to whether or not the equation is described in a forward- or backward-looking way. For example, the adaptive expectations model, Eq. (3-4) of Chapter 3, was described with a structure like Eq. (4-1). By contrast, the money demand Eq. (3-2) of Chapter 3 had a structure like Eq. (4-3). Both are arbitrarily transformable, as Eqs (4-1), (4-2) and (4-3) demonstrate.

The conclusion is that whether or not an equation is written forwards or backwards can in no way dictate whether an equation is solved forwards or backwards. The main purpose of this chapter is to explain *precisely* why some equations are solved forwards and others backwards. It is not, in fact, a magical unique property of rational expectations—one could equally well solve forwards in other contexts, as we shall see. Indeed, a rational model could, given certain assumptions, be solved in a backward-looking way. Important lesson number one is that it has absolutely nothing to do with the way an equation is written.

The natural way to solve Eq. (4-1) is to adopt a backward-looking method. For most people this would seem the only appropriate way to solve a difference equation. Why is this? Our view of time is implicitly unidirectional and the natural first instinct is to think of Eq. (4-1) as starting from somewhere in the past and then running forward through time. This leads us to locate the backward-looking technique without giving the mental processes involved as much as a second thought. It is because we are most comfortable in this mode of thought that we find it difficult and slightly counter-intuitive to solve forwards. However, once the reasons are well understood, there should be no problem with the latter method. It is rather like driving in reverse using only the mirror as a direction-finder. It is difficult at first, but once you become accustomed to it, it is not much more difficult than ordinary driving.

The first solution method is best described as the 'up-and-at-'em' technique. This works just so far, and more elegant techniques are required for the more complex cases. The 'up-and-at-'em' method does have the virtue of showing exactly and directly what is being done. Incidentally, the following method works for any value of λ, including 1. Substitute out Y_{t-1} in Eq. (4-1) to derive:

$$Y_t = a + \lambda(a + \lambda Y_{t-2}). \tag{4-4}$$

Now substitute out Y_{t-2} and carry on successive substitutions to derive after $T-1$ such iterations:

$$Y_t = a \sum_{i=0}^{T-1} \lambda^i + \lambda^T Y_{t-T}. \tag{4-5}$$

Those familiar with this elementary textbook case know that there are two ways of describing the solution to a difference equation. A general solution is one that satisfies or is consistent with Eq. (4-1). There are an infinite number of such solutions. A particular solution is one that satisfies Eq. (4-1) and, in addition, satisfies an initial condition or starting value. Without this information about the starting value for Y_t, it is clearly impossible to describe the precise path of Y_t through time. If the starting value was 10, Y_t would follow one precise path, whereas if the starting value was -100, it would follow another. A particular solution describes a precise path for a given starting condition, whereas the general solution describes the infinite set of possible particular solutions. In the absence of information about a starting value, obviously the best that can be done is to give a general solution to any difference equation. Clearly, a general solution is only half the story, and it will turn out that the initial conditions or side values play the crucial role in our understanding of how rational expectations models are solved. There is, therefore, purpose behind all this pedantry at this stage of the exposition. If the discussion seems to insult your intelligence at this stage, please bear with it!

Suppose Y_{t-T} just happens to be the starting value for the equation—thus Y_{t-T} is determined somewhere outside or is exogenous to the system described by Eq. (4-1). In this case, Eq. (4-5) is the particular solution to Eq. (4-1). Equation (4-5) does not look like the familiar textbook result, but in point of fact it is exactly the same. It would be a highly alarming situation if it were not! To see this, note that

$$S = a \sum_{i=0}^{T-1} \lambda^i = a(1 + \lambda + \lambda^2 + \cdots + \lambda^{T-1}). \tag{4-6}$$

Except when $\lambda = 1$, it follows that

$$S(1 - \lambda) = a - a\lambda^T. \tag{4-7}$$

Hence:

$$a \sum_{i=0}^{T-1} \lambda^i = \bar{Y} - \lambda^T \bar{Y} \tag{4-8}$$

where $\bar{Y} = a/(1 - \lambda)$ is the equilibrium value of the equation, that is when $Y_t = Y_{t-1}$. Hence, Eq. (4-5) can be expressed equivalently as

$$Y_t = \bar{Y} + \lambda^T(Y_{t-T} - \bar{Y}). \tag{4-9}$$

This would be

$$Y_t = \bar{Y} + \lambda^t(Y_0 - \bar{Y}) \tag{4-10}$$

if the starting value was Y_0, exactly t periods before Y_t. This is the usual textbook result, and is exactly Eq. (4-5) once more. As has been said, this solution technique is the natural first-choice method. Time is unidirectional and forward-looking, and it makes sense to think of a dynamic system starting somewhere in the past and projecting it forwards. Rational expectations often turns this on its head to some extent, so it is a good idea to understand clearly what the backwards technique is really about.

Now solve Eq. (4-1) in an unfamiliar way. Instead of iterating backwards, iterate forwards. This is easily done by substituting out Y_{t+1}, using the Eq. (4-3) version. After $T - 1$ forward iterations the following expression is derived:

$$Y_t = -a \sum_{i=1}^{T} \left(\frac{1}{\lambda}\right)^i + \left(\frac{1}{\lambda}\right)^T Y_{t+T}. \tag{4-11}$$

Notice that Eq. (4-11) qualifies as a general solution of Eq. (4-1) just as much as Eq. (4-5), since both are consistent with Eq. (4-1). However, if the starting value for the system lies in the past such as Y_0 or Y_{t-T}, then Eq. (4-11) could never locate the particular solution. Forward projection, though logically possible, gets us absolutely nowhere. We have simply shot off in the wrong direction. Equation (4-11) is disconnected from the past, which is where the starting value is presumed to lie.

Suppose, however, Eq. (4-1) had to satisfy a final condition instead of a starting value. In other words, we think of the system travelling *towards* a fixed point rather than coming from a fixed point. This is the essence of why a system would be solved forwards. If Y_{t+T} was the specified exogenous final condition, then Eq. (4-11) would be the particular solution of Eq. (4-1). The backward-projection method could then never locate the particular solution. Going backwards would have been shooting off in the wrong direction in this case.

Equation (4-11) can be manipulated to derive an equation which looks like Eq. (4-9) or Eq. (4-10). Applying exactly the same manipulations as was done in Eqs (4-6) to (4-8), it follows that

$$-a \sum_{i=1}^{T} \left(\frac{1}{\lambda}\right)^{i} = \bar{Y} - \frac{\bar{Y}}{\lambda^{T}} \tag{4-12}$$

where $\bar{Y} = a/(1 - \lambda)$ as before. Hence:

$$Y_t = \bar{Y} + \left(\frac{1}{\lambda}\right)^{T} (Y_{t+T} - \bar{Y}) \tag{4-13}$$

which 'looks forward' to the final condition Y_{t+T}. The key to whether Eq. (4-5) or (4-11) is a particular solution is therefore entirely determined by a prior belief or assertion about where a starting value or final condition should lie (henceforth we shall use the non-committal term 'side condition'). It is the economic dimension of the problem that should determine this, not mathematical convenience.

Side condition is a much more useful description than either starting value or final condition. The latter terms imply that the system does not operate either before or beyond the starting value or the final condition. There is no reason why side conditions should be restricted in this way. For example, in Eq. (4-13) Y_t looks forward to Y_{t+T} and there is no reason why future values such as Y_{t+j} (with $j > T$) cannot be projected beyond Y_{t+T}, though in other circumstances one might want to restrict the time domain up to just Y_{t+T}. A similar process could hold with backward projection, with the system obliged to pass through Y_0 to give a particular solution but holding in periods before $j = -t$.

Leaving aside the above digression, important lesson number two has now been demonstrated. If a rational expectations model is solved forwards, of which the New Classical theory of the price level of Chapter 3 provides an excellent example, it implies a prior belief that the side condition for the particular solution is disconnected from the past. There can be no other explanation for the forward-looking method.

Before moving on to consider a specific example, the following possible source of confusion should be noted. Suppose $|\lambda| < 1$. Clearly, Eq. (4-10) is a stable difference equation, in the sense that $Y_{t+j} \to \bar{Y}$ as $j \to \infty$. Now it looks as if Eq. (4-13) is an *unstable* equation with $|\lambda| < 1$ and given the $(1/\lambda)^T$ power in the equation. A little thought shows that this is not so. $Y_{t+j} \to \bar{Y}$ as j increases just as before. Consider the expression for Y_{t+j}. This is:

$$Y_{t+j} = \bar{Y} + \left(\frac{1}{\lambda}\right)^{T-j} (Y_{t+T} - \bar{Y}). \tag{4-14}$$

Since $(1/\lambda)^{T-j} \to 0$ as $j \to \infty$, the claim that Eq. (4-13) is stable is met. Consequently, statements of the kind, 'The equation is stable solved backwards, but unstable solved forwards', are slightly misleading.

PROBLEMS

4-1 Consider the equation $Y_t = a + Y_{t-1}$. What is the particular solution for Y_t if:

(*a*) $Y_{t-T} = 0$?
(*b*) $Y_{t+T} = 0$?

4-2 Consider the equation $Y_t = a + \lambda Y_{t-1}$, where $|\lambda| < 1$. A side condition is specified for Y_{t-T}. What restrictions must be placed on the value for Y_{t-T} if:

(*a*) Y_{t-j} is to be a finite number as $j \to \infty$?
(*b*) Y_{t+j} is to be a finite number as $j \to \infty$?
(*c*) How do these results change if $|\lambda| > 1$?
(*d*) How do the results change if the side condition is placed on Y_{t+T}?

4-2 FORWARD PROJECTION: AN EXAMPLE

Solving forwards is not the exclusive preserve of rational expectations, as the following simple model should make clear. It also illustrates the point that it should be the economic context which points us in the right direction as to how to solve the problem. As has been said, the natural way to solve a dynamic system is the backwards method, which is bound to be the most common case corresponding to our actual experience of how the world operates. It is not the only way. To be specific, the economics should direct us as to where in time (future or past) a side condition is located.

Here is the example which makes us think forwards, not backwards. Miss X wants to raise a loan now (where now is denoted as time $= t$). Based on her salary, she can afford a fixed monthly real repayment of size R. The question is: What is the maximum amount that Miss X can raise right now? If B_t is the amount raised, then the following must hold:

$$B_{t+1} = (1 + \rho)B_t - R \tag{4-15}$$

where ρ is the real rate of interest and B_{t+1} is the outstanding amount left of the loan one period later. This is a first-order equation in B_t and the mathematics of the problem tell us that there can be no particular solution for this—and hence no specific value for B_t—unless a side condition is specified. As with most loans, we shall specify a final condition that the loan must be fully paid off T periods hence. Hence the final condition is $B_{t+T} = 0$. We therefore seek a particular solution which satisfies Eq. (4-15) and the final condition $B_{t+T} = 0$. Clearly, the time domain of the problem is from t to $t + T$ and Eq. (4-15) does not apply either before t or beyond $t + T$. The fact that $1 + \rho > 1$, making Eq. (4-15) an unstable difference equation, is neither here nor there given the restricted time domain. This problem is solved quite naturally by forward iteration to give the particular solution:

$$B_t = R \sum_{i=1}^{T} \frac{1}{(1 + \rho)^i} + \frac{B_{t+T}}{(1 + \rho)^T}. \tag{4-16}$$

Noting that B_{t+T} is specified as 0, this can be transformed into a form like Eq. (4-13), to give the required value for B_t:

$$B_t = \frac{R}{\rho} - \frac{R/\rho}{(1 + \rho)^T}.$$ (4-17)

Thus the outstanding amount declines to zero as B_t moves towards the final date B_{t+T}. The important point is that we sought a forward solution because the side condition lay in the future. Although possible (see the solution to Chapter 1, Problem 1-12(a)), it would have been counter-intuitive to solve backwards in this example. It shows that solving forwards is very often the appropriate technique and there is nothing particularly mysterious about it.

PROBLEMS

4-3 An individual borrows £1000 at a fixed real rate of interest of 2 per cent. Calculate the fixed annual real repayment if the loan must be fully repaid in ten years. How would inflation affect this result?

4-4 An individual borrows a fixed sum and agrees the following repayment scheme: payments are such as to ensure $B_{t+j}/B_{t+j-1} = k$ for all $j > 0$, where B_{t+j} is the outstanding *real* debt and k is a fraction <1. What rate of inflation would ensure that nominal repayments would be constant? Show that this is independent of the real rate of interest.

4-3 TIME DOMAINS, STABILITY AND BOUNDEDNESS

Once again at the risk of appearing excessively pedantic, Fig. 4-1 helps conceptualize the various solution techniques for any difference or differential equation. Time moves forward from left to right along the line, with Y_t representing the present. A future value such as Y_{t+j} lies to the right of Y_t and a past value such as Y_{t-j} lies to the left of Y_t.

The time domain is the period over which the equation is supposed to hold. In some contexts the largest possible time domain might be conceptually appropriate, that is from $t - \infty$ to $t + \infty$. In other contexts a subset of this domain might be used. For example, the problem of the last section only made sense over the restricted time domain t to $t + T$. In many rational expectations models, involving a second-order difference equation, the time domain is often restricted from t to $t + \infty$, with a historical value of Y_t, namely last period's value Y_{t-1}, as one of the side conditions. The time domain is not often given explicit attention when formulating most models, yet it can become important, as we shall see, when particular solutions for Y_t are to be chosen. It is also important in determining whether or not the current value of Y_t (the value we are often interested in) will be an equilibrium value such as $\bar{Y}$ or something else. This should become clear when more complicated higher order systems are discussed. For the moment, these assertions might appear somewhat opaque.

There are four methods for solving Y_t, shown in Fig. 4-1 as A, B, C and D. Method A says start at Y_t and work backwards. Equation (4-5) is an example of this approach. Of course, having located the particular solution by this method, there is nothing to prevent us from projecting the system forwards beyond Y_t to find out what will happen to Y_t in future periods. That thought-experiment should not be confused as being different from the backward-looking solution method.

Method B says start somewhere in the past and work forward until Y_t is reached. Method A and Method B are just arithmetical transformations of each other. B, the 'past future' method, should not be confused with Methods C or D, which are truly forward-looking. For example, starting from the initial condition Y_{t-T}, Eq. (4-5) can be re-derived by forward iteration as:

$$Y_{t-T} = -a \sum_{i=1}^{T} \left(\frac{1}{\lambda}\right)^i + \left(\frac{1}{\lambda}\right)^T Y_t. \tag{4-18}$$

Equations (4-18) and (4-5) are just arithmetical transformations of each other and both are backward-looking.

Method C is truly forward-looking and Eq. (4-11) is an example of it. Once again, D and C are just arithmetical transformations of each other. Although this may be somewhat laboured, it does clarify thoughts, especially for higher order cases to be discussed later in this chapter. For example, later on it will be shown how a second-order equation requires two side conditions. Consequently, the solution could involve a mixture of elements of A and C if one side condition is backward-looking and the other forward-looking.

Now let us return to the question of the stability of Eq. (4-5). It was argued that Eq. (4-5) was stable if $|\lambda| < 1$ since $Y_{t+j} \to \bar{Y}$ as $j \to \infty$. Now suppose the time domain of the equation is extended to $t + \infty$ to $t - \infty$. A useful concept is the sequence $\{Y_{t-j}\}$. This sequence means the values $Y_t, Y_{t-1}, \ldots, Y_{t-j}$ with $j \to \infty$. Clearly, $\{Y_{t-j}\}$ describes 'past' behaviour and similarly the sequence $\{Y_{t+j}\}$ can be used to describe 'future' behaviour. Unless Y_{t-T} happens to be $\bar{Y}$, $\{Y_{t-j}\}$ will be unbounded when $|\lambda| < 1$. (A bounded sequence is simply one that for some finite number Z, $\{Y_{t-j}\} < Z$.) Now, in some contexts, boundedness for the $\{Y_{t-j}\}$ sequence might be a requirement for a meaningful economic solution. With $|\lambda| < 1$, Eq. (4-5) is unstable, looking backwards in the sense that $\{Y_{t-j}\}$ is unbounded, *except* if $Y_{t-T} = \bar{Y}$. In this case, the initial condition setting $Y_{t-T} = \bar{Y}$ could be *imposed* to ensure the leftwards (backwards in time) boundedness of $\{Y_{t-j}\}$. Obviously, $\{Y_{t+j}\}$ is bounded whatever the value of Y_{t-T} and is the 'natural' method of thinking about stability. Concern about $\{Y_{t-j}\}$ requires a two-directional view of time to infer something

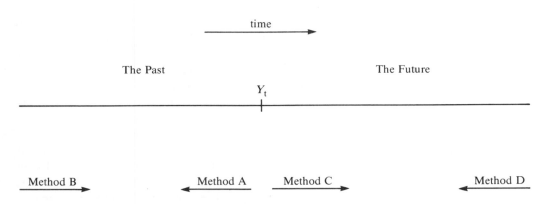

Figure 4-1 Schema of solution methods

about stability and, it must be said, is not entirely convincing. What is being invoked here is a type of Samuelson correspondence principle. The correspondence principle is the idea that since the world does not, in general, exhibit instability, we can rule out parameter values that would lead to unstable behaviour. Here the argument is extended somewhat to claim that the world never *was* unstable and never will be. If $Y_{t-T} \neq \bar{Y}$, then projecting backwards through time the world was, in a manner of speaking, unstable in the past—hence such behaviour is ruled out by requiring $Y_{t-T} = \bar{Y}$.

Do we really care about stability in this sense? It is surely reasonable to care more about where we are going to than where we have come from. Thus, even if the time domain is the unrestricted one, it is still reasonable to assert that Eq. (4-5) is stable even though $Y_{t-T} \neq \bar{Y}$. The standard treatments assert that this is so, because we implicitly have a unidirectional, forward-looking view of time. The mathematics places no constraints but actual experience of the world might reasonably cause us to question the idea of two-sided boundedness being in any way useful. Notice, however, that if the time domain is restricted on the left-hand side—that is, the model applies only from some *finite* time in the past—then we need not involve ourselves in such arcane issues. Y_t need not be restricted to the equilibrium value, since the now restricted $\{Y_{t-j}\}$ sequence will be bounded no matter what the value of Y_{t-T}.

All the above points apply in exactly the same way to the forward-looking solution, Eq. (4-11), and we consider this for the case when $|\lambda| > 1$. In this case Eq. (4-11) is unstable, since, unless $Y_{t+T} = \bar{Y}$, then $|Y_{t+j}| \to \infty$ as $j \to \infty$. Notice, symmetrically with the $|\lambda| < 1$ case, the $\{Y_{t-j}\}$ sequence is always bounded. Since the rational expectations case will have a structure like Eq. (4-11), let us concentrate on this case. In many instances $|\lambda| > 1$ will also be a property of such systems. Paradoxically, such a property will be regarded not as a problem but as a highly desirable feature. Suppose it is argued that the $\{Y_{t+j}\}$ sequence must be bounded. If that is so then there is only one possible value of Y_{t+T} that will ensure this—namely, setting $Y_{t+T} = \bar{Y}$. This is the essence of the rational expectations method, since the requirement for boundedness ensures a *unique* choice for this side condition. Naturally enough, the boundedness requirement must be carefully justified, and few would argue that it is appropriate or correct in every instance. Notice, as with the backward-looking case, if the time domain is restricted to be somewhat less than the infinite future we do not have to be restricted to the equilibrium view, since the restricted $\{Y_{t+j}\}$ is always bounded.

Suppose, by contrast, $|\lambda| < 1$ and the time domain is the unrestricted one from t to $t + \infty$. In this case, $\{Y_{t+j}\}$ is bounded no matter what the choice of Y_{t+T}. It is then argued that this makes solving the problem rather more difficult because there is no criterion by which to pin down Y_{t+T}. All this should become clear as we proceed.

Chapter 3 examined two ways of expectations formation, the forward-looking rational method and the backward-looking adaptive method. The forward-looking method involves a normalization like $Y_{t+T} = \bar{Y}$ and it turns out that the backward-looking method involves exactly the same type of normalization. Now the backward normalization is difficult to justify because it involves an argument that a backward-looking $\{Y_{t-j}\}$ sequence should be bounded. As has been said, this is not a very comfortable notion. The rational case involves the more natural idea that the forward sequence be bounded. In other words, rational expectations forces us to confront serious problems that exist in other mechanisms which we would not have thought of before. The last part of Section 4-7 explores the adaptive expectations model once again to emphasize this particular point.

PROBLEM

4-5 Consider the difference equation $Y_t = a + \lambda Y_{t-1}$, which is restricted to the time domain $-T$ to $+T$. The side condition is specified for Y_0. Is there a specific value for Y_0 that will ensure that, in all circumstances, $Y_{-T} = Y_T$?

4-4 FORCING VARIABLES

In Eq. (4-1), the only exogenous variable is the constant term a. For many economic problems this is too restrictive. Chapter 3, for example, did not restrict the expected money supply to be constant in all future periods. A more general specification of Eq. (4-1) is

$$Y_t = bX_t + \lambda Y_{t-1}. \tag{4-19}$$

X_t is an exogenous variable, determined outside the system and is no longer restricted to be the same period by period. X_t is sometimes known as a forcing variable, since it 'forces' the behaviour of the dynamic system. In other contexts X_t could be interpreted as a random component of a difference equation. Such an equation is then a stochastic difference equation and is the familiar linear regression equation with a lagged dependent variable:

$$Y_t = \lambda Y_{t-1} + u_t \tag{4-20}$$

where u_t is a disturbance term that is assumed to exhibit certain statistical properties; for example, it might be assumed to have a zero mean and a constant variance for its possible values. There is no difference between Eqs (4-19) and (4-20) beyond this. We shall stick to Eq. (4-19), interpreting X_t in an essentially non-stochastic way. It turns out that, under reasonable assumptions, the presence of additive uncertainty like u_t does not make the solution of rational expectations models any more difficult.

Equation (4-19) is no more difficult to solve than Eq. (4-1) by either forward or backward iteration. Backward iteration gives the result:

$$Y_t = b \sum_{i=0}^{T-1} \lambda^i X_{t-i} + \lambda^T Y_{t-T}. \tag{4-21}$$

The point about Eq. (4-21) is that it can no longer be transformed into the familiar textbook results such as Eqs (4-9) or (4-10), unless special assumptions about the behaviour of the $\{X_{t-j}\}$ sequence are made. The concept of an equilibrium value $\bar{Y}$ simply cannot be applied here, though we shall, of course, be extremely interested in exploring analogous properties that are strongly related to the equilibrium solution $\bar{Y}$. Thus, at one level forcing variables add little complication, but at another level they complicate a lot, because considerably more care is required in discussing what is meant by the model being 'in equilibrium'—an analogous property to $Y_t = \bar{Y}$; or being 'out of equilibrium'—an analogous property to $Y_t \neq \bar{Y}$.

Stability has the connotation of the system converging towards some fixed point—but this is unhelpful in the present context since there is no need for Y_t to converge to a fixed point, no matter what value λ takes. Clearly $|\lambda| < 1$ suggests that Eq. (4-21) possesses some equilibrium property, albeit rather more difficult to state precisely. In the previous section we discussed stability in terms of either (or both) the $\{Y_{t-j}\}$ or $\{Y_{t+j}\}$ sequence being bounded. This idea might be useful here, since, as has been said, we cannot invoke the idea of $Y_{t+j} \to \bar{Y}$ as $j \to \infty$. Thus, suppose $|\lambda| < 1$ in Eq. (4-21). Clearly the last term $\to 0$ as we project the system forwards. Does that not mean that the $\{Y_{t+j}\}$ sequence is bounded, whereas if $|\lambda| > 1$, then the $\{Y_{t+j}\}$ sequence would not be bounded? Unfortunately, no. Y_{t+j} involves the term $\sum \lambda^i X_{t+j-i}$. Now as $j \to \infty$, the $\{\sum \lambda^i X_{t+j-i}\}$ sequence need not necessarily be bounded, irrespective of any normalization placed on Y_{t-T}. An obvious example would be if $X_{t+j+1} = X_{t+j}(1 + g)$ for $j > 0$, hence X_{t+j} grows at the uniform rate g for all j. In this case with $|\lambda| < 1$, the $\{Y_{t+j}\}$ sequence would eventually converge to grow at the rate g, which contradicts the definition of a bounded sequence.

In the forward-looking case with $|\lambda| > 1$, we considered the idea of imposing a side condition to ensure stability, or in the present context a bounded $\{Y_{t+j}\}$ sequence. Now the present difficulty becomes rather more acute. It may be that there is no side condition that will ensure a bounded $\{Y_{t+j}\}$ sequence, given the behaviour of $\{X_{t+j}\}$. The upshot of this discussion is that the case for imposing particular normalizations on rational expectations models is weakened, not strengthened. However, the difficulty is not insurmountable and we shall tackle it directly when the specific theory of the price level of Chapter 3 is explored in Section 4-7.

PROBLEM

4-6 Consider the difference equation $Y_t = X_t + \lambda Y_{t-1}$, where λ is a positive parameter and X_t is a forcing variable which behaves according to $X_{t+j+1} = (1 + \beta)X_{t+j}$ for $j \geq -t$ and where β is a positive constant. Y_0 and X_0 are the respective starting values. Show that $Y_{t+j} \to$ a steady growth rate of β as $j \to \infty$ if $|\lambda| < 1$.

4-5 THE RATIONAL EXPECTATIONS INTERPRETATION: A PRELIMINARY LOOK

Suppose the model, written forwards, is

$$Y_t = bX_t + \lambda Y_{t+1}. \tag{4-22}$$

Further, suppose it has been decided that the forward method of solution is appropriate. This implies a belief that the side condition is forward-looking. The time domain is from t to $t + \infty$, where t can be thought of as the present. The first point is that the precise size of the future values of the X_t forcing variable may not be known, given currently available information. Thus the future path of Y_t cannot be precisely determined, only at best its expected future path. A special case is when the future values of the X_t variable are presumed to be known. In this case the exact path for Y_t can be determined and this special case is known as a perfect foresight model. Quite often rational expectations models are formulated as perfect foresight models as this offers a convenient simplification without discarding too much detail.

In general, therefore, when Eq. (4-22) is solved forwards, it is an equation in *expectations*. For example, a future term could be

$$E_t Y_{t+s} = b E_t X_{t+s} + \lambda E_t Y_{t+s+1} \tag{4-23}$$

where, as in Chapter 3, $E_t Y_{t+s}$ is the expected value of Y_{t+s} based on information available at time t, and $E_t X_{t+s}$ is the expected value of the forcing variable. The concern is the behaviour of the $\{E_t Y_{t+s}\}$ sequence from $s = 0$ to $+\infty$. Obviously, unless there is perfect foresight, Eq. (4-22) is a potential contradiction, since it claims that today's value of Y_t is determined by the actual, but unknown, future value of Y_{t+1}. A less than perfect foresight economic model might therefore be of the form

$$Y_t = b X_t + \lambda E_t Y_{t+1}. \tag{4-24}$$

Notice that, although, at best, we can make statements about the $\{E_t Y_{t+s}\}$ sequence rather than $\{Y_{t+s}\}$, we may determine the current value Y_t in the above case if X_t is known information at that time.

Equation (4-22) is frequently generalized in one further way by adding a disturbance term u_t in the manner of Eq. (4-20):

$$Y_t = b X_t + \lambda E_t Y_{t+1} + u_t. \tag{4-25}$$

The random component can be assumed to be a 'white noise' process with a zero mean. Consequently, if the system is projected forwards, a typical term will be Eq. (4-23) again, since $E_t u_{t+s} = 0$ for all $s > 0$. Solving Eq. (4-25) is therefore effectively the same as in the presence of no additive uncertainty.

One slight modification is to be clear whether u_t is known information at time t. The usual interpretation of Eq. (4-25) is that the realization of u_t is not part of the currently available information set. To make this absolutely clear, Eq. (4-25) might be more comfortably expressed as

$$Y_t = b E_{t-1} X_t + \lambda E_{t-1} Y_{t+1} + u_t. \tag{4-25'}$$

Thus $Y_t - E_{t-1} Y_t = u_t$ is the random component. Dating information at $t - 1$ makes this clear and models containing such stochastic elements are often expressed in this way. An equation like (4-25') would be solved for $E_{t-1} Y_t$, where Y_t is just u_t plus $E_{t-1} Y_t$. Section 4-9 gives an example. We have now reached the limits of the 'up-and-at-'em' technique. For more complex cases it simply does not work, and more elegant solution methods are required. This involves the use of lag and forward operators.

PROBLEM

4-7 Model: $Y_t = a + \lambda Y_{t+1} + u_t$, where u_{t+j} is an independent random variable of zero mean for all $j \geq 0$. The side condition is $Y_{t+T} = A$.

(a) Calculate $E_{t-1} Y_t$ and Y_t.
(b) How would these results modify if the model was $Y_t = a + \lambda E_{t-1} Y_{t+1} + u_t$?

4-6 THE LAG AND FORWARD OPERATORS

Linear operators are very useful mathematical tools. The idea is that a symbol is defined in a particular way to indicate a particular mathematical operation. The operator can then be shown to have certain properties and to obey (if one is careful) the usual laws of algebra, just like real numbers. The operator can then be separated from its associated variable and treated 'as if' it is a variable in its own right. This is what makes them such a useful and appealing mathematical tool. The lag and forward operators are two such cases. The actual mathematics to formally justify their use is somewhat advanced, so some of what follows must be taken on trust—though at an elementary, intuitive level it is easy to see why they work in the way that they do.

The lag operator, denoted as L, is defined in the following way:

$$LX_t = X_{t-1}. \tag{4-26}$$

Thus X_{t-2} is simply $L(LX_t)$ or $L^2 X_t$ and $L^n X_t$ is X_{t-n}. Now consider $\sum_{i=0}^{T-1} \lambda^i X_{t-1}$ from Eq. (4-21). Using the L operator, this could be written as

$$\sum_{i=0}^{T-1} \lambda^i X_{t-i} = \sum_{i=0}^{T-1} \lambda^i L^i X_t. \tag{4-27}$$

In general, any sequence could be written as

$$\sum_{i=0}^{T-1} b_i X_{t-i} = \sum_{i=0}^{T-1} b_i L^i X_t = B(L) X_t \tag{4-28}$$

where $B(L) = \sum_{i=0}^{T-1} b_i L^i$ is a finite polynomial in L. One polynomial sequence, which will be critical to the solution method, will be the infinite polynomial sequence

$$A(L) = \sum_{i=0}^{\infty} \lambda^i L^i. \tag{4-29}$$

The useful point about $A(L)$ is that it can often be written as

$$A(L) X_t = (1 - \lambda L)^{-1} X_t = \sum_{i=0}^{\infty} \lambda^i L^i X_t. \tag{4-30}$$

The point about the above representation is that $(1 - \lambda L)^{-1}$ can be 'separated' from its associated X_t and this property will prove very useful for locating solutions. (Strictly, one should write $(L^0 - \lambda L)^{-1}$ rather than $(1 - \lambda L)^{-1}$ because we have an algebra of operators and one cannot really subtract an operator from a scalar. However, the former representation is the one most frequently used and will be followed here.)

To see why Eq. (4-30) 'works', multiply through by $(1 - \lambda L)$. This is

$$X_t = (1 - \lambda L)(1 - \lambda L)^{-1} X_t = (1 - \lambda L) \sum_{i=0}^{\infty} \lambda^i L^i X_t$$

$$= (1 + \lambda L + \lambda^2 L^2 + \cdots) Xt - X_t(\lambda L + \lambda^2 L^2 + \cdots). \tag{4-31}$$

Another suggestive analogy is to think of the $\lambda^i L^i$ sequence as a geometric series of factor λL. The geometric series $1 + b + b^2 + \cdots$ sums to $1/(1 - b)$ for $|b| < 1$. Treating $1 + \lambda L + (\lambda L)^2 + \cdots$ in exactly the same way gives $(1 - \lambda L)^{-1}$. This suggests that Eq.

(4-30) is most useful when it is a convergent sequence. Now let us solve Eq. (4-1) using the useful lag operator construct. Equation (4-1) is written as $(1 - \lambda L) Y_t = a$. Hence,

$$Y_t = (1 - \lambda L)^{-1} a + c\lambda^t. \tag{4-32}$$

Equation (4-32) is the general solution and the only mysterious part of this is the $c\lambda^t$ term. Remember that a general solution is any equation that is consistent with $(1 - \lambda L) Y_t = a$. Multiplying Eq. (4-32) by $(1 - \lambda L)$ gives

$$(1 - \lambda L) Y_t = (1 - \lambda L)(1 - \lambda L)^{-1} a + c(1 - \lambda L)\lambda^t = a. \tag{4-33}$$

This follows because $(1 - \lambda L)c\lambda^t$ is zero (note: $\lambda L c\lambda^t = \lambda c\lambda^{t-1} = c\lambda^t$). Thus Eq. (4-33) is consistent with Eq. (4-32) and hence it is a general solution. A specific value for c would give a particular solution. Rest assured that Eq. (4-33) can be transformed into exactly the same thing as Eq. (4-10), which is a particular solution with Y_0 as the initial condition. From Eq. (4-32), noting that $(1 - \lambda L)^{-1} a$ is just $a/(1 - \lambda) = \bar{Y}$, it follows that $Y_0 = \bar{Y} + c$ and Eq. (4-10) emerges directly. Hence there is nothing actually different about solutions expressed in lag operator form. It would be surprising, to say the least, if there were.

The forward operator, denoted as F (sometimes called the shift operator), is defined in an analogous way:

$$F X_t = X_{t+1}. \tag{4-34}$$

Clearly the F operator will be extremely useful for solving difference equations forwards and has similar properties to the L operator. In fact it should be obvious from the definition that $F = L^{-1}$. A property like Eq. (4-30) pertains:

$$(1 - \lambda F)^{-1} X_t = \sum_{i=0}^{\infty} \lambda^i F^i X_t. \tag{4-35}$$

Two further transformations, which give useful relationships between the L and F operators, are

$$(1 - \lambda F)^{-1} = (1 - \lambda^{-1} L)^{-1}(-\lambda^{-1} L) \tag{4-36}$$

and

$$(1 - \lambda L)^{-1} = (1 - \lambda^{-1} F)^{-1}(-\lambda^{-1} F). \tag{4-37}$$

Both the above expressions are achieved by multiplying the l.h.s. of Eqs (4-36) and (4-37) by $(-\lambda^{-1} L)^{-1}(-\lambda^{-1} L)$ and $(-\lambda^{-1} F)^{-1}(-\lambda^{-1} F)$ respectively, and noting that $LF\lambda = \lambda$. These transformations will prove to be extremely useful.

These transformations are clearly suggested by the fact that $1/(1 - \lambda) = -\lambda^{-1}/(1 - \lambda^{-1})$. Notice that if $|\lambda| < 1$, then the former sequence can be expanded as the convergent geometric sequence $(1 + \lambda + \lambda^2 + \cdots)$ whereas it is clear that $-\lambda^{-1}(1 + \lambda^{-1} + (\lambda^{-1})^2 + \cdots)$ is not a convergent expansion. Similarly, if $|\lambda^{-1}| < 1$ then the latter expansion is convergent and equals $-\lambda^{-1}/(1 - \lambda^{-1})$, whereas the former expansion is not convergent.

Referring to Eqs (4-36) and (4-37), this suggests that a forward or backward expansion might be chosen on the basis of whichever gave a convergent sequence. However, the earlier discussion warned against basing the decision on such arbitrary criteria. The forward expansion is chosen if a side condition looks forwards and the backward expansion if the side condition looks to the past. Nothing else counts. Now consider the forward solution to Eq. (4-19). Equation (4-19) can be written as

$$Y_t = \lambda^{-1} Y_{t+1} - b\lambda^{-1} X_{t+1} \tag{4-38}$$

or

$$(1 - \lambda^{-1}F)Y_t = -b\lambda^{-1}FX_t. \tag{4-39}$$

Hence a general solution is

$$Y_t = (1 - \lambda^{-1}F)^{-1}(-b\lambda^{-1}FX_t) + c\lambda^t \tag{4-40}$$

where c is some particularizing constant. Notice it is $c\lambda^t$ and *not* $c(\lambda^{-1})^t$. This is because only $c\lambda^t = 0$ when multiplied through by $(1 - \lambda^{-1}F)$. Solved backwards, the alternative general solution to Eq. (4-19) is

$$Y_t = (1 - \lambda L)^{-1} bX_t + c\lambda^t. \tag{4-41}$$

Notice that the forward solution equation (Eq. (4-40)) can be derived directly from Eq. (4-41) using transformation (4-37) and shows the usefulness of this move. However, it must be stressed that such transformations cannot be done on a whim or for solution convenience. Side conditions determine whether to look forwards or backwards for a particular solution.

Now let us check that Eqs (4-41) and (4-21) are equivalent when Y_{t-T} is the side condition. Since Eq. (4-41) must satisfy Y_{t-T}, then

$$Y_{t-T} = (1 - \lambda L)^{-1}(bX_{t-T}) + c\lambda^{t-T}. \tag{4-42}$$

Hence c is given by

$$c = [Y_{t-T} - (1 - \lambda L)^{-1}(bX_{t-T})]\lambda^{T-t}. \tag{4-43}$$

Substitute back into Eq. (4-41) to derive

$$Y_t = (1 - \lambda L)^{-1}b(X_t - \lambda^T X_{t-T}) + \lambda^T Y_{t-T}. \tag{4-44}$$

Thus,

$$Y_t = b \sum_{i=0}^{T-1} \lambda^i X_{t-i} + \lambda^T Y_{t-T} \tag{4-45}$$

which is Eq. (4.21) once again. If, by contrast, Y_{t+T} is a final definitizing condition, readers can (see Problem 4-8) transform Eq. (4-40) into

$$Y_t = -b \sum_{i=1}^{T} \left(\frac{1}{\lambda}\right)^i X_{t+i} + \left(\frac{1}{\lambda}\right)^T Y_{t+T}. \tag{4-46}$$

Notice that $c\lambda^t$ appears in Eq. (4-40) and $(1/\lambda)^T Y_{t+T}$ appears in Eq. (4-46). There should be no confusion here. Both equations are equivalent.

It turns out that the $c\lambda^t$ term will be critical to the solution of models involving rational expectations. The 'fundamentals' solution imposes the particularization $c = 0$. We have already gone a long way towards understanding why this is so. The next section re-examines the model of Chapter 3 to explore the solution more deeply using the methods developed in this section.

PROBLEMS

4-8 Transform Eq. (4-40) into Eq. (4-46).

4-9 Another frequently used operator is the difference operator Δ. ΔY_t is defined in the following way: $\Delta Y_t = Y_{t+1} - Y_t$. The backward difference operator is defined as $\nabla Y_t = Y_{t-1} - Y_t$. Show that the following relationships hold:

(a) $\Delta = -F\nabla$;
(b) $\nabla = -\Delta L$;
(c) $(\Delta + 1)(\nabla + 1) = 1$.

4-7 THE NEW CLASSICAL VIEW OF PRICES ONCE AGAIN

Recall Eq. (3-2) of Chapter 3:

$$P_t = \frac{M_t}{\alpha_1} + \left(\frac{\alpha_2}{\alpha_1}\right)_t P_{t+1}. \tag{4-47}$$

The rational expectations version of this can be written as

$$P_t = aM_t + bE_t P_{t+1} \tag{4-48}$$

where $E_t P_{t+1}$ is the rational expectation of $_t P_{t+1}$, $a = 1/\alpha_1$ and $b = \alpha_2/\alpha_1 < 1$. As Sec. 4-5 has made clear, the forward projection of Eq. (4-48) is an equation in *expectations*. We are concerned with the sequence $\{E_t P_{t+j}\}$, that is P_t, $E_t P_{t+1}$, $E_t P_{t+2}$ and so on. The equation, except in the special case of perfect foresight, does not explain the sequence $\{P_{t+j}\}$, that is P_t, P_{t+1}, P_{t+2} and so on.

Equation (4-48) is just a first-order difference equation with $E_t M_{t+j}$ a typical value of the forcing variable—'the money supply expected at time $t + j$, based on information available at time t'; and $E_t P_{t+j}$ the typical term—'the price level expected at time $t + j$, based on information available at time t'. The particular solution is chosen on the basis of giving the $\{E_t P_{t+j}\}$ sequence a desirable property. The time domain is t to $t + \infty$. Recall the fundamentals solution:

$$P_t = aM_t + a\sum_{i=1}^{\infty} b^i E_t M_{t+i}. \tag{4-49}$$

Now solve Eq. (4-48) using the methods of Sec. 4-6:

$$(1 - bE_t F)P_t = aM_t. \tag{4-50}$$

Thus:

$$P_t = (1 - bE_t F)^{-1}(aM_t) + c\left(\frac{1}{b}\right)^t \tag{4-51}$$

or

$$P_t = a\sum_{i=0}^{\infty} b^i E_t M_{t+i} + c\left(\frac{1}{b}\right)^t. \tag{4-52}$$

Equation (4-52) is the general solution and it is readily seen that Eq. (4-49) is the particular solution which sets $c = 0$. (Note that Eq. (4-52) is summed from $i = 0$ and that $E_t M_t$ is just M_t once more.) The first term of Eq. (4-52) is known as the 'fundamentals' part of the solution and $c(1/b)^t$ is known suggestively as the 'bubble'. In effect, Eq. (4-49) rules out bubbles. Actually, the deterministic form of the bubble $c(1/b)^t$ is not the only way of describing a bubble. The bubble can be given a stochastic specification with a probability that it will burst in any future period and which is consistent with an equation in forward expectations. This idea is not pursued here, except to say that it further emphasizes that the fundamentals solution is not the only possible one.

The first point to emphasize is that not only is Eq. (4-49) a particular solution, but also this particularization is unconnected with the past. This is a strong assumption, but must necessarily follow if one iterates forwards to locate a particular solution. The current price level adjusts immediately to accommodate beliefs about future monetary policy. It is in no way driven by previous history. Is this claim justified? It is difficult to point to factors that make the claim self-evident. One should be absolutely clear about the embodied auxiliary hypothesis.

Now consider the justification for imposing $c = 0$. This requires a lot of care. With $c \neq 0$ and $1/b > 1$, then the expected price level would either grow or decrease without limit. For example, $E_t P_{t+j}$ would be

$$E_t P_{t+j} = a \sum_{i=0}^{\infty} b^i E_t M_{t+j+i} + c \left(\frac{1}{b} \right)^{t+j}. \tag{4-53}$$

As $j \to \infty$, then clearly the last term grows without limit if $c > 0$, and decreases without limit if $c < 0$.

This explains the use of the term 'bubble' to describe the process. Whether to call such bubbles irrational and rule them out at the outset, is therefore the issue. In another context, Eq. (4-52) could refer to an equity or asset price, where the first term represents the present value of expected dividend payments (see Problem 4-10). This would be the fundamentals price of the stock—ignoring issues of risk. Now it might be rational to pay over the odds if one was certain that a bubble in prices would obtain—as reflected by a positive value for c. Thus c reflects the herd instinct, a self-fulfilling prophecy of the kind, 'Buy now because the price is bound to go up tomorrow, irrespective of the fundamentals.' The smart investor now no longer bases decisions on fundamentals, because it no longer pays to be smart if everyone else is stupid. Keynes likened the process to a beauty contest. The idea is to rank a series of faces in ascending order of beauty to win a prize. The fundamentals approach would be to use *objective* criteria. However, Keynes pointed out an alternative strategy, which is that, in order to win, it is necessary for your choice to coincide with the judges' opinions. Fundamentals are then ignored, and the idea is to second-guess the views of the judges.

The speculation of the housing market, discussed in Chapter 1, is an excellent example of prices driven by a bubble and the stockmarket is replete with many such examples. The smart investor follows the bubble, jumping off before the bubble bursts. Is the investor behaving irrationally? The argument that it is purely irrational is difficult to sustain and, after all, Eq. (4-52) with $c \neq 0$ is *consistent* with the theory of the price level. However, most of us would conclude that there is something 'fishy' and not quite right about bubbles. A personal view is that bubbles are generally the product of arrogance and greed. Individual investors and 'City slickers' sincerely believe that they are the smart ones and everyone else is stupid. When money is made, it is due to their own amazing skill, and when money is lost, it is just bad luck. The reality is that bubbles are driven by mass hysteria and greed. Setting $c = 0$ takes the sin out of economic processes! A more conventional view is to regard bubbles as the product of rational human behaviour.

The fundamentals solution rules out bubbles, but the discussion serves to show that setting $c = 0$ is not an immediately obvious conclusion. This doubt is reinforced by the following consideration. Even if $c = 0$ is imposed on Eq. (4-52), it is possible that the $\{E_t P_{t+j}\}$ sequence could grow without limit. Indeed, for the UK economy, the economist's best guess is that this is the expectation path for prices any sensible agent would hold! In Chapter 3, using the fundamentals solution with $c = 0$ imposed, just such an example was given. A constant expected growth rate in the money supply of g implied a constant expected inflation rate of g. Such a solution makes perfectly good sense, but does imply an unbounded sequence in the expected future price level. Thus the argument for setting $c = 0$, because it rules out 'explosive' behaviour in expectations, is unconvincing and sloppy. The sloppy line of reasoning arises because most people only consider the case of a constant value for the forcing variable. Suppose $E_t M_{t+j} = M$ was a constant for all j, then the general solution could be written as

$$P_t = \bar{P} + c\left(\frac{1}{b}\right)^t \qquad (4\text{-}54)$$

where $\bar{P} = aM/(1 - b)$ is the equilibrium price level. This makes clear the inherent perversity of the bubble—despite a constant M, prices grow or decrease without limit unless $c = 0$ were imposed. Setting $c = 0$ is, therefore, closely related to ruling out non-equilibrium solutions, though the notion of 'equilibrium' is somewhat tenuous in the case of a non-constant forcing variable. Setting $c = 0$ can, therefore, be justified on the basis that it is the only case that allows the possibility of a bounded sequence in expectations.

What does $c = 0$ mean? One need not actually take any fixed position on this, other than the assertion that the side value cannot be in the past. Suppose P_{t+T} was the imposed side condition. We know from Sec. 4-6 that an equivalent representation of Eq. (4-52) is

$$P_t = a \sum_{i=0}^{T-1} b^i E_t M_{t+i} + b^T P_{t+T}. \qquad (4\text{-}55)$$

The above contains sufficient information to particularize the solution for P_t but there is nothing to prevent projection beyond P_{t+T}, if the time domain is t to $t + \infty$. If $c = 0$ is a requirement, then P_{t+T} must satisfy

$$P_{t+T} = a \sum_{i=0}^{\infty} b^i E_t M_{t+T+i}. \qquad (4\text{-}56)$$

Notice that if the time domain is restricted to a finite future period, there is no need to impose $c = 0$, because no matter what choice is made, the restricted $\{E_t P_{t+j}\}$ sequence would always be bounded, no matter what value c took.

Sometimes the line of reasoning used to justify Eq. (4-49) is to consider the case which sets $T = 0$, with P_t regarded as the starting value to ensure the possibility of a bounded sequence in future expectations. The interpretation is: 'What must P_t be right now to ensure a desirable property about the $\{E_t P_{t+j}\}$ sequence?' There is nothing in particular to favour this interpretation over any other, except convenience of exposition. It is equivalent to setting $c = 0$. Any other future value could be designated as the side condition, providing it implied $c = 0$. The important point is that the particularization is forward-looking, driven by the requirement for boundedness.

Several further points about the fundamentals solution are in order here. First, for P_t to be well defined requires that the $\sum_{i=0}^{\infty} b^i E_t M_{t+i}$ term be finite. For example, if M is expected to grow at the rate g for ever, then P_t is not defined if $b(1 + g) > 1$. Generally speaking, the fact that $b < 1$ should ensure that P_t is defined, but this need not always be so. For this reason, Eq. (4-49) seems unsuitable as a vehicle to explain hyper-inflation when g is likely to be large. Yet it is the hyper-inflation case for which the rational expectations version of the Cagan equation has been popularized. A second observation is to re-emphasize the point already made in Chapter 3. The fundamentals solution and the normalization depend on the assumption of an infinite future time horizon. It is not relevant if people *in fact* operate with finite and probably quite short time horizons. This simply points up the fact that, although rational expectations may be the logical way to form expectations, logic and reality are not necessarily the same thing.

Suppose, in fact, $b > 1$, which means a stable difference equation in the conventional sense. It was pointed out that this can cause serious problems because $c(1/b)^t$ will converge no matter what the choice of c. (Equation (4-13) explicitly illustrated this for the constant forcing variable case.) With $b > 1$, in most circumstances we would not have a sensible theory of the price level because a constant M would imply a negative equilibrium price. However, suspend disbelief for a moment. For example, with $b > 1$ and $E_t M_{t+i}$ *declining* at a sufficiently fast rate, the fundamentals solution does give a finite positive P_t, so credulity is not unbearably strained.

How does rational expectations cope with such a problem? 'Brethren, here is a great difficulty; let us look it firmly in the face and pass on', is probably about as far as anyone has considered it until now. One tactic might be to look backwards for a solution and use a historical value of the price level as the side condition. In the present model, such a move is effectively precluded—the economic context simply rules out interpreting the demand for money in this way. In other contexts, however, the issue may not be so clear cut. The next section concerns second-order difference equations and will, in certain cases, exploit historical values as a method of pinning down particular solutions. However, it must be emphasized that the choice of going forwards, as in Eq. (4-49), or looking backwards for a side condition is not, and should not be, simply a matter of mathematical convenience depending on whatever value of b a model happens to throw up. It is one's beliefs about the economic processes that should determine the solution method, and not the value of b.

This section is concluded by looking at the adaptive expectations model once more. The purpose is to emphasize that the problems discussed are not unique to rational expectations; backward-looking extrapolative predictors face a common set of problems. Recall the first-order adaptive expectations rule, Eq. (3-3) of Chapter 3:

$$(1 - \lambda L)P_t^* = (1 - \lambda)P_{t-1}, \quad 0 \le \lambda \le 1 \tag{4-57}$$

where P_{t-1} is now the forcing variable. The above rule only makes sense if the time domain is restricted from the present to 'somewhere' in the past. The fundamentals solution is derived by repeated lagging and substitution:

$$P_t^* = [1 - \lambda] \sum_{i=0}^{\infty} \lambda^i P_{t-i-1}. \tag{4-58}$$

Here the time domain is presumed to be t to $t - \infty$. Notice the complete symmetry with rational expectations, except that now we look backwards. Equation (4-58) is a particular solution. The general solution is

$$P_t^* = [1 - \lambda] \sum_{i=0}^{\infty} \lambda^i P_{t-i-1} + c\lambda^t \tag{4-59}$$

with $c\lambda^t$ the equivalent of the bubble. Just like Eq. (4-49), Eq. (4-58) is the particular solution which sets $c = 0$. It is actually quite hard to come up with any totally convincing explanation for this normalization since λ is not > 1. Section 4-3 questioned the notion of two-sided boundedness. One simply may not care that the sequence $\{P_{t-j}^*\}$ should be a bounded one. One slightly heretical view might be to impose another normalization other than $c = 0$. For example, we saw in Chapter 3 that the extrapolative predictor was likely to make systematic errors over some observed sequence of prices. A possible alternative would be to impose the normalization that made P_{t-j}^* on average correct over the period of study.

The following is an alternative line of reasoning in support of the correctness of Eq. (4-58). Suppose the model has been true for ever with a starting value infinitely far back in the past. By the time t arrives the model is bound to have organized itself into the fundamentals solution. All in all, extrapolative predictors face exactly the same problems as forward-looking rational expectations predictors, and in some respects backward projection has rather more conceptual difficulties. Fixing some future expectation is entirely possible, since expectations as such exist entirely in the mind and correspond to nothing actual in the world. For backward-looking models this is more tricky. History being history gives us almost an infinity of fixed points from which to choose a starting value. Do we choose P_{t-1}, P_{t-2}, or what?

If the time domain is restricted to commence sometime after $t - \infty$, then adaptive expectations need not exhibit the equilibrium property as exemplified by the fundamentals solution—exactly as occurs with a restricted future time domain in the rational case. The next section concerns more complex models where solutions can look both backwards and forwards. When the time domain is restricted—particularly in the backwards part of the solution—once again the model need not exhibit an equilibrium property.

PROBLEMS

4-10 A riskless asset offers a fixed rate of return r. An equity offers profits of Z_t and a proportionate expected capital gain of $(E_t P_{t+1} - P_t)/P_t$, where P_t is the current price of the equity and $E_t P_{t+1}$ is the rational expectation of the price at $t + 1$ based on current information. Calculate the fundamentals price of the equity, assuming that the expected return on the equity and the safe asset are the same.

4-11 Suppose the current price earnings ($=$profits) ratio of an equity was 10 to 1, whereas the price earnings ratio of another was 30 to 1. What does that imply about relative expected future profit performance of the two equities?

4-12 Show how the presence of a speculative bubble could cause the current price to exceed the fundamentals price.

4-8 THE SECOND-ORDER CASE

In a sense, first-order difference equations oblige one to take a strong 'either–or' view of how the world behaves. Since there is only one side condition to be specified, there has to be either a forward solution or a backward one. There can be no half-way house. Second-order difference equations, by contrast, offer the possibility of a more flexible approach. With two side conditions to be specified, there is the possibility of a 'mixed' solution which involves forward and backward elements. The logic is quite inexorable; if one side condition is located in the past and the other in the future, then the solution must involve both past and future values of the forcing variables. These possibilities are now explored. Consider the second-order difference equation

$$Y_t - s_1 Y_{t-1} - s_2 Y_{t-2} = aX_t. \tag{4-60}$$

Using the L operator, write this as

$$(1 - s_1 L - s_2 L^2) Y_t = aX_t. \tag{4-61}$$

In the rational expectations context, future values of Y_t will be an equation in expectations, unless perfect foresight is assumed. For convenience, we shall simply refer to Y_{t+j} and X_{t+j} without any loss of generality.

Very often an economic model will not be specified as a second-order difference equation, but rather as a pair of simultaneous first-order difference equations. In fact, the two structures are completely equivalent. A pair of first-order simultaneous difference equations can be expressed as a second-order difference equation, and *vice versa*. Thus the discussion of the second-order case covers many more cases than might at first be thought. To see this equivalence, consider the simultaneous first-order difference equation in two variables Y_t and Z_t:

$$(1 - a_{11}L)Y_t = a_{12}LZ_t + bR_t$$
$$(1 - a_{22}L)Z_t = a_{21}LY_t + cS_t \tag{4-62}$$

where R_t and S_t are forcing variables. Now:

$$Z_t = (1 - a_{22}L)^{-1} a_{21} L Y_t + cS_t^1 \tag{4-63}$$

where S_t^1 is $(1 - a_{22}L)^{-1} S_t$. Substitute Eq. (4-63) into the first of Eqs (4-62):

$$(1 - a_{11}L)Y_t = (1 - a_{22}L)^{-1} a_{12} a_{21} L^2 Y_t + dX_t^1 \tag{4-64}$$

where $dX_t^1 = a_{12}cLS_t^1 + bR_t$. It follows that the two-equation system is expressible as

$$(1 - s_1 L - s_2 L^2) Y_t = aX_t \tag{4-65}$$

where $s_1 = a_{11} + a_{22}$ and $s_2 = a_{12}a_{21} - a_{11}a_{22}$ and $aX_t = (1 - a_{22}L) dX_t^1$. The above result generalizes in an obvious way. An n-equation first-order system is expressible as an nth-order single equation. This section will concentrate on the solution of a single second-order equation, noting that the discussion applies to the simultaneous form (4-62). Section 4-12, which considers the continuous time analogue of a second-order system, will, in the interests of variety, concentrate on the simultaneous equation case.

The solution to Eq. (4-61) can be represented in (at least) six different ways. It is important to have a clear understanding of these and their relationships, since the side conditions will dictate which representation is appropriate. Confusion can occur, as will be illustrated, if, for example, a backward representation is chosen when one or more of the side conditions are forward-looking. Based on the earlier discussion, the logic of which representation to choose is dictated by prior beliefs about the two side conditions for Y_t.

Method 1: solve backwards

($\Rightarrow$A prior belief that both side conditions are located in the past—the future has no role in driving the system.)

Factorize Eq. (4-60) to derive:

$$(1 - \lambda_1 L)(1 - \lambda_2 L) Y_t = a X_t \tag{4-66}$$

where $\lambda_1 \lambda_2 = -s_2$ and $\lambda_1 + \lambda_2 = s_1$. The general solution is therefore:

$$Y_t = (1 - \lambda_1 L)^{-1}(1 - \lambda_2 L)^{-1} a X_t + c_1 \lambda_1^t + c_2 \lambda_2^t. \tag{4-67}$$

The terms $c_1 \lambda_1^t$ and $c_2 \lambda_2^t$ appear because

$$(1 - \lambda_1 L)(1 - \lambda_2 L) c_1 \lambda_1^t = (1 - \lambda_1 L)(1 - \lambda_2 L) c_2 \lambda_2^t = 0.$$

Equation (4-67) can be further factorized as

$$Y_t = (1 - \lambda_1 L)^{-1} a_1 X_t + (1 - \lambda_2 L)^{-1} a_2 X_t + c_1 \lambda_1^t + c_2 \lambda_2^t \tag{4-68}$$

where $a_1 = a \lambda_1 /(\lambda_1 - \lambda_2)$ and $a_2 = -a \lambda_2 /(\lambda_1 - \lambda_2)$. Expanding $(1 - \lambda_1 L)^{-1}$ and $(1 - \lambda_2 L)^{-1}$ gives

$$Y_t = a_1 \sum_{i=0}^{\infty} \lambda_1^i X_{t-i} + a_2 \sum_{i=0}^{\infty} \lambda_2^i X_{t-i} + c_1 \lambda_1^t + c_2 \lambda_2^t \tag{4-69}$$

which makes it absolutely clear that the solution is backward-looking.

λ_1 and λ_2 are determined as follows: $\lambda_2 = s_1 - \lambda_1$; therefore $\lambda_1(s_1 - \lambda_1) = -s_2$. Hence the following must be true:

$$\lambda_1^2 - s_1 \lambda_1 - s_2 = 0. \tag{4-70}$$

This is a quadratic equation and in general there are two values that will satisfy this equation. Equation (4-70) is also true for λ_2, hence λ_1 and λ_2 are the two values that satisfy the quadratic $\lambda^2 - s_1 \lambda - s_2 = 0$. Hence:

$$\lambda_1, \lambda_2 = \frac{s_1}{2} \pm \frac{1}{2}\sqrt{s_1^2 + 4s_2}. \tag{4-71}$$

(In the simultaneous equation case, λ_1 and λ_2 are just the eigenvalues of the $[a_{ij}]$ matrix—this will be discussed further in Sec. 4-12.) If $s_1^2 + 4s_2 < 0$, then the roots are imaginary. If $s_1^2 = -4s_2$ then we have repeated real roots. Both of these have implications for the representation of Eq. (4-60). Since there are quite enough points to put across already, it is assumed from now on that λ_1 and λ_2 are real and distinct. The appendix to Chapter 5 gives some more information on the complex root case.

Equation (4-69) is a general solution, and for a particular solution one would particularize c_1 and c_2. Notice, however, that we solve backwards not because $|\lambda_1| < 1$ and $|\lambda_2| < 1$, but because of a prior belief that two side conditions lie in the past. If, for example, $|\lambda_1| > 1$ and $|\lambda_2| > 1$, we would not just be able to say, 'let's solve forwards, then'. It is the economics of the problem that should direct the solution procedure, not the values of $|\lambda_1|$ and $|\lambda_2|$. The merits of the normalization $c_1 = c_2 = 0$ when $|\lambda_1| < 1$ and $|\lambda_2| < 1$ have already been discussed in the first-order backward-looking case, and all the issues discussed there can be applied here. There is no necessity to repeat this discussion.

Method 2: solve forwards

($\Rightarrow$A prior belief that both side conditions are forward-looking—the past has no role to play in driving the system.)

Remembering F is the forward operator, $FX_t = X_{t+1}$, multiply Eq. (4-61) through by F^2 and divide by $-1/s_2$ to derive:

$$\left(1 + \left(\frac{s_1}{s_2}\right)F - \left(\frac{1}{s_2}\right)F^2\right)Y_t = -\left(\frac{a}{s_2}\right)F^2X_t. \tag{4-72}$$

Factorize:

$$(1 - \delta_1 F)(1 - \delta_2 F)Y_t = -\left(\frac{a}{s_2}\right)F^2X_t \tag{4-73}$$

where $\delta_1\delta_2 = -1/s_2$ and $\delta_1 + \delta_2 = -s_1/s_2$. This implies that $\delta_1 = 1/\lambda_1$ and $\delta_2 = 1/\lambda_2$. The general solution is, therefore,

$$Y_t = (1 - \delta_1 F)^{-1}(1 - \delta_2 F)^{-1}\left(-\frac{a}{s_2}\right)F^2X_t + c_1\left(\frac{1}{\delta_1}\right)^t + c_2\left(\frac{1}{\delta_2}\right)^t \tag{4-74}$$

noting that

$$(1 - \delta_1 F)(1 - \delta_2 F)c_1\left(\frac{1}{\delta_1}\right)^t = (1 - \delta_1 F)(1 - \delta_2 F)c_2\left(\frac{1}{\delta_2}\right)^t = 0.$$

In terms of λ_1 and λ_2, the forward solution can be expressed as

$$Y_t = (1 - \lambda_1^{-1}F)^{-1}(1 - \lambda_2^{-1}F)^{-1}a\lambda_1^{-1}\lambda_2^{-1}F^2X_t + c_1\lambda_1^t + c_2\lambda_2^t. \tag{4-75}$$

Actually, this result can be reached directly using the transformation $(1 - \lambda_1 L)^{-1} = (-\lambda_1^{-1}F)(1 - \lambda_1^{-1}F)^{-1}$. Equation (4-75) follows immediately. Using this transformation on Eq. (4-68) gives

$$Y_t = -\left(\frac{a_1}{\lambda_1}\right)\sum_{i=0}^{\infty}\left(\frac{1}{\lambda_1}\right)^iX_{t+1+i} - \left(\frac{a_2}{\lambda_2}\right)\sum_{i=0}^{\infty}\left(\frac{1}{\lambda_2}\right)^iX_{t+1+i} + c_1\lambda_1^t + c_2\lambda_2^t. \tag{4-76}$$

This expresses Y_t as a function of the future values of the forcing variable. In a rational expectations context, this should be interpreted as the expectation of the future values of the forcing variable impinging upon (or causing) current behaviour, since actual values will not be known except in perfect foresight. This idea of the future causing the present is entirely natural to economists, but not necessarily to those whose lives are devoted to the analysis of purely mechanical systems such as engineers. Consequently, an engineer might regard discussion about the time dating of solutions as unimportant hair splitting; for economists such issues are crucial.

If $|\lambda_1|$ and $|\lambda_2| > 1$, the possibility of boundedness requires the particularization $c_1 = c_2 = 0$, as previously discussed. Note how similar all this is to the simple first-order case; one solves forwards because of the belief that side conditions are forward-looking. The fact that $|\lambda_1|$ and $|\lambda_2| > 1$ possibly ensures a sensible result, but in no way determines the solution technique. The next method is the most interesting because this is where the complexities, different from the first-order case, arise. It is the 'typical' second-order rational expectations model.

Method 3: the mixed case

($\Rightarrow$A prior belief that one side condition looks to the past and the other to the future. The current value of Y_t is driven by both past and future values of the forcing variable.)

To obtain the solution, write Eq. (4-68) in mixed form, as

$$Y_t = (1 - \lambda_1^{-1}F)^{-1}\left(-\frac{a_1}{\lambda_1}\right)FX_t + (1 - \lambda_2 L)^{-1}a_2 X_t + c_1\lambda_1^t + c_2\lambda_2^t \qquad (4\text{-}77)$$

or, by expanding,

$$Y_t = \left(-\frac{a_1}{\lambda_1}\right)\sum_{i=0}^{\infty}\left(\frac{1}{\lambda_1}\right)^i X_{t+1+i} + a_2\sum_{i=0}^{\infty}(\lambda_2)^i X_{t-i} + c_1\lambda_1^t + c_2\lambda_2^t \qquad (4\text{-}78)$$

which makes clear the dependence of Y_t on past history as well as future prospects. It offers the possibility of an eclectic position, being neither entirely forward-looking nor entirely backward-looking. Obviously, if $|\lambda_1|$ and $|\lambda_2| > 1$ or $|\lambda_1|$ and $|\lambda_2| < 1$ then Eq. (4-78) is, in general, unbounded, no matter what normalization is imposed on c_1 and c_2. Representation (4-78), in general, gives a 'sensible' result only if $|\lambda_1| > 1$ and $|\lambda_2| < 1$. The case of $|\lambda_1| > 1$ and $|\lambda_2| < 1$ is called a saddlepoint.

Equations (4-69), (4-76) and (4-78) are the three explicit solutions, with each one appropriate depending on the location of the side conditions. Particular solutions impose values on c_1 and c_2. More often than not, however, solutions are not presented in one of these three ways. Often, the equation is 'half solved', and the result presented in the form of a first-order difference equation. If the time domain is $t - \infty$ to $t + \infty$, this is not formally correct because this is not the fully worked-out solution, unlike Eqs (4-69), (4-76) and (4-78). This can, as will shortly be seen, lead to confusion, particularly in interpretation. The issue will be discussed with respect to Method 3—the ideas are readily applicable to the first two methods. Method 3, however, reveals the most interesting of the subtleties involved. The mixed solution can be represented as

$$Y_t = (1 - \lambda_1^{-1}F)^{-1}(1 - \lambda_2 L)^{-1}(-a\lambda_1^{-1}FX_t) + c_1\lambda_1^t + c_2\lambda_2^t. \qquad (4\text{-}79)$$

Multiply through by $(1 - \lambda_2 L)$ to derive

$$(1 - \lambda_2 L)Y_t = (1 - \lambda_1^{-1}F)^{-1}(-a\lambda_1^{-1}FX_t) + c\lambda_1^t \qquad (4\text{-}80)$$

or

$$Y_t = \lambda_2 Y_{t-1} - a\lambda_1^{-1} \sum_{i=0}^{\infty} \left(\frac{1}{\lambda_1}\right)^i X_{t+1+i} \tag{4-81}$$

where the particularization $c = 0$ has been imposed. Notice that Eq. (4-81) is simply an alternative and incomplete way of representing Eq. (4-78) which reduces a second-order difference equation to first difference form. However, in the context of a rational expectations model, Eq. (4-81) may be an appropriate representation; and we shall return to this issue shortly.

The choice of Eq. (4-81) is entirely arbitrary, and one could equally well choose the alternative backward-looking representation:

$$(1 - \lambda_1^{-1}F)Y_t = (1 - \lambda_2 L)^{-1}(-a\lambda_1^{-1}FX_t) + c\lambda_2^t \tag{4-82}$$

or, with $c = 0$,

$$Y_t = \lambda_1^{-1}Y_{t+1} - a\lambda_1^{-1} \sum_{i=0}^{\infty} \lambda_2^i X_{t+1-i}. \tag{4-83}$$

Now lag Eq. (4-83) one period and rearrange terms to give

$$Y_t = \lambda_1 Y_{t-1} + a \sum_{i=0}^{\infty} \lambda_2^i X_{t-i}. \tag{4-84}$$

Representation (4-81) asserts that the current value depends on its own past value and the expected future prospects, whereas Eq. (4-84) asserts that Y_t is determined by its own past value and the past history of the forcing variable!

A believer in rational expectations would no doubt emphasize representation (4-81), whereas an unreformed Keynesian, addicted to adaptive expectations, would emphasize representation (4-84). Of course the distinction is inherently silly, since Eqs (4-81) and (4-84) are exactly the same thing, namely, incomplete ways of describing Eq. (4-78). The best way to understand these apparent paradoxes is to think of the latter representations as applying over a more restricted time domain, whereas Eq. (4-78) applies over the wider domain $t - \infty$ to $t + \infty$. Thus Eq. (4-81) would be appropriate if the time domain were from t to $t + \infty$ and if Y_{t-1} is the chosen historical value as the backward-looking side condition and $c = 0$ imposes the forward side condition, driven by a requirement for boundedness of $\{Y_{t+j}\}$. Seen in this light, Eq. (4-84) is now inappropriate since it carries with it the connotation that both side conditions are backward-looking.

Representation (4-81) is the one most frequently put forward as the solution to models of second-order rational expectations. Our discussion shows that Eq. (4-81) should not be given a false claim of universality and regarded as the *only* possible solution. We do not always have to look for a saddlepoint property as if this is some magical essential ingredient of rational expectations. First, saddlepoints can be described in different ways, witness representation (4-78). Secondly, representation (4-76) is, in the proper context, a perfectly acceptable solution to a rational expectations model. Rational expectations is merely the claim that predictions are the same as the model's forecasts and, indeed, there is nothing in this to preclude a model being either (a) stable, (b) unstable or (c) a saddlepoint.

Under rational expectations, models must do double duty; if we have a theory for the value of an economic variable, then the theory must also encompass forecasts of that variable. By this criterion, the adaptive expectations model of Sec. 4-7 is clearly irrational, since any forecast P^*_{t+j} immediately runs into a potential consistency problem. However, many people seem to confuse this with the idea that all backward-looking models are irrational. Finally, notice that representation (4-81) (unlike Eq. (4-78), when $c_1 = c_2 = 0$ is imposed) need not have an equilibrium property. The restricted time domain t to $t + \infty$ with Y_{t-1} a starting value, no matter what value this takes, allows the possibility of a bounded $\{Y_{t+j}\}$ sequence, depending on the behaviour of the second term of Eq. (4-81).

PROBLEMS

4-13 Consider the equation $Y_t - 2.5Y_{t-1} + Y_{t-2} = 10$, where t refers to the 'present'. Discuss the solution to this equation, where the additional information is that the future path of Y_t is bounded.
4-14 Model: $(1 - \frac{1}{2}F)(1 - \frac{1}{3}F)Y_t = X_t$. $X_{t+j} = 0.5X_{t+j-1}$ for all j. Discuss the solution for Y_t. The side conditions are specified such that the current value Y_t is defined and its future path is bounded.

4-9 THE OVERLAPPING CONTRACTS MODEL

This section reinforces some of the important lessons of the second-order case by examining a famous model that embodies rational expectations. This is the overlapping contracts model associated with Fischer and Taylor. Now that we are armed with the knowledge provided by the foregoing sections, this should be a trivial problem to solve and, more importantly, we should understand why it is solved in this way.

The overlapping contracts idea falls into the category of a New Keynesian model. Here the force of the rational expectations hypothesis is accepted and allows expectations to be formed in this way, rather than following a mechanical rule such as adaptive expectations. However, not all the tenets of the Keynesian agenda are rejected and the particular aspect that is focused upon is the idea of price rigidity in the short run. Thus New Keynesians throw some institutional grit into the smooth 'prices everywhere and always flexible, markets always clearing' New Classical representation of the world. Because many New Keynesians accept the central part of the New Classical agenda, namely rational expectations, their work and ideas are inevitably taken seriously and greatly respected by New Classicals. Pure Post-Keynesians who dismiss rational expectations and work within a rigid price disequilibrium framework are, by contrast, not taken seriously at all. New Keynesians, respecting rational expectations, represent a halfway house and keep one foot comfortably in each camp. Chapter 8 reviews some more New Keynesian themes in greater detail.

For many New Classicals the Achilles' heel of New Keynesian ideas is to explain the reason for price rigidity. They would argue that such rigidities are themselves irrational and inefficient and would therefore be eliminated. New Keynesians, like Post-Keynesians, take a somewhat more relaxed position on this. For them it is often sufficient to assert the existence of the institutional reality of rigid prices. Their claim is that it is silly to ignore what we can all see with our own eyes, and to ignore such institutional grit makes a large difference. 'I can't exactly explain why this arises, but what I do know for sure is that it is out there', seems a perfectly sensible and defensible position, more especially if it is seen to make a large difference to model solutions.

The first institutional *datum* that drives the overlapping contract model is that negotiated wages run for a finite period of time and are typically fixed in nominal terms for the length of the contract. Thus each contract group is locked into a fixed nominal wage in the short run at least. The second institutional *datum* is the fact that not every group negotiates its contract at the same point each year. There is no grand annual wage settlement, an institutional reform which some have advocated for wage bargaining. Contracts overlap and thus, when negotiating a settlement, each group must recognize that its own contract will (*a*) overlap with contracts previously negotiated and (*b*) overlap with contracts that have yet to be negotiated in the future. Taylor and Fischer apply the idea of rationality to the above institutional process.

To be specific, suppose there are two groups, A and B, each negotiating a year-long nominal wage contract. Group A settles each 1 January, and group B settles each 1 July. Figure 4-2 illustrates the process. Time is split into discrete six-monthly blocks, and we consider the problem facing group A negotiating its twelve-monthly contract at time t. As can be seen from the figure, the first six months of A's contract will overlap with B's contract negotiated at time $t - 1$. Furthermore, the last six months of A's contract will overlap with the contract B will negotiate at time $t + 1$. Now apply the idea of rational expectations to this process. Group A will note that group B faces an exactly symmetrical problem with its own. Thus group A will see that when B negotiates at $t + 1$, it will take into account A's current contract as well as A's expected future contract. This basic process would, under rational expectations, iterate forwards *ad infinitum*.

The structure, therefore, depends on *both* A and B holding rational expectations and *believing* that the other negotiates on a rational basis. When formalized, a second-order difference equation will emerge. Since the contract looks both *backwards* to the wage at $t - 1$ and forwards as well, intuition strongly suggests that Method 3 will be in the frame. In fact, the structure will be like representation (4-81), where B's contract at $t - 1$ is treated as the backward side condition and the other side condition is imposed to ensure boundedness. Now let us put flesh on this intuitive view of the overlapping contracts model. It follows Taylor's exposition closely. Nominal wage determination is given by

$$x_t = bx_{t-1} + dE_{t-1}x_{t+1} + \gamma(bE_{t-1}y_t + dE_{t-1}y_{t+1}) + \varepsilon_t. \qquad (4\text{-}85)$$

This is hardly given a rigorous micro foundation, but is strongly suggested by the previous discussion. The term x_t is the log of the current nominal wage expressed as a deviation from its trend. This depends on x_{t-1} and $E_{t-1}x_{t+1}$, the expectation of the future contract. Since the equation contains a random term ε_t, dating information from $t - 1$ makes clear it is not part of the current information set (see the discussion of Eq. (4-25′)).

The terms $E_{t-1}y_t$ and $E_{t-1}y_{t+1}$ are 'forcing variables', but not truly so because they will be seen to depend on x_t. The term y_t is a measure of excess demand, measured as the

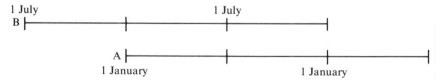

Figure 4-2 Overlapping contracts

deviation of the log of real output from its trend. This is why x_t is expressed in deviation form because it is being driven not by a level but by a deviation from trend output. The parameters b and d are assumed to sum to 1. Thus $b = d = \frac{1}{2}$ would give equal weights to the lead and lag contract. There is no need to assume such symmetry and, as d increases, more weight is given to the future contract. The model explores how persistence in wages and output varies as the weighting moves across the lag and lead contracts. Intuition suggests that, as $d \to 1$, persistence should decline and this, indeed, turns out to be the case.

The following three equations complete the model. First:

$$m_t = y_t + w_t - v_t. \tag{4-86}$$

This equation is the demand for the log of nominal money and w_t is the (log) wage rate here used as a convenient proxy for the price level. Both m_t and w_t are in deviation form and v_t is another random element. The term w_t is just a simple average of the existing contracts, namely :

$$w_t = \frac{x_t + x_{t-1}}{2}. \tag{4-87}$$

Finally, there is a money supply rule:

$$m_t = g w_t. \tag{4-88}$$

Under rational expectations, agents are assumed to know the authorities' reaction function. It follows that g is a measure of how much authorities accommodate fluctuations in the wage (price) level. The case $g = 0$ would be no accommodation and $g = 1$ would be complete accommodation—cases of 'over-accommodation' are ruled out. Combining Eqs (4-88) and (4-86) gives

$$y_t = -\beta w_t + v_t \tag{4-89}$$

where $\beta = 1 - g$.

The rest, as they say, is just a case of arithmetic! It can be seen that combining Eqs (4-87) and (4-89) and substituting into Eq. (4-85) gives

$$bx_{t-1} - cE_{t-1}x_t + dE_{t-1}x_{t+1} = 0 \tag{4-90}$$

where $c = (1 + 0.5\gamma\beta)/(1 - 0.5\gamma\beta)$ and noting that $E_{t-1}\varepsilon_t = 0$, $E_{t-1}v_t = 0$ and $b + d = 1$. This is a second-order difference equation where there is now no forcing variable—which is neither surprising nor a source of alarm, since everything is expressed in deviation terms. Equilibrium is zero in this context.

Two side conditions are required for Eq. (4-90) to have a particular solution and strongly suggests the 'mixed' case as the solution. The solution will, therefore, be of the same type as Eq. (4-81), with one of the side conditions specified as the historical value x_{t-1}. The solution does not, therefore, constrain us to an equilibrium view. Following Eq. (4-81), the general solution to Eq. (4-90) is

$$E_{t-1}x_t = \lambda_1 x_{t-1} + a\lambda_2^t \tag{4-91}$$

where a is a constant term. If Eq. (4-89) does indeed define a saddlepoint then the particularization $a = 0$ can be imposed to ensure the boundedness of the $\{E_{t-1}x_{t+j}\}$

sequence. This is, in fact, what is done where λ_1 and λ_2 are given by

$$\lambda_1, \lambda_2 = \frac{c \pm \sqrt{c^2 - 4bd}}{2d} \tag{4-92}$$

since c is assumed to satisfy >1 and $b = 1 - d$, then $c^2 - 4bd$ is always positive because $4bd$ has a maximum value of 1. Thus λ_1 and λ_2 must both be real and positive since $\sqrt{c^2 - 4bd} < c$. This is a saddlepoint, and taking the root λ_1 as <1 and 'suppressing' $\lambda_2 > 1$ gives the solution for $E_{t-1}x_t$:

$$E_{t-1}x_t = \lambda_1 x_{t-1}. \tag{4-93}$$

By taking expectations of Eq. (4-85) it is clear that x_t is just $E_{t-1}x_t + \varepsilon_t$. The solution for w_t is

$$w_t = \lambda_1 w_{t-1} + \frac{\varepsilon_t + \varepsilon_{t-1}}{2} \tag{4-94}$$

and for y_t the solution is

$$y_t = \lambda_1 y_{t-1} + v_t - \lambda_1 v_{t-1} - \frac{\beta(\varepsilon_t + \varepsilon_{t-1})}{2}. \tag{4-95}$$

Thus the model predicts persistence in both nominal wages and output. Output deviations are not a random fluctuation with a zero mean. High output today tends to be associated with high output tomorrow. Such a conclusion does not arise in many New Classical models. This is not surprising, since such models assume equilibrium, market clearing conditions with flexible prices and no involuntary rationing. Here, the practice of looking backwards to the last contract generates momentum in output. Notice that this momentum occurs no matter what the value of g. No accommodation—that is with $g = 0$ and m_t just subject to random fluctuations—still gives persistence in output. As $g \to 1$, that is as we tend towards complete accommodation, so $c \to 1$. Consequently, g alters the degree of persistence but has no qualitative effect on the result.

What drives the persistence is the parameter b. If b were zero there would be no persistence. This can be seen immediately from Eq. (4-90), which would reduce to the first-order equation

$$-cE_{t-1}x_t + E_{t-1}x_{t+1} = 0 \tag{4-96}$$

with $c > 1$ and no forcing term, the solution is

$$E_{t-1}x_t = 0 \tag{4-97}$$

which obviously implies no persistence.

The overlapping contracts model has other important implications. The first point is that it reinforces the case for gradualism and one needs no fancy mathematics to understand the logic of this. Given that group A is locked into a fixed nominal wage contract from 1 January, if the government changed the monetary rule suddenly on 1 July, it would be quite easy for group B to adjust, but impossible for A. Consequently, the real wage could be considerably different from what was intended. Large output fluctuations would be the consequence.

The second implication is for the 'rules versus discretion' debate. This whole issue will be dealt with more thoroughly in Chapter 7, but the following points can be made here. Suppose there was a large negative shock to v_t. According to Eq. (4-95) this would lead to a large fall in real output—a fall that is likely to persist for several periods. Again, suppose that this nasty surprise occurred on 1 July. Group B can accommodate its bargain to the shock, but again group A is locked in. The authorities, by announcing a well-understood change to the rule, could mitigate the output loss; that is what discretion in monetary policy is all about. For example, the negative shock—such as an oil crisis—might require real wage reductions, which would be difficult to achieve with a fixed nominal wage. The authorities could engineer such a real wage reduction by a judicious monetary expansion. Again group B would be unaffected, since it could alter its contract to take account of the new set of circumstances.

New Classicals sometimes argue that overlapping contracts are an epiphenomenon and therefore not quite as important as might at first appear. Fixed nominal wage contracts are only observed during periods of relative price stability. During times of high inflation, long-term contracts tend to disappear—a rational response by optimizing agents. At the peak of the UK's inflation in 1971, unions were seen to negotiate more than one wage claim per year. Thus overlapping wage contracts may only exist when they do not actually matter. Nevertheless, it is still a very interesting approach to wage determination.

PROBLEM

4-15 A partial adjustment price model is specified as $P_t^* = aM_t + bE_tP_{t+1}$, where P_t^* is the equilibrium price level, $b < 1$ and E_tP_{t+1} is the rational expectation of the future price level. The actual price level adjusts according to $P_t - P_{t-1} = 0.5(P_t^* - P_{t-1})$. Calculate a solution for the current price level, P_t.

4-10 CONTINUOUS TIME: THE FIRST-ORDER CASE

Rational expectations models can be equally well formulated in continuous time, like most dynamic economic systems. The following discussion should draw out many of the points of similarity between discrete time and continuous time systems. In view of this, many of the previous arguments need not, therefore, be reiterated. The present section discusses underlying principles and the next section gives two examples. The analogue of the first-order linear difference equation is the linear first-order differential equation:

$$\frac{\mathrm{d}y(t)}{\mathrm{d}t} = a + bx(t) + \lambda y(t). \tag{4-98}$$

This is the analogue of Eq. (4-19), where Eq. (4-98) includes both a constant term a and a time-dependent forcing variable $x(t)$. Together these drive $y(t)$, whose rate of change is the time derivative $\mathrm{d}y(t)/\mathrm{d}t$.

In the discrete time case, both the L and F operators proved to be extremely useful. In continuous time, it will be extremely useful to use another operator, denoted as D and known as the differential operator. This is defined as:

$$Dy(t) = \frac{dy(t)}{dt}. \tag{4-99}$$

Like the L and F operators, the D operator has useful properties which enable it to be treated 'as if' it were an algebraic entity. It can then, subject to certain restrictions, be separated from the variable with which it was originally associated and treated like an ordinary variable in its own right, just like L and F. The precise mathematical foundations for these rules are not explored, but if accepted they certainly make the solution of linear differential equations a much more straightforward business. Using the D operator, Eq. (4-98) can be written as

$$(D - \lambda)y(t) = a + bx(t). \tag{4-100}$$

The general solution is therefore

$$y(t) = (D - \lambda)^{-1}a + (D - \lambda)^{-1}bx(t) + c\,e^{\lambda t}. \tag{4-101}$$

A general solution is one which is consistent with Eq. (4-98) or with its equivalent Eq. (4-100). Multiplying Eq. (4-101) by $(D - \lambda)$ retrieves Eq. (4-100) because $(D - \lambda)c\,e^{\lambda t} = c\lambda e^{\lambda t} - c\lambda e^{\lambda t} = 0$. The $c\,e^{\lambda t}$ term is therefore analogous to the $c\lambda^t$ term in the general solution of a first-order difference equation. As before, a definite solution involves choosing a particular value for c. Exactly as before, the forward-looking method involves a particularization unconnected with the past and a backward representation involves a particularization unconnected with the future.

As a first stage, let us retrieve the equivalent of Eq. (4-10) from Eq. (4-101). For this case, let the forcing variable $x(t) = 0$, which reduces to the familiar textbook case involving a constant term alone. First solve for $(D - \lambda)^{-1}a$, assuming $\lambda \neq 0$. This is:

$$(D - \lambda)^{-1}a = (1 - \lambda D)^{-1}\left(-\frac{a}{\lambda}\right) = -(1 + \lambda D + (\lambda D)^2 + \cdots)\left(\frac{a}{\lambda}\right). \tag{4-102}$$

Since $D(a/\lambda)$ and all higher powers $= 0$, then

$$(D - \lambda)^{-1}a = -\frac{a}{\lambda} = \bar{y} \tag{4-103}$$

or

$$y(t) = \bar{y} + c\,e^{\lambda t}. \tag{4-104}$$

The (backward-looking) textbook case specifies a starting value $y(0)$. Thus c must satisfy

$$y(0) = \bar{y} + c. \tag{4-105}$$

Thus Eq. (4-103) can be written in familiar form as

$$y(t) = \bar{y} + (y(0) - \bar{y})e^{\lambda t} \tag{4-106}$$

which is the analogue of Eq. (4-10). Stability now involves the question of whether λ is positive or negative. A positive λ implies instability and a negative λ implies stability. These conditions are, it should be noted, not precisely the same as the difference equation case.

Now consider the role of $x(t)$. As before, this can be 'summed' backwards or forwards, depending on whether the solution is backward- or forward-looking. The choice is dictated by whether the particularization of c is backward- or forward-looking, exactly as before. The backward-looking way has

$$(\mathbf{D} - \lambda)^{-1} bx(t) = b \int_{-\infty}^{t} e^{(t-s)\lambda} x(s) \, ds. \tag{4-107}$$

This is equivalent to Eq. (4-30) and this integral must be convergent if Eq. (4-107) is to be defined. Most often $\lambda < 0$ will ensure this. The forward-looking way has

$$(\mathbf{D} - \lambda)^{-1} bx(t) = -b \int_{t}^{\infty} e^{(t-s)\lambda} x(s) \, ds. \tag{4-108}$$

This is equivalent to Eq. (4-35) and must be convergent if Eq. (4-108) is to be defined. Again $\lambda > 0$ is 'more likely' to ensure this. The mathematics involved in deriving the above results are somewhat advanced and are not pursued here.

Thus the general solution to Eq. (4-101) can be written in a backward-looking way as

$$y(t) = -\frac{a}{\lambda} + b \int_{-\infty}^{t} e^{(t-s)\lambda} x(s) \, ds + c \, e^{\lambda t} \tag{4-109}$$

or in a forward-looking way as

$$y(t) = -\frac{a}{\lambda} - b \int_{t}^{\infty} e^{(t-s)\lambda} x(s) \, ds + c \, e^{\lambda t}. \tag{4-110}$$

Equation (4-109) is the analogue of Eq. (4-41) and Eq. (4-110) is the analogue of Eq. (4-40). All the issues concerning the particularization of c apply equally well here.

Expressions (4-107) and (4-108) are somewhat conceptual and getting an explicit solution, given actual functional forms of $x(s)$, can be difficult. To illustrate that Eq. (4-107) may converge whereas Eq. (4-108) may diverge, and *vice versa*, consider the special case with $\lambda < 0$ and $bx(s)$ is a constant $= b$. Expression (4-107) becomes

$$b \left[\frac{e^{(t-s)\lambda}}{-\lambda} \right]_{-\infty}^{t} = -\frac{b}{\lambda} \tag{4-111}$$

whereas Eq. (4-108) is not defined. With $\lambda > 0$, expression (4-108) becomes

$$-b \left[\frac{e^{(t-s)\lambda}}{-\lambda} \right]_{t}^{\infty} = -\frac{b}{\lambda} \tag{4-112}$$

whereas Eq. (4-107) is not defined. However, as before, the solution method should be dictated by a belief about the location of a side condition.

PROBLEM

4-16 Consider the differential equation $(\mathbf{D} - \lambda)y(t) = bt$, where $\lambda > 0$. Derive the fundamentals forward-looking solution.

4-11 FIRST-ORDER CONTINUOUS CASE: TWO EXAMPLES

By modifying Eq. (3-1) of Chapter 3 in an obvious way, the rational expectations version of the Cagan money demand equation can be formulated in continuous time as

$$DE_t P(t + s) = -\alpha E_t M(t + s) + \lambda E_t P(t + s).$$

(4-113)

The time domain is $s = 0$ to $+\infty$, D is the differential operator. Both α and λ are positive constants and Eq. (4-113) is, as before, an equation in expectations based on information at time t, where $E_t P(t) = P(t)$. As before, the solution is the forward-looking one, where representation (4-110) is appropriate. The general solution is therefore

$$P(t) = \alpha \int_t^\infty e^{(t-s)\lambda} E_t M(s) \, ds + c \, e^{\lambda t}.$$

(4-114)

This is equivalent to Eq. (4-52). As before, the fundamentals solution would impose the particularization $c = 0$.

The second example concerns a rational expectations theory of the exchange rate and illustrates that apparently diverse issues have a common problem structure. The spot rate of one currency against another is assumed to be driven by the following:

$$E_t S(t + s) = E_t Z(t + s) + \gamma DE_t S(t + s)$$

(4-115)

where

$S(t + s) =$ the domestic currency price of one unit of foreign exchange, expressed in logs at time $t + s$; $E_t S(t + s)$ is today's estimate of this rate;

$Z(t + s) =$ the information set which affects the spot rate at $t + s$; this could include just about anything—interest rates, balance of payments, oil crises, wars, rumours, and so on;

$DE_t S(t + s) =$ the expected change in the spot rate.

Equation (4-115) has a structure exactly like Eq. (4-113) and is an equation in expectations, based on information available at time t. The last term in Eq. (4-115) captures the idea of $S(t)$ reflecting an asset price. γ is a positive constant and expresses the idea that if it is believed that an asset's price will rise in the future, this will be immediately discounted into the spot price. The parameter γ, therefore, measures the elasticity of responsiveness to expected future events. Just as with Eq. (4-113), the general solution for $S(t)$ is

$$S(t) = \left(\frac{1}{\gamma}\right) \int_t^\infty e^{(t-s)/\gamma} E_t Z(s) \, ds + c \, e^{(1/\gamma)t}.$$

(4-116)

The theory implies that the spot rate is driven by the whole expected path of $Z(s)$, discounted at the rate $1/\gamma$. As with the New Classical theory of prices, this gives rise to a rich set of predictions. The fundamentals solution would impose $c = 0$; however, Eq. (4-116) could be used as a basis for discussion of speculative bubbles, which are surely a feature of exchange markets. There is a discrete time analogue to this model, which will be discussed in Chapter 7.

PROBLEMS

4-17 A continuous time analogue of the adaptive expectations model considered in Sec. 4-7 can be expressed as $DP^*(t) = \lambda[P(t) - P^*(t)]$, where $P^*(t)$ is the expected price level, $P(t)$ is the price level and $0 < \lambda < 1$. Derive a general expression for $P^*(t)$.

4-18 Suppose $P(t) = P(0)(1 + e^{-gt})$, where g is a positive constant but with $\lambda > g$. Derive an explicit solution for $P^*(t)$.

4-12 CONTINUOUS TIME: THE SECOND-ORDER CASE

As in the discrete case there is a direct equivalence between a pair of simultaneous linear first-order differential equations and a second-order linear differential equation. In the discrete case, the main effort was devoted to solving the second-order case. Here we shall concentrate on the case of a pair of simultaneous equations; in particular, the use of phase diagrams as a way of representing a graphical solution will be explored. Many rational expectations models are presented in this way, and it is useful to have an explicit idea of what is happening.

First, however, the single equation second-order case can be briefly discussed. Again, in view of much of the previous discussion, few of the methodological issues need be reiterated. The second-order case can be written as

$$D^2 y(t) + s_1 Dy(t) + s_2 y(t) = bx(t) \tag{4-117}$$

where, as before, $x(t)$ is the forcing variable. This can be factorized as

$$(D - \lambda_1)(D - \lambda_2)y(t) = bx(t) \tag{4-118}$$

where $\lambda_1 + \lambda_2 = -s_1$ and $\lambda_1 \lambda_2 = s_2$. Explicit values for λ_1 and λ_2 are given by

$$\lambda_1, \lambda_2 = \frac{-s_1 \pm \sqrt{s_1^2 - 4s_2}}{2}. \tag{4-119}$$

We shall concentrate on the case of real, distinct roots. The general solution to Eq. (4-118) is

$$y(t) = (D - \lambda_1)^{-1}(D - \lambda_2)^{-1}bx(t) + c_1 e^{\lambda_1 t} + c_2 e^{\lambda_2 t} \tag{4-120}$$

where c_1 and c_2 are two particularizing constants. Two side conditions must be specified for a particular solution. Equation (4-120) replicates Eq. (4-118) because

$$(D - \lambda_1)(D - \lambda_2)c_1 e^{\lambda_1 t} = (D - \lambda_1)(D - \lambda_2)c_2 e^{\lambda_2 t} = 0.$$

Note that

$$(D - \lambda_1)^{-1}(D - \lambda_2)^{-1} = \frac{1}{\lambda_1 - \lambda_2}[(D - \lambda_1)^{-1} - (D - \lambda_2)^{-1}]. \tag{4-121}$$

Thus Eq. (4-120) can be written as

$$y(t) = (D - \lambda_1)^{-1}ax(t) - (D - \lambda_2)^{-1}ax(t) + c_1 e^{\lambda_1 t} + c_2 e^{\lambda_2 t} \tag{4-122}$$

where $a = b/(\lambda_1 - \lambda_2)$. There are three representations for Eq. (4-122) equivalent to Eqs (4-69), (4-76) and (4-78). As these are entirely obvious, they will not be stated here. The merits or otherwise of the normalizations $c_1 = c_2 = 0$ have also been discussed already. As before, 'half solving' is sometimes a useful representation for the mixed case:

$$(D - \lambda_1)y(t) = (D - \lambda_2)^{-1}bx(t) + c\,e^{\lambda_2 t} \tag{4-123}$$

with $\lambda_2 > 0$, then the 'fundamentals' solution can be represented as

$$y(t) = \left(\frac{b}{\lambda_1}\right)\int_t^\infty e^{(t-s)\lambda_2}x(s)\,ds + \left(\frac{1}{\lambda_1}\right)Dy(t) \tag{4-124}$$

where $Dy(t)$ is the second side condition. This is equivalent to representation (4-81). What is being done here should become clearer when the simultaneous first-order case has been discussed in the next section. $Dy(t)$ then becomes a historical value like Y_{t-1} in Eq. (4-81).

PROBLEM

4-19 A second-order differential equation is given by: $(D - 3)(D + 4)y(t) = -12$. The first side condition specifies $y(0) = 10$ and the second is imposed to ensure a bounded path for $y(t)$. Find the solution for $y(t)$.

4-13 SIMULTANEOUS DIFFERENTIAL EQUATIONS

The system to be analysed is described by the equations

$$\begin{aligned} Dy_1 &= a_{11}y_1 + a_{12}y_2 + b_1 \\ Dy_2 &= a_{21}y_1 + a_{22}y_2 + b_2 \end{aligned} \tag{4-125}$$

where y_1 and y_2 are the time-dependent endogenous variables. Dy_1 and Dy_2 are time derivatives and both b_1 and b_2 are constants. Since the intention here is to concentrate on graphical techniques, the case of non-constant forcing variables is excluded.

One approach to Eqs (4-125) would be to convert to a second-order differential equation, as was done with the difference equation case, and then proceed as indicated in Sec. 4-12. This can be achieved as follows. Multiply the first equation of (4-125) by D to derive

$$D^2y_1 = a_{11}\,Dy_1 + a_{12}\,Dy_2. \tag{4-126}$$

Now use the second equation of (4-125) to substitute out Dy_2 above:

$$D^2y_1 - a_{11}\,Dy_1 = a_{12}a_{21}y_1 + a_{12}a_{22}y_2 + a_{12}b_2. \tag{4-127}$$

Now use the first equation of (4-125) to substitute out y_2. This gives:

$$D^2y_1 - a_{11}Dy_1 = a_{12}a_{21}y_1 + a_{22}(Dy_1 - a_{11}y_1 - b_1) + a_{12}b_2. \tag{4-128}$$

Gathering terms gives an equation exactly equivalent to Eq. (4-117).

$$D^2y_1 + s_1\,Dy_1 + s_2y_1 = b_3 \tag{4-129}$$

where $s_1 = -(a_{11} + a_{22})$, $s_2 = (a_{11}a_{22} - a_{12}a_{21})$ and $b_3 = a_{12}b_2 - a_{22}b_1$. Note that the roots of Eq. (4-129) (given by Eq. (4-119)) are also given by the eigenvalues of the $[a_{ij}]$ matrix associated with simultaneous Eqs (4-125). The eigenvalues are the values of λ_1 and

λ_2 that satisfy the following determinant:

$$\begin{vmatrix} a_{11} - \lambda & a_{12} \\ a_{21} & a_{22} - \lambda \end{vmatrix} = 0. \tag{4-130}$$

Expanding gives

$$\lambda^2 - (a_{11} + a_{22})\lambda + (a_{11}a_{22} - a_{12}a_{21}) = 0. \tag{4-131}$$

Therefore,

$$\lambda_1, \lambda_2 = \frac{\operatorname{tr} A \pm \sqrt{(\operatorname{tr} A)^2 - 4|A|}}{2} \tag{4-132}$$

where A is

$$A = \begin{bmatrix} a_{11} & a_{12} \\ a_{21} & a_{22} \end{bmatrix} \tag{4-133}$$

and tr A is the sum of the diagonal elements $= a_{11} + a_{22}$. Thus a saddlepoint is easily identified if det $A < 0$ since this implies $\lambda_1 > 0$ and $\lambda_2 < 0$. Furthermore, the system is stable if tr $A < 0$ and det $A > 0$; and unstable if tr $A > 0$ and det $A > 0$. In the case of a saddlepoint, it is clear that λ_1 and λ_2 must both be real. The following discussion concentrates on the case of saddlepoints, since this is the 'typical' rational expectations case. However, the previous discussion warned against taking such a narrow view and readers can, as an exercise, figure out other cases for themselves.

The strategy will be to consider the problem formally, before discussing graphical representations. To save on arithmetic and without loss of generality, set $b_1 = b_2 = 0$. Thus y_1 and y_2 can be regarded as being expressed in deviation from equilibrium form. The general solution to Eqs (4-125) must therefore be

$$\begin{aligned} y_1 &= K_{11}\,e^{\lambda_1 t} + K_{12}\,e^{\lambda_2 t} \\ y_2 &= K_{21}\,e^{\lambda_1 t} + K_{22}\,e^{\lambda_2 t} \end{aligned} \tag{4-134}$$

where $\lambda_1 < 0$ and $\lambda_2 > 0$ is assumed. The parameters K_{11}, K_{12}, K_{21} and K_{22} are the exact equivalent of c_1 and c_2 in Eq. (4-122). Since it only requires two side conditions to particularize the solution, only two of K_{11}, K_{12}, K_{21} and K_{22} can be independent parameters. If $y_1(0)$ and $y_2(0)$ are the starting values, then these parameters can be determined as follows. At $t = 0$, from Eqs (4-134) we know that:

$$\begin{aligned} y_1(0) &= K_{11} + K_{12} \\ y_2(0) &= K_{21} + K_{22} \end{aligned} \tag{4-135}$$

noting that $e^{\lambda_1 0} = e^{\lambda_2 0} = 1$. Furthermore, at $t = 0$, we know that

$$\begin{aligned} Dy_1(0) &= K_{11}\lambda_1 + K_{12}\lambda_2 \\ Dy_2(0) &= K_{21}\lambda_1 + K_{22}\lambda_2. \end{aligned} \tag{4-136}$$

Substituting $Dy_1(0)$ and $Dy_2(0)$ from Eqs (4-125), the following must hold:

$$\begin{aligned} a_{11}y_1(0) + a_{12}y_2(0) &= K_{11}\lambda_1 + K_{12}\lambda_2 \\ a_{21}y_1(0) + a_{22}y_2(0) &= K_{21}\lambda_1 + K_{22}\lambda_2. \end{aligned} \tag{4-137}$$

This gives us sufficient information to particularize K_{11}, K_{12}, K_{21} and K_{22}, if $y_1(0)$ and $y_2(0)$ are known. Notice, as in all previous cases, we are not necessarily tied to $y_1(0)$ and $y_2(0)$ as the side conditions.

In a rational expectations model the concern is the particularization that sets $K_{12} = K_{22} = 0$. As before, this is exactly equivalent to setting $c_2 = 0$ in Eq. (4-122). The justification is exactly the same as in all previous discussion on the issue and hopefully by now the reader should be aware that we are simply examining the same problem once more in a slightly different context. In the present case, the usual methodology is the following. One side condition will be one historical value, say $y_2(0)$. Now locate that *unique* value of $y_1(0)$ which will make $K_{12} = K_{22} = 0$. The justification is that this is the only value which ensures that the future projection of y_1 and y_2 will converge to its equilibrium value (in this case 0, since $b_1 = b_2 = 0$). Be clear what is being done. All the discussion, caveats, etc., of the previous sections apply equally well here. The particularization $K_{12} = K_{22} = 0$ is based on a *forward* projection in expectations, as earlier discussion should have made abundantly clear.

Now consider a graphical representation of the foregoing case using phase diagrams. Although discussion is limited to the linear case, one advantage of phase diagrams is that useful qualitative information can often be gleaned even if the system is non-linear. Section 5-3 of Chapter 5 gives an example of this for a non-linear system. (See also Problem 4-20.) The first thing to consider is the demarcation line for the first equation of (4-125). The demarcation line has the property that $Dy_1 = 0$. This occurs when

$$y_2 = \left(-\frac{a_{11}}{a_{12}} \right) y_1. \tag{4-138}$$

The slope depends on the sign of $-a_{11}/a_{12}$ and Fig. 4-3 illustrates one possibility with an upward-sloping line, going through the origin. The next stage is to plot the streamlines associated with this. The streamlines show how y_1 will move for any given value of y_2 when y_1 is not on its demarcation line. This is given by

$$\frac{\partial Dy_1}{\partial y_1}\bigg|_{y_2} = a_{11}. \tag{4-139}$$

Assume that this is greater than zero. The streamlines are shown as the horizontal arrows moving away from the demarcation line. To the right of the demarcation line y_1 has increased in value, and from Eq. (4-139) this means Dy_1 will be positive and therefore y_1 will be increasing; hence the direction shown. The streamline moves away from the left of the demarcation line by a similar line of reasoning.

Figure 4-4 carries out a similar exercise for the second equation. The demarcation line is given by

$$y_2 = \left(-\frac{a_{21}}{a_{22}} \right) y_1. \tag{4-140}$$

This is assumed negative. The streamlines are governed by

$$\frac{\partial Dy_2}{\partial y_2}\bigg|_{y_1} = a_{22}. \tag{4-141}$$

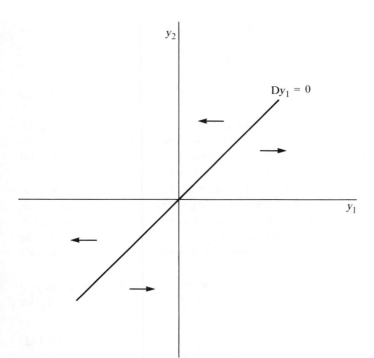

Figure 4-3 Dy_1 demarcation line

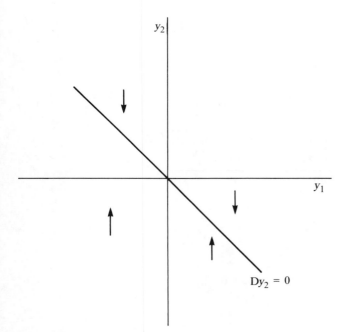

Figure 4-4 Dy_2 demarcation line

Figure 4-4 assumes $a_{22} < 0$. It takes little thought to work out that the streamlines are the vertical arrows moving towards the demarcation line. The assumptions imply that both a_{12} and a_{21} are negative. It is also easy to check that this must imply a saddlepoint because $\det A < 0$. Notice this is the only requirement for a saddlepoint and this could also occur if both the demarcation lines were upward-sloping or if both were downward-sloping. The example just picks up on one possible case.

Figure 4-5 puts Figs 4-3 and 4-4 together to complete the phase diagram, which illustrates the dynamic behaviour of the system as a whole. Equilibrium, in this case the origin, is where both demarcation lines intersect. The previous discussion showed that for a given historical value $y_2(0)$ there is a unique value of $y_1(0)$ from which the system would converge to its equilibrium. This saddlepoint line is shown as the arrowed line, somewhat steeper than the $Dy_1 = 0$ demarcation line. Thus if $y_2(0)$ is the given historical value, shown on the y_2 axis in Fig. 4-5, then the $y_1(0)$ value shown is the required value to ensure that the system will converge towards equilibrium. Any other value for $y_1(0)$ and the system will veer off away from equilibrium. Obviously a different $y_2(0)$ would require a different $y_1(0)$ value.

The fact of the saddlepoint line being steeper than the $Dy_1 = 0$ demarcation line can be seen as follows. Given that $K_{12} = K_{22} = 0$, then $y_1(0)$ must equal K_{11}. From Eq. (4-137) it follows that

$$a_{11}y_1(0) + a_{12}y_2(0) = y_1(0)\lambda_1. \tag{4-142}$$

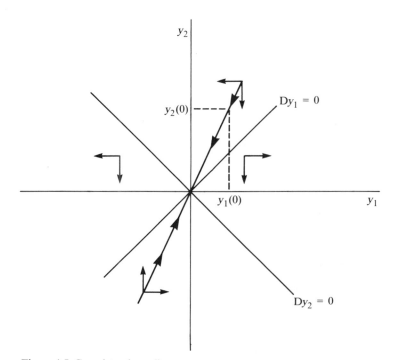

Figure 4-5 Complete phase diagram

Hence,

$$y_2(0) = \frac{(\lambda_1 - a_{11})y_1(0)}{a_{12}}. \tag{4-143}$$

Comparing this with Eq. (4-138) and noting that $\lambda_1 < 0$, it follows that Eq. (4-143) is steeper than Eq. (4-138). This confirms that what the streamlines already suggest must be the case. The next section discusses a particularly illuminating rational expectations example which also makes use of phase diagrams.

PROBLEM

4-20 Consider the following non-linear simultaneous differential equation system:

$$Dy_1 = y_1^2 - 2y_1 + y_2 - 10$$
$$Dy_2 = -2y_1 + y_2 - 6.$$

By drawing a phase diagram, show that this has two local equilibria, of which one is a saddlepoint and the other is unstable.

4-14 EXCHANGE RATE OVERSHOOTING

Dornbusch's exchange rate overshooting model is deservedly famous. It gave an insight into why, with fully flexible exchange rates, actual rates might be more volatile than might have been expected—hence the term overshooting. Given reasonable assumptions about the goods market and the market for foreign exchange, Dornbusch showed how the exchange rate might overshoot its final equilibrium value in response to a domestic disturbance. It is precisely because speculators exploit every available profit opportunity that the exchange rate overshoots. It is not the result of speculative bubbles.

Dornbusch's insights are extremely important. When the Bretton Woods system of fixed rates collapsed around 1971, the conventional wisdom was that extreme rates of exchange rate volatility would not be observed. Stabilizing speculation would smooth large fluctuations when a currency faced 'lumpy' trading inflows and outflows. In fact, almost the opposite happened, with fluctuations which appeared irrational and purely speculative. Dornbusch's ideas were a direct response to those events and he showed how over-depreciation and over-appreciation could be explained as a rational optimizing process.

The framework is basically New Keynesian. Dornbusch argued that the goods market was characterized by sluggish price adjustment. He asserted this as an institutional reality and as such it had important implications for exchange rates. Again, the idea is not to explain this price sluggishness but merely to derive its logical consequences, just as Taylor exploited the idea for his overlapping contracts model. Dornbusch's second assumption was that asset markets were not characterized by any such institutional sluggishness. Dornbusch needed to point no further than to the extremes of volatility in exchange rates as impressive testimony to the accuracy of this assumption. Dornbusch's insight was that if one market behaves imperfectly, in the sense of not adjusting immediately to a disturbance, this imperfection has consequences for the market that does not adjust slowly. In a sense the perfect market becomes the slack variable which must over-adjust to accommodate the sluggish market. The two markets cannot be considered in isolation.

Before formalities, it is useful to give an intuitive overview of the Dornbusch result. The critical equation is the following interest arbitrage condition which must hold at all times:

$$De = r - r^*. \tag{4-144}$$

D is the differential operator and e is the log of the exchange rate, expressed as the domestic currency price of one unit of foreign exchange (the number of pounds, if that is the domestic currency, needed to purchase one dollar). The domestic interest rate is r and the world rate, assumed to be fixed, is r^*. If domestic rates exceed the world rate, then Eq. (4-144) asserts that the exchange rate must be depreciating. (Note that $De > 0$ implies an increasing number of pounds per dollar, and thus a depreciating domestic currency.) For example, if the domestic interest rate was 10 per cent and the world rate 5 per cent, then, unless the exchange rate were depreciating at 5 per cent on an annual basis, there would be a certain profit to be made by borrowing the foreign currency and investing it in the domestic economy. The interest arbitrage condition simply asserts that the exchange rate adjusts instantaneously to eliminate such profit opportunities. Dornbusch also assumes perfect foresight, so actual and expected paths are the same. There is no risk in the model.

Now suppose a domestic monetary disturbance, taking the form of an increase in the money supply. The equilibrium exchange is determined by the ratio of foreign to domestic money, and consequently the long-run position requires that the exchange rate must depreciate in proportion to the increase in the domestic money supply. This is the law of Purchasing Power Parity. In the short run, things are rather different. With output fixed and price adjustment slow, a rise in the money supply must cause a fall in domestic interest rates, since this is the only variable available to take up the slack to clear the money market. Since $r - r^*$ is now negative, the exchange rate must be appreciating, as can be seen from Eq. (4-144). This is overshooting in a nutshell. The monetary disturbance causes an instantaneous depreciation of the currency, but, more importantly, the currency must depreciate by *more* than its final equilibrium value.

As the price level adjusts upwards towards its equilibrium value, the exchange rate appreciates slowly to its new equilibrium as domestic interest rates rise. Price sluggishness in the goods market therefore serves to exaggerate the volatility in the exchange rate. In the absence of this price sluggishness, there would be no overshooting. It is because the interest arbitrage condition must hold that the overshooting occurs. Under Dornbusch's assumptions, *irrationality* would be the case when no overshooting occurred!

Now let us consider the matter a little more formally. Dornbusch, in fact, uses subtle methods to derive the solution, but the problem can be tackled directly using the technology of the previous sections. The phase diagram to be used will be characterized in (log) price and (log) exchange rate space. The demand for real balances is given by

$$h - p = -\lambda r + \phi \bar{y} \tag{4-145}$$

where h is the log of the money supply, p is the log of the price level, r is domestic interest rates as before and $\bar{y}$ is the fixed full-employment level. Dornbusch actually relaxes this latter assumption somewhat without detriment to the overall argument. Consequently, Eq. (4-145) is a convenient linearization which enables the system to be expressed as a pair of linear simultaneous differential equations.

Substitute out r from Eq. (4-144) using Eq. (4-145) to derive

$$De = a_{12}p + b_1 \qquad (4\text{-}146)$$

where $a_{12} = 1/\lambda > 0$ and $b_1 = (\phi\bar{y})/\lambda - h/\lambda - r^*$. The demarcation line is shown in Fig. 4-6 when $De = 0$ and is a horizontal line where $p = -b_1/a_{12}$. The streamlines are also shown. Since $a_{12} > 0$, then $De > 0$ above the demarcation line and $De < 0$ below the demarcation line. Notice that e does not appear on the right-hand side of Eq. (4-146), reflecting the fact that this market is not characterized by slow adjustment.

Now consider the sluggish goods market. Here prices rise and fall slowly in response to excess demand or excess supply. Demand is given by

$$Z = u + \delta(e - p) - \sigma r + fy^* + \gamma\bar{y}. \qquad (4\text{-}147)$$

Think of this as an IS schedule with a foreign sector. The term u is an autonomous expenditure term, and $e - p$ is the log of the real exchange rate. (The foreign price level is fixed at $P^* = 1$, thus its log is 0.) The term y^* is foreign output, here assumed to be exogenous. The response parameters to all these sources of demand are δ, σ, f and γ respectively. Sluggish price adjustment to excess demand is expressed by the following equation:

$$Dp = \pi[Z - \bar{y}] \qquad (4\text{-}148)$$

where π is the speed of response. Substitute out r using Eq. (4-145) once again to derive the second of the two equation systems:

$$Dp = b_2 + a_{21}e + a_{22}p \qquad (4\text{-}149)$$

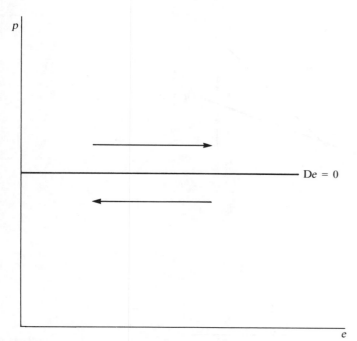

Figure 4-6 Exchange market

where $b_2 = \text{constant} = \pi[u + fy^* + (\gamma - 1 - \sigma\phi/\lambda)\bar{y} + \sigma h/\lambda]$, $a_{21} = \pi\delta$ and $a_{22} = -\pi(\delta + \sigma/\lambda)$. The demarcation line is shown in Fig. 4-7. This has slope $-a_{21}/a_{22} = \delta/(\delta + \sigma/\lambda)$ which is >0 but <1. The streamlines point towards the demarcation line because $a_{22} < 0$.

Figure 4-8 gives the complete phase diagram, combining Figs 4-6 and 4-7. The streamlines indicate a saddlepoint, and this is confirmed by noting that det $A < 0$, where

$$A = \begin{bmatrix} 0 & 1/\lambda \\ \pi\delta & -\pi[\delta + \sigma/\lambda] \end{bmatrix}. \tag{4-150}$$

Equilibrium is shown as the point Q and the saddlepoint line is shown as AA. The mechanics are now easily explained. Suppose the initial equilibrium position is $p(0)$ and $e(0)$. Now suppose that there is a domestic monetary disturbance that takes the form of an increase in h. Both the Dp and De demarcation lines shift upwards. Final equilibrium must, however, be located on the 45° line because the exchange rate and price level are in the long run homogeneous of degree 1. The final equilibrium point is shown as Q.

Now explore the dynamics. One side condition is simply the historical value $p(0)$. Dornbusch chooses the fundamentals solution to pin down the second side condition. The exchange rate adjusts instantaneously to ensure that the future path will converge to the equilibrium Q. There is only one exchange rate that will ensure that, which is shown as $e(0)'$. Any other exchange rate and the system would shoot off on an unstable path. Notice that $e(0)'$ necessarily involves overshooting; the exchange rate over-depreciates before slowly appreciating towards its equilibrium value Q along the saddlepoint line. The solution

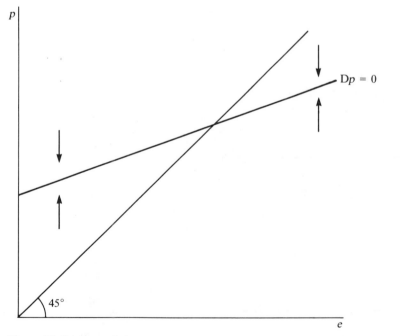

Figure 4-7 Goods market

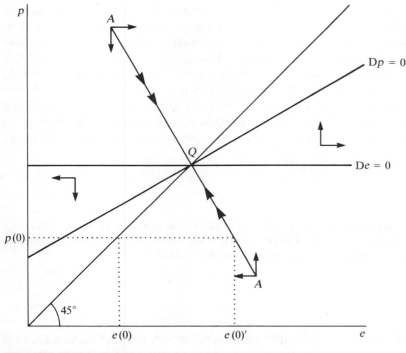

Figure 4-8 The Dornbusch model

embodies rationality and there is nothing surprising or perverse about this outcome. The exchange markets would reflect this rationality. Thus the forward rate should trade at a premium to the spot rate, since it is now known that the currency must appreciate in the future.

More formally, the saddlepoint line is derived exactly as described in Sec. 4-13. The general solution is

$$
\begin{aligned}
De &= \bar{e} + K_{11}\, e^{\beta_1 t} + K_{12}\, e^{\beta_2 t} \\
Dp &= \bar{p} + K_{21}\, e^{\beta_1 t} + K_{22}\, e^{\beta_2 t}.
\end{aligned}
\tag{4-151}
$$

Obviously e on the r.h.s. of Eq. (4-151) refers to the exponential and not the exchange rate, and β_1 and β_2 are determined by the eigenvalues of A which are easily derived from Eq. (4-132):

$$
\beta_1, \beta_2 = \frac{-\pi(\delta + \sigma/\lambda) \pm \sqrt{[-\pi(\delta + \sigma/\lambda)]^2 + 4\pi\delta/\lambda}}{2}.
\tag{4-152}
$$

The fundamentals solution, putting the system on the saddlepoint line, sets $K_{12} = K_{22} = 0$ (equivalent to $e(0)'$). Thus the speed of adjustment is given by the negative root of Eq. (4-152).

Dornbusch's analysis gives important insights about exchange rate behaviour. The source of exchange rate volatility is domestic monetary disorder, not a fault of the collective psyche among the players on the foreign exchange markets. Consequently, the way to eliminate the volatility is to do something about domestic internal policies rather than arbitrarily interfere with the free functioning of foreign exchange markets. Many see excessive exchange rate volatility as inherently damaging, and no doubt there is some truth in this observation. Direct interference is advocated, but this, according to Dornbusch's analysis, is a futile treatment of symptoms and not a cure. Clearly it is important to know whether exchange rate volatility is an artefact generated by the players or represents something fundamental, *à la* Dornbusch. At least Dornbusch shows that many of the conclusions about exchange rate behaviour—that it is all mindless speculation—are superficial to say the least.

PROBLEM

4-21 Suppose that the interest arbitrage condition, Eq. (4-144), is modified to be the following: $De = r - r^* + \alpha e$, where α is a parameter. The Dornbusch model remains as before in other respects. Discuss the exchange rate dynamics for the various possible values of α.

4-15 SUMMARY

This chapter has dealt with some quite difficult material, which must be tackled if one is interested in pursuing the subject in depth. It has tried to unravel the logical structure underpinning some common rational expectations forms and to show that 'obvious' solutions are not quite so 'obvious' after all. Hopefully, it has provided readers with a useful 'tool-kit' with which to unravel a broad class of structures and to build models of their own.

ESSAY TOPICS

4-1 'In a rational expectations model the "fundamentals solution" must always prevail.' Discuss.

4-2 'The source of exchange rate volatility is domestic monetary disorder. Therefore, acting directly on the exchange rate is at best irrelevant and at worst damaging.' Discuss.

4-3 Do 'New Keynesian' ideas restore the case for gradualism in the control of inflation?

4-4 'The problem with rational expectations is that it suggests how agents *ought* to form their expectations, rather than how they actually *do* form their expectations.' Discuss.

4-5 What is your forecast for the inflation rate over the next twelve months? On what basis did you derive your answer?

READING

Much of the material for this chapter, particularly Secs 4-6 and 4-8, is derived from Sargent (1987a). Readers who want a more advanced treatment cannot do better than read his text. A good introduction to difference and differential equations is to be found in Chiang (1984) and Allen (1959). The latter reference has a particularly useful chapter on the use of operators. Useful alternative references on solution methods are Blanchard and Fischer (1989) (particularly the appendix to Chapter 5), Holden *et al.* (1985) and Begg (1982). Hopefully, the reader should see how all these treatments relate to the methods described here. Blanchard and Fischer also have a good discussion of stochastic bubbles. The money demand function of Sec. 4-7 derives from Cagan (1956); the overlapping contracts model of Sec. 4-9 is taken from Taylor (1979); and an easy discussion of the model is to be found in Hall and Taylor (1986). Fischer (1977) is another good example of overlapping contracts. The exchange rate model of Sec. 4-9 is based on Frenkel (1981). Mussa (1979) is an extremely readable account of the asset market approach to exchange rate determination. The overshooting model of Sec. 4-14 is from Dornbusch (1976) and can also be found in Dornbusch (1980).

BUSINESS CYCLES

Business cycles are all about the volatility or fluctuations in real output and employment. All recorded economic history in capitalist countries has been characterized by times of 'good trade' and 'bad trade'. This tendency for economies to lurch uncomfortably from 'boom' to 'bust' rather than follow a smooth progression has dominated the research agenda of some of the brightest and best economists of the twentieth century.

Figure 5-1 shows the unemployment rate in the UK from 1850 to 1990. Clearly, there are innumerable measurement problems here: statistical data in the nineteenth century are not accurate; changes in definition mean that the unemployment rate in 1990 is hardly comparable with 1980, let alone with 1850. Nevertheless, since the concern is to look at the broad picture rather than fine detail, Fig. 5-1 provides useful information. Business cycle theory attempts to elicit the big forces that drive real aggregate economic data, such as those contained in Fig. 5-1, instead of concentrating on unemployment as an *individual* experience.

Figure 5-1 achieves three ends. First, it confirms that business cycles exist. Over the period there have been nineteen well-defined cycles lasting, on average, seven years. They are endemic and it would be facile to pretend they did not occur. 'Boom' and 'bust' are probably better terms than the phrase 'business cycle'. The problem with the latter term is that it carries the connotation of regularity and smoothness in the process of fluctuation, where, in truth, no such regularity exists. Much effort has been devoted to trying to find such regularities in the data and these attempts do tend to become barren exercises in search of a statistical artefact. Look at the same piece of information for long enough and one can convince oneself of anything.

The second important point to notice is the serial correlation, persistence or momentum in the data. Business cycles are not characterized by random blips around some normal level, but have the characteristic of persistence. Thus, if output or employment is below normal in one year, there is a tendency for this to persist for several periods and similarly

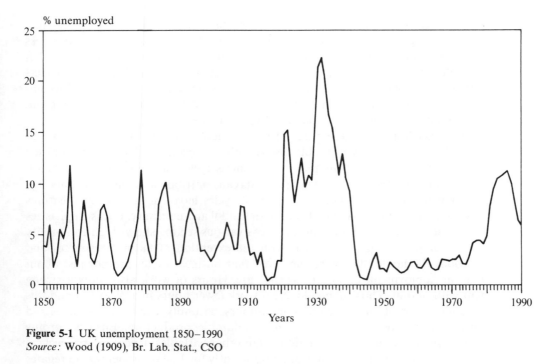

Figure 5-1 UK unemployment 1850–1990
Source: Wood (1909), Br. Lab. Stat., CSO

for times when output or employment are above normal. A business cycle theory, if it is to be credible, must therefore contain two elements: there must be (1) a mechanism to explain the source of the disturbance; and (2) a mechanism to explain persistence—the propagation mechanism, as it has come to be known.

The third feature is that the severity of cycles seems to have diminished after the Second World War, which is not just unique to the UK. Some argue that this points up the success of Keynesian activist economic policy, whereas others maintain this was more a case of good luck than good judgement. Against this, it has been claimed that the poor quality of historic economic data exaggerated the fluctuations in earlier times. Notwithstanding this point, it should be noted that the 1979–86 recession matched anything except the great 1930s slump. There are, therefore, no grounds for complacency or for believing that we now understand enough about the problem to be able to say that severe slumps will never happen again. Lucas, a name that will feature prominently in this chapter and someone who has made major contributions to recent theory, has cautioned that 'at any given time there will be phenomena that are well-understood from the point of view of the economic theory that we have and other phenomena that are not'. He was specifically referring to the state of business cycle theory.

The fourth feature of Fig. 5-1 is that rises and falls in unemployment can be sudden and dramatic. The fact that what once seemed an intractable unemployment problem can disappear in a short space of time casts doubt on some of the so-called 'hysteresis' theories of unemployment. Hysteresis, in this context, means there is not one single equilibrium or natural rate of unemployment (at least in the short run), rather the equilibrium itself varies with the actual level of unemployment. One possible cause of hysteresis is the idea that, if unemployment is high, those unemployed deteriorate to the extent that they become less employable in the future. Unemployed people are akin to mothballed machinery; if left idle long enough they simply cannot be made to work again. Clearly, if true, such effects would tend to increase the natural rate of unemployment as the actual level of unemployment increases. Figure 5-1 shows that such effects are not, in practice, particularly important. Chapter 8 will look at one other example of a hysteresis theory.

Having discerned some broad features, the next question to ask is whether business cycles form a subject that can be profitably discussed by the economic theorist as opposed to the economic historian. Some claim that each business cycle is a one-off historical event, unique in itself. Thus only historians and not theorists can contribute to their understanding. Lucas argues that this is not so, claiming that most cycles have enough *common* features to make the search for an encompassing theory both fruitful and necessary. Lucas emphasizes the following common features. First, output across various sectors shows high conformity with all sectors tending to move together, with the exception of natural resources and agricultural goods. It should also be remembered that business cycles are not just about movements in unemployment, important as they are. Hours of work also show a strong co-movement with output. Those in employment work fewer hours in a recession and this accounts for a good part of the reduction in man-hours. Secondly, consumer durables and capital goods show greater fluctuations than non-durable production. Business profits show high conformity and greater fluctuations than other variables. Prices are procyclical as well as short-run interest rates. Finally, and importantly for Lucas, monetary aggregates are procyclical with the velocity of circulation increasing in the boom phase of the cycle.

A good analogy might be to compare business cycles to warfare. A historian might argue that the First World War was caused by factors x, y and z, whereas the Vietnam War had a separate and distinctive set of causes. At this level, each war is a unique event with its own specific causes. However, an alternative analysis might suggest that, because wars have occurred with such frequency throughout history, something more fundamental might underlie every war. Man's psychological make-up makes it prone to warfare which demands a 'deeper' analysis than the proximate causes described by historians. This is what business cycle theorists are trying to provide and they should not be seen as being in competition with the historian.

It was the great slump of the 1930s which inspired Keynes to write *The General Theory*. Keynesian business cycle models were refined in the late 1930s and 1940s by Samuelson, Hicks and Metzler among others and it is hard to believe that these latter efforts are now half a century old. They represent a landmark, attempting to give a complete 'deep' analysis of the cycle using internally consistent mathematical models. Section 5-1 will look at one example of this genre. Although subject to much criticism, this model is recognizably modern. However, no theory should be commended or criticized by reason of that fact alone.

The 1950s and 1960s saw the monetarist counter-revolution, spearheaded by Friedman and the Chicago School. This saw monetary factors and, in particular, monetary contractions as the proximate cause of slumps. More recently, the rational expectations revolution has led to the development of complex and sophisticated equilibrium theories. These ideas will form a part of this chapter, which is most closely associated with Lucas. The ideas of Lucas can be seen as a logical development of Friedman's Monetarism. Lucas also deliberately looks to revive an older tradition associated with Hayek and the Austrian school. Notice particularly how Lucas emphasized monetary factors in his list of those factors common to most business cycles. Monetary disturbances are critical to the Lucas cycle.

It is probably because understanding business cycles is a truly difficult problem that it has attracted the best minds of the profession, keen to study 'deep' questions. Despite this massive intellectual effort, it is useful to bear in mind what has been achieved so far. Lucas sums it up thus: '[What we have] at best is a workable approximation that is useful in answering a limited set of questions.' There is absolutely no doubt that the problem will continue to attract the best minds in the future.

Most discussions of business cycles assume that they are *ipso facto* a 'bad thing'. Behind most theories lies a more or less open polemical agenda whereby, if only this and that did not happen or if the authorities behaved in this as opposed to that way, business cycles could be considerably muted, if not eliminated. Lucas, for example, states that, 'attempts to document and account for regular cyclical movements need not be connected in any way to a presumption that such movements are an *inevitable* feature of capitalist economies'.

In fact, it may be that economies without 'booms' or 'busts' are, like the elusive philosophers' stone or perfect happiness, simply a naive Utopian dream. Recent theory, an approach to which Lucas is not unsympathetic, suggests that economies have a natural cycle or resonance. Undoubtedly, misguided policy actions by the authorities can exacerbate fluctuations, but the point is that 'boom' and 'bust' would still occur even if the authorities were doing the best they could at all times. This type of approach has become known as real business cycle theory. In fact, the title is somewhat confusing, because early Keynesian models have also been described as real business cycles, and the two are most definitely not the same. Modern real business cycle theory emphasizes the fact of an irreducible minimum cycle. This contribution will be discussed in Sec. 5-3.

A useful analogy here would be to compare the economy to a rocking-chair. One theoretical approach is to see the rocking-chair as being kicked or disturbed from without. It rocks back and forth until equilibrium is restored or it responds to yet more external shocks. The alternative is to see no external shock, but rather the chair rocks back and forth as if powered by an internal motor. This is the essence of the modern real business cycle theory. On this view, then, business cycles need not be pathological phenomena. Since 1850 living standards for the average family have been transformed from a condition of drudgery and degradation, to one of good health, well-rewarded work and considerable leisure time, despite the endemic cycles exemplified in Fig. 5-1. Business cycles may be an unpleasant Faustian pact with the 'capitalist devil'; a necessary price paid in the past and to be paid in the future in order to secure the unimaginable increases in wealth only the capitalist system can provide. This contrasts with the superficial appeal of command socialist economies, which guarantee a job for life but which, in reality, impoverish their own citizens.

Just how costly are business cycles? After all, if the sums involved are trivial, devoting scarce intellectual resources to studying the problem is a misallocation. Lucas attempts, not with any pretence at great sophistication, to answer the question. Think of a typical consumer viewing the future. That person can expect on average a steady growth in real consumption, but, because of the expectation of business cycles, this consumption stream is subject to a certain amount of risk. There is a finite probability at any point in time of being unable to consume along the trend growth line. Now, it is generally accepted that most consumers regard risk as undesirable; all things being equal, more risk means less utility.

The acid test of something that is disliked is that individuals are prepared to pay something to have less of it. Lucas asks how much extra consumption this typical consumer would require to swop a riskless for a risky stream—precisely the opportunity cost of the business cycle. (Incidentally, the argument presented here is purely heuristic; Chapter 6 looks at risk in a much more systematic way.) To do this Lucas makes reasonable assumptions about the size of risk to be faced and the value the consumer would place on such 'units' of risk. Having done this, he then asks what addition to consumption now and in every future period the consumer would require in order to face a risky consumption stream in place of a trend growth consumption stream. The answer turns out to be surprisingly small, just one-tenth of 1 per cent of GNP! This is a far smaller figure than the deadweight loss calculated from a steady inflation rate of 10 per cent—exactly five times smaller, to be precise. Notice that Lucas is not asking whether such trade-offs are feasible. It is simply an accounting exercise to ask how much a typical individual is prepared to pay.

Lucas, not least because he has devoted considerable time to the study of business cycles, was somewhat surprised by the smallness of the numbers involved. He did recognize a number of potential flaws in the analysis. First, unemployment is very much an individual experience. Calculations for the typical individual are reasonable if there is only a small variation around them, but that is not the case. The majority go through their economic lives effectively untouched by the hazard of recession, whereas for a significant minority the hazards are disproportionately large. 'Small earthquake in Peru—only five dead', is an insignificant event as long as one is not one of the five dead. The second point is that, as can be seen from Fig. 5-1, the intensity of most business cycles was generally lower after the Second World War, and this was also true for the USA, on which Lucas based his calculations. The two post-1979 recessions show that small slumps in the future cannot be taken for granted. Using pre-1939 variances, Lucas calculated the deadweight loss as one half of 1 per cent. This is a much larger figure, but is still surprisingly small.

For Lucas, then, business cycles, although a formidable intellectual challenge, are relatively insignificant events, no worse than a mild cold. He implicitly challenges the Keynesian assumption that somehow unemployment is worse than inflation. Against Lucas, it has to be said that the 'folk memory' of slumps is that they are not insignificant events and the fact that times of slump attract such considerable political debate and media attention suggests that the 'folk memory' is a better guide to costs than any attempted economic calculus. With any statistical calculation the question should always be asked: 'Does this answer make sense?'

We are now in a position to look at some formal models. The great dividing line in modelling is whether one adopts the equilibrium approach, which characterizes the rational expectations school, or whether one adopts a non-equilibrium approach. Section 5-1 will examine a typical fix-price Keynesian model which was very influential in its time and is an archetypical non-equilibrium model. This is the Metzler inventory cycle, which is one of the best examples of the genre—and it would probably be foolish to ignore some of its insights even now. The main purpose, however, is to highlight differences between the non-equilibrium and equilibrium approaches.

5-1 THE INVENTORY CYCLE

The first point is that there is not just one inventory cycle model; Metzler looks at a whole variety of cases. Here we concentrate on one simple case, as this is sufficient to tell us enough about the modelling 'style' of this category. Problem 5-1 invites the reader to consider a more complicated case. Metzler's inventory cycle model is a fix-price model and this assumption above all makes it distinctively Keynesian and a non-equilibrium model. According to Metzler, 'any discrepancy between output and consumer demand may be met by inventory fluctuations rather than price changes'. Thus there is no question of prices adjusting to clear markets. The dichotomy between microeconomics and macroeconomics is complete and glaring here; by construction the price mechanism has been thrown overboard. The interesting thing about reading Metzler is that virtually no attention is paid to this assumption. It was as if Keynes had settled the matter and the fix-price assumption was such common ground that little or no explicit attention needed to be devoted to it.

The fix-price tradition lives on, albeit in a much more sophisticated form, in disequilibrium post-Keynesian economics. In the previous chapter we examined two classic New Keynesian models which involved price rigidity to some degree. Much of the New Keynesian agenda seeks to give a well-grounded microtheoretic justification for such price rigidities, some of which are reviewed in Chapter 8. However, the important point to note at this stage is the fix-price non-market-clearing tradition exemplified by Metzler. This contrasts with the flex-price market-clearing tradition exemplified by Lucas and other equilibrium theorists.

The inventory cycle is based on the following assumptions. There is no lag between real output and real income. Thus, income at time t is made up of three elements:

$$Y_t = u_t + s_t + v_0 \qquad (5\text{-}1)$$

where Y_t is real income ($=$ real output), u_t is production for sale, s_t is production for inventory and v_0 is fixed autonomous investment. Entrepreneurs are assumed to believe that sales this period will be last period's consumption. Note that this is an entirely arbitrary and mechanical rule, based on the idea that it 'seems plausible' rather than on any well-defined optimizing process. Lucas and the rational expectations school would simply highlight the utter naivety and crassness of such mechanical and robotic behaviour on the part of entrepreneurs. Do they never learn? Just why should they behave with such permanent myopia, no matter what the economic outcome (namely cycles)? Lucas objects to modelling economic agents as tin toys to be wound up by theorists and watched clattering off the edge of a table—as though that gave any insight into how the world operates. The assumption is, therefore,

$$u_t = C_{t-1} = \beta Y_{t-1} \qquad (5\text{-}2)$$

where C_{t-1} is last period's consumption, which is a linear function of income in that period. Production for inventory follows an equally mechanical 'plausible' rule, which is assumed to be just the difference between actual and anticipated sales in period $t - 1$. This could either be positive or negative and Metzler further assumes that inventories never run out—if consumption exceeds production, there are always sufficient stocks to meet demand.

The intuition of the Metzler rule is quite simple. Suppose sales are 20 units above what was anticipated. The extra is met by running down stocks by 20 units. Next period inventory production is stepped up by 20 units to restore stocks to their normal level. At time $t - 1$ anticipated sales were βY_{t-2}, whereas actual sales were βY_{t-1}. Thus:

$$s_t = \beta Y_{t-1} - \beta Y_{t-2}. \tag{5-3}$$

Combining Eqs (5-1), (5-2) and (5-3) gives the second-order difference equation:

$$Y_t - 2\beta Y_{t-1} + \beta Y_{t-2} = v_0. \tag{5-4}$$

This difference equation is the heart of the inventory cycle and is solved entirely conventionally, that is with two historical starting values for Y_t. The solution is

$$Y_t = \bar{Y} + c_1 \lambda_1^t + c_2 \lambda_2^t \tag{5-5}$$

where $\bar{Y}$ is equilibrium output ($= v_0/(1 - \beta)$) and λ_1, λ_2 are given by

$$\lambda_1, \lambda_2 = \beta \pm \sqrt{\beta^2 - \beta}. \tag{5-6}$$

Since β is the marginal propensity to consume and is less than 1, it follows that $\beta^2 - \beta < 0$. Hence λ_1, λ_2 are conjugate, complex roots. Therefore, Eq. (5-5) follows a cycle defined by

$$Y_t = \bar{Y} + AR^t \cos(\theta t + \varepsilon). \tag{5-7}$$

(For readers unfamiliar with this type of derivation, the appendix fills in some details.)

Figure 5-2 shows the type of cycle implied by Eq. (5-7). The critical parameter is the dampening factor R, since this determines whether the cycle is convergent towards $\bar{Y}$ or explosive. Clearly, $R < 1$ implies a damped cycle, and since $R = \sqrt{\beta}$ (see the appendix if you are not sure of this) and $\beta < 1$, a non-explosive cycle is guaranteed.

The other parameters are A, θ and ε. Both A, the amplitude, and ε, the phase, are determined by the initial conditions and their effect on the cycle is illustrated in Fig. 5-2. The period is $2\pi/\theta$, which is the time required to complete one whole cycle. Thus, a high θ means a higher frequency with more 'squeezed' oscillations. This, along with R, is determined from the characteristic equation.

The Metzler inventory cycle is among the most imaginative of the early Keynesian models. Although recent theories are highly critical of this type of approach, it must be said that the propagation mechanisms of these recent models have some common elements with Keynesian real business cycles. It might be said that the early Keynesians were more concerned with the *propagation* mechanism, paying less heed to a rigorous theory of the source of disturbance. Recent theories pay much closer attention to the source of the cycle.

Metzler was no fool. He was well aware of the mechanical nature of his inventory cycle. He therefore put forward alternative schemes of increasing sophistication, the result of which were cycles of corresponding complexity. However, for Lucas and the New Classicals such stratagems are irrelevant. For them the whole approach is mistaken and inherently flawed. No matter how sophisticated, a mechanical rule of behaviour is just that—a mechanical rule. The correct framework should view agents as rational consistent optimizers, aware of the economic environment in which they operate and the consequences

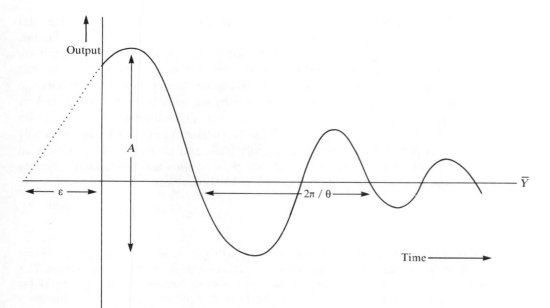

Figure 5-2 The Metzler inventory cycle

of their actions. Behaviour is not arbitrary but purposeful and logical. In short, agents hold rational expectations. Lucas dismissed Keynesian structures like Metzler's as 'jerry-built'.

The ideas of Lucas and the later real business cycle are so-called *equilibrium* theories in strong contrast to the early Keynesian models, of which Metzler is one example. It is now appropriate to be more precise as to what is meant by the term 'equilibrium theory'. Unfortunately, the term does not have a single interpretation and can mean different things to different people. One view, which might be characterized as Keynesian, considers equilibrium as a point of rest from which a system has no tendency to move. There could be a severe recession with large numbers of involuntary unemployed workers willing to work at the prevailing wage but unable to find jobs, yet the economy might still be considered to be in equilibrium. As long as there is no tendency for the situation facing rationed agents to change, then this state of affairs is described as an equilibrium.

Lucas, in strong contrast, takes a different view of what is meant by equilibrium. For him, equilibrium essentially means market clearing. Thus, a market characterized by rationing in which buyers and sellers are unable to buy and sell all they wish at the given prices would not be in equilibrium. The fix-price assumption of Keynesian business cycle theories and the later work of post-Keynesians allow for non-market-clearing situations. Often these are characterized as 'equilibria' or 'temporary equilibria', by which is meant no tendency to change given the fixed prices. Lucas is in a world of flexible prices where such situations could not prevail. Prices would adjust to ensure market clearing.

It is immediately clear that operating within a fix-price paradigm makes it quite easy to generate less than full employment. Cycles are basically situations of disequilibrium, where disequilibrium is used in the sense of non-market clearing. Given fixed prices and a price vector that is 'wrong' really loads the dice very much in the theorist's favour. Lucas claims to hark back to a tradition established by Hayek and the Austrian school. It must be said that he establishes a set of ground rules that make it much more difficult for the theorist at the outset. If the assumption is that markets always clear, then a simplistic reaction would be to say that Lucas has thrown the baby out with the bathwater. If markets clear, how can there be a cycle? Lucas sets himself a truly difficult problem, yet he argues that the task is worth while and important. If the Keynesian framework is fundamentally flawed, then all its policy prescriptions are equally facile and incorrect. The causes of an equilibrium cycle are more subtle, and the policy prescriptions are correspondingly very different from the activist, interventionist doctrines of Keynesians.

PROBLEM

5-1 The Metzler inventory cycle is modified as follows. Producers aim to maintain a constant proportion of stocks to sales, where expected sales in period t are last period's consumption. This is expressed as kC_{t-1}, where k is the desired ratio of stocks to consumption. Actual stocks are $K_t = kC_{t-1} - (C_t - C_{t-1})$, since $(C_t - C_{t-1})$ is the forecast error in expected sales. Inventory production is, therefore, $s_t = kC_{t-1} - K_{t-1}$. Explore the properties of the implied business cycle, assuming all other features of the Metzler cycle remain the same.

5-2 THE LUCAS MONETARY CYCLE

The key to the Lucas cycle is limited information. Given the assumption of equilibrium, if there were perfect information there would be no cycle. Thus Lucas holds out the possibility of eliminating or at least attenuating the cycle by improving upon the quality of information available to agents in the economy. Specifically, if monetary policy was made precise and if agents suffered no confusion as to what the authorities were trying to do, then much if not all of the cycle could be eliminated. In other words, the policy prescription is for simple, well-understood policy rules and not for active, piecemeal intervention. The latter would simply generate the very confusion that must be avoided. The contrast with discretionary Keynesian policy or 'fine tuning' could not be more complete.

In the Lucas model, microeconomics works! Agents make real decisions about which quantities to supply and demand based on relative prices. They do not suffer from money illusion. Agents *to the limit of the information available to them* are consistent optimizers. They do not make systematic forecast errors—to be precise, they hold rational expectations. Finally, institutional constraints are ignored; prices are freely flexible and markets clear. To quote Lucas, 'One would like a theory which accounts for the observed movements in quantities ... as an optimizing response to observed movements in prices.'

Having made these points, it must be mentioned that Lucas is not at all hostile to some models which embody a degree of nominal price rigidity. The danger of textbook expositions such as this is that readers can often be misled into making sweeping generalizations on the lines of 'Keynesians believe prices are always rigid, whereas Lucas believes they are flexible and markets clear.' Lucas writes in an inquisitorial rather than dogmatic way, believing that there are some quite competently worked out models involving price rigidities, whereas there are others which are woeful and pretty ropey. Lucas is not quite sure at this stage how useful such lines of enquiry will prove, but some certainly seem very promising.

As has been said, the key to the Lucas cycle is less than perfect information. Given that agents respond to changes in relative prices, they have to distinguish between a rise in general prices—assuming the norm is inflation—and a rise in relative prices. The problem is that price changes become a noisy signal unable to communicate accurately what is a general price rise and what is a relative price rise. Suppose, for example, an entrepreneur observes a rise in price for his product or service of 15 per cent. Is this because of general inflation of 15 per cent or a favourable shift in demand for the type of service or product offered? What the entrepreneur observes is the 15 per cent rise in price and that person must make a 'best guess' as to whether the market has moved favourably or unfavourably. Clearly, the supply response will be different depending on whether the price rise is just part of a general inflation or is a true rise in relative prices. The latter category could be further subdivided into a temporary rise in relative prices or a permanent rise. Again the supply response is likely to be different in both situations. Lucas sees agents as making the best of a bad job and optimizing in a systematic manner, rather than behaving in a random manner or obeying simple mechanical rules. It is entirely possible that such optimizing behaviour can generate cycles, as will be seen.

It is now appropriate to be a little more formal. The Lucas prototype posits a world of little 'island economies', of which there are n, each producing an identical product so there are no aggregation problems. Each microeconomy has its own supply schedule, which looks like this:

$$Y_i = Y^* + g(P_i - P_\varepsilon), \quad i = 1,\dots,n \tag{5-8}$$

where Y_i = output of the ith economy, Y^* is normal output, P_i is the price of the ith island's product and P_ε is the worker/entrepreneur's expectation of the general price level. Thus, Eq. (5-8) asserts that if P_i exceeds P_ε the island will produce more; and if P_i is less than P_ε, the island will produce less, where $g > 0$ measures the degree of response.

Lucas holds that Eq. (5-8) is a reasonable description of micro behaviour, and for our purposes we do not have to enquire too deeply for its foundation. The main task is to build an aggregate supply schedule from the summation of all the individual micro schedules. One justification for Eq. (5-8) is the idea of intertemporal substitution. This is the proposition that there should be a large positive supply response if prices are *temporarily* high. Workers, for example, are observed to work long overtime hours in response to relatively small overtime premia when such opportunities are transitory. Thus intertemporal substitution is the idea of making hay while the sun shines. Work and produce as much as you can when relative prices are favourable; indulge in extra leisure and produce less when relative prices are unfavourable.

Notice that Eq. (5-8) is really oversimplified because the supply response g is likely to be much higher for temporary as opposed to permanent price rises. If someone told me I could earn £500 per hour for one month only, I would undoubtedly work all the hours I possibly could, whereas my response would be much less dramatic if I were told that £500 per hour was available for always. Despite this, Eq. (5-8) will do for the present. Equation (5-8) is a micro supply schedule and Lucas shows that the aggregate supply schedule, given noisy signalling, will mirror this micro schedule. In other words, there is the possibility of a cycle since aggregate output is not constrained to equal the normal level nY^*. *Prima facie*, this is a somewhat surprising result because one might reason as follows. On some islands, prices will be temporarily high with $P_i > P_\varepsilon$ and Y_i being correspondingly higher than normal. On other islands prices will be temporarily low and the Y_i also low. With rational expectations the average price $= (1/n)\sum P_i$ should be P_ε and thus the pluses and minuses should cancel with average output $= nY^*$. There should be no business cycle.

Lucas shows that the above line of reasoning is faulty and this serves to demonstrate the subtlety of his approach. There are two sources of price disturbance. The first comes from *monetary* factors and this affects the general price level. The second is the relative price effect and is 'island specific'. However, the average relative price effect is zero. Thus P_i is given by

$$P_i = P + Z_i \qquad (5\text{-}9)$$

where P is the general price level, Z_i is the relative price effect and, by definition, $\sum Z_i = 0$ across all the islands. The next stage is to make some assumptions about the distributions of P and Z_i. First, the mean and variance of P are given by

$$P \sim (\hat{P}, \sigma_u^2). \qquad (5\text{-}10)$$

Agents are assumed to know the mean of the price level and its variance. Because monetary policy is confused, agents do not know in advance what the exact realization of P will be. If they did know this, then monetary policy would be so transparent that σ_u^2 would be zero and there would be no distribution for P. There would be no business cycle if that happened, as will shortly be seen. A similar assumption to Eq. (5-10) is made about the distribution of Z_i:

$$Z_i \sim (0, \sigma_e^2). \qquad (5\text{-}11)$$

Here the mean is zero and the variance is σ_e^2.

Now focus in on the problem that the typical island economy faces. The information available is P_i, but what the island really wants to know is the exact breakdown between P and Z_i. Because monetary policy is noisy, this information is not precisely available. Technically, the island faces the classic signal extraction problem. The island observes a single signal P_i made up of two components, P and Z_i. Something is known about the relative distributions—namely σ_u^2 and σ_e^2—and on this basis the island wants to make the most informed guess it can about the size of P and Z_i. Clearly, unless the guess happens to be very lucky, the island entrepreneur will make some mistakes.

Now one solution might be for the island to reason that the best estimate for P is $\hat{P}$—after all this is the mean value of the distribution—and then guess at Z_i as being $P_i - \hat{P}$. However, to do this ignores important information and the island can actually do rather better than this. Simply relying on $\hat{P}$ ignores the useful information available from a knowledge of P_i. The island might reason that if a high P_i has occurred, this means a high P is more likely; and conversely, if a low P_i has been observed. That judgement would be based on the relative sizes of σ_u^2 and σ_e^2. The unconditional expectation of P is $\hat{P}$, but a better forecast would be the conditional expectation given a knowledge of P_i. This conditional expectation is written as $E\{P|P_i\}$. Since Lucas claims that agents use all information efficiently, this conditional forecast is the best that can be done and the conditional forecast will be used as the best guess of P_ε.

Before showing exactly what $E\{P|P_i\}$ is, let us see how far intuition can point us in the right direction. Suppose σ_u^2 was five times higher than σ_e^2. Now suppose a high value for P_i was observed. Since the overall spread of the P distribution is five times that of the Z_i distribution, it would be reasonable to argue that most (five-sixths, to be exact) of this high P_i is due to a high realization of P, rather than a high Z_i. Thus the relative variances offer a suggestive way of weighting one's beliefs to derive the conditional mean. Hence $E\{P|P_i\}$ would be given by $\frac{5}{6}$ $(= \sigma_u^2/(\sigma_u^2 + \sigma_e^2))$ times P_i plus $\frac{1}{6}$ times $\hat{P}$. Obviously, if σ_u^2 and σ_e^2 were not known, there would be no way of improving the forecast over $\hat{P}$. The following demonstrates the correctness of the above intuition and the related assumptions. (Readers can ignore what follows if they are prepared to accept Eq. (5-20) and can carry on from there without loss of continuity.)

Suppose $X \sim (\mu, \Sigma)$ where X is an $n \times 1$ vector of random variables, μ is an $n \times 1$ vector of means and Σ is an $n \times n$ variance–covariance matrix. Given this, then $AX \sim (A\mu, A\Sigma A')$ where A is an $n \times n$ matrix of constants and A' is the transpose of A. (This result is stated and not proved.) In our case we have:

$$\begin{bmatrix} P \\ Z_i \end{bmatrix} \sim \begin{bmatrix} \hat{P} \\ 0 \end{bmatrix}, \quad \begin{bmatrix} \sigma_u^2 & 0 \\ 0 & \sigma_e^2 \end{bmatrix} \tag{5-12}$$

which assumes P and Z_i are uncorrelated. We wish to know the distribution of

$$\begin{bmatrix} P \\ P + Z_i \end{bmatrix} = \begin{bmatrix} 1 & 0 \\ 1 & 1 \end{bmatrix} \begin{bmatrix} P \\ Z_i \end{bmatrix}. \tag{5-13}$$

Clearly the mean of the random variable $P + Z_i$ is just $\hat{P}$ and the variance–covariance matrix is

$$A\Sigma A' = \begin{bmatrix} 1 & 0 \\ 1 & 1 \end{bmatrix} \begin{bmatrix} \sigma_u^2 & 0 \\ 0 & \sigma_e^2 \end{bmatrix} \begin{bmatrix} 1 & 1 \\ 0 & 1 \end{bmatrix} = \begin{bmatrix} \sigma_u^2 & \sigma_u^2 \\ \sigma_u^2 & \sigma_u^2 + \sigma_e^2 \end{bmatrix}. \tag{5-14}$$

Hence $\text{var}(P + Z_i) = \sigma_u^2 + \sigma_e^2$ and $\text{Cov}(P, P + Z_i) = \sigma_u^2$. Now consider the linear regression:

$$P = a + b(P + Z_i) + \delta \tag{5-15}$$

where δ is a residual term. In the limit:

$$b = \frac{\text{Cov}(P, P + Z_i)}{\text{Var}(P + Z_i)} = \frac{\sigma_u^2}{\sigma_u^2 + \sigma_e^2}. \tag{5-16}$$

The regression line also goes through the mean, thus:

$$a = \hat{P} - b\hat{P} \tag{5-17}$$

noting that the mean of $P + Z_i$ is just $\hat{P}$. Hence,

$$P = \hat{P} - \frac{\sigma_u^2 \hat{P}}{\sigma_u^2 + \sigma_e^2} + \frac{\sigma_u^2 P_i}{\sigma_u^2 + \sigma_e^2} + \delta \tag{5-18}$$

or

$$P = \frac{\sigma_e^2 \hat{P}}{\sigma_u^2 + \sigma_e^2} + \frac{\sigma_u^2 P_i}{\sigma_u^2 + \sigma_e^2} + \delta. \tag{5-19}$$

Thus the conditional mean of P, given a particular value for P_i, is simply:

$$P_\varepsilon = E\{P|P_i\} = \frac{\sigma_e^2 \hat{P}}{\sigma_u^2 + \sigma_e^2} + \frac{\sigma_u^2 P_i}{\sigma_u^2 + \sigma_e^2} \tag{5-20}$$

which is just the intuitive result alluded to previously. Having indicated the solution to the signal extraction problem, the hard work has now been done and our task is easy from here on!

Substitute out P_ε from Eq. (5-8) using Eq. (5-20):

$$Y_i = Y^* + g(P_i - (1 - b)\hat{P} - bP_i). \tag{5-21}$$

Hence,

$$Y_i = Y^* + g(1 - b)(P_i - \hat{P}) \tag{5-22}$$

where b is the ratio of the variances as shown in Eq. (5-16). Now derive the aggregate supply schedule by summing over all markets:

$$\sum_{i=1}^{n} Y_i = Y = nY^* + \gamma(P - \hat{P}) \tag{5-23}$$

where $\gamma = ng(1 - b)$, noting that $\sum(P_i - \hat{P}) = \sum(P + Z_i - \hat{P}) = n(P - \hat{P})$. Equation (5-23) is the famous Lucas price surprise aggregate supply schedule—the equation that launched at least a thousand articles and a hundred books!

Equation (5-23) shows that even though markets clear, output is not constrained to be at the natural rate or normal level nY^*. If the price surprise, measured as the difference $P - \hat{P}$, is positive then output is above normal and, conversely, output is below normal if there is a negative price surprise. It is clearly the beginnings of an equilibrium business cycle. The intuition for Eq. (5-23) is really quite simple. At any one point in time a monetary policy resulting in a high P means that all individual islands tend to make the same mistake in interpreting this as a rise in prices in their favour. Consequently, aggregate output increases, and with a surprisingly strict monetary stance it decreases. Notice this does not contradict the assumption of rational expectations. Agents do not make systematic errors; expected output at any point in time is always nY^*, as can be seen from Eq. (5-23), noting that $E\{P - \hat{P}\} = 0$.

Given the equilibrium framework, there can be no involuntary unemployment in the Lucas prototype business cycle. Lucas becomes somewhat irritated by criticisms on the lines, 'The good thing about Keynesian models is that unemployment can be involuntary, whereas the bad thing about the equilibrium approach is that unemployment is voluntary.' As Lucas points out, the fact that markets clear does not necessarily imply that people like being unemployed, just as the fact that when food markets clear it does not make the hungry feel any better about their situation. Debates about when unemployment is voluntary or involuntary can quickly degenerate into sterile semantics and become especially difficult when studied from the point of view of the individual job-searcher.

Equation (5-23) is an equation in price level surprises, but it can easily be re-interpreted as an equation in inflation surprises. It is really a matter of convenience whether to interpret the Lucas schedule in level terms or to gear it up into an equation in inflation surprises. The following trick, due to Laidler, shows how this can be done. The previous model could easily be reformulated in log terms as:

$$Y = nY^* + \gamma(\ln P - \ln \hat{P}). \tag{5-24}$$

Add and subtract log of the price level lagged one period to derive:

$$Y = nY^* + \gamma\left[\ln\left(\frac{P}{P_{-1}}\right) - \ln\left(\frac{\hat{P}}{P_{-1}}\right)\right]. \tag{5-25}$$

Now $\ln(P/P_{-1})$ is to an excellent approximation the inflation rate equal to $(P - P_{-1})/P_{-1}$ and similarly $\ln(\hat{P}/P_{-1})$ is the expected inflation rate (try some examples to confirm this). Hence, the Lucas supply schedule, depending on the purpose at hand, can be formulated in level terms as in Eq. (5-23) or inflation terms as in Eq. (5-25).

Now, consider Eq. (5-23) to see that it makes sense in the light of the assumptions of the Lucas theory. First suppose $\sigma_u^2 = 0$. Although this means $b = 0$, it also implies $P = \hat{P}$ always and there will be no business cycle. The micro functions, as shown by Eq. (5-8) will still 'churn around' with some producing more than normal when Z_i is positive and others less when Z_i is negative. This is the Lucas ideal, since $\sigma_u^2 = 0$ means there is no signal extraction problem and the price mechanism works as it is meant to do, communicating accurate information about relative prices.

Notice that it is not inflation *per se* that generates the aggregate business cycle, but the *uncertainty* about the inflation rate. The expected inflation rate could be zero, yet σ_u^2 be large, generating large output discrepancies. By contrast, a high expected inflation rate could be associated with a low σ_u^2 and smaller fluctuations. For Lucas it is *unanticipated* inflation which is the most costly part. However, in practice, high inflation is more likely to be associated with greater degrees of uncertainty than low rates of inflation. Hence the importance of sound monetary policy to promote price stability. For Lucas one of the costs of inflation is that it messes up the price mechanism, making it function ineffectively and generating business cycles.

This helps explain why Lucas and New Classicals attach considerable importance to fixed rules in the conduct of economic policy. The attempt to 'fine tune' merely creates confusion, which in turn generates unnecessary fluctuations. Fixed rules offer a better guarantee of a steady, presumably low, certain inflation performance. This issue, which is a central part of the New Classical agenda, will be returned to in Chapter 7.

The second case is when $\sigma_e^2 = 0$. It follows that $b = 1$ and $\gamma = 0$. There is no business cycle because by construction all the Z_i are zero. Hence there are no micro fluctuations and no aggregate fluctuations. Clearly, this is a trivial case. The final case is an interesting *curiosum* which is the case of $\sigma_u^2 \to \infty$. It can be seen that $b \to 1$ and $\gamma \to 0$ in this case and again there is no business cycle. A high σ_u^2 is the case of a totally reckless monetary authority which creates an infinite degree of uncertainty in the body politic. Thus it appears that putting Militant Tendency in charge of the Bank of England would have the same beneficial effect as Milton Friedman!

There is, in fact, nothing surprising about the above result and it demonstrates the richness of the Lucas approach. A totally reckless monetary policy is economic terrorism. Agents believe that any delivered inflation rate is a *general* price rise and not a Z_i change. Consequently, all the micro functions are wiped out and each individual island will produce Y^* with P_ε set to P_i always. Obviously, although at an aggregate level things look fine, at a micro level such a policy is disastrous. This is a case of an economy locked in a concrete straitjacket, with no individual sector responding to changing consumer demand. What this shows is that eliminating *aggregate* fluctuations is not, *ipso facto*, desirable. Much of macroeconomics, particularly on stabilization policy, seems to suggest that it is. There is more than one way of skinning a cat and, as has been seen, the cat can be skinned the wrong way. An economy producing a steady level of output of products nobody wants to buy is hardly a desirable objective.

Equation (5-23) on its own is hardly a complete story of the business cycle. It establishes an excellent source for the cycle—namely monetary disturbances, but as yet contains no propagation mechanism. Since $P - \hat{P}$ is a 'white noise' term, Eq. (5-23) predicts random blips in output around the natural level. However, the discussion of Fig. 5-1 established that an important feature of business cycles is persistence or momentum. An equation such as (5-23) would not fit any set of data particularly well and reasonable results are only to be obtained when a propagation term is included, such as

$$Y - nY^* = \gamma(P - \hat{P}) + \lambda(Y_{-1} - nY^*), \quad 0 < \lambda < 1. \tag{5-26}$$

Clearly, the lagged output term Y_{-1} is a minimal requirement for persistence, but, of course, Eq. (5-26) is an entirely *ad hoc* construction.

Lucas was well aware that his theory required a satisfactory explanation for cycle persistence, but it must be said that the main effort went into establishing a satisfactory source for aggregate disturbances. One simple explanation is that money shocks themselves are positively correlated. This is not satisfactory on two counts. First, it is somewhat antithetical to the assumptions of rational expectations. Smart agents should quickly learn that monetary shocks are serially correlated, which would eliminate the potential serial correlation. Secondly, even if there were serially correlated shocks, these should be reflected in a series of positive or negative values in $P - \hat{P}$, and there is still no justification for the lagged output term.

To explain the persistence, Lucas points to the larger cyclical volatility of durable goods, particularly capital equipment—in effect an accelerator principle. The model described here is over-simplified to the extent that there is just a single relative price effect Z_i. In reality, Z_i is more complicated than that, with agents required to distinguish a *permanent* rise in relative prices from a *temporary* rise. In effect, there is a three-way signal extraction problem. A rise in relative prices thought to be permanent will have the strongest effect on capital accumulation and projects once initiated take time to complete and are costly to cancel. Furthermore, 'he who dares, wins'—with the right investment decision at the right time the returns can be huge. Consequently, Lucas argues that 'a quick current response to what seems to others a weak signal is often the key to a successful investment'.

In this way the cycle will generate momentum. A monetary surprise can generate large over-investment, which takes time to work its way through the system. The downturn can similarly be extended, with previous over-investment now taking its time to work its way out of the system.

PROBLEM

5-2 The Lucas supply schedule is given by $Y = Y^* + \xi(1 - b)(P - \hat{P})$, where ξ is a parameter and $b = \sigma_u^2/(\sigma_u^2 + \sigma_\varepsilon^2)$. The expected price level is $\hat{P}$ (or alternatively the expected inflation rate) and $E\{P - \hat{P}\}^2$ is σ_u^2.

(a) Write out $Y - Y^*$ and hence derive $E\{Y - Y^*\}^2$.

(b) Assuming that σ_ε^2 is a constant, work out the value of σ_u^2 that will give the maximum variance of the fluctuations. Try to give some intuition for this result.

5-3 THE REAL BUSINESS CYCLE

Lucas is quite sympathetic to the ideas embodied in modern real business cycle theory. (It is called modern here to distinguish it from earlier Keynesian models, which are also real business cycles.) The driving force is random technological shocks. The essence of technological progress is that it does not evolve with a smooth exponential growth rate but rather is somewhat unpredictable and random. Growth theory, as it developed from the late 1950s and 1960s, misleadingly modelled the growth process as if technological progress could be described as a smooth progression. In reality, the economy is repeatedly subjected to technological shocks. It is these technological shocks that are both the source and the propagation mechanism of the business cycle. This approach is most often associated with Kydland and Prescott, though there have been important contributions from others.

For Prescott, business cycles are natural phenomena and not necessarily a sign of any pathological malfunction of the economy. Like the Lucas framework, the emphasis is above all on adopting an equilibrium approach. Output fluctuations are optimal responses by rational agents who are in no way artificially rationed. To quote Prescott, 'Given the nature of the changing production possibility set, it would be puzzling if the economy did not display these large fluctuations in output and employment.'

For Prescott, no matter how well designed any set of macroeconomic policies, there will still be cycles as long as there is a random element to technical advance. Consequently, 'costly efforts at stabilization are likely to be counterproductive. Economic fluctuations are optimal responses to uncertainty in the rate of technological change.' Although Lucas finds this basic idea promising, he regards the neglect of monetary factors as a serious omission. Real business cycle theory can cast no light on inflation and the co-movements of output and prices. Lucas sees a well-thought-out integrated monetary sector grafted onto the technology cycle as the logical step forward, but cautions that such a model 'is, at present, slightly beyond the frontier of what is technically possible'.

If what Lucas suggests is beyond what is feasible, then current real business cycle theory is certainly close to the limits. Real business cycle theory is mathematically daunting. Having said that, if one is prepared to sacrifice one part of the elaborate real business cycle structure, it is easy enough to show the essential favour of the approach. Real business cycles are really very sophisticated growth models. Indeed, Prescott regarded it as a *grave* theoretical error to have separated growth theory and business cycle theory and to have treated them as if they were separate topics. Prescott advocates a unified approach. Stripped to its essentials, the real business cycle simply builds on the early neoclassical growth models such as those of Solow and Swan, which appeared in the latter half of the 1950s.

These early growth models had two basic characteristics, of which real business cycle theory is highly critical. The first has already been alluded to, which is the assumption of smooth technical advance. The second characteristic, which also typified Keynesian business cycle models, is mechanical and arbitrary rules of behaviour. For example, in the Solow growth model, savings, come what may, are always a constant fraction of income. Real business cycle theory replaces these mechanical rules with full-blooded rational expectations. Thus the consumer will formulate a consumption plan contingent on presently available information to maximize the present value of expected utility. This optimal plan will be subject to repeated revision as new information becomes available. It is the incorporation of rationality that makes such models so daunting.

What is proposed here is to offer a compromise. A growth model is analysed which embodies non-smooth technical advance, but which still adopts the mechanical rules of early growth models. This sacrifices quite a lot, but has the clear advantage of getting across the essential nature of the process in a much more accessible way. Indeed, adding 'lumpy' technical advance to a standard neoclassical growth model hardly involves much difficulty at all. It is easy to see how such shocks can generate cycles with inbuilt momentum or persistence.

The first task is, therefore, to review the standard Solow neoclassical growth model. This consists of three elements. First, there is a constant growth rate in the working population described by

$$L(t) = L(0)e^{nt} \tag{5-27}$$

where $L(t)$ is the current population and n is the *smooth* exponential growth rate. The second feature is a production function, which exhibits constant returns to scale, given by

$$Q(t) = f(K(t), L(t)e^{\lambda t}) \tag{5-28}$$

where $Q(t)$ is output, $K(t)$ is the capital stock and $L(t)$ is employment once more. Technical advance, which is of the Harrod-neutral labour augmenting kind, also occurs at the smooth rate λ. For simplicity, there is no depreciation and since this is a one-sector model, current savings represent additions to the capital stock. Hence:

$$\frac{dK(t)}{dt} = sQ(t) \tag{5-29}$$

where s is the savings ratio. Equation (5-29) is the mechanical rule and the task is to solve the dynamic system embodied in the above three equations. The labour supply in efficiency units can be defined as

$$\bar{L}(t) = L(t)e^{\lambda t}. \tag{5-30}$$

It is convenient to work in per efficiency unit terms, so redefine Eq. (5-28) as

$$q(t) = f(k(t)) \tag{5-31}$$

where $q(t) = Q(t)/\bar{L}(t)$ and $k(t)$ is capital per efficiency unit $(= K(t)/\bar{L}(t))$. The transformation (5-31) exploits the assumption of constant returns to scale. By definition,

$$\ln k(t) = \ln K(t) - \ln \bar{L}(t). \tag{5-32}$$

Hence, after differentiation,

$$\frac{Dk(t)}{k(t)} = \frac{sQ(t)}{K(t)} - (n + \lambda) \tag{5-33}$$

where $Dk(t) = dk(t)/dt$. Equation (5-33) can be rearranged to give

$$Dk(t) = sf(k(t)) - (n + \lambda)k(t). \tag{5-34}$$

This is a first-order non-linear differential equation—non-linear because of the $f(k(t))$ term. However, a qualitative graphic solution shows that Eq. (5-34) is stable, with an equilibrium value of $k(t)$ satisfying $sf(k^*) = (n + \lambda)k^*$.

The graphical solution is shown in Fig. 5-3, which plots $sf(k(t))$ and $(n + \lambda)k(t)$ as separate curves. The latter is just a straight line of slope $(n + \lambda)$ and the former cuts this line from above, assuming a well-behaved production function $f(k(t))$. Equilibrium occurs when $Dk(t) = 0$, that is, when $sf(k(t)) = (n + \lambda)k(t)$ and k^* is the value of $k(t)$ satisfying this.

This is shown as the point when capital per labour efficiency unit is k^*. Clearly, this equilibrium is stable, since to the left of k^*, savings per efficiency unit and described by the curve $sf(k(t))$ exceed $(n + \lambda)k(t)$ and hence $Dk(t) > 0$. Points to the right of k^* imply $Dk(t) < 0$ and the system will be moving back towards k^*. No explicit functional form for the path of k out of equilibrium can be given in the absence of a precise specification of $f(k(t))$. The problem asks you to derive a precise path for the Cobb Douglas case. Equilibrium can be expressed as the famous Solow condition:

$$\frac{s}{v} = n + \lambda \tag{5-35}$$

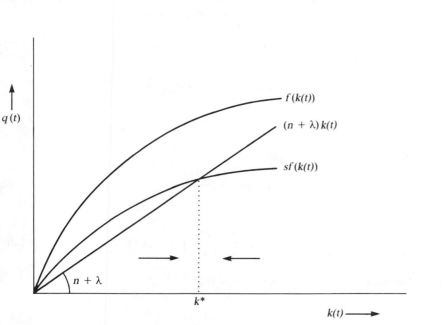

Figure 5-3 The neoclassical growth model

where v is the capital-to-output ratio:

$$v = \frac{k^*}{f(k^*)} = \frac{K(t)}{L(t)e^{\lambda t}f(k^*)} = \frac{K(t)}{Q(t)}. \tag{5-36}$$

The steady state k^* implies that $K(t)$ grows at the rate $n + \lambda$, output at $n + \lambda$ and output and capital per head at the rate of technical advance λ. With smooth technical advance there are no cycles. But note that the model contains all the requirements for an inbuilt propagation mechanism. Suppose, for example, due to some shock $k(t)$ was above k^*. Output will therefore be above its trend growth rate path. Given the differential equation, $k(t)$ will now converge back to k^*, but this will not occur instantaneously. Consequently, there is a natural tendency for momentum or serial correlation in output and other series when the system is subjected to shocks.

Before pursuing the main theme, an interesting digression is to locate the so-called golden rule consumption path. Consumption per efficiency unit is the difference between the $f(k(t))$ line and the $sf(k(t))$ line. Clearly, if $s = 0$ there would be no consumption, since there would be no capital stock. Similarly, if $s = 1$ there would be no consumption because everything would be saved! The golden rule locates the value of s which gives, in the steady state, the maximum value of consumption per head. It is important to note that consumption per head always grows at the rate λ in a steady state, irrespective of the value of s (aside from the extreme cases); the golden rule locates the maximum level of consumption per head that can grow at the rate λ.

In fact, the golden rule can be found quite easily from Fig. 5-3. Consumption per efficiency unit is just the gap between $f(k(t))$ and $sf(k(t))$. Since the steady state must occur along the $(n + \lambda)k(t)$ line, consumption per head at any point in time must be highest at the maximum gap. This occurs when $df(k^*)/dk^* = f'(k^*) = n + \lambda$. More formally, consider an explicit expression for consumption per head in a steady state:

$$(1 - s)\frac{Q(t)}{L(t)} = (1 - s)f(k^*)e^{\lambda t} = [f(k^*) - (n + \lambda)k^*]e^{\lambda t}. \tag{5-37}$$

The golden rule requires this to be maximized. Hence, differentiating gives

$$f'(k^*) = \rho = n + \lambda = \frac{s}{v} \tag{5-38}$$

where ρ is the profit rate. To see this, note that

$$Q(t) = L(t)e^{\lambda t}f(k^*). \tag{5-39}$$

Hence,

$$\rho = \frac{\partial Q(t)}{\partial K(t)} = L(t)e^{\lambda t}f'(k^*)\left[\frac{dk^*}{dK(t)}\right] = f'(k^*). \tag{5-40}$$

The golden rule therefore has $s = \rho v$, which means that

$$sQ(t) = \frac{\rho Q(t)k^*}{f(k^*)} = \rho K(t). \tag{5-41}$$

Hence the golden rule requires that

$$S = \Pi \qquad (5\text{-}42)$$

where S are total savings and Π are total profits. Golden rules are to economists what magic numbers are to mathematicians, and are likewise the subject of much fascinating discussion.

No explicit solution of Eq. (5-34) is possible unless a specific functional form is given for $f(k(t))$. However, the interest here is in qualitative information and, in particular, to understand the source and propagation mechanism of the technology cycle. Given this goal, it is not necessary to make specific assumptions about $f(k(t))$, beyond assuming a well-behaved production function. The aim is to explore the general lie of the land rather than to produce a detailed map. A simple way to embody technology shocks is to modify the production function, Eq. (5-28), to

$$Q(t) = \gamma(t)f(K(t), L(t)e^{\lambda t}). \qquad (5\text{-}43)$$

The term $\gamma(t)$ embodies the idea of non-smooth technical advance. On average, $\gamma(t)$ would take the value unity, but sometimes it will be in excess of unity, reflecting a period in which there was a 'technological burst'. Periods with $\gamma(t)$ less than unity reflect times of technological slack. Figure 5-4 illustrates a possible case that Eq. (5-43) tries to capture. It shows how output might evolve for a constant $K(t)$ and $L(t)$ but with a varying $\gamma(t)$. With this modification, Eq. (5-34) is easily seen to become

$$Dk(t) = s\gamma(t)f(k(t)) - (n + \lambda)k(t). \qquad (5\text{-}44)$$

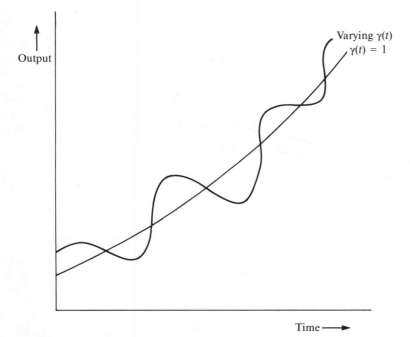

Figure 5-4 Technological shocks

Needless to say, the dynamics of Eq. (5-44) are potentially a lot more complicated than Eq. (5-34). The crucial point to put across is not, however, very difficult to comprehend—namely, the fact of momentum or persistence in output in response to technology shocks. Figure 5-5 illustrates this. It reproduces Fig. 5-3, shown as the $sf(k(t))$ curve which obviously has $\gamma(t) = 1$. Also shown is a case where $\gamma(t) > 1$. Imagine that $\gamma(t) = 1$ had been maintained for a considerable time, so that the system was at the equilibrium point k^*. Now allow a positive technology shock with $\gamma(t) > 1$. It can be seen that the system will now start to move towards the new attractor k^{**}. Clearly, as the system moves towards its new attractor, output will be growing somewhat faster than its underlying trend rate $n + \lambda$.

Now let us see how persistence arises. Suppose $\gamma(t)$ reverts back to unity. Consequently, the original technology 'burst' has disappeared from the system. Output, however, will not immediately revert back to its old equilibrium trend path. The new attractor is the original k^*, and since $k(t) > k^*$, output will continue to be above the trend path even though the technology shock is no longer apparent. Eventually, output will revert to its trend rate, provided that there are no further shocks. Technology shocks, consequently, give *both* a source for the cycle and contain an inbuilt propagation mechanism, which gives this theory some advantage over the Lucas monetary business cycle described in the previous section.

The intuition behind the real cycle is thus surprisingly simple despite the complex structures built to explain them. Agents form a consumption plan based on available information and optimizing behaviour. A positive technological shock ensues, which results in a surprisingly high real wage. Optimal behaviour dictates that at least part of this wage surprise is saved, not consumed. Consequently, the capital stock is higher than it would

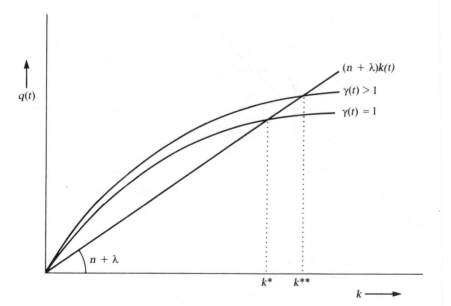

Figure 5-5 The real business cycle

otherwise be. Now, with the technology shock no longer present, its effects still linger in subsequent periods, because the higher than normal capital stock results in higher subsequent saving, higher capital and a continuing higher than normal output.

Population growth shocks could also lead to a cycle similar to the technology cycle. This is hardly surprising, given the fact that steady-state growth in a Solow model is just a composite of population growth and technological growth, $n + \lambda$. Consider a modified Eq. (5-27):

$$\frac{DL(t)}{L(t)} = n + \delta(t) \tag{5-45}$$

where $\delta(t) > 0$ indicates higher than normal growth and $\delta(t) < 0$ less than normal. Equation (5-34) is then modified to

$$Dk(t) = sf(k(t)) - (n + \lambda + \delta(t))k(t). \tag{5-46}$$

Here the cycle and persistence are generated by a pivoting of the $(n + \lambda + \delta(t))k(t)$ line as $\delta(t)$ varies.

As yet, the technology cycle is incomplete. Although a plausible story for output variations has been described, notice that the Solow growth model always assumes full employment; so far there is no unemployment story. Basically, the explanation of this latter point is the standard one of most equilibrium business cycle models, namely intertemporal substitution. When wages and (or) interest rates are temporarily high, there is a strong incentive to supply more labour now and consume more leisure when wages and interest rates are temporarily low. Such considerations reinforce the output variations and give rise to employment fluctuations. Referring back to Fig. 5-5, when $\gamma(t) > 1$ (here interpreted as a positive technological shock), wages are surprisingly high, growing somewhat faster than the trend rate λ. The interest rate is also temporarily high. The claim is that this will cause additional labour supply and have the opposite effect when output is below normal. In this theory, as in Lucas, the unemployed are everywhere and always a volunteer army. In a recent survey, Nickell concluded that estimated short-run labour supply elasticities are simply too small to support the intertemporal substitution idea fully.

Obviously, actual real business cycle models are a lot more complicated than described here. Kydland and Prescott, for example, lay particular emphasis on the fact that deferred consumption is not immediately convertible into capital, as is assumed here. The labour supply function is also unusual in that current utility involves lagged values of previous leisure, reinforcing intertemporal effects. Part of the Kydland and Prescott research agenda is to try to give, as far as possible, plausible parameter values for their equations and see how far their highly abstract constructions mimic actual business cycle behaviour, output, unemployment, hours of work and so on. Prescott concludes that, though far from perfect, 'the match between theory and observation is excellent'.

Despite its technical mastery, real business theory does have its critics, leaving aside the question of whether or not the equilibrium approach is itself a heroic over-simplification. Hoover makes the point that simply making a model more or less mimic actual behaviour is trivial. Rival theories could also be made to mimic actual data. As always in empirical work, researchers are reluctant to reveal the precise number of man-hours expended before the excellent match between theory and observation was achieved.

Hoover makes the second point that it is very difficult to formally identify a technological shock. Although productivity growth shows a strong procyclical trend, with output per head higher than the trend at the peaks, the problem is that much of this is the *result* of booms and slumps, and not the cause. For a variety of reasons, it takes time for businesses to adjust their labour stocks downwards in a slump to the most cost-efficient level. Firms are said to hoard labour, which lowers productivity. Simply taking deviations from a trend as an indicator of technology shocks is a dangerous exercise in circular reasoning. Technology shocks may indeed exist, but it is simply always going to be somewhat problematical to identify them exactly.

That concludes the review of the equilibrium business cycle. It certainly represents a sharp counterpoint to the smug Keynesianism of the 1950s and 1960s. In a sense the equilibrium approach, with its strong emphasis on *laissez-faire*, non-intervention and freedom of choice, is a reaction against the patrician class of interventionists. It is tempting to sympathize with the equilibrium approach as a political agenda. An interventionist philosophy implies that there will be a class of interveners. This implies giving considerable power and prestige to an élite caste at the centre. It is always irritating to observe an élite caste benignly claiming to be doing good for others, sacrificing the best of themselves on behalf of the lower orders, while in reality doing well for themselves. Identikit capitalists selfishly pursuing their own interests are much less hypocritical figures.

Being wrong for the best of motives still means being wrong, no matter how much one might sympathize with the philosophy. Phelps sums it up thus:

Lying behind this enterprise, I suspect, is a methodological motive: to show that economics can proceed throughout, on the axiom that the world is Pareto-optimal. So one watches in fascination as some of our most brilliant people engage in this odds-defying experiment, and I must admit to being in some suspense myself over how far they get before it is widely judged that Pareto optimality can go no further.

A Keynesian, without necessarily being smug, need only point to Fig. 5-1 and note that cycles were least severe when Keynesian ideas were in the ascendant. Keynesians need only say, 'It is you, not us, that have the most explaining to do.'

PROBLEM

5-3 In a one-commodity Solow growth model, output is given by

$$Q(t) = (K(t))^\alpha (L(t))^{1-\alpha}$$

where $Q(t)$ is output, $K(t)$ is the capital stock and $L(t)$ is employment. Employment grows at the smooth exponential rate n per annum and there is no technical advance. Savings are a constant proportion of output.

(*a*) Derive the golden rule *per capita* capital stock.
(*b*) Show that the golden rule savings ratio s is just α.
(*c*) Derive an explicit solution for the out of equilibrium behaviour of the *per capita* capital stock.
(*d*) Suppose the initial *per capita* stock was 200 units. How long would it take for the *per capita* capital stock to reach 90 per cent of its equilibrium value, assuming that the golden rule savings ratio prevailed? Assume $n = 0.02$ and $\alpha = 0.4$.

5-4 SUMMARY

This chapter has shown that the term 'equilibrium' can be used in two distinct senses by economists. For a Keynesian it means a point of rest, not necessarily at full employment. For New Classicals it essentially means market clearing. These issues are of supreme importance since it broadly defines opposing camps of 'interventionists', who believe in active macroeconomic management, and a contrasting 'hands off' approach with a strong belief in the self-organizing power of free markets.

APPENDIX

Solving Eq. (5-7)

λ_1 and λ_2 are given by $\beta + vi$ and $\beta - vi$, where $v = \sqrt{\beta - \beta^2}$ and $i = \sqrt{-1}$. The trick is to express these in polar coordinates. Thus:

$$\beta \pm vi = R(\cos \theta \pm i \sin \theta) \tag{A5-1}$$

where $\sin \theta = v/R$ and $\cos \theta = \beta/R$. There is nothing mysterious about this. The complex number $\beta + vi$ is pinned down by a knowledge of β and v. Equation (A5-1) simply re-expresses this, using θ and R as the 'equivalent' of β and v. For convenience, θ is expressed in radians where $360°$, the whole circle, is simply 2π radians. Figure A5-1 shows the relationship between β and v and the polar coordinates. For further reference note that

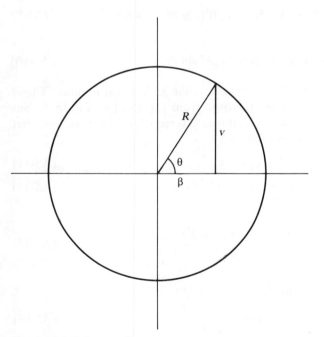

Figure A5-1 Polar coordinates

the Pythagoras theorem requires that

$$R = \sqrt{\beta^2 + v^2}.$$ (A5-2)

Now since $v^2 = \beta - \beta^2$, it follows that $R = \sqrt{\beta}$.

The next stage is to note that

$$(\beta \pm vi)^t = R^t(\cos \theta t \pm i \sin \theta t).$$ (A5-3)

This is De Moivre's theorem and can be derived as follows. First note the following trigonometric relationships, which are stated without proof:

$$\cos(\theta_1 + \theta_2) = \cos \theta_1 \cos \theta_2 - \sin \theta_1 \sin \theta_2$$ (A5-4)

$$\sin(\theta_1 + \theta_2) = \sin \theta_1 \cos \theta_2 + \cos \theta_1 \sin \theta_2.$$ (A5-5)

Now evaluate $(\beta + vi)^2$ by squaring (A5-1) directly. This gives:

$$(\beta + vi)^2 = R^2(\cos \theta \cos \theta + 2i \sin \theta \cos \theta + i^2 \sin \theta \sin \theta).$$ (A5-6)

Noting that $i^2 = -1$ and applying Eq. (A5-4) to the first and third terms and Eq. (A5-5) to the middle term, gives

$$(\beta + vi)^2 = R^2(\cos 2\theta + i \sin 2\theta).$$ (A5-7)

Generalizing in an obvious way gives

$$(\beta \pm vi)^t = R^t(\cos \theta t \pm i \sin \theta t).$$ (A5-8)

The solution to Eq. (5-5) can therefore be written as

$$Y_t = \bar{Y} + c_1 R^t(\cos \theta t + i \sin \theta t) + c_2 R^t(\cos \theta t - i \sin \theta t)$$ (A5-9)

or

$$Y_t = \bar{Y} + A_1 R^t \cos \theta t - A_2 R^t \sin \theta t$$ (A5-10)

where $A_1 = c_1 + c_2$ and $A_2 = i(c_2 - c_1)$. Note, however, that A_2 is a real number. Thus i can be regarded as a 'catalyst' which enables us to go from Eq. (5-6) to Eq. (5-7), but which, in the final analysis, disappears from the solution. To see why A_2 is real, note that from the starting values Y_0 and Y_1 it follows that

$$Y_0 = \bar{Y} + c_1 + c_2$$ (A5-11)

$$Y_1 = \bar{Y} + c_1(\beta + vi) + c_2(\beta - vi).$$ (A5-12)

Readers can easily verify that

$$i(c_2 - c_1) = \frac{\bar{Y} - Y_1 + (Y_0 - \bar{Y})\beta}{v}$$ (A5-13)

which is real.

Now write A_1 and A_2 in polar coordinates as

$$A_1 = A \cos \varepsilon$$ (A5-14)

$$A_2 = A \sin \varepsilon.$$ (A5-15)

Substituting these into Eq. (A5-10) gives

$$Y_t = \bar{Y} + AR^t(\cos \theta t \cos \varepsilon - \sin \theta t \sin \varepsilon) \qquad (A5\text{-}16)$$

which, using Eq. (A5-4) again, can be written compactly as

$$Y_t = \bar{Y} + AR^t(\cos \theta t + \varepsilon) \qquad (A5\text{-}17)$$

where A and ε are determined by the initial conditions and are the amplitude and phase of the cycle respectively. R is known as the damping factor and is determined, along with θ, from λ_1 and λ_2. The damping factor is of particular interest, since this will determine whether the cycle is explosive or converges. Obviously, if $R < 1$ then the cycle is damped. We know that R is just $\sqrt{\beta}$, hence it is very easy to tell whether the cycle converges just by inspection of the coefficient associated with Y_{t-2}. This is true, incidentally, not just in this instance but of any second-order linear difference equation with complex roots.

The period is $2\pi/\theta$, since $t = 2\pi/\theta$ is the time required to complete one cycle. From Fig. A5-1 it can be seen that $\tan \theta = v/\beta$, which enables θ to be calculated from the characteristic equation of Eq. (5-4).

ESSAY TOPICS

5-1 What distinguishes the 'equilibrium' approach to business cycles from the 'disequilibrium' approach?

5-2 Can the business cycle ever be eliminated?

5-3 Outline the common features and the main differences between the real business cycle and the Lucas monetary cycle.

5-4 'Business cycles are best understood by economic historians and not by theorists.' Discuss.

5-5 'Without a satisfactory theory to explain the momentum or persistence inherent in business cycles, then such explanations are seriously deficient.' Discuss.

READING

As with most of the topics in this book, Hoover (1988) offers an excellent discussion of the topics. The early data from Fig. 5-1 are from Wood (1909) and the discussion on the costs of business cycles is taken from Lucas (1987). The latter reference is a particularly useful summary of the Lucas assessment of alternative approaches. The early business cycle model is taken from Metzler (1941). Samuelson (1939) and Hicks (1950) are also classic references of this genre. For solution methods, Allen (1959) once again is extremely useful and Chapter 4 of that text gives an excellent discussion of complex numbers. There are many excellent discussions of the Lucas business cycle. Lucas (1977) is a highly readable, non-technical account, whereas Lucas (1973) is somewhat more technical and offers some empirical support. Hall and Taylor (1986) give a good account at a more moderate level than here and Attfield *et al.* (1985) is slightly more advanced and offers a comprehensive review of the empirical evidence. Lucas claims Hayek (1933) to be the true progenitor of his ideas, with Friedman and Schwarz (1963) the progenitor of the monetary dimension of the cycle. The classic reference for the real business cycle is Kydland and Prescott (1982).

It has to be said that this is one for mathematical mandarins only. Prescott (1986) is somewhat more discursive, but still fairly difficult. Blanchard and Fischer (1989) offer an excellent account at one level of difficulty beyond this text, and is highly recommended. Nickell (1990) also presents a real business cycle. It is useful in that the issues are viewed from a labour economics perspective rather than a purely macroeconomic one and discusses evidence for intertemporal substitution. My account of the real business cycle is based on the growth models of Solow (1956) and Swan (1956). Allen (1967) gives a comprehensive review of growth theory, which Prescott claims is the progenitor of the real business cycle. Finally, Taylor (1974) and Leslie and Laing (1978) discuss labour hoarding and the issue of non-constant technical advance. The final quotation is from Phelps (1990), which is easy bedtime reading. A recent and important text, adopting neither a purely classical view (equilibrium is non-market clearing) nor Keynesian (there is a long-run natural rate of unemployment) is Layard *et al.* (1991). This text offers considerable empirical evidence of UK and OECD country labour market experience since 1945 and puts considerable emphasis on the issue of hysteresis.

6

UNCERTAINTY

In an excellent text, *Uncertainty in Microeconomics*, John Hey stressed the importance of uncertainty. 'Uncertainty is everywhere; it pervades every facet of life. Uncertainty affects everyone. From the cradle to the grave we are all confronted by uncertainty; however hard we may try to avoid it, the problem of taking decisions in partial ignorance of their consequences remains ever present.' Uncertainty pervades macroeconomics—it is not just a feature of microeconomic decision-making! The Lucas business cycle of the previous chapter is a good example of decision-making in the presence of uncertainty and of how partial ignorance can change economic outcomes. This chapter will give several other examples.

Much of macroeconomic theory is conducted within a framework of perfect information or certainty. This is just a convenient simplification, useful for some purposes, but inadequate in many other contexts. The general reality is that decisions must be taken when the exact consequences will not be known in advance. Economic decision-making is more often than not a question of gambling or taking chances. One approach to uncertainty is to argue that since outcomes are not predictable, choices might as well be random and therefore we should just trust our fortunes to pure luck alone. If this were the case, economists might as well pack their bags and train for a new career. The *raison d'être* of economic theory is that agents are systematic, purposeful maximizers, even in the presence of uncertainty. Analysing such behaviour is difficult, but not impossible.

The dominant, but by no means exclusive, paradigm within the profession for the systematic treatment of uncertainty is the von Neumann–Morgenstern utility theory, or 'expected utility maximization', as it is often called. This will be referred to as the VM approach in what follows. The VM approach is applied so often and in such a variety of contexts that it can be classified as a basic analytical tool. It is essential knowledge for any economist claiming to be well trained. Once learned, the VM approach can be applied to a variety of problems involving uncertainty. The problem is that many learn to *apply* the idea mechanically, without ever bothering to understand precisely what is involved. This chapter aims to give a thorough understanding of the underlying principles that make the VM approach work in the way that it does.

In an uncertain world modelling agents as expected value maximizers, rather than expected utility maximizers, means more often than not giving an inaccurate description of how people behave. Consider the following example, involving the government in a choice between two policy regimes, A and B. Regime A is a gamble offering unemployment of 20 per cent with probability 1/2 and unemployment of 8 per cent with probability 1/2. Such a regime might be the sudden policy change case illustrated in Fig. 3-5 of Chapter 3. If the policy is believed, then the economy goes to U^*, giving 8 per cent unemployment in this example; if not, the economy goes to Z, giving 20 per cent unemployment. Regime B, by contrast, offers 15 per cent unemployment with certainty. Which policy regime should be chosen? Under regime A, expected unemployment is the lowest, namely 14 per cent—that is, half of 20 per cent plus half of 8 per cent. If the criterion was to minimize expected unemployment, then regime A is certainly the best one. However, regime A involves more risk than regime B. There is a 50 per cent probability of ending up with an unemployment rate higher than that guaranteed by regime B. The government might actually prefer regime B because of the lower risks involved. Any theory of uncertainty which has claims to *generality* must take account of such risk factors affecting decision-making. The whole point about the VM approach is that it does take account of the riskiness of outcomes and treats them in a systematic way. Modelling agents as expected value maximizers (or, in the context of the example, an expected value minimizer) are likely to be very inaccurate, as the example just given has demonstrated.

Sections 6-1 and 6-2 give the theoretical basis for the VM approach and describe what exactly a VM utility indicator is. The subsequent sections examine two classic macroeconomic applications of the idea. The first is Tobin's theory of portfolio choice and the second examines the instrument–objective problem in the presence of uncertainty, first developed by Brainard. In fact, it turns out that both problems have a common structure, despite analysing such disparate problems. Very often, good economic research is about identifying the common structure of a wide range of seemingly separate problems.

6-1 THE THEORY OF EXPECTED UTILITY MAXIMIZATION

The strategy will be to describe precisely what a VM utility indicator is, why it works and the assumptions required to make it work. Suppose in a particular problem context there are a set of basic outcomes labelled $Z_1, Z_2, \ldots$ up to Z_n. Each of the set of n basic outcomes can be perfectly general, for example Z_i could consist of a quite complicated bundle of commodities—so many cars, so many bottles of whisky and so on. In some problem contexts, the Z_i could consist of something rather simpler, such as units of wealth or money. Thus Z_i could be £5000, Z_j £2000 and so on. Later, the Z_i will be interpreted in this specific way, but the important point to note at this juncture is that the VM utility theory is *general* and the Z_i need not always be interpreted in a specific monetary way.

Consider the usual ordinal utility indicator, here denoted as $U(\ )$. This obeys the rule which says that if $U(Z_i) > U(Z_j)$, then the commodity bundle Z_i is preferred to Z_j and if $U(Z_i) = U(Z_j)$, then the individual is indifferent between these two commodity bundles.

That's all there is to it. Since we shall be using the terms 'is preferred to' and 'is indifferent to' rather frequently, we might as well adopt a convenient shorthand to summarize the above phrases. Let Z_i P $Z_j \equiv$ 'the individual prefers Z_i to Z_j' and Z_i I $Z_j \equiv$ 'the individual is indifferent between Z_i and Z_j'. Using this notation, two key properties of an ordinal utility indicator are the following. $U(Z_i) > U(Z_j)$ if and only if Z_i P Z_j and $U(Z_i) = U(Z_j)$ if and only if Z_i I Z_j. An obvious extra piece of notation would be $U(Z_i) \geq U(Z_j)$ if and only if Z_i IP $Z_j \equiv$ 'the individual is indifferent between or prefers Z_i to Z_j'.

A VM utility indicator will be denoted as $V(\ )$ to distinguish it from the usual ordinal utility indicator. It is important to realize that a VM utility indicator and the ordinal utility indicator are not the same. In fact, the VM utility indicator is rather more powerful in that it could also serve as an ordinal utility indicator in problems restricted to certainty. By contrast, an ordinal utility indicator would not, in general, be admissible in problems involving uncertainty. The immediate task is to explain why this is so and to clarify what a VM utility indicator is.

Without any loss of generality, let the basic outcomes be ranked from Z_1 (the most preferable) to Z_n (the least preferable). Thus Z_1 IP Z_2, Z_2 IP Z_3 and so on down to Z_{n-1} IP Z_n, though to make the theory non-trivial we should impose Z_1 P Z_n. The key to understanding the VM utility indicator and expected utility maximization is to consider a thought experiment in which each of the $V(Z_i)$ can be interpreted as *equivalent probabilities*.

Let us define a 'standard gamble' as one which offers the agent a chance of the best alternative Z_1 with probability p and a chance of the worst alternative Z_n with probability $1 - p$. Now consider a particular Z_i and compare this with the set of gambles formed by allowing p to vary from 1 to 0. Since Z_1 IP Z_i, being offered Z_1 with probability 1 would certainly be IP Z_i. Similarly, since Z_i IP Z_n, being offered Z_i with probability 1 would certainly be IP Z_n. The claim is that there will be a certain probability between 1 and 0 (inclusive) at which the individual would be indifferent between the offer of Z_i and the standard gamble. Denote this probability as v_i. This indifference can be summarized using the following notation:

$$Z_i \text{ I}[v_i Z_1; (1 - v_i)Z_n] \qquad (6\text{-}1)$$

where $[v_i Z_1; (1 - v_i)Z_n]$ represents the gamble or lottery ticket in question. A v_i can be found for each of the Z_i. Clearly, v_1 is 1 because Z_1 is only equivalent to the standard gamble which offers Z_1 with certainty. By the same reasoning $v_n = 0$. Hence,

$$V(Z_1) = 1 \qquad (6\text{-}2)$$

and

$$V(Z_n) = 0. \qquad (6\text{-}3)$$

For other alternatives the v_i may take intermediate values. Such v_i can be used as a VM utility indicator. Thus $V(Z_i) = v_i$. Once this point is grasped, one is a long way towards understanding the VM approach. Just think of the VM indicator as representing equivalent probabilities. It will be seen later that this indicator is not unique. Equations (6-2) and (6-3) represent a convenient scaling that enables us to retain the equivalent probability interpretation.

If the plausible condition that preferences among standard gambles are ranked according to the probability p of securing the good outcome rather than the bad (this is called the monotonicity assumption), the VM indicator will also be admissible as an ordinal utility indicator. This follows because if $v_i \geq v_j$ then, from the monotonicity assumption, Z_i IP Z_j. Thus the v_i satisfy the required property for an ordinal utility indicator expressing preferences across certain outcomes. But the converse is not necessarily true; an ordinal utility indicator that only respects preferences among certain outcomes need not be consistent with the values produced by the foregoing thought experiment to produce the VM utility indicator, even if it is required to satisfy $U(Z_1) = 1$ and $U(Z_n) = 0$. The VM utility indicator is clearly different from the ordinal $U(\ )$ indicator and is, in a real sense, more 'useful'. Note that any particular v_i probability is entirely subjective. It does not, in any sense, measure an objective probability that such an outcome will occur. It is simply the answer to a thought experiment which makes the individual indifferent between a certain outcome and the gamble described by Eq. (6-1). Different individuals are likely to have different values for v_i.

An example helps show at an intuitive level why the v_i are a promising way of incorporating attitudes to risk. Suppose Z_1 represents £1000, Z_n represents £0 and Z_i represents £500. The actuarial fair gamble would be the one which offered an expected return equal to Z_i. Obviously, this would be Z_1 with probability $1/2$ and Z_n with probability $1/2$. Now the v_i need not be, and in general would not be, equal to the actuarial fair gamble $1/2$. A risk-averse individual might set v_i far in excess of $1/2$ before being indifferent between Z_i and the standard gamble. For example, it is entirely possible that a highly risk-averse individual might only be indifferent between £500 with certainty and the gamble offering £0 with probability 0.01 and £1000 with probability 0.99. Thus $V(500) = 0.99$ in this case. A risk lover, by contrast, sets v_i below the actuarial fair gamble.

The VM approach is all about worlds characterized by uncertainty and it is hardly surprising that the thought experiment used to construct the utility indicator involves comparing risky outcomes. If you believe that individuals are incapable of the calculus just described, then the VM approach is not for you. Of course, we do not have to claim that individuals literally calculate the v_i probabilities, only that they behave 'as if' they are capable of handling such probability concepts. A world-class snooker or pool player can still pot balls without any understanding of the laws of Newtonian physics.

The VM utility indicator can be evaluated for each of the Z_i and is denoted as $V(Z)$. An uncertain world, involving the basic outcomes $Z_1, \ldots, Z_n$, can be described by a series of lottery tickets or gambles. It sounds artificial but it is actually a sensible way of characterizing uncertainty, when decisions must be made in advance of precise knowledge about outcomes. Suppose there are K such lottery tickets, where the L^j ticket is described by

$$L^j = [p_1^j Z_1; p_2^j Z_2; \cdots; p_n^j Z_n].$$ (6-4)

The probability of Z_1 occurring is p_1^j and so on, with the probabilities summing to 1 and, of course, some of the probabilities could be zero. Note, most importantly, that the probability terms in Eq. (6-4) are not in any way connected with the v_i terms described by Eq. (6-1). The former terms reflect the individual's beliefs as to the likelihood of any particular set of outcomes. For example, the L^j could reflect the roll of a die in which case the probabilities in Eq. (6-4) would be set at $1/6$ (at least, most rational individuals would set them at $1/6$). An alternative lottery ticket L^i could reflect the toss of a coin, in which case the probabilities would be set at $1/2$.

The individual's decision problem is as follows. Out of the K lottery tickets on offer, one must be chosen. The VM utility indicator gives an easy way of deciding which among the K lottery tickets will be preferable. Describing the world as making a choice among a set of available lottery tickets accurately reflects the presence of uncertainty. Many decisions must be made *ex ante*, before the state of nature is revealed. Choices are described as access to lottery tickets because there is uncertainty as to what state of nature will prevail when the decision is made. Once the choice of lottery ticket is made, then the *ex post* state of nature is revealed, which is one among the Z_i set of basic outcomes. Notice that *ex post* the individual may regret the *ex ante* choice of lottery ticket, but that is not the point. Going back to the regime A or regime B unemployment example, the government might *ex ante* decide on regime A as the best choice. *Ex post*, if the realized state of nature was unemployment of 20 per cent, obviously the government would regret not having chosen regime B in the first place. Uncertainty is all about being wrong sometimes for the best of reasons! Given the same circumstances, the government would choose regime A once again.

The individual will choose that lottery ticket which is *ex ante* the most preferable. The beauty of the VM approach is that it gives an extremely easy way of calculating the most preferable choice. For each L^j calculate the following:

$$V(L^j) = \sum_{i=1}^{n} p_i^j V(Z_i). \tag{6-5}$$

Notice that the right-hand side of Eq. (6-5) is just the expected value of the VM utilities of the basic outcomes, where the 'utilities' are, note, just the v_i probabilities as defined by Eqs (6-1), (6-2) and (6-3). The VM approach shows that $V(L^j) \geq V(L^i)$ if and only if L^j IP L^i. This is an amazingly powerful result because it gives an extremely easy way of locating the best choice—namely, it must be the one with the highest expected utility as defined by Eq. (6-5). This explains why the VM approach often goes under the alternative title of 'expected utility maximization'.

In many economic contexts the basic outcomes could be monetary values—though this is not necessary, as has been stressed. In this case, the shape of the VM utility indicator can be given a useful interpretation. To give an example of this, let $V(\pi)$ be a VM utility indicator for a firm's profits. This is shown as a concave function in Fig. 6-1 where the upper level of profits is shown as π_1 and the lower level as π_N. Figure 6-1 assigns a utility of 1 to π_1 and a utility of 0 to π_N. (As mentioned, this scaling is arbitrary, as will shortly be seen, but it is useful to keep it at this stage so that the $V(\pi)$ indicator can be directly interpreted in terms of equivalent probabilities.) Consider $V(\pi_i)$, where π_i lies somewhere between π_1 and π_N—not necessarily halfway. Remember $V(\pi_i)$ is just the probability v_i which makes this firm indifferent between the certain π_i and the lottery ticket described by $[v_i\pi_1; (1 - v_i)\pi_N]$. Now the actuarial fair gamble is the probability which makes the expected value of the gamble $= \pi_i$. This is the p_i with the property

$$p_i\pi_1 + (1 - p_i)\pi_N = \pi_i. \tag{6-6}$$

Given this, it takes little thought to recognize that p_i for any π_i simply lies along the straight line segment between π_1 and π_N. The p_i for the particular π_i in question is illustrated in Fig. 6-1. The fact that $V(\pi_i) > p_i$ in Fig. 6-1 indicates risk aversion. The firm is not prepared to accept the actuarial fair gamble. The odds would have to be shifted in the firm's favour—namely, to at least v_i—before the gamble would be accepted.

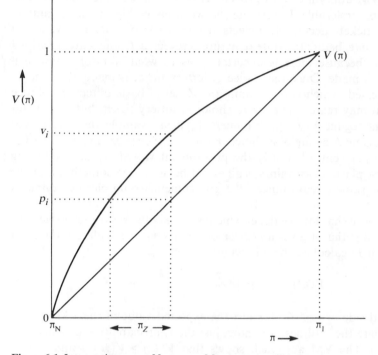

Figure 6-1 Interpreting a von Neumann–Morgenstern utility function

An alternative interpretation of Fig. 6-1, which amounts to the same thing, is the following. If the firm was offered π_i with certainty it would get $V(\pi_i) = v_i$. If, however, offered the lottery ticket $[p_i\pi_i; (1 - p_i)\pi_N]$ this would then give an expected utility of $p_i V(\pi_1) + (1 - p_i)V(\pi_N) = p_i$. Since $V(\pi_i)$ exceeds p_i the firm prefers the risk-free certain outcome π_i to the lottery ticket. Shown also is the amount π_Z, which is the risk premium. This is the fall in profits below the actuarial fair gamble that the firm is prepared to accept in order to avoid risk. The conclusion of this discussion is that a risk-averse firm can be described as having a concave utility function with $V'(\pi) > 0$ and $V''(\pi) < 0$. By contrast, a risk-neutral firm would have a linear utility function, and a risk-loving firm a convex function with $V''(\pi) > 0$.

Before describing why the VM approach works, let us consider an example to demonstrate its power. As the example is somewhat difficult in places, readers can proceed directly to Sec. 6-2 if they wish. The example considers the employment decision of a firm facing uncertain outcomes, first discussed by Sandmo. The firm's profits are given by

$$\pi = \bar{Z}f(l) - Wl \qquad (6\text{-}7)$$

where $\bar{Z}$ is the price of output, l is employment and W the money wage. In a certain world $\bar{Z}$ is fixed, so profits are maximized when

$$\frac{\mathrm{d}\pi}{\mathrm{d}l} = \bar{Z}f'(l^*) - W = 0 \qquad (6\text{-}8)$$

where l^* indicates the optimal l. The firm employs labour to the point where the marginal revenue product equals the money wage. Both the labour and product markets are assumed to be competitive in this example.

Now introduce uncertainty. This takes the form of the price being a random variable Z taking the values $Z_1, \ldots, Z_n$ with probabilities $p_1, \ldots, p_n$ respectively. Actually, Z could equally well be described as a continuous random variable, but we shall persevere with the discrete case, which the earlier theory has assumed. The choice of l must now be made before the precise value of Z is known. Each choice of l gives access to a particular lottery ticket. For example, a particular choice of employment denoted as l^j would give the lottery ticket

$$L^j = [p_1 \pi_1^j; p_2 \pi_2^j; \cdots; p_n \pi_N^j] \tag{6-9}$$

where

$$\pi_i^j = Z_i f(l^j) - W l^j. \tag{6-10}$$

Out of all the lottery tickets associated with the various values of l^j, which will the firm choose? The answer, according to the VM theory, is the one giving the highest level of expected utility. Let $V(\pi)$ be a VM utility indicator with $V' > 0$ and $V'' < 0$ to indicate a risk-averse firm. The problem, therefore, resolves itself to

$$\underset{l}{\text{Max:}} \quad E\{V(\pi)\} = \sum_{i=1}^{n} p_i V(Z_i f(l) - W l) = E\{V(Z f(l) - W l)\}. \tag{6-11}$$

Do not be intimidated by Eq. (6-11). This is no more difficult than Eq. (6-7); the differences are that Eq. (6-11) has n terms, whereas Eq. (6-7) has just one and π is replaced by $V(\pi)$. Differentiating gives

$$\frac{dE\{V(\pi)\}}{dl} = \sum_{i=1}^{n} p_i(Z_i f'(l^{**}) - W)V'(\pi) = 0 \tag{6-12}$$

where l^{**} is the new optimal choice of l. Assume that the second-order condition for a maximum also holds. Equation (6-12) can be written more succinctly as:

$$\frac{dE\{V(\pi)\}}{dl} = E\{(Z f'(l^{**}) - W)V'(\pi)\} = 0. \tag{6-13}$$

Notice that once Eq. (6-11) has been solved by laboriously writing out the expected value in longhand and then retrieving Eq. (6-13), the stochastic optimization result can be derived directly by treating the expectation exactly as if it were a problem like Eq. (6-7) but remembering always to retain the E operator in front of the expression. Of itself, Eq. (6-13) is not particularly useful until it is compared with some benchmark case. The obvious benchmark is the behaviour of the risk-neutral firm. The risk-neutral firm maximizes expected profits. This problem is

$$\underset{l}{\text{Max:}} \quad E\{\pi\} = \sum_{i=1}^{n} p_i(Z_i f(l) - W l). \tag{6-14}$$

Hence,

$$\frac{dE\{\pi\}}{dl} = \sum_{i=1}^{n} p_i(Z_i f'(l^*) - W) = \bar{Z} f'(l^*) - W = 0 \tag{6-15}$$

where $\bar{Z}$ is the mean of $Z = \sum p_i Z_i$. Equation (6-15) says that the risk-neutral firm chooses its employment level to make the expected marginal product equal to the wage. *Ex post*, if the realization of Z exceeds $\bar{Z}$, the marginal product will exceed the wage and the firm will regret not having hired more labour, and if the realization of Z is below $\bar{Z}$, the firm will regret having hired so much labour. The best decision for the risk-neutral firm is embodied in Eq. (6-15). Some manipulation is necessary to compare this to the risk-averse decision in Eq. (6-13). First note:

$$(Z - \bar{Z})V'(\pi) < (Z - \bar{Z})V'(E\{\pi\}) \quad \text{when } Z > \bar{Z}. \tag{6-16}$$

This is because of risk aversion. If $Z > \bar{Z}$, then $\pi > E\{\pi\}$ and $V'(\pi) < V'(E\{\pi\})$, as can be seen from the concave shape of Fig. 6-1. Surprisingly, exactly the same inequality holds when $Z < \bar{Z}$. Why is this? When $Z < \bar{Z}$, $V'(\pi) > V'(E\{\pi\})$, but now $Z - \bar{Z}$ is negative. Multiplying $V'(\pi)$ by the *negative* number $Z - \bar{Z}$ means that inequality (6-16) must continue to hold. So inequality (6-16) holds for all values of Z, other than $Z = \bar{Z}$. Taking expectations gives

$$E\{(Z - \bar{Z})V'(\pi)\} < E\{(Z - \bar{Z})V'(E\{\pi\})\}. \tag{6-17}$$

But the r.h.s. of Eq. (6-17) is zero because $V'(E\{\pi\})$ is non-stochastic and $E\{Z - \bar{Z}\} = \bar{Z} - \bar{Z} = 0$. Hence,

$$E\{(Z - \bar{Z})V'(\pi)\} < 0. \tag{6-18}$$

Equation (6-13) can be re-expressed by subtracting $\bar{Z}f'(l^{**})E\{V'(\pi)\}$ from both sides. This gives

$$f'(l^{**})E\{(Z - \bar{Z})V'(\pi)\} = (W - \bar{Z}f'(l^{**}))E\{V'(\pi)\}. \tag{6-19}$$

The l.h.s. is negative (see Eq. (6-18)), hence $W - \bar{Z}f'(l^{**})$ must also be negative. The firm therefore employs *less* labour than the risk-neutral firm, given the diminishing marginal product of labour.

The intuition for this should be clear. A smaller labour force will punish bad states of nature less severely than a larger labour force. A risk-averse firm wishes to avoid (insofar as it is possible) making large losses by having too much labour on its books. Of course, the reverse side of the coin is that by having a smaller labour force at the outset, the firm will be unable to reap the maximum profit should a good state of nature ensue. The risk-averse firm must trade-off some expected profits in return for minimizing damage on the downside, so to speak. Such behaviour is surely a feature of many companies. However, it should be said that there is now a large literature, called 'implicit contracts', on the subject of how a firm might share risks with its labour force, which has important macroeconomic consequences. Chapter 8 explores some of these. This example has served to show how the expected utility calculus can be usefully applied to problems of considerable complexity.

PROBLEM

6-1 An agent has a von Neumann–Morgenstern utility indicator given by ln Z, where Z represents some basic monetary outcome.

(*a*) Does this utility indicator show risk aversion?

(*b*) The agent is offered the choice of two lottery tickets. The first gives 30 with probability $1/3$, 60 with probability $1/3$ and 90 with probability $1/3$. The second gives 0 with probability $1/3$, 60 with probability $1/3$ and 150 with probability $1/3$. With the utility indicator ln Z, which lottery ticket will be chosen?

(*c*) Calculate the risk premium associated with the lottery ticket offering 100 with probability $1/2$ and 200 with probability $1/2$ for ln Z.

(*d*) $V(\pi)$ is a von Neumann–Morgenstern utility indicator with the property of risk aversion. By plotting a diagram, show why $E\{V(\pi)\} < V(E\{\pi\})$. Give some explanation for this result.

6-2 PROOF OF THE VM EXPECTED UTILITY HYPOTHESIS

So far three assumptions have been made. First, the basic outcomes can be ranked in relation to each other. Secondly, preferences are transitive. Thus if Z_i IP Z_j and Z_j IP Z_k, this implies Z_i IP Z_k. The third is the continuity assumption, which is the claim that there does indeed exist a v_i for all Z_i, with the property Z_i I$[v_i Z_1; (1 - v_i)Z_n]$. Three further assumptions are required. The first and most controversial of these is the so-called 'independence of irrelevant alternatives' assumption. Suppose that Z_i I L, where L is some lottery ticket as described by Eq. (6-4). The independence assumption states that an individual will be indifferent between any two lottery tickets which differ only in the respect of one containing Z_i and the other containing L. Thus, given

$$L^1 = [p_1 Z_1; \ldots; p_i Z_i; \ldots; p_n Z_n] \tag{6-20}$$

and

$$L^2 = [p_1 Z_1; \ldots; p_i L; \ldots; p_n Z_n] \tag{6-21}$$

the independence assumption says L^1 I L^2 if Z_i I L. It is this critical assumption that makes the expected utility maximand, Eq. (6-5), always *linear* in the probabilities unlike the VM utilities themselves. Not everyone accepts that this is a reasonable description of actual behaviour. Experiments suggest that individuals do not always choose in a way consistent with this assumption.

The fifth assumption is the claim that agents can accurately calculate probabilities. They are not fooled by complex probabilistic alternatives. Consider the lottery ticket:

$$L^1 = [pC; (1 - p)Z_j] \tag{6-22}$$

where C is just any other lottery ticket such as

$$C = [qZ_i; (1 - q)Z_k]. \tag{6-23}$$

If offered the lottery ticket

$$L^2 = [pqZ_i; (p - pq)Z_k; (1 - p)Z_j] \tag{6-24}$$

the agent would be indifferent between L^1 and L^2. The above would apply to any combination of lottery tickets no matter how complex.

The final assumption is that of 'monotonicity' or rationality. This states that individuals prefer those gambles which offer the highest chance of winning. This has already been alluded to in the discussion of the relation between the ordinal indicator connected with certainty problems and the VM indicator. To be more formal about this, we already know that Z_1 P Z_n. Now comparing:

$$L^1 = [pZ_1; (1-p)Z_n] \quad \text{and} \quad L^2 = [qZ_1; (1-q)Z_n] \tag{6-25}$$

then L^1 P L^2 if and only if $p > q$.

These six assumptions are sufficient for the VM method to work. To show why, the first stage is to reduce any general lottery ticket to an equivalent one involving only the standard gamble between Z_1 and Z_n. Equivalent in this context means that the agent is indifferent between the two. Consider any lottery ticket

$$L = [p_1 Z_1; \ldots; p_i Z_i; \ldots; p_n Z_n]. \tag{6-26}$$

Assume the individual is indifferent between the following (standard gamble) lottery ticket and Z_i:

$$C_i = [v_i Z_1; (1-v_i)Z_n] \text{ I } Z_i. \tag{6-27}$$

Note *very carefully* that v_i is just the VM utility indicator of Z_i defined in Eq. (6-1). The independence of irrelevant alternatives assumption means that the following indifference relationship holds for L:

$$L \text{ I} [p_1 Z_1; \ldots; p_i C_i; \ldots; p_n Z_n]. \tag{6-28}$$

Apply Eq. (6-27) to all the Z_i to derive

$$L \text{ I} [p_1 C_1; \ldots; p_i C_i; \ldots; p_n C_n]. \tag{6-29}$$

Now apply the fifth assumption, which is that agents accurately apply the probability rule. Since the C_i are just combinations of Z_1 and Z_n, this gives

$$L \text{ I} \left[\sum_{i=1}^{n} p_i v_i Z_1; \left(1 - \sum_{i=1}^{n} p_i v_i \right) Z_n \right]. \tag{6-30}$$

Notice that $\sum p_i v_i = E\{V(L)\}$, which appears in Eq. (6-30), is nothing more than the expected utility of the lottery ticket L. So what has been proved so far? Given *any* lottery ticket L, the agent would be indifferent between this and another lottery ticket involving just Z_1 and Z_n providing that the probability of winning Z_1 was *exactly* the expected utility of L and the probability of winning Z_n necessarily 1 minus the expected utility of L. This is the key result, and the justification for using VM utilities is now virtually all over but for crossing the t's. Consider two lottery tickets

$$L^i \text{ I} [E\{V(L^i)\}Z_1; (1 - E\{V(L^i)\}Z_n] \tag{6-31}$$

and

$$L^j \text{ I} [E\{V(L^j)\}Z_1; (1 - E\{V(L^j)\}Z_n]. \tag{6-32}$$

Assumption six tells us which of these will be preferable. Remembering that $E\{V(L^i)\}$, the expected utility of the lottery ticket L^i, is just a probability associated with Z_1, then L^i IP L^j if and only if $E\{V(L^i)\} \geq E\{V(L^j)\}$. This proves the VM result. Any set of lottery tickets can be ranked in order of preference by simply calculating the expected value of the VM utility index. The one with the highest expected utility is the preferable one.

The useful scaling assumption $V(Z_1) = 1$ and $V(Z_n) = 0$ enabled the direct interpretation of any $V(Z_i)$ utility as a probability. However, the argument is valid for any values of $V(Z_1)$ and $V(Z_n)$ (providing only that $V(Z_1) > V(Z_n)$), so there is no *unique* VM utility indicator for any set of lottery tickets. To see this, suppose we work with another VM utility indicator $S(Z)$ with the property

$$S(Z_i) = a + bv_i = a + bV(Z_i), \quad b > 0 \tag{6-33}$$

then $S(Z)$ would also serve equally well as a VM utility indicator. Consider the expected utilities of the lottery tickets described in Eqs (6-31) and (6-32) using the new VM indicator. The difference in expected utilities is $E\{S(L^i)\} - E\{S(L^j)\}$ which is easily seen to be $b[E\{V(L^i)\} - E\{V(L^j)\}]$. Since b is a positive constant, $S(\ )$ will rank lotteries identically with the $V(\ )$ indicator. This shows that the VM utility indicator is unique only up to a linear transformation. As with the ordinal utility indicator of consumer demand theory, the concept of marginal utility has no significance. Diminishing or increasing marginal utility—the second derivative—does, however, have significance unlike ordinal utility theory; in Fig. 6-1 we indicated how it could be interpreted as showing attitudes towards risk.

PROBLEM

6-2 (*This is intended to make you think about the controversial 'independence of irrelevant alternatives' assumption.*) Suppose an agent is indifferent between the certain offer of £1 million and the gamble offering £1 billion with probability 0.8 and £0 with probability 0.2. Show that this implies that the agent is indifferent to £1 billion with probability 0.08 and £0 with probability 0.92 and the second gamble offering only £1 million with probability 0.1 and £0 with probability 0.9. Does this result agree with how people might actually behave?

6-3 FUNCTIONAL FORMS OF THE VM UTILITY INDICATOR

The discussion is restricted to the most common utility indicator $V(W)$, having the single argument W, usually but not always units of wealth or money. $V(W)$ is the general specification and for many purposes this is all that is required, beyond specifying whether the agent is a risk lover ($V'' > 0$) or is risk averse ($V'' < 0$). The example at the end of Sec. 6-1 illustrates this general approach and how useful results can be obtained. A basic principle of any theorist is that of *Occam's razor*: make the least number of assumptions to obtain a particular result. Minimalism implies a more powerful theory.

In many other contexts, working with a specific functional form for $V(W)$ will be a useful and necessary approximation, akin to assuming a Cobb Douglas production function or a Stone–Geary ordinal utility indicator. The first important type is the quadratic utility function. This specifies

$$V(W) = a + bW - 0.5cW^2, \quad b, c > 0 \tag{6-34}$$

where

$$V'(W) = b - cW > 0 \tag{6-35}$$

and

$$V''(W) = -c < 0. \tag{6-36}$$

Clearly, for $V'(W)$ to be positive requires b to be large enough for the range of possible values of W. Equation (6-36) assumes risk aversion, but risk loving could be assumed where necessary.

The useful feature of the quadratic utility function is that it allows risk to be characterized in an extremely suggestive way. Suppose that W is distributed with a mean of μ and variance of σ^2. With a quadratic utility function we can consider those combinations of μ and σ which give the same level of expected utility—or, to put it another way, once we know the mean and standard deviation of W we shall know the expected utility of W. Expected utility is

$$E\{V(W)\} = a + bE\{W\} - 0.5cE\{W^2\} \tag{6-37}$$

or

$$E\{V(W)\} = a + b\mu - 0.5c(\sigma^2 + \mu^2). \tag{6-38}$$

Equation (6-38) follows because the variance of W is $E\{W - \mu\}^2 \equiv \sigma^2 = E\{W^2\} - \mu^2$. Now totally differentiate Eq. (6-38):

$$dE\{V(W)\} = (b - c\mu)\,d\mu - c\sigma\,d\sigma. \tag{6-39}$$

On an indifference curve $dE\{V(W)\} = 0$, hence:

$$\frac{d\mu}{d\sigma} = \frac{c\sigma}{b - c\mu} > 0 \tag{6-40}$$

noting that $b - c\mu > 0$ from Eq. (6-35). The indifference curves slope upwards. The second derivative is

$$\frac{d^2\mu}{d\sigma^2} = \frac{c}{b - c\mu} + \frac{c^3\sigma^2}{(b - c\mu)^3} > 0. \tag{6-41}$$

Consequently, the indifference curves have the shape shown in Fig. 6-2. The mean return of W can be regarded as the 'good' and the standard deviation of the return on W can be regarded as the 'bad'. A higher σ means more risk, which must be compensated for by a higher mean return μ in the case of risk aversion. Notice that because $d\mu/d\sigma = 0$ when $\sigma = 0$, as can be seen from Eq. (6-40), then the indifference curves must start horizontal.

In general, this is the only case when risk can be specifically identified with the standard deviation of the distribution. The exception is the case when the distribution of W is just a two-parameter distribution. In this case, once the mean and standard deviation are known, everything else is known about the distribution. The normal distribution is the classic example of a two-parameter distribution. Indifference curves like Fig. 6-2 can then be drawn irrespective of the functional form of $V(W)$. The justification for this is not pursued here.

Another frequently used functional form is the Arrow–Pratt constant relative risk-aversion utility function. This is given by

$$V(W) = a + bW^{1-\gamma}. \tag{6-42}$$

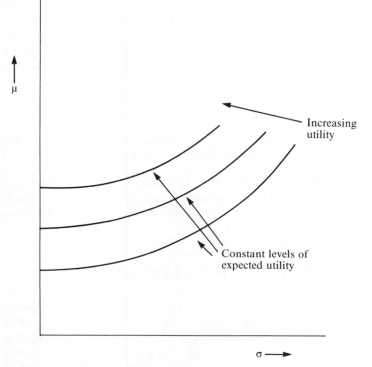

Figure 6-2 The quadratic utility function

Since any VM utility function is only unique up to a linear transformation, we might as well work with

$$V(W) = \frac{1}{1-\gamma} W^{1-\gamma}. \tag{6-43}$$

γ is the parameter of risk aversion, higher values of which indicate a greater degree of aversion. In the special case where $\gamma = 1$, the utility function reduces to the logarithmic function. This can be seen by first differentiating Eq. (6-43) and then setting $\gamma = 1$ and integrating back. Note that

$$V'(W) = W^{-\gamma} > 0 \tag{6-44}$$

and

$$V''(W) = -\gamma W^{-\gamma-1} < 0. \tag{6-45}$$

The particular property of the Arrow–Pratt utility function is that the negative of the elasticity of the marginal utility is constant ($= \gamma$). Thus:

$$-\frac{WV''(W)}{V'(W)} = \gamma. \tag{6-46}$$

Attitude to risk is, therefore, embodied in the single parameter γ. This was, in fact, the utility function adopted by Lucas to derive his estimate for the cost of macroeconomic fluctuations described in Chapter 5. The figure of around one-tenth of 1 per cent of GNP was based on the assumption of $\gamma = 20$, which is a high degree of risk aversion to give a very low cost. Lower values of γ would have made the cost of fluctuations even lower.

PROBLEMS

6-3 What must be the shape of the indifference curves of a quadratic utility function showing risk-loving behaviour? Are indifference curves convex to the origin ever possible with a quadratic utility indicator?

6-4 An individual's preferences are described by $(1 - \gamma)^{-1} C^{(1 - \gamma)}$, where C is consumption. The coefficient of risk-aversion parameter, γ, is 2. What proportion of consumption while employed is the individual prepared to give up to avoid a 5 per cent unemployment risk, if unemployment leads to a 50 per cent reduction in consumption?

6-4 APPLICATIONS OF EXPECTED UTILITY MAXIMIZATION

The first application will be Tobin's theory of portfolio choice. This is one of the classic articles in economic theory and Tobin is the father of the modern theory of finance. Tobin's theory was prompted by a general dissatisfaction with the Keynesian speculative motive for holding money and concerns how an individual investor might allocate wealth across different assets. In the simplest possible case there are just two assets; the first is a *certain* asset offering no return but no risk. We might as well call this certain asset money, though because of unpredictable inflation it is not necessarily true that money is a riskless asset. The second is an asset which offers a rate of return, but this return is risky, so there is a probability of a capital loss and an overall negative return as well as the possibility of capital gains giving higher than normal returns.

The Keynesian analysis predicted an all-or-nothing choice. If the agent believed that the overall expected return on the risky asset (including interest payments and capital gain) was positive, then all wealth would be placed in the risky asset. Otherwise, all wealth would be held as money. The problem with this approach is immediately apparent; in general, individuals hold diversified portfolios and do not put all their eggs into one basket in the way suggested by the Keynesian speculative motive. Tobin used the VM approach to explain diversified portfolios. Agents seek to maximize the expected utility of wealth, as described by the VM theory. He further assumed that the utility function was quadratic, or, alternatively, that wealth could be described as a two-parameter distribution. Consequently, indifference curves showing constant levels of expected utility could be shown in mean-standard deviation space, exactly as shown in Fig. 6-2.

To complete Tobin's theory, therefore, all that needs to be shown is the budget constraint. In the context of this particular problem, the trade-off will be between units of mean return and units of standard deviation. If the individual placed all wealth in money, the mean return would just be the original investment and a zero standard deviation, hence no risk. If all wealth was placed in the risky asset, this would offer the chance of the highest mean return but correspondingly the highest standard deviation or risk. The individual will choose that combination from the available set—the budget constraint—which maximizes expected utility.

The budget constraint is derived as follows. First, note the following relationship:

$$W = (W_0 - A) + A(1 + r + g) \tag{6-47}$$

where W is wealth. The initial endowment is W_0, which is allocated across bonds (the risky asset) at cost A and what remains, $W_0 - A$, is held as cash. The bond offers a rate of interest r, but there is also a risk to the return reflected in the random variable g. This is distributed with a mean of zero and a standard deviation of σ_g. The investor makes his or her decision *prior* to the realization of g. If, for example, the realization of g was such that $1 + r + g = 0$, then the investor would have lost all his or her money in the risky asset and realized wealth would simply be the amount held in cash. Actually, the set-up does not prevent $1 + r + g$ being negative—the investor could lose more than the original investment. Very few investments have this property (being an underwriter at Lloyds is one notable exception, as some of the erstwhile rich have discovered to their cost). The constraint $1 + r + g \geq 0$ could be imposed, however, such a consideration is really an unimportant embellishment to Tobin's theory. From Eq. (6-47) is derived the budget constraint. First, the mean return is

$$E\{W\} = \mu = W_0 + Ar \tag{6-48}$$

noting that $E\{g\} = 0$. Secondly, the standard deviation of return is

$$\sqrt{E\{W - E\{W\}\}^2} = \sigma = A\sigma_g. \tag{6-49}$$

Eliminating A then gives the budget constraint

$$\mu = W_0 + \left(\frac{r}{\sigma_g}\right)\sigma. \tag{6-50}$$

Figure 6-3 illustrates this. The indifference curves are exactly as in Fig. 6-2 and the budget constraint is the straight line with intercept W_0 and slope r/σ_g. The investor can allocate a portfolio anywhere along this line. If all of W_0 was allocated to A, this would offer the expected return $W_0(1 + r)$ and a maximum risk of $W_0\sigma_g$ as shown. The investor can choose anywhere on the line segment joining these points. It was established earlier that the indifference curves must start horizontal, consequently the investor must allocate at least part of W_0 to the risky asset. This is an uncomfortably strong conclusion, since introspection leads us to conclude that not all investors would wish to do this. The assumption of quadratic preferences appears to impose too much structure on the model.

The chosen point is the one that maximizes expected utility. Clearly, this implies the possibility of a *diversified* portfolio and Fig. 6-3 illustrates such a case, with expected utility maximized at D. The theory does not *necessarily* imply a diversified portfolio for risk-averse investors. A risk-averse individual may still choose to place all his or her wealth in all bonds, but not, as we have seen, all money. In terms of Fig. 6-3, all bonds would just be a corner solution, with the highest indifference curve at the top edge of the budget constraint.

Just as in ordinary consumer demand theory, the change in demand for the risky asset can be split into an income and substitution effect as the 'price' of risk alters. In the present context, this price is just the slope r/σ_g. A higher r or lower σ_g makes bonds less 'expensive' relative to money. The substitution effect should lead to more bonds being purchased but

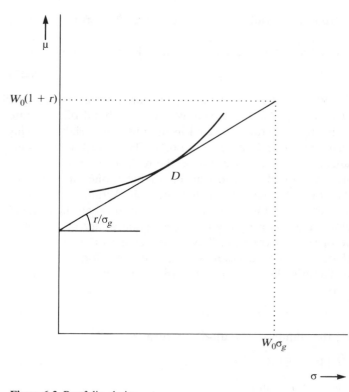

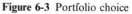

Figure 6-3 Portfolio choice

the possibility of a Giffen good arises with a large negative income effect dominating the substitution effect. Readers are invited to illustrate these possibilities.

Tobin's theory is easily generalized to describe portfolio choice problems across a broad class of risky assets—something which Tobin did in his original article. We shall consider the next most complex problem where the choice is between two risky assets. Obviously, nothing happens to the indifference curves, only the budget constraint becomes more complicated. Equation (6-47) is modified to

$$W = (W_0 - A)(1 + r_1 + g_1) + A(1 + r_2 + g_2) \tag{6-51}$$

where r_1 and $g_1 \sim (0, \sigma_{g_1}^2)$ refer to the first risky asset and r_2 and $g_2 \sim (0, \sigma_{g_2}^2)$ refer to the second. From this it follows that

$$E\{W\} = \mu = W_0 + (W_0 - A)r_1 + Ar_2 \tag{6-52}$$

and

$$E\{W - E\{W\}\}^2 = \sigma^2 = (W_0 - A)^2\sigma_{g_1}^2 + A^2\sigma_{g_2}^2 \tag{6-53}$$

where the above assumes a zero correlation between returns for both assets. A non-zero correlation would add extra complexity, so we shall concentrate on the above case of uncorrelated returns.

To help locate the shape of the budget constraint, consider that value of A which gives the lowest possible risk, that is the lowest value for σ^2. This occurs when

$$\frac{d\sigma^2}{dA} = -2(W_0 - A^*)\sigma_{g_1}^2 + 2A^*\sigma_{g_2}^2 = 0 \tag{6-54}$$

or

$$A^* = \frac{W_0\sigma_{g_1}^2}{\sigma_{g_1}^2 + \sigma_{g_2}^2} < W_0 \tag{6-55}$$

where A^* is the minimum risk choice of A. This shows that risk is minimized with a *mixed* portfolio. Figure 6-4 illustrates the budget constraint. If everything was held in the first asset, this would offer an expected return of $W_0(1 + r_1)$ and a risk of $W_0\sigma_{g_1}$. This is shown as A_1. If everything was held in the second asset, this would offer the return $W_0(1 + r_2)$ and risk $W_0\sigma_{g_2}$. This is shown as A_2. We have already seen that risk is minimized with the mixed portfolio A^* also shown. Hence, the budget constraint has the shape shown.

The important point to note about this more complicated problem is that a diversified portfolio still might be the best strategy, even though the returns to both assets are uncorrelated. One might have thought that diversification was only likely to be best when asset returns were negatively correlated—a low return on one asset more likely to be offset by a high return on another. The optimal choice must be somewhere between A^* and A_2 and this could indeed imply a diversified portfolio if the highest indifference curve is tangential along this line segment. Notice that the investor will never hold an undiversified

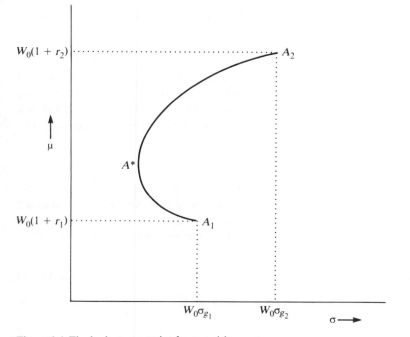

Figure 6-4 The budget constraint for two risky assets

portfolio consisting only of the lower expected yield asset; all points between A_1 and A^* are inefficient.

The second application of expected utility maximization will be to examine the instrument–objective problem in a stochastic setting. The interesting point about this problem is that we end up with an equation almost the same as Eq. (6-55). A technique, once well understood, can be applied to diverse problems. The simplest possible stabilization problem would be

$$Y = aP + \bar{u} \qquad (6\text{-}56)$$

where Y is the objective or target variable, P is the instrument, which is sometimes described as the control or policy variable, and a and $\bar{u}$ are parameters. At this level, the stabilization problem is a trivial one. If Y^* is the target value for Y, then setting

$$P^* = \frac{Y^* - \bar{u}}{a} \qquad (6\text{-}57)$$

achieves the objective exactly. Furthermore, suppose, instead of Eq. (6-56), the following was the case:

$$Y = a_1 P_1 + a_2 P_2 + \bar{u}. \qquad (6\text{-}58)$$

Now there are two instruments to achieve one objective. In this non-stochastic setting, there is instrument redundancy. With either P_1 or P_2 not used, the objective Y^* can still be achieved. The interesting thing about the stochastic setting is that instrument redundancy may no longer hold. It is not always a good idea to be a one-club politician! In general, the more instruments used, the better the outcomes. The main objective of this section is to show this.

To fix thoughts, the single-instrument problem will be considered first. Suppose, in contrast to Eq. (6-56), that the following holds:

$$Y = aP + u, \quad u \sim (\bar{u}, \sigma_u^2). \qquad (6\text{-}59)$$

There is now additive uncertainty, because u is now a random variable with the distribution shown. It will be impossible, unless one is very lucky, to hit the target value Y^* every time. It is now necessary to specify a preference function for the authorities. As with Tobin's portfolio choice theory, this is given a specific functional form, namely quadratic. The authorities seek to maximize

$$E\{V(Y, Y^*)\} = -E\{Y - Y^*\}^2. \qquad (6\text{-}60)$$

There is nothing sacrosanct about this objective function, it just happens to be easy to use. $Y - Y^*$ represents the deviations from the target and the authorities want to make these as small as possible. Equation (6-60) says make the square of these deviations as small as possible, and putting a minus sign in front is just a convenience to turn the problem from one of minimization to maximization. First note:

$$E\{V\} = -E\{Y - Y^*\}^2 = -E\{Y - \bar{Y} + \bar{Y} - Y^*\}^2 = -\sigma_y^2 - (\bar{Y} - Y^*)^2 \qquad (6\text{-}61)$$

where $\bar{Y} = E\{Y\}$ and $\sigma_y^2 = E\{Y - \bar{Y}\}^2$ is the variance of Y. From Eq. (6-59), we know that $\bar{Y} = aP + \bar{u}$ and that $\sigma_u^2 = \sigma_y^2$. Hence,

$$E\{V\} = -\sigma_u^2 - (aP + \bar{u} - Y^*)^2. \qquad (6\text{-}62)$$

We choose the value of P which maximizes $E\{V\}$. Hence,

$$\frac{dE\{V\}}{dP} = -2a(aP^* + \bar{u} - Y^*) = 0 \tag{6-63}$$

or

$$P^* = \frac{Y^* - \bar{u}}{a} \tag{6-64}$$

where P^* is the optimal value of the instrument.

Notice that this result is effectively the same as the non-stochastic case Eq. (6-57), though, of course, Y^* will not be achieved unless the realization of u is $\bar{u}$. This is an illustration of the phenomenon of *certainty equivalence*, which is a very useful property of many stochastic problems. Certainty equivalence occurs when the authorities maximize their preferences by acting as if the stochastic variables take their mean values and treating the problem as if it were a non-stochastic optimization. Here setting $u = \bar{u}$ and choosing P^* according to Eq. (6-57) maximizes preferences.

It would be a mistake to think that certainty equivalence always arises in the presence of additive uncertainty. It also requires the presence of a symmetric preference function whereby undershooting the target is punished just as much as overshooting. It is intuitively obvious that a non-symmetric preference function will weaken the case for certainty equivalence. If Y represents real output, then a reasonable preference function might wish to punish overshooting the target rather less than undershooting. Given this asymmetric preference function, it is clear that P^* would be set so that $\bar{Y}$ exceeds the target Y^*.

Next consider a case of multiplicative uncertainty:

$$Y = aP, \quad a \sim (\bar{a}, \sigma_a^2). \tag{6-65}$$

The additive part has been dropped to save on arithmetic. Here there is uncertainty about the coefficient associated with P and this is surely an appropriate way to represent uncertainty. Most econometric models can never be specific about the *exact* values of coefficients. Note that the certainty equivalent result would be $P^* = Y^*/\bar{a}$. Note also that

$$\sigma_y^2 = \sigma_a^2 P^2 \quad \text{and} \quad \bar{Y} = \bar{a}P. \tag{6-66}$$

Substitute into Eq. (6-61) once more to derive

$$E\{V\} = -\sigma_a^2 P^2 - (\bar{a}P - Y^*)^2. \tag{6-67}$$

Differentiating gives

$$\frac{dE\{V\}}{dP} = -2\sigma_a^2 P^{**} - 2\bar{a}(\bar{a}P^{**} - Y^*) = 0 \tag{6-68}$$

or

$$P^{**} = \frac{\bar{a}Y^*}{\bar{a}^2 + \sigma_a^2} < \frac{Y^*}{\bar{a}} \tag{6-69}$$

where P^{**} is the new optimal value for the instrument. The important point about this result is that certainty equivalence no longer applies. P^{**} lies below the certainty equivalent value P^*. Consequently, setting P so that Y on average undershoots the target value Y^* maximizes the authorities' objective function. The higher σ_a^2, the greater the degree of undershooting required.

This result can be shown diagrammatically and is the analogue of Fig. 6-3. First, totally differentiate Eq. (6-61) to derive

$$dE\{V\} = -2\sigma_y\,d\sigma_y - 2(\bar{Y} - Y^*)\,d\bar{Y}. \tag{6-70}$$

On an indifference curve $dE\{V\} = 0$; hence,

$$\frac{d\bar{Y}}{d\sigma_y} = \frac{\sigma_y}{Y^* - \bar{Y}}. \tag{6-71}$$

This is negative when $\bar{Y} > Y^*$ and positive when $Y^* > \bar{Y}$. The indifference curves are shown in Fig. 6-5 as the semicircles around Y^* and moving outwards represents decreasing expected utility.

Next comes the 'budget constraint'. This is derived from Eq. (6-66), which after P has been eliminated gives

$$\bar{Y} = \left(\frac{\bar{a}}{\sigma_a}\right)\sigma_y. \tag{6-72}$$

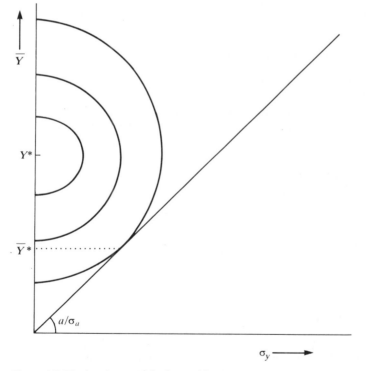

Figure 6-5 The instrument-objective problem

The trade-off between $\bar{Y}$ and σ_y is therefore shown as the line from the origin with a slope $\bar{a}/\sigma_a$. Expected utility is maximized on the highest indifference curve tangential to this line. This confirms Eq. (6-69) once more. Expected utility is maximized at $\bar{Y}*$, which lies below $Y*$. Only if the budget constraint was vertical would certainty equivalence hold. Note that as $\sigma_a \to 0$ we get nearer to the certainty equivalence. Additive uncertainty would give a vertical budget line and readers are invited to show this.

Now consider the combination policy. The problem is specified as

$$Y = a_1 P_1 + a_2 P_2 \tag{6-73}$$

where both a_1 and a_2 are stochastic and where, for convenience once again, additive uncertainty has been ignored. Let $E\{a_1\} = E\{a_2\} = 1$. Again this assumption is made to save arithmetic and is ensured by a suitable choice of units for P_1 and P_2. Assume also that a_1 and a_2 are uncorrelated with each other and that the relevant variances are σ_{a1}^2 and σ_{a2}^2. It will now be shown that a combination policy, using both instruments P_1 and P_2, will maximize the authorities' preference function, despite the fact that they are independent instruments. Given these assumptions it follows that:

$$\sigma_y^2 = \sigma_{a1}^2 P_1^2 + \sigma_{a2}^2 P_2^2 \tag{6-74}$$

and

$$\bar{Y} = P_1 + P_2. \tag{6-75}$$

Substituting into Eq. (6-61) gives

$$E\{V\} = -\sigma_{a1}^2 P_1^2 - \sigma_{a2}^2 P_2^2 - (P_1 + P_2 - Y*)^2 \tag{6-76}$$

where P_1 and P_2 are chosen to maximize this. This requires

$$\frac{\partial E\{V\}}{\partial P_1} = -2\sigma_{a1}^2 P_1^* - 2(P_1^* + P_2^* - Y*) = 0 \tag{6-77}$$

$$\frac{\partial E\{V\}}{\partial P_2} = -2\sigma_{a2}^2 P_2^* - 2(P_1^* + P_2^* - Y*) = 0 \tag{6-78}$$

where P_1^* and P_2^* are the optimal values of the instruments. Subtracting gives

$$\sigma_{a1}^2 P_1^* - \sigma_{a2}^2 P_2^* = 0 \tag{6-79}$$

or

$$\frac{P_1^*}{P_1^* + P_2^*} = \frac{\sigma_{a2}^2}{\sigma_{a1}^2 + \sigma_{a2}^2}. \tag{6-80}$$

This shows that a combination policy is best, giving the lowest variance around $Y*$. Neither of the instruments should be set to zero. Instrument redundancy no longer applies. Notice how similar Eq. (6-80) is to Eq. (6-55), which is no coincidence because essentially both problems have the same structure. Both seek to maximize a quadratic utility function and both use two independent instruments to achieve this. It is not surprising that the same basic finding occurs, namely that a diversified portfolio of instruments is better than a single instrument.

PROBLEMS

6-5 Consider the model $Y = a_1 P_1 + a_2 P_2 + u$, where P_1 and P_2 are instruments. Both a_1 and a_2 are non-stochastic and, for convenience, are set to unity. By contrast, u is stochastic with a mean of $\hat{u}$ and a variance of σ^2. Is instrument redundancy a feature of this particular problem?

6-6 Preferences are described by $V(W) = W - cW^2$, where W is wealth. The budget constraint is described by $W = W_0 - A + A(1 + r + g)$, where W_0 is the initial endowment and A is the amount allocated to the risky asset, where g is a stochastic term of zero mean and variance σ^2. Assuming an internal solution, calculate an explicit solution for the choice of A.

6-5 SUMMARY

The main purpose of this chapter has been to elucidate an essential part of any economist's kit of problem-solving tools to deal with the question of uncertainty. The logical basis of expected utility maximization has been explained and the idea has been applied to two areas. However, there are innumerable applications in a whole variety of contexts and the next two chapters, among other things, will use this principle in several further ways.

ESSAY TOPICS

6-1 Is 'expected utility maximization' an adequate analytical framework to describe agents' behaviour in the presence of uncertainty?

6-2 Why, if at all, is a von Neumann–Morgenstern utility indicator superior to the usual ordinal utility indicator?

6-3 'In any realistic situation the problem of instrument redundancy does not arise.' Discuss.

6-4 Explain Tobin's theory of liquidity preference. Why is it an improvement over the Keynesian speculative motive?

6-5 Explain the concept of 'certainty equivalence'. What conditions are necessary for it to hold?

READING

Two excellent sources on the theory of expected utility maximization, which form the basis for this chapter, are Hey (1979) and Baumol (1965). Baumol is the slightly easier of the two, whereas Hey gives an extremely comprehensive coverage of the approach with many examples. Luce and Raiffa (1957) is another classic reference. The example concerning the risk-averse firm is taken from Sandmo (1971), which contains much further discussion of this most interesting problem. Tobin (1958) is the classic reference on the portfolio choice problem. Laidler (1985) provides a gentle introduction, as well as a broad coverage of the whole demand for money topic. Ryan (1978) gives a very comprehensive account of the theory of portfolio choice, going far beyond what is done here. The instrument-objective problem under stochastic conditions is taken from Brainard (1967). Theil (1968) is a comprehensive book and especially good on certainty equivalence. Poole (1970) is another classic article and a good application of Brainard's point about a combination policy, in general, working best. For the current status of expected utility theory in current thinking try Schoemaker (1982) and Machina (1987).

SOME IMPLICATIONS OF RATIONAL
EXPECTATIONS FOR MACROECONOMICS

The rational expectations hypothesis, because it views the behaviour of the economy in such a different way from earlier theories, has revolutionized macroeconomics. This has had radical consequences and even sceptics are forced to confront important issues, hitherto unthought of. This chapter reviews three further major implications of rational expectations. They are the rules versus discretion debate, the Lucas Critique of policy evaluation and, finally, the prediction, associated with particular models, that many economic time series will tend to follow a random walk.

7-1 RULES VERSUS DISCRETION

The idea that economic policy should follow fixed rules has already been discussed in previous chapters. This debate has a long history, stretching back to at least the 1950s, but the ground rules have shifted considerably since then. 'Traditional' Monetarists, such as Milton Friedman, who are sceptical of full-blown rational expectations, also favour rules in economic policy. According to New Classicals, rules should: (*a*) be simple; (*b*) be pre-announced and widely disseminated; (*c*) be widely understood; and (*d*) have commitment behind them. So both camps give similar policy advice on this issue, but the rationale for the fixed rule prescription is very different. The purpose here is to give an explicit discussion of these issues, concentrating on the New Classical perspective. What exactly is meant by a rule, and what exactly is meant by discretion?

Early discussion of this topic by New Classicals was somewhat muddled. It was the later seminal work of Kydland and Prescott that really defined the matter. The early work will be reviewed first, if only to point out some sources of potential confusion. There are two types of rule. The simplest type is a non-feedback or non-contingent rule: this says the policy variable should stay on its prescribed path, no matter what the economic circumstances. The x per cent monetary growth rule of Milton Friedman is a good example. The second type of rule is the feedback or contingent rule. Such rules could, in principle, be extremely complicated; for example, 'Monetary growth of x per cent per annum, but x per cent minus some specified amount depending on some inflation threshold, and x per cent plus some specified amount if the unemployment rate rises above some specified threshold.' The important point to note is that feedback and non-feedback rules are generically of the same type, although, on the whole, New Classicals favour rules which are the least complicated. Feedback rules should *not* be confused with discretion. A feedback rule is more complicated than a non-feedback rule, but they are both rules nevertheless.

Discretion or 'fine tuning' is the idea that policy rules can change in the light of circumstances; policy makers give themselves the option of ditching any pre-announced policy regime at any time they see fit. By contrast, all rules, contingent rules included, have *commitment* behind them, whereas discretion means there is no commitment behind any pre-announced regime. Contingent rules specify in advance how the authorities will react to changed circumstances; discretion reserves the right to change one's mind whenever one sees fit.

This all seems to make discretion slightly disreputable and undesirable; indeed, part of the New Classical agenda is to suggest that economic policy is too important to be left in the hands of 'mere' politicians, for whom discretion is regarded as a way of life. However, there are powerful arguments favouring discretion which transcend the somewhat narrow economist viewpoint, and Chapter 9 will review some of these. The purpose of the present discussion is to explain the economic case for non-discretion in economic policy.

The first classic and accessible discussion is the work of Sargent and Wallace. The idea is to contrast a Keynesian world before rational expectations with the world after rational expectations came on the scene. The Keynesian world is characterized by the equation

$$Y_t = \alpha + \lambda Y_{t-1} + \beta m_t + u_t. \tag{7-1}$$

Y_t is output and m_t is a policy instrument, here considered as a money supply rule. The last term is the residual, here assumed to be 'white noise' of variance σ^2. The important point about the equation is that m_t has a systematic, predictable effect on Y_t. The lagged dependent variable Y_{t-1} gives momentum to output fluctuations and the policy goal is to minimize these fluctuations as far as possible. This is a typical 'Brainard' type problem, as discussed in Chapter 6.

Equation (7-1) does not claim to be a realistic description, but the point is that the 'deep' structure of many pre-rational expectations' models will look something like this. British Keynesians, such as Kaldor, would not have accepted that m_t has a predictable effect on output, whereas US Keynesians probably would. Indeed, many 'traditional' Monetarists would accept that systematic monetary policy has a short-run impact on output. However, the precise model is hardly the point here, Eq. (7-1) is intended to capture the *general* point that a policy variable, under the control of the authorities, directly affects output.

The objective of the authorities is to minimize the quadratic objective function $E\{Y_t - Y^*\}^2$, where Y^* is the target output level. The policy rule is

$$m_t = g_0 + g_1 Y_{t-1} \tag{7-2}$$

where the idea is to choose a value for g_0 and g_1 to minimize the objective function. A non-contingent rule would be the case which set $g_1 = 0$. Equation (7-2) specifies a linear reaction function. Although no formal proof is offered, it is not surprising that a linear rule is best, given that Eq. (7-1) is also linear. Given the symmetric preference function and additive uncertainty, certainty equivalence will apply. Thus one condition for choosing g_0 and g_1 is that $E\{Y_t\} = Y^*$. Hence,

$$E\{Y_t\} = Y^* = \frac{\alpha + \beta g_0}{1 - (\lambda + \beta g_1)}. \tag{7-3}$$

The variance is given by

$$E\{Y_t - Y^*\}^2 = \frac{\sigma^2}{1 - (\lambda + \beta g_1)^2}. \tag{7-4}$$

(In case the reader is unfamiliar with this type of derivation, both the above equations are demonstrated in the appendix.) Equation (7-4) is minimized when $\lambda + \beta g_1 = 0$, which implies the contingent rule $g_1 = -\lambda/\beta$. From Eq. (7-3), $g_0 = (Y^* - \alpha)/\beta$, and substituting into Eq. (7-1) gives

$$Y_t = Y^* + u_t. \tag{7-5}$$

In principle, a feedback rule can eliminate all fluctuation in output down to the irreducible 'white noise' component u_t. This case for activist intervention is characterized as the conventional view by Sargent and Wallace. However, it is important to note that the above has nothing to do with discretion *per se*, but rather it prescribes a feedback rule because it produces better outcomes than a non-feedback rule.

The world of rational expectations is characterized by the idea that only policy surprises can affect real outcomes. An equation such as (7-1) is, on this view, fundamentally mis-specified. Sargent and Wallace re-specify Eq. (7-1) as

$$Y_t = \xi_0 + \xi_1(m_t - E_{t-1}m_t) + \xi_2 Y_{t-1} + u_t. \tag{7-6}$$

$E_{t-1}m_t$ is the rational expectation of m_t based on information at time $t - 1$. Since m_t is the realized policy, then $m_t - E_{t-1}m_t$ is just the policy surprise. Such an equation is based on the familiar Lucas supply schedule discussed in Chapter 5. The policy rule is

$$m_t = g_0 + g_1 Y_{t-1} + \varepsilon_t. \tag{7-7}$$

The unpredictable part of policy is described by the 'white noise' process ε_t. Under rational expectations, agents are presumed to know the parameters g_0 and g_1. Monetary policy, therefore, consists of two parts, a systematic part which is known to everyone and a 'surprise' component which is not. To give an example, when the Conservatives were returned to power in 1979, a strict monetary regime was widely advertised with precise targets specified in the so-called 'Medium Term Financial Strategy'. Presumably, this systematic change in policy was known to all. At the same time there was widespread uncertainty because of important changes in banking regulations that occurred at the same time. This rendered many monetary aggregates unreliable indicators of the true monetary stance. The authorities engaged in large-scale over-funding of the budget deficit to try to stay within the money supply growth targets specified in the financial strategy. A safe conclusion is that monetary policy was surprisingly strict at that time. Equation (7-7) would have had a large negative ε_t at that time. The point of Eq. (7-7) is that such surprises are basically random and cannot be systematically engineered.

In reality, the requirements to 'fully know' the model are quite large. Equation (7-6) is basically static, as is the monetary rule embodied in Eq. (7-7). Once g_0 and g_1 change, agents are presumed to believe they will stay at these new values for ever. Chapter 3 argued for a much more general view of monetary policy, embodying the whole future path of the monetary rule. Such complexities surely make it less self-evident that systematic changes to the monetary rule become known to the public immediately. Be that as it may, it follows that

$$E_{t-1} M_t = g_0 + g_1 Y_{t-1}. \tag{7-8}$$

Substituting into Eq. (7-6) gives

$$Y_t = \xi_0 + \xi_1 \varepsilon_t + \xi_2 Y_{t-1} + u_t. \tag{7-9}$$

Since Eq. (7-9) does not contain m_t, monetary policy has no real effect on output, only its surprise component ε_t. By definition, a surprise cannot be systematically engineered.

Care is required about the scope of what Eq. (7-9) demonstrates over the Keynesian world. It does not show that rules work better than discretion, but rather it shows that a contingent rule is *irrelevant* and will work no better than a fixed non-feedback rule. The parameters g_0 and g_1 do not appear in Eq. (7-9) and hence any feedback rule, no matter how often it changed, would give the same result as setting $g_1 = 0$. The claim of Eq. (7-8) is that agents are always smart enough to figure out the rule as soon as the authorities change it.

The assertion of the superiority of rules over discretion, therefore, requires the Sargent and Wallace analysis to be interpreted with some imagination. There is nothing wrong in that. Economic models should not be regarded as being set in concrete, with a mean-spirited refusal to think beyond internally consistent implications; rather, they should serve as useful guiding lights and points of reference for a looser, less formal discussion. Let us proceed on this basis. Simple rules are likely to be better understood compared to feedback rules, especially if the latter are subject to frequent discretionary change. The variance of ε_t in Eq. (7-7) is most likely to be smallest for the simplest rule. Frequent changes in policy create uncertainty, and agents—though rational, doing the best they can and not making any systematic errors in the context of this model—are nevertheless unlikely to predict particularly well. Consequently, simple rules would generate the smallest fluctuations in output.

Traditional Monetarism emphasizes extrapolation from past observations of inflation in forming expectations. Given this, even perfectly anticipated monetary policy would have some systematic effect on output, albeit in the short term. Consequently, the way in which agents form their expectations is crucial to the 'rules versus discretion' debate. Even so, traditional Monetarists generally advocate simple non-feedback policy rules. As Barro once wryly remarked, it is often a good idea to listen to what Milton Friedman advocates, though his reasons may not be entirely cogent to an out-and-out New Classical! Traditionalists advocate simple rules on the pragmatic grounds that not enough is known about the structure of the economy to make 'fine tuning' successful. Traditionalists argue that monetary policy operates with 'long and variable lags' so that 'fine tuning' to produce short-run gains is unlikely to achieve any desirable result. However, traditionalists must, in principle, be committed to 'fine tuning' if eventually enough becomes known to make short-run activism predictable. New Classicals deny even the principle of 'fine tuning'.

Equations (7-6) to (7-9) put the policy ineffectiveness proposition in its sharpest form. The presence of rational expectations is necessary but not sufficient for policy ineffectiveness. To give an example, the overlapping contracts model, described in Chapter 4, embodies rational expectations, yet retains a role for intervention. The overlapping contracts model throws some institutional grit into the smooth neoclassical machinery. Specifically, the idea of nominal price rigidity over the finite period of the contract is sufficient leverage to re-establish the case for intervention in the light of circumstances. The intuition behind this is simple enough to see. Short-term price rigidity prevents market clearing as circumstances change during the period of the contract. Given that monetary policy can operate within the contract period, activist monetary policy becomes an aid to market clearing.

A second argument deployed against policy ineffectiveness is asymmetric information. This is the idea that the authorities are more aware of the monetary regime than the public and can engineer monetary policy in a way which is surprising to the public but not to themselves. Suppose, instead of Eq. (7-7), that the following is the case:

$$m_t = g_0 + g_1 Y_{t-1} + \varepsilon_t + \gamma_t \tag{7-10}$$

where γ_t is under the control of the authorities, but unknown to the public. This seems to restore policy effectiveness, enabling the authorities to operate a benign monetary policy to improve economic outcomes. Unfortunately, that is not the end of the matter.

A monetary authority with a good reputation could easily announce a policy regime of $m_t = g_0 + g_1 Y_{t-1}$, which is believed by the public, and then deliver a γ_t surprise. On a one-off basis such a strategy works. However, what happens when the authorities try it a second time? The authorities' reputation will be diminished and their policy pronouncements will be that much less believed. No doubt they will try to confuse the public by claiming that, last time, γ_t was really just part of ε_t. Eventually the public will cease to believe the authorities and γ_t will then be a wasted and useless weapon. Indeed, the public may very well come to 'expect' to be surprised, which poses a further dilemma for the authorities. If they fail to deliver what the public expects, even though they have announced something else, inferior outcomes can be the result. Equation (7-10) is therefore a useful lead into the 'rules versus discretion' debate proper. The discussion also serves to show that structural equations concerning the effects of policy cannot be written down in the absence of information about the authorities' reputation for telling the truth. New Classicals claim that part of Britain's malaise is the poor reputation of policy makers. The economy will only be successful when the good name of the policy makers has been restored. That means eschewing the γ_t weapon if it is available.

It was the path-breaking work of Kydland and Prescott that explained precisely what was involved in the 'rules versus discretion' debate. The contribution of Sargent and Wallace fudged the issue somewhat, as we have seen. For Kydland and Prescott the heart of the matter is the time inconsistency of economic policy, and this important concept will now be explained. This is an issue that few of us think about directly, yet it permeates our lives at every level. In fact, we all have an informal understanding of time inconsistency, through practical experience. Let us first consider several such examples before establishing a more formal structure.

Each year, a famous London store advertises an important sale. It is announced that the doors will open at 9 a.m. on 1 January. Inevitably, a long queue forms well in advance of the official opening time. Queueing is a pure waste of scarce resources which could be avoided if the store reneged on its original promise and opened its doors early. Think of the official opening time as the policy rule and opening early as the exercise of discretion. The question is, why does the store not exercise discretion, even though there are large benefits to be gained from doing so?

Everyone can give a commonsense explanation, which already goes a long way towards unravelling the mystery of time inconsistency. The argument would be, 'Certainly, you can open the doors early and for sure there will be considerable one-off gains. But what happens next year? This year's queue was based on the certain belief that the doors would open at 9 a.m. on 1 January. Next year the queue will start even earlier because the public will expect you to renege on your agreement once more. Opening early creates uncertainty in future years, leading to a worse outcome than the one which obtains at the present, which is queues but at least the certain expectation of a particular opening time. Exercising discretion is a poisoned chalice.'

The time inconsistency in the above problem arises because once the policy has been announced, and providing the public believe the store will stick to its agreement, there is then a short-run gain to be had by reneging on the original agreement. Notice that the reneging comes from the most *benign* of motives, not from selfishness. The gains accrue (in the short term at least) to the very people with whom the store has entered into an agreement, which it now has the option to renege upon.

Here is an example where a time-inconsistent optimal policy run with absolutely no discretion is just too risky to agree to. One problem with being super-rich is the danger of being kidnapped and held to ransom for a vast sum. To avoid this, the super-rich can either spend considerable amounts on elaborate security or pretend to be poor to avoid the attentions of potential kidnappers. The latter strategy seems particularly futile, since it destroys the point of becoming rich in the first place. The optimal policy, which would avoid all these costs, would be for super-rich individuals to announce, with the maximum publicity, that if they are kidnapped, in no circumstances will any ransom be paid. If potential kidnappers believe there is absolute commitment behind this statement, the super-rich individuals can enjoy their wealth without the expense and hassle of elaborate security or the inconvenience of pretending to be poor. Unfortunately, such a policy carries with it a high degree of time inconsistency. If the same individual is kidnapped, and suffers all the horrors involved, the first-best strategy may be to pay up after all! Discretion *is* sometimes the better part of valour. The optimal policy really has no credibility behind it. Kidnappers know that they can exploit the sentimentality of human nature—the friends or relatives of the victim will believe that by reneging they help this particular individual, even though it results in danger to potential victims in future.

Finally, here is a case where dynamic inconsistency led to tragedy. At popular football games the authorities announce that no one without a ticket will be admitted to the game. If credible, fans without tickets will not show up for the game. The authorities must reinforce that credibility by strictly enforcing the rule, even at the risk of public disorder from those not admitted. In the past the authorities have reneged by admitting them at the last moment as large crowds gather without tickets, threatening violence and disorder. The result was large groups without tickets travelling to games because they knew the policy of non-admission was not credible. The tragic consequence was the Hillsborough football disaster in which 95 innocent fans with tickets, and who had arrived early, were crushed to death by those behind.

The important point to note in all these examples is the tension between an optimal policy and *ex post* reneging. The optimal policy only works provided people believe there will be no subsequent reneging. Reneging produces some short-run advantages, but then the optimal policy no longer works, because behaviour changes at the outset if people no longer believe that agreements made will be kept to. Kydland and Prescott's insight was to show that the potential time inconsistency of optimal policies applies equally well in the economic sphere. Even though discretion appears to give the policy maker additional degrees of freedom, enabling short-run advantages to be gained in the light of circumstances, it is still worth while to operate according to fixed rules.

Kydland and Prescott's policy example is made up of three elements. First, there is an inflation–unemployment trade-off, based on a Lucas surprise supply function

$$U_t = \lambda(X_t^\varepsilon - X_t) + U^* \qquad (7\text{-}11)$$

where U_t is unemployment, U^* the natural rate, X_t^ε expected inflation and X_t actual inflation. Positive inflation surprises reduce unemployment below the natural rate. For a given X_t^ε, Eq. (7-11) defines a negative relationship between unemployment and inflation. Figure 7-1 illustrates this trade-off for $X_t^\varepsilon = 0$ and $X_t^\varepsilon = b$. The latter line is obviously a vertical displacement of the former by the amount b. The natural rate U^* is shown at the origin. The second feature is a welfare function. Society regards both inflation and

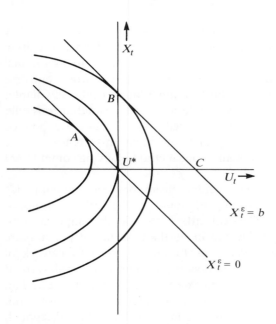

Figure 7-1 Rules versus discretion

unemployment as evils, reflected by

$$S = f(X_t, U_t) \qquad \frac{\partial S}{\partial X_t}, \frac{\partial S}{\partial U_t} < 0. \tag{7-12}$$

Indifference curves for S are also shown in Fig. 7-1, with utility increasing in the westward direction. The final feature is that agents hold rational expectations. Given the present set-up of no uncertainty, this means $X_t = X_t^\varepsilon$. Outcomes must lie along the vertical axis with unemployment at U^* always.

Now let us explore the time inconsistency of the optimal policy. Suppose the government announces a policy of zero inflation and an unemployment target of U^* and, furthermore, announces that it intends to stick to these targets with no reneging. Such targets are clearly feasible and agents will set $X_t^\varepsilon = 0$ providing they *believe* the government is committed to its policy. In such circumstances $X_t = 0$ and U^* will be obtained. The time inconsistency is, however, immediately apparent from Fig. 7-1. Given that $X_t^\varepsilon = 0$, the authorities might believe themselves able to trade along the short-run supply curve and obtain A, which offers a higher level of welfare than the optimal policy. Reneging on the original promise and delivering some surprise inflation offers the possibility of a short-term gain in welfare to all. Without sincere commitment behind the original policy, time inconsistency causes the optimal policy to unravel. A is actually unobtainable because it is inconsistent with the rational expectations assumption. Agents now expect the authorities to renege, meaning that they can no longer trade along the original $X_t^\varepsilon = 0$ supply line. Under discretion, when agents believe the government can and will change its mind, the only internally consistent outcome is at B. Here $X_t = X_t^\varepsilon$ once more and there is no incentive for the government to induce any inflation surprise since this would lead to an outcome that was inferior to B. In the futile attempt to reach A, the authorities arrive at an outcome that is worse than the optimal policy.

Because there is no commitment behind the policy, agents come to expect policy reneging. A benign authority is virtually obliged to accommodate this. Under discretion the public expect $X_t^\varepsilon = b$. If, at this stage, the authorities actually stuck to its original commitment and delivered zero inflation, this would then lead to an even worse outcome of C. Recall the discussion on public borrowing at high nominal interest rates in Chapter 1. The inconsistency of a policy announcement of zero inflation and the simultaneous offer of interest rates that were consistent only with high delivered inflation rates, was pointed out. The high rates of interest offered effectively signalled an intention to renege on the zero-inflation announcement. Indexation can be seen as one method of giving commitment to policy pronouncements.

Time inconsistency is, therefore, all about the inherent tension between optimal policy and the incentive to indulge in some one-off cheating, no doubt for the best of reasons, to produce some large gains. This is why New Classicals attach considerable importance to rules and why they advocate institutions that would make the reneging of policy more difficult. In effect, there should be an 'economic constitution'—a strict framework of regulation under which any elected government must operate. Two important rules would be a legal requirement for a balanced budget, except in exceptional circumstances, and an independent central bank with control over monetary policy. An independent central bank of 'the great and the good'—presumably dominated by like-minded New Classicals, though this is rarely made clear—is advocated.

Unfortunately, there is an equally inherent tension between the New Classical doctrine of strict rules and the right of people to change economic policy through the ballot box. It is surprising how a creed, based on free markets and individual choice, seeks to restrict freedom in the most fundamental way by denying people the right to vote out those in charge of the most crucial aspects of economic policy. The doctrine of giving up such hard-won democratic rights is based on the arrogant presumption that policy will be run so well that the people would never dream of wanting to criticize, let alone throw out, those to whom they entrust their economic destiny. It is exactly the same authoritarianism that Hayek, the noted thinker and defender of the free enterprise system, warned would be the undesirable consequence of socialist collectivism:

Parliaments come to be regarded as ineffective 'talking shops' ... The conviction grows that if efficient planning is to be done, the direction must be 'taken out of politics' and placed in the hands of experts, permanent officials or independent autonomous bodies. (Hayek, 1944, p. 46)

Chapter 9 tries to put these arguments into some sort of perspective. Like most things, it never is that simple.

The path-breaking analysis of Kydland and Prescott opens up an extremely interesting area of debate that goes far beyond 'mere' economics. It brings to the forefront the way in which a government's perceived reputation affects economic outcomes. Kydland and Prescott's example is one of extremes. In the first case, the government's announcements are trusted absolutely and U^* and $X_t = 0$ are obtainable. In the second instance the government is distrusted absolutely and the suboptimal U^* and $X_t = b$ are obtained. In real-life situations, a government's reputation lies somewhere between the two extremes, with its current reputation based on previous performance—what the press euphemistically refer to as the 'credibility gap'. This opens up the possibility of some quite complex policy games as the government and public interact. There is now a substantial literature on this, but this will not be explored further here.

PROBLEM

7-1 Welfare is described by $S = -U_t^2 - X_t^2$, where U_t is unemployment and X_t is the rate of inflation. The trade-off between the rate of inflation and unemployment is described by $U_t = \lambda(X_t^\varepsilon - X_t) + U^*$, where X_t^ε is the expected inflation rate and U^* is the natural rate of unemployment. Expectations are rational.

(a) Show that the optimal policy $X_t^\varepsilon = X_t = 0$ and $U_t = U^*$ are obtainable and calculate the implied value of S.
(b) Show that this is time-inconsistent by calculating the 'first best' solution, which assumes $X_t^\varepsilon = 0$, independent of the choice of X_t. Calculate the implied value of S. Is this higher or lower than that obtained in (a)?
(c) Calculate the discretionary (time-consistent) equilibrium and the implied value of S. Is this higher or lower than that obtained in (a)?

7-2 THE LUCAS CRITIQUE OF POLICY EVALUATION

What underpins the Lucas Critique is actually rather similar to the 'rules versus discretion' debate. Section 7-1 was all about changing policy in the mistaken belief that agents will not alter their expectations when policy changes. The same idea is applied by Lucas to the predictions made by many macroeconometric models. These models, according to Lucas, have an abysmal forecasting performance, because they incorrectly assume that agents' beliefs are invariant to the policy regime. Lucas regarded his critique as a devastating attack, rendering much of the traditional agenda as wrong—as plain and as simple as that! The immediate task is to describe the critique in general terms and then to give two illuminating examples.

The usual approach involves estimating an equation or set of equations over some historical period. In stylistic terms, Lucas suggests that such an equation could be described by

$$Y_t = F(Y_{t-1}, X_t, \theta, \varepsilon_t) \qquad (7\text{-}13)$$

where Y_t is the target variable, X_t is the policy variable and θ are the parameters of the F function. The econometric model estimates the critical θ parameters by fitting the data over some historical period. These parameters purport to explain how Y_t will alter in response to changes in X_t. The ε_t term is the residual component of the fitted equation.

Traditional practice asserts that the θ are invariant to the policy regime that is in operation. For Lucas, this claim is flawed. The θ parameters, in general, must alter as the policy regime changes. As a consequence, macroeconometric policy simulations at best need to be treated with caution and at worst are incorrect. Counter-factual policy simulations use Eq. (7-13) to forecast performance for a different set of values for X_t, based on θ. These simulations are useless, because θ changes as X_t alters. Even though models such as Eq. (7-13) might fit well over some historical period, such equations are inappropriate for forecasting or policy analysis. To give a specific example, money demand functions have been estimated for many countries and over many different historical periods. A well-defined θ was synonymous with stability. Lucas claims that such findings are of limited interest and relevance for policy purposes.

Equation (7-13) is correctly specified as

$$Y_t = F(Y_{t-1}, X_t, \theta(\lambda), \varepsilon_t) \qquad (7\text{-}14)$$

where λ now represents the policy regime. Changes in X_t change λ, and to forecast correctly one needs to know the response of θ to λ. Estimating θ in the traditional way is inappropriate, since that only gives some historical average of previous policy regimes, quite useless for forecasting purposes. Notice that the Lucas Critique is not totally dependent on rational expectations. All that is required is for θ to be dependent on λ *to some degree*. The Lucas claim of a serious problem inherent in the traditional agenda is not, therefore, an immodest one.

The basic point behind the Lucas Critique is easily seen by extending the Sargent and Wallace model on rules versus discretion. We already know that the true structure is given by Eq. (7-9). This takes into account how the structure alters in response to policy change and there is no role for the policy variable m_t to systematically affect Y_t. Many estimated models will, however, misleadingly appear to give a systematic role for m_t. To see this, substitute out $E_{t-1}m_t$ from Eq. (7-6), replacing it with $g_0 + g_1 Y_{t-1}$ to derive

$$Y_t = a + bY_{t-1} + \xi_1 m_t + u_t \qquad (7\text{-}15)$$

where $a = \xi_0 - \xi_1 g_0$ and $b = \xi_2 - \xi_1 g_1$. Suppose g_0 and g_1 were fairly constant over some historical period. Clearly, Eq. (7-15) would fit the data extremely well. Quite misleadingly, it appears as if m_t 'causes' Y_t, which we know to be untrue. A change in policy is wrongly forecast to affect Y_t with coefficient ξ_1. This is simply a statistical artefact; it holds *only as long as $E_{t-1}m_t$ does not change.* Under rational expectations this presumption is false—if the monetary rule changes, so must $E_{t-1}m_t$. The traditional agenda assumes that $E_{t-1}m_t$—or variables like this—do not alter as the regime changes. The point is a devastating attack on traditional macroeconometric practice.

What drives the Lucas Critique is the same as what underlies time inconsistency. Seeking a time-inconsistent first-best by reneging on policy promises makes the false presumption that agents do not alter their expectations of policy in the face of policy reneging. In the Lucas Critique, Eq. (7-15) works only if agents maintain a similarly unchanged expectation of policy, even though policy changes. Rational expectations points up the absurdity of these positions.

In his original article, Lucas considers several examples of varying complexity, although what underpins each is exactly the same disarmingly simple principle. The greatest economic insights are always disarmingly simple. One of the most interesting of Lucas' examples is the inflation–output trade-off. Standard econometrics might make it appear as though there is a stable trade-off between inflation and output—the original non-expectations augmented Phillips curve of yore—whereas in reality no such trade-off exists. It really is quite fascinating stuff. The true structure of the economy is reflected by a Lucas surprise supply schedule:

$$Y_t = \beta(P_t - E_{t-1}P_t) + \bar{Y} \tag{7-16}$$

where $\bar{Y}$ is the natural rate of output and P_t is the log of the price level, hence $P_t - E_{t-1}P_t$ is the inflation surprise. Suppose inflation has taken the following path over the historical period under study:

$$P_t = P_{t-1} + \varepsilon_t, \quad \varepsilon_t \sim (\pi, \sigma^2). \tag{7-17}$$

Here inflation takes the mean value of π, but fluctuates around this value as reflected by the distribution of ε_t. The rational expectations forecast $E_{t-1}P_t$ is

$$E_{t-1}P_t = P_{t-1} + \pi. \tag{7-18}$$

Substituting into Eq. (7-16) gives the correct 'deep' structure

$$Y_t = \beta\delta_t + \bar{Y} \tag{7-19}$$

where $\delta_t = \varepsilon_t - \pi$ is just a random term. Clearly, Eq. (7-19) emphasizes that there is no permanent trade-off between inflation and unemployment. This is the correct and true 'deep' structure of the economy. Now substitute out $E_{t-1}P_t$ alone to derive

$$Y_t = \beta(P_t - P_{t-1}) - \beta\pi + \bar{Y}. \tag{7-20}$$

Since $\beta\pi$ is a constant, Eq. (7-20) will appear to fit the data extremely well. $P_t - P_{t-1}$ is the *actual* inflation rate and there appears, quite falsely, to be a trade-off between output and the inflation rate. This would only be true if, when the authorities raised the mean inflation above π, agents continued to believe that the original mean value of the ε_t distribution prevailed, that is, $E_{t-1}P_t$ remained as before. Most traditionally estimated Phillips curves, purporting to demonstrate a long-run trade-off, are literally meaningless because the estimated equations are falsely assumed to be independent of the policy regime.

Lucas gives other examples from a wide area of economics, but they all boil down to the same thing. Counter-factual policy simulations are wrong if they fail to take account of the fact that agents' expectations will change when the policy regime is changed. Although highly critical of much current econometric practice, Lucas is not against empirical economics. He would advocate a search for the 'deep' structures such as Eq. (7-19). These are structures which are truly independent of the policy regime. Then, he says, do the econometrics. Despite the power of the Lucas Critique, much econometric practice continues to ignore it—many of the large UK forecasting models are a case in point. The defence made is that policy changes are small and (or) they are not perceived by agents, so that equations such as (7-15) and (7-20) will do for policy and forecasting purposes. This defence does seem a trifle disingenuous since the UK economy has been characterized by dramatic policy reversals in recent years.

PROBLEM

7-2 A 'traditional' supply schedule is stylized as $Y_t = A + \alpha m_t + u_t$, where A is a constant, Y_t is output, m_t is the money supply and u_t is a random white-noise term. The money supply rule is $m_t = m_{t-1} + \varepsilon_t$, where ε_t is also a white-noise process. The money supply rule is common knowledge, hence $E_{t-1} m_t = m_{t-1}$. Show that

$$Y_t = A + \alpha \sum_{i=0}^{\infty} S_{t-i} + u_t$$

where S_t is money surprise ($= m_t - E_{t-1} m_t$). Comment on this result.

7-3 RANDOM WALKS

A random walk is defined as

$$Y_t = Y_{t-1} + u_t \tag{7-21}$$

where u_t is a 'white noise' process, with the following properties:

$$E(u_t) = 0 \quad \text{for all } t.$$
$$E(u_t u_s) = 0 \quad \text{for all } s \text{ and } t, t \neq s. \tag{7-22}$$
$$E(u_t^2) = \sigma^2 \quad \text{for all } t.$$

It is easy to see why Eq. (7-21) is called a random walk, because the position of Y_t is given by where it was yesterday, namely at Y_{t-1}, plus some totally unpredictable random component. The best prediction for Y_t, given information available at $t - 1$, is simply Y_{t-1}. A prediction of rational expectations is that many economic time series should follow a random walk. This section reviews two examples of this. The first concerns exchange rates and the second concerns the consumption function. It illustrates once again how seemingly disparate questions have a common problem structure.

In a system of flexible exchange rates, the market for foreign exchange is claimed to be efficient. Efficient markets utilize all the available information on anything that influences prices. The second assumption of market efficiency is that prices, in this case the exchange rate, are fully flexible and markets clear. Finally, expectations are rational. The efficient market hypothesis is, in fact, a much older tradition than rational expectations, but is easily recast in terms of the newer theory. The important point is that market efficiency is somewhat stronger than rational expectations, because of the additional assumptions of fully flexible prices and market clearing. Not all models embodying rational expectations need have these properties.

There are innumerable theories of the exchange rate, and the present model, which embodies the efficient market hypothesis, is part of what has become known as the asset market approach. The sheer volume of transactions in foreign exchange is quite staggering, at around twice Britain's GNP *per day*. The vast majority of these transactions are not for the purposes of foreign trade and the great advantage of the asset market approach is that it seems to be 'plugged into' the actual world of traders and speculators who deal in foreign exchange. It captures the role of information and demonstrates how exchange rates can apparently move so rapidly in response to new information.

A continuous-time version of the model was described in Chapter 4. The discrete-time version specifies

$$S_t = Z_t + b(E_t S_{t+1} - S_t) \tag{7-23}$$

where S_t is the log of the spot rate (there is a technical reason called Seigel's paradox, not explored here, why specifying in level terms would be inappropriate); Z_t is current information which affects the spot rate; and $E_t S_{t+1}$ is the rational expectation of tomorrow's spot rate. The weakness of Eq. (7-23) is its generality. Since Z_t can contain virtually anything, it is always possible to rationalize *ex post* any exchange movement. A strong test of Eq. (7-23) would be to predict in advance how S_t would react to pre-specified items of new information.

Because Z_t is a 'broad church', potentially encompassing many different types of causal variables, at one level the model might satisfy the *technical* requirements for rationality, yet at another level the determination of exchange rates might be deeply irrational—in the layman's sense of the word. Speculators have an alarming habit of convincing themselves that certain trivial items of information have an incredibly important bearing on the exchange rate. The fact that the model is grounded in rational expectations does not contradict the fact that exchange markets could simply be driven by the stupidity and greed of the players involved. Economic theorists are more comfortable with the idea of Z_t coming from some well-specified model of the exchange rate based on fundamentals. For example, a 'flow of funds' theory would emphasize the balance of payments; a monetary theory would regard the relative supplies of foreign and domestic money as important. Taking an eclectic view of Z_t has the danger of vacuity in the final analysis.

Readers can quickly verify the fact that the 'fundamentals' rational expectations solution of Eq. (7-23) is

$$S_t = \left(\frac{Z_t}{1+b}\right) + \left(\frac{1}{1+b}\right) \sum_{i=1}^{\infty} \left(\frac{b}{1+b}\right)^i E_t Z_{t+i}. \tag{7-24}$$

The spot rate is driven by currently available information and today's best guess of all future information 'discounted' at the rate $b/(1+b)$.

Equation (7-24) does *not* predict that S_t follows a random walk. Some claim that over fairly long periods a random walk is an accurate description of the behaviour of some exchange rates. To see why a random walk need not occur, hypothesize some plausible behaviour for Z_t. For example, a monetary theory of exchange rates would emphasize relative money supplies as a key argument of the Z_t vector. Let $Z_t = M_t$, where M_t is the log of the relative money supplies. Furthermore, suppose that

$$M_{t+j} = M_{t+j-1}(1 + g) \quad \text{for all } j \geq 1. \tag{7-25}$$

Substituting into Eq. (7-24), S_t is easily derived as

$$S_t = \frac{M_t}{1 - bg} \tag{7-26}$$

and

$$S_{t+1} = \frac{(1 + g)M_t}{1 - bg}. \tag{7-27}$$

Hence,

$$S_{t+1} = (1 + g)S_t \tag{7-28}$$

which is certainly not a random walk. The UK pound, for example, fell consistently against the Deutschmark from 1971. The fact that this was not a random walk was confirmed by the behaviour of the forward rate which consistently traded at a discount to the spot rate—the market therefore expected the spot rate to fall, and it did. A falling pound over long periods does not definitively disprove a random walk, the crucial point is the forward discount, which is *prima facie* inconsistent with the random walk idea.

What is predicted to be a random walk is the following:

$$S_{t+1} = E_t S_{t+1} + u_{t+1} \tag{7-29}$$

where S_{t+1} is the (log) spot rate one period ahead, $E_t S_{t+1}$ is the future (log) spot rate based on currently available information and u_{t+1} is white noise. Since there is a well-organized forward market in exchange rates, $E_t S_{t+1}$ is equated with the current forward rate. Hence,

$$S_{t+1} = F_t + u_{t+1} \tag{7-30}$$

where F_t is the (log) forward rate. (The forward rate is simply the right to buy or sell foreign exchange, at a price fixed today, at some specified time in the future, most usually three months.) Since F_t is readily available information, an equation such as (7-30) is easily tested. From Eq. (7-24):

$$E_t S_{t+1} = \left(\frac{E_t Z_{t+1}}{1 + b}\right) + \left(\frac{1}{1 + b}\right) \sum_{i=1}^{\infty} \left(\frac{b}{1 + b}\right)^i E_t Z_{t+i+1}. \tag{7-31}$$

Hence,

$$S_{t+1} - E_t S_{t+1} = \left(\frac{Z_{t+1} - E_t Z_{t+1}}{1 + b}\right) + \left(\frac{1}{1 + b}\right) \sum_{i=1}^{\infty} \left(\frac{b}{1 + b}\right)^i (E_{t+1} Z_{t+i+1} - E_t Z_{t+i+1}). \tag{7-32}$$

The terms on the right-hand side of Eq. (7-32) represent pure news, the irreducible forecast errors. If, for example, $Z_{t+1} - E_t Z_{t+1}$ was anything other than 'white noise', such information would, under rational expectations, immediately be embedded in $E_t Z_{t+1}$, making $Z_{t+1} - E_t Z_{t+1}$ an unpredictable component once more. Equations (7-31) and (7-32) therefore reflect the assumption of market efficiency, and Eqs (7-29) and (7-30) are immediately implied. Equation (7-30), therefore, says that the current forward rate is the best predictor of the future spot rate and a better predictor than the current spot rate. Having said that, fitted equations such as (7-30) tend to be dominated by noise. Typically, around 90 per cent of the variation of S_{t+1} is accounted for by u_{t+1}, which is another way of saying that it is 'news' which dominates the behaviour of exchange rates.

Not everyone accepts the random walk model of exchange rates in its purest form and the empirical evidence is not completely clear cut on the issue. Work in the late 1970s and early 1980s seemed to support the random walk idea quite strongly, but the consensus subsequent to this is that the empirical evidence is not supportive of the idea. One reason suggested why the pure random walk model may not work is the presence of risk. Those who take positions in the forward market demand to be compensated for the risks involved. Consequently,

$$F_t = E_t S_{t+1} + \delta \tag{7-33}$$

where δ is a risk premium. If true, this clearly modifies the random walk model. Finally, note that models such as Eq. (7-24) can be applied to many other asset markets.

We now turn to the second example of a random walk which concerns the consumption function. The implications of rational expectations for the lifecycle theories of consumption were first noticed by Hall. In certain circumstances a random walk is predicted and, as an empirical matter, it is claimed that the random walk version describes the data better than possible alternatives. The standard lifecycle model allows the consumer to maximize utility subject to an intertemporal budget constraint. The problem can be described by

$$\text{Max:} \quad \sum_{\tau=0}^{T-t} \left(\frac{1}{1+\delta} \right)^\tau U(C_{t+\tau}) \tag{7-34}$$

subject to the intertemporal budget constraint

$$\sum_{\tau=0}^{T-t} \left(\frac{1}{1+r} \right)^\tau (C_{t+\tau} - R_{t+\tau}) = A_t. \tag{7-35}$$

$U(C_{t+\tau})$ is utility of consumption in the $(t+\tau)$th period. The subjective rate of time preference is δ, and Eq. (7-34) defines an additively separable intertemporal utility function over the remaining $T - t$ periods of economic life. The budget constraint simply says that current assets A_t must equal the present value of consumption minus receipts ($= R_{t+\tau}$), where r is the rate of interest.

The consumer will choose a $C_t, C_{t+1}, \ldots, C_T$ to maximize Eq. (7-34) subject to Eq. (7-35). The problem assumes a perfect capital market with the consumer free to borrow or lend as much as necessary in a particular period, provided only that the lifetime intertemporal constraint is satisfied. Versions of this problem have led to the lifecycle hypothesis associated most closely with Modigliani and Brumberg and most famously to the Friedman permanent income hypothesis, which was briefly discussed in Chapter 3. Hall considered exactly the same problem, except that he added uncertainty. Current receipts R_t are known information, but future receipts are uncertain. $U(C_{t+\tau})$ is now a von Neumann–Morgenstern utility function, as described in Chapter 6. The consumer maximizes the expected value of Eq. (7-34) subject to the stochastic intertemporal budget constraint.

The dynamic stochastic programme now defined by Eqs (7-34) and (7-35) is a truly difficult problem, but with some advanced mathematical techniques it can, indeed, be solved. Essentially the consumer will devise a consumption plan between now and the end of his or her economic life. Because of uncertainty, this plan will not be set in concrete but will be subject to continuous revision as the consumer's lifetime proceeds and the information set is updated. To get the flavour of the Hall approach, which derives Hall's key result exactly, a two-period version of the stochastic intertemporal consumption problem is considered. Utility is given by

$$Z = U(C_t) + \left(\frac{1}{1+\delta}\right)U(C_{t+1}). \tag{7-36}$$

The budget constraint, where for convenience $A_t = 0$, is given by

$$C_{t+1} = R_{t+1} + (R_t - C_t)(1 + r). \tag{7-37}$$

R_t, receipts in the current period, are known information, whereas R_{t+1} is uncertain. This is the crucial stochastic element in the optimization which, in a multi-period context, would make the solution rather less than immediately obvious. The consumer will maximize the expected value of Z, subject to the stochastic budget constraint Eq. (7-37). The consumer chooses an optimal value for C_t to maximize $E\{Z\}$. The value for C_{t+1} cannot be precisely predicted at this stage and is basically dependent on the *realization* of R_{t+1}, given the value for C_t.

Substitute out C_{t+1} from Eq. (7-36) using Eq. (7-37) to obtain the following expression for $E\{Z\}$:

$$E\{Z\} = U(C_t) + \left(\frac{1}{1+\delta}\right)E\{U(R_{t+1} + [R_t - C_t][1 + r])\}. \tag{7-38}$$

Now choose a C_t to maximize this. The first-order condition requires

$$\frac{dE\{Z\}}{dC_t} = U'(C_t) - \left(\frac{1+r}{1+\delta}\right)E\{U'(C_{t+1})\} = 0. \tag{7-39}$$

This is Hall's famous result. Since neither R_{t+1} nor R_t appears in Eq. (7-39) the best prediction of C_{t+1} requires a knowledge only of C_t. Other variables are irrelevant.

Some further assumptions are required before a random walk is the prediction. First assume that the utility function is quadratic with $U(C) = aC - \frac{1}{2}bC^2$. Equation (7-39) becomes

$$a - bC_t - \left(\frac{1+r}{1+\delta}\right)[a - bE\{C_{t+1}\}] = 0. \tag{7-40}$$

The random walk requires the further assumption that $r = \delta$. Given this, Eq. (7-39) simplifies to

$$E\{C_{t+1}\} = C_t \tag{7-41}$$

or

$$C_{t+1} = C_t + u_{t+1} \tag{7-42}$$

where u_{t+1} is a 'white noise' term.

Hall's approach to the consumption function is extremely elegant. Tests of the model involve showing that no other variable, apart from the lagged value of consumption, significantly improves the performance of the model. The random walk is *additional* to this and involves showing that no other functional form involving the lagged value of consumption works better than the random walk specification. Hall found reasonable support for the random walk version of Eq. (7-39). He found that the lagged value of corporate stock significantly improved the model performance. Consequently, the rational expectations version of the consumption function in its *purest* form is not supported.

This is hardly surprising, because the assumptions required for Eq. (7-39) are very strong. Foremost among these is the absence of capital constraints, which is a highly questionable assumption. It is difficult for those with few non-human assets to borrow. Secondly, the degree of uncertainty assumed by Hall is actually rather limited. The rate of interest is assumed to be non-stochastic and individual time preference is assumed constant throughout the lifecycle.

PROBLEM

7-3 An individual lives for two periods with utility function $\ln C_t + (1 + \delta)^{-1} \ln C_{t+1}$, where C_t is consumption in the tth period and δ reflects time preference. The budget constraint is given by $C_{t+1} = R_{t+1} + (R_t - C_t)(1 + r)$, where receipts in the tth period are R_t and r is the rate of interest. The realization of R_{t+1} is not known in advance of the decision on C_t, but has a known distribution.

(a) Show that C_t is the best predictor of C_{t+1}.
(b) Does C_{t+1} follow a random walk if $r = \delta$?
(c) Show that C_t is independent of r if R_{t+1} is known to be zero. When would $C_t = \frac{1}{2}R_{t+1}$? Is C_{t+1} a random walk?

7-4 SUMMARY

This chapter has shown just how interesting the rational expectations approach can be. It leads to conventional views being completely turned upside-down in just about every area of the subject. It is too early to say whether any elected politician, without committing electoral suicide, could respond to an economic shock with the statement, 'I shall stick to the rule and do nothing.' Nigel Lawson, the then UK Chancellor, responded to the 1987 stockmarket crisis with dramatic interest rate cuts in anticipation of a slump that never came. The result was an unintended and damaging inflationary boom. According to those who advocate rules, this is impressive testimony to the folly of trying to do good, yet ending up doing harm.

APPENDIX

Equation (7-1) is a first-order stochastic difference equation of the form

$$Y_t = a + bY_{t-1} + u_t \tag{A7-1}$$

where $E\{u_t\} = 0$ and $E\{u_t u_s\} = 0$ when $t \neq s$ and $E\{u_t u_s\} = \sigma^2$ when $t = s$. Using the lag operator notation of Chapter 4, the solution for Y_t can be written directly as

$$Y_t = (1 - bL)^{-1}a + (1 - bL)^{-1}u_t. \tag{A7-2}$$

Taking expectations, and noting that $E\{u_t\} = 0$, gives

$$E\{Y_t\} = (1 - bL)^{-1}a = \frac{a}{1 - b}. \tag{A7-3}$$

Now consider the variance; this is

$$E\{Y_t - E\{Y_t\}\}^2 = E\{(1 - bL)^{-1}u_t\}^2 = E\{(1 - bL)^{-1}u_t(1 - bL)^{-1}u_t\}. \tag{A7-4}$$

Expanding gives

$$E\{Y_t - E\{Y_t\}\}^2 = E\left\{ \sum_{i=0}^{\infty} b^i u_{t-i} \sum_{j=0}^{\infty} b^j u_{t-j} \right\}. \tag{A7-5}$$

This can be simplified, noting that $E\{u_t u_s\} = 0$ when $t \neq s$ and $= \sigma^2$ when $t = s$, to give

$$E\{Y_t - E\{Y_t\}\}^2 = \sigma^2 \sum_{i=0}^{\infty} (b^2)^i = \frac{\sigma^2}{1 - b^2}. \tag{A7-6}$$

Note that this is an asymptotic variance and not, for example, $E\{Y_t - Y_{t-1}\}^2$, conditional on Y_{t-1}. Are we always interested in minimizing an asymptotic variance? Notice also that (A7-6) implies that the asymptotic variance of a random walk is infinite. Drunks take note!

ESSAY TOPICS

7-1 'Monetary policy is too important to be left in the hands of politicians.' Discuss.
7-2 'In practice, it is impossible for the authorities to make any pre-defined monetary aggregate follow a precise rule. Consequently the "rules versus discretion debate" is of limited practical relevance.' Discuss.
7-3 Describe some examples of time inconsistency, either in the economic sphere or elsewhere. (*Definitely not those shown in this chapter already!*) Are optimal policies always time-inconsistent?
7-4 How devastating is the 'Lucas Critique' for standard econometric practice?
7-5 The consumption function has, at various times, been described in the following three ways:

$$C_t = kY_t^d + u_t$$

$$C_t = kY_t^p + u_t$$

$$C_t = C_{t-1} + u_t$$

where C_t is consumption, Y_t^d is disposable income and Y_t^p is permanent income, with u_t a random component. Discuss the relative merits of each of these specifications.

READING

Once again, Hoover (1988) provides considerable flesh to the arguments presented here and the discussion of Eq. (7-10) is based on this. The classic articles discussed in the 'rules versus discretion' debate are Sargent and Wallace (1976) and Kydland and Prescott (1977). Barro (1986) provides a useful non-mathematical survey and Barro and Gordon (1983) present a fully worked out reputational model which extends the ideas of Kydland and Prescott. A good example of a text which confuses contingent rules with discretion is Stevenson *et al.* (1988). The quote is from Hayek (1944). The discussion of the Lucas Critique is from Lucas (1976). Again, this is not so difficult to read compared to some of this author's articles! It is also interesting to note how the late 1970s was a period of many classic articles in economics. The random walk exchange rate model is based on Frenkel (1981) and Mussa (1979). Attfield *et al.* (1985) offer a good discussion of Seigel's paradox. MacDonald and Taylor (1989) give a comprehensive survey of this area. Hall (1978) is the source for the random walk consumption model. Blanchard and Fischer (1989) discuss a more general derivation of the random walk result and Sargent (1987b) is another step up beyond this. This is a very difficult reference, for mandarins only! Begg (1982) presents an alternative and interesting way of deriving the random walk consumption model. Muellbauer (1983) offers a comprehensive theoretical and empirical critique of Hall using British data. Modigliani and Brumberg (1954) and Friedman (1957) are two classic references on the lifecycle approach to consumption.

SOME NEW KEYNESIAN THEMES

This chapter contains a hotchpotch of ideas, which are given the title 'New Keynesian'. There is not one single all-encompassing New Keynesian model; rather, the label is attached to models which share some important common features. We have already come across some examples in earlier chapters. Taxonomies are often irritating and authors often object to being labelled New Keynesian, New Classical, or whatever. Friedman once said he was happy to be labelled a Keynesian. It is the ideas that are important, not the label.

Central to New Keynesianism is the idea that market imperfections resulting from institutional factors are not just important but *central* to economic processes. This fact applies to all markets to a greater or lesser extent, but particular emphasis is placed on the labour market. The normal rules of the competitive paradigm simply do not apply. The assumption of rational expectations is also routinely made by New Keynesians, but this need not always be a feature. For example, much of the recent work of Solow could be labelled 'New Keynesian', but he certainly does not have much sympathy with rational expectations.

For many New Keynesians, the labour market is not an impersonal, inanimate instrumental institution. It is not just the means whereby labour-power is transformed into income to achieve the ultimate goal of consumption, but it is also a social institution. Work gives people self-esteem and defines what they are. A machine will, within limits, perform tolerably well no matter how it is treated. Not so with human beings. Productivity is inextricably linked with how workers perceive the way in which they are treated and notions such as 'fairness' and 'justice' apply, which could not be applied to machines or to other markets.

At the turn of the century, the doctrine of 'scientific management' was developed in the USA. This was the idea that workers and their productivity could be completely controlled by the employer. The doctrine is now more or less totally repudiated, though it does have a modern echo in the form of time-and-motion studies. No employer can totally control the workforce. Monitoring performance is expensive and difficult and more often than not counter-productive. The modern worker is no longer prepared to be deferential and subservient, which therefore means subtle tactics on the part of management to maximize performance. The labour bargain is therefore not just the intersection of a supply and demand curve, but is far more complex. Add to this lack of information, transaction costs of various kinds and a whole new area is opened up for the theorist to explore.

In short, New Keynesianism throws bucketfuls of grit into the smooth-running neoclassical paradigms. The point of doing this is to show that such institutional detail does make a difference. The neoclassical agenda in the main stripped away what was considered to be unessential detail—judging that most problems were difficult enough already. Neoclassicals claimed to have revealed the basic economic resource allocation problem. The article of faith was that adding back institutional reality would not change things much. The New Keynesian agenda implicitly challenges this presumption. None of this is particularly new, however. Industrial relations and industrial psychology have been considering such issues since time immemorial. What is new is the attempt to place these constraints within a systematic optimizing framework and the elaboration of internally consistent formal models, where any obvious profit opportunity has been exploited. In the words of Lucas, there are no $500 bills lying around just waiting to be picked up. To that extent New Keynesians, New Classicals, Neoclassicals, or whatever label is attached, are not in competition with one another.

New Keynesian macroeconomics asks the following type of question. Do institutional constraints generate involuntary unemployment? Do they help explain the observation of nominal price rigidities in the short run? Is policy effectiveness restored when institutional constraints are present? The stakes are obviously quite high, addressing precisely the same questions over which Keynes took issue with his neoclassical colleagues in a former age.

This chapter will review five separate New Keynesian ideas. Before looking at specifics, two notes of caution are in order. First, there is a danger, when one is imbued into New Keynesian modes of thought, to go the other way and reject all the insights of the competitive paradigm. Chapter 2 showed that, by assuming competition, many useful and interesting insights are derived which, in addition, are strongly supported by empirical evidence. In the long term the forces of competition do show through. The second word of caution concerns the lack of empirical evidence to support many New Keynesian models. Often they become a theoretical playground with little justification for the institutional assumptions beyond a type of 'this sounds plausible' argument. If industrial relations used to be measurement without theory, much New Keynesianism is theory without measurement. Perhaps the right way forward is careful investigation to justify the various institutional constructions used in the models.

8-1 THE GAME THEORETIC APPROACH

The following elegant example, due to Solow, captures the idea of not being a sneak in the labour market. Unemployed workers refuse to undercut the going wage rate, even though such a wage would secure a job that is above their own reservation wage. (The reservation wage is a term frequently used by labour economists; it is simply the critical wage below which one is not prepared to work.) Solow shows how such behaviour can be motivated by self-interest. Suppose the reservation wage is w_0 and that convention has established a wage w in excess of w_0. Furthermore, suppose that only a fraction of the labour pool is hired at the prevailing wage:

$$e(w) < e(w_0) < 1 \qquad (8\text{-}1)$$

where $e(w)$ is the fraction hired. The question is this. Why do the unemployed not undercut in order to secure a job?

By refusing to undercut the workers show solidarity and the firm is obliged to pay w in all subsequent periods. If the workers do undercut, the firm learns that solidarity is weak and it can successfully apply a punishment strategy of wage-cutting in subsequent periods. The model, therefore, draws attention to the long-term nature of the labour bargain; it is this long-term nature which impinges upon current behaviour, resulting in non-market-clearing equilibria. Industrial relations experts frequently emphasize the long-term nature of the employment relationship to explain why the wage bargain appears 'irrational' in the short run.

A worker who undercuts by a small amount this period receives (nearly) w and w_0 in subsequent periods. The present value of this is

$$w + w_0(d + d^2 + \cdots + d^T) \qquad (8\text{-}2)$$

where $d < 1$ is the discount rate and there are $T + 1$ periods of employment. The present value of Eq. (8-2) is

$$w + kw_0 \qquad (8\text{-}3)$$

where $k = d(1 - d^T)/(1 - d)$. Now consider what happens if the worker refuses to undercut the going wage. This period w_0 is received, but in subsequent periods there is a probability $e(w)$ of securing a high-paying job. This offers the following expected present value:

$$w_0 + \{e(w)w + [1 - e(w)]w_0\}\{d + d^2 + \cdots + d^T\} \qquad (8\text{-}4)$$

$$= w_0 + k\{e(w)w + [1 - e(w)]w_0\}. \qquad (8\text{-}5)$$

This strategy is preferred as long as the value of Eq. (8-5) exceeds Eq. (8-3). It is easy to show that this requires

$$[w - w_0][1 - ke(w)] < 0. \qquad (8\text{-}6)$$

Since $w > w_0$, then not undercutting pays provided that $e(w) > 1/k$. Given k, there is a *range* of w up to a critical value where undercutting does not pay. The higher is k, the higher is this critical amount. A high k means placing more weight on the future, which obviously reduces the incentive to undercut.

Unemployment can hardly be described as involuntary in this framework. If agents choose not to undercut, then they prefer to gamble on the chance of a higher-paying job in future periods. If there are unlucky outcomes, they may regret their previous decision to gamble. Thus, although agents may not like being unemployed and describe their predicament as 'involuntary', the point is that next time round they still prefer to gamble. This discussion points up the Lucas observation that very often the distinction between 'voluntary' and 'involuntary' unemployment becomes a sterile debate in semantics.

An unsatisfactory feature of the model is the random draw nature of employment; employed and unemployed have an equal chance of securing a job in future periods. In reality, complex seniority rules prevail and 'random draw' is an unsatisfactory feature of many New Keynesian models. Incorporating and justifying the institutional reality of seniority rules and job tenure is an active area of research, but, as can be imagined, one that it is difficult to formalize. A further problem concerns the finite life assumption, since there is every incentive for the worker to undercut in the very last period. It is generally agreed that solutions to finite life games can 'unravel' by this type of argument. Despite these criticisms, there is something highly suggestive about the Solow approach. Unions are generally reluctant to negotiate wage cuts, even though higher employment for their members might result in the short run. They see such tactics as sacrificing an important point of principle.

On an individual basis, there is probably some limited discretion in wage negotiation when seeking a job. However, most people apply for a job where there is a well-defined remuneration package—read any 'Jobs Vacant' column in any newspaper. Offering to work for *less* than the advertised rate is simply not done. There are undoubtedly many reasons for this phenomenon, apart from the argument put forward here. The whole point of this and other analyses is to explain the observation of short-run wage stickiness in response to aggregate demand shifts.

PROBLEM

8-1 Show that the no wage undercutting condition $e(w) > 1/k$ is independent of the degree of risk aversion among the workers.

8-2 TRANSACTION COSTS

Transaction costs are a simple way of justifying short-run nominal price rigidity. If there are costs associated with changing prices, it is sometimes worth while not to change them, even though it would be optimal to do so in the absence of these costs. Transaction costs can be of several types. First are the obvious 'menu' costs, which are simply the bureaucratic expenses of altering price labels. For example, the largest UK building society, the Halifax, estimates that it costs around £1 million to change its mortgage rate for borrowers. To save on this, the society has introduced one single annual review of rates rather than altering rates several times a year, as in the past.

The second type of cost is less tangible. Employers may be reluctant to cut wages for fear of damaging employee morale and productivity. Firms are reluctant to lower prices for the same reason. Automobile manufacturers find that discounting erodes the customer loyalty of those who bought at the earlier, higher, price. Furthermore, a Tobin effect can occur which is the idea of postponing purchase in the hope of yet further price discounts. All in all, exploring the theme of transaction costs seems a promising area.

The firm is viewed as having some monopoly power and is consequently a price-setter rather than a price-taker. Secondly, there is a *fixed* transaction cost element in price-changing, independent of the size of the price change. Obviously, a more general approach might wish to introduce a variable cost element, but it turns out that the fixed cost element is the important one. This echoes Baumol's famous transactions demand for money theory in which fixed costs and not variable costs turn out to be critical.

One of the points emphasized in this literature is that it requires only *small* transaction costs to induce price rigidity. If firms are profit-maximizing at one initial price, then, when they are faced with a shock, the change in profits that is induced is only of the second order of smallness. Consequently, the profit 'penalty' for not changing prices in the face of the shock can be small. Put another way, only relatively 'large' changes in price are worth while. Moderate shocks will induce no price-changing behaviour—an extremely important insight. To see this, consider the following static problem involving the familiar price-setting monopolist. Profits are given by

$$\pi = (a - bq)q \tag{8-7}$$

where $p = a - bq$ is a downward-sloping demand curve and q is output. Zero production costs are assumed. (For the effect of positive marginal production costs, see Problem 8-3 at the end of this chapter.) With Eq. (8-7) optimal (profit-maximizing) output is easily derived as $a/2b$, price is $a/2$ and profits are $a^2/4b$. Now suppose a finite shock of Δa to demand. In the absence of any transaction costs, the firm will adjust both price and output. The change in price is $\Delta a/2$ and the new level of profits is easily derived as

$$\pi^A = \frac{(a + \Delta a)^2}{4b} = \frac{a^2}{4b} + \frac{(\Delta a)^2}{4b} + \frac{a\,\Delta a}{2b}. \tag{8-8}$$

Now suppose, because it is expensive to adjust prices, that the firm can only adjust its output in response to the demand shock. Profits in this case are

$$\pi^F = pq = \frac{p(a + \Delta a - p)}{b}. \tag{8-9}$$

Substituting in the *original* level of p, profits are, therefore,

$$\pi^F = \left(\frac{a}{2}\right)\frac{(a + \Delta a) - a/2}{b} = \frac{a^2}{4b} + \frac{a\,\Delta a}{2b}. \tag{8-10}$$

The penalty for not adjusting profits is

$$\pi^A - \pi^F = \frac{(\Delta a)^2}{4b}. \tag{8-11}$$

This is of the second order of smallness relative to Δa. If the transaction cost of changing prices was above this, it would not be worth while to change prices.

The above insight is made clearer by expressing values in relative terms. Let $\gamma = (\Delta a)^2/4b$ be the critical value of the fixed transaction cost, above which it is not worth while to change prices. Note that

$$\frac{\gamma}{\pi} = \left(\frac{\Delta a}{a}\right)^2. \tag{8-12}$$

If it was worth while to adjust the price, then given the fixed transaction cost the firm might as well adjust optimally. Hence,

$$\frac{\Delta p}{p} = \frac{\Delta a}{a}. \tag{8-13}$$

Thus, if γ/π was just 1 per cent, then the size of the shock $\Delta a/a$ has to be such as to induce a 10 per cent change in the optimal price, before it is worth while to make the price change. It is in this sense that small transaction costs lead to fairly rigid price behaviour.

A second point to emphasize is that, although the consequences for the micro unit can be of the second order of smallness, the macroeconomic consequences can be large when set within a general equilibrium context. The welfare costs are, therefore, not of the second order. An idea of why can be gleaned by examining the output consequences of the shock in the previous problem. Think of Δa as a downward shock, reflecting a downturn in economic fortunes. Transaction costs exacerbate the resultant cyclical fluctuation. If the price was fully adjusted, the fall in output would be

$$\frac{\Delta q}{q} = \frac{\Delta p}{p} = \frac{\Delta a}{a}. \tag{8-14}$$

However, if the price was not adjusted, the proportionate fall in output is

$$\frac{\Delta q^F}{q} = \frac{2\Delta a}{a}. \tag{8-15}$$

Hence the additional fall in output is

$$\frac{\Delta q^F}{q} - \frac{\Delta q}{q} = \frac{\Delta a}{a}. \tag{8-16}$$

Hence a small transaction cost could potentially lead to large output falls. For example, with $\gamma/\pi = 1$ per cent again, *additional* output falls of up to 10 per cent are possible. Notice the following slightly paradoxical finding. Small changes in policy inducing small shocks can apparently have larger consequences than large changes, because the latter induce price-changing behaviour!

These results are a feature of optimizing behaviour. At a maximum the neighbouring territory is often fairly flat and one has to move some way before encountering dramatic falls in value. However, the result is not *always* true and it is sometimes misleadingly held up as a universal law. Problem 8-2 (p. 202), which modifies Eq. (8-7) slightly, makes this clear. Some maxima have 'sharp' peaks and small changes can have a large effect on the value of a function.

The example was also static. If any price change was expected to be sustained over several periods, it may be worth while to adjust now for the rewards of future additional profits. The so-termed *Ss* model attempts just such a dynamic analysis. Although the mathematical mechanics are difficult, the basic reason for the result is no more difficult to follow than this simple static example. There will be an upper *S* bound and a lower *s* bound within which there will be rigid prices.

Although these ideas are interesting, no one has tried to quantify such costs accurately. It does appear that some industries, when faced with frequent shocks, do adjust their prices frequently in response. They develop cost-saving means of reducing menu costs. Petrol prices are a classic example, with filling-stations able and willing to adjust prices on an almost daily basis. Finally, notice that the transaction costs idea motivates *nominal* price rigidity unlike other optimizing frameworks which generally motivate *real* price rigidity of some kind. This is important because it is the observation of nominal rigidities which is the most difficult to theoretically justify.

PROBLEMS

8-2 The firm's profit function is given by $\pi = (a - bq)q - F$, where π are profits, q is output and F are fixed production costs. How does F modify the conclusions about transaction costs, in particular the result that a 1 per cent transaction cost to profits ratio would require a shock sufficient to induce a 10 per cent change in the optimal price before any adjustment was made?

8-3 The firm's profit function in Problem 8-2 is modified to $\pi = (a - bq)q - cq$, where c is a marginal production cost. Show how the results on transaction costs are affected by the presence of c.

8-3 INSIDER–OUTSIDER THEORY

The advantage of this approach is that it readily and directly explains the phenomenon of involuntary unemployment. Insider–Outsider theory actually builds on a somewhat older tradition of segmented or dual labour markets. Many New Keynesian themes have their antecedents in an older, less formalistic, more anecdotal literature. The maxim of Insider–Outsider theory is that, 'Possession is nine tenths of the law.' Those with a job (insiders) have an inherent advantage over those without insider jobs (outsiders). Outsiders may be unemployed or consigned to a residual category of undesirable and poor-paying secondary sector jobs. Insider–Outsider theory takes a dim view of human nature. Insiders conspire against outsiders to prevent (insofar as it is possible) their recruitment and to bid up their own wages. There is nothing malign in this; they are motivated by individualistic self-interest.

Insiders, therefore, have some limited monopoly power over the employer, which they exploit to their own advantage. This insider power can take place at various levels, which all serve to reinforce one another. First, they can make it expensive to sack an insider. The more expensive this is, clearly the less incentive the employer has to replace a high-paid insider with a low-paid outsider. Secondly, through cooperation with each other and harassment of entrants (newly recruited outsiders) they can make the latter relatively less productive. Again, this serves to discourage the recruitment of outsiders. Finally, by making things potentially unpleasant for outsiders, they bid up the outsider reservation wage to compensate for the disutility of the harassment.

The *modus operandi* of the Insider–Outsider model can be seen by assuming just one of the above three processes. We concentrate on just the last, with the first two in effect making it 'as if' the outsider reservation wage is higher than it would otherwise be. (Problem 8-4 on page 206 considers additional sources of insider power.) The following terminology is used:

W_I = Insider wage.
R_I = Insider reservation wage.
H = Monetary value of the disutility of harassment by insiders.
R_E = Outsider reservation wage $(= R_I + H)$.
m = Incumbent workforce of insiders.
L_I = Numbers of insiders employed $(L_I \leq m)$.
L_E = Numbers of outsiders employed $(L_E \geq 0)$.
$\theta f(L_I + L_E)$ = Output.
θ = Productivity shift parameter, assumed fixed in the first instance.

The only restriction on wage-setting by insiders is that the wage cannot be set so high as to make it worth while for the firm to sack its insiders, replacing them with outsiders. If any outsider is recruited, all the insiders must be retained and if some insiders are dismissed then no outsiders will be recruited. This puts a limit on insider wage-setting power. To see how the problem evolves, the firm's profit-maximization problem is given by

$$\text{Max:} \quad \pi = \theta f(L_I + L_E) - W_I L_I - R_E L_E \qquad (8\text{-}17)$$

subject to the constraints

$$L_I \leq m, \qquad L_E \geq 0, \qquad L_I > 0. \qquad (8\text{-}18)$$

The firm chooses L_I and L_E to maximize π, subject to the constraints. For the moment, the insider wage, W_I, is assumed to be exogenous.

The solution is best seen with the aid of Fig. 8-1. The horizontal axis shows the labour force, $L_I + L_E$. The wage rate is shown on the vertical axis and the marginal product of labour, $\theta f'(L_I + L_E)$ is shown as the downward-sloping line. Also shown are three possible sizes for the incumbent workforce of insiders. They are 'small', m_a; 'intermediate', m_b; and 'large', m_c. The insider wage is shown as W_I and the outsider wage as R_E.

Consider the first case of a small incumbent workforce. Here the marginal product exceeds R_E at m_a and it is worth while to recruit outsiders to the point A where $\theta f' = R_E$. All insiders are retained because $\theta f' > W_I$ at A. Note that it is important that W_I does not exceed R_E, otherwise the firm would find it worth while to dismiss all its insiders and hire outsiders. This puts a restriction on the maximum insider wage. The second case is the intermediate labour force m_b. Here the marginal product exceeds W_I, hence it is worth while to retain all the insiders. No outsiders are recruited because the marginal product lies below R_E. This set-up gives an immediate insight as to why involuntary unemployment might be the result. In the absence of harassment, with an intermediate labour force outsiders would be hired. Furthermore, with a small incumbent labour force there would be some additional hiring of outsiders beyond the point A. The final case is of a large incumbent workforce m_c. Here marginal product lies below W_I and the profit-maximizing firm will dismiss some insiders with employment set at C. Obviously, no outsiders are hired in this case.

The complete Insider–Outsider model endogenizes W_I, which insiders are assumed to manipulate to their maximum advantage. The firm is assumed to retain complete discretion on employment. Employer discretion on employment is referred to as a 'right to manage' contract. Consider first the case of m_c. Here the wage would fall to the reservation level

R_I. If it were above this, some insiders would be dismissed, even though they would prefer employment. Consequently, there is an incentive to opt for a lower wage. Thus R_I represents the lower bound for W_I. Note that some insiders could still be dismissed even though W_I falls to R_I. Next consider the case of the intermediate workforce m_b. Here the wage would be driven up to the point W^*, illustrated in Fig. 8-1. A wage up to W^* means that no insiders are dismissed. It cannot go above this because some insiders would then be dismissed. Finally, consider the case of m_a. The presence of R_E places an upper limit on $W_I = R_I + H$. Above this all insiders would be dismissed. The insider wage W^* is therefore bounded between R_I and R_E. It is clearly in the insiders' interests to make H as large as possible.

A more appealing—but entirely equivalent—way of characterizing the solution is to have a constant level of the incumbent labour force, but different values of θ, shifting the labour demand schedule. High and low values of θ then represent the upswing and downswing respectively of the economic cycle. On this interpretation low values of θ imply the lower bound reservation wage on W^*, with the possibility of dismissal for some insiders. Intermediate values imply the retention of all insiders, with $dW^*/d\theta > 0$ in this range. Thus, unlike the competitive paradigm, where output and employment expand in the upswing, in Insider–Outsider theory this productivity gain is more or less dissipated in

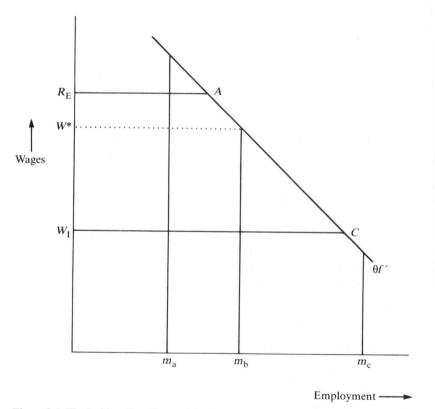

Figure 8-1 The Insider–Outsider model

the form of higher wages rather than additional recruitment. Hiring only occurs at high values of θ, when the R_E constraint is hit. Tests of the hypothesis basically involve these predictions and, secondly, the idea that firms 'doing well' pay higher wages beyond what pure competition would predict.

Another important implication of Insider–Outsider theory is that there no longer appears to be a natural rate of unemployment; employment, with some qualifications, is predicted to follow a random walk. To see this, an element of uncertainty has to be introduced into the present model. Suppose there is an incumbent workforce of m_b and that the best guess of θ is the line shown in Fig. 8-1. Insiders are assumed to negotiate a wage W^* on the basis of this best guess or expected value of θ. Now suppose a moderately bad state of nature is realized. The negotiated wage remains at W^* and, with the firm retaining the right to manage, some insiders are dismissed. This means that in the next period there will be a smaller incumbent labour force. With the same distribution of θ, the best guess for labour demand remains the line shown in Fig. 8-1. Dismissed insiders are assumed to have a negligible influence and, given this fact, the new (smaller) incumbent labour force will negotiate a higher wage above W^*. The effect of moderately good states of nature is more problematical. If the marginal cost of hiring remains at R_E then there need be no hiring, except for sufficiently large positive demand shocks to make it worth while to hire at R_E. So there need be no symmetric response in employment. However, if the firm could hire at W^* (possible if there were a pool of laid-off insiders, with first choice on hires over outsiders), then a more symmetric employment response is possible. It takes little thought to see that employment could then follow a random walk with the 'white noise' depending on the realization of θ.

Even then, this random walk conclusion has to be tempered somewhat because of the R_I and R_E wedge. If the initial value of the incumbent force of insiders is low, on average some hiring would be expected, because W^* would not be set above R_E. With a high incumbent force of insiders, some firing would be expected on average, because W^* would not be set below R_I. So the random walk prediction is only an approximation, but a good one if the R_I to R_E wedge is large. The important point, however, is not the precise form but the fact there is no longer a single 'equilibrium' level of unemployment.

The present discussion takes a somewhat naive view of insider behaviour, but does nevertheless serve to show some potentially interesting possibilities arising from the approach. The random walk model assumes considerable myopia on the part of insiders if they view their relationship with an employer as long term. Presumably, the whole essence of exploiting insider advantage is to secure long-term employment. Currently employed insiders would know that recruitment this period will, in general, mean lower wages for all next period. Yet such an effect is assumed not to impinge on the current negotiation. Similarly, insiders might be expected to take account of the threat of dismissal in future periods if the relationship is long term. Here the dynamic problem has just been considered as a sequence of segmented static optimizations. Finally, the criticism that is true of much New Keynesian theory is also applicable to Insider–Outsider theory. Virtually no evidence is brought to show whether insiders actually behave in the way suggested. Given the innumerable man-hours devoted to developing a theory of considerable elegance and power, it might seem a good idea to whizz by the odd factory or two to find out just what degrees of selfishness insiders are really capable of!

PROBLEM

8-4 The Insider–Outsider problem is modified in the following way. First, there is a per worker firing cost of C associated with dismissing insiders. Secondly, insiders cooperate with each other and harass outsiders so that the production function is modified to $\theta f(AL_I + BL_E)$, where A is a 'cooperation' parameter and B is an 'harassment' parameter with $A > B$. The model remains unchanged in other respects. Show how the results of the static Insider–Outsider model are modified.

8-4 EFFICIENCY WAGES

Insider–Outsider theory looks at the labour bargain from the point of view of the employee. Efficiency wage theory looks at the labour bargain from the employer's point of view. The central feature is that worker productivity is related positively to the wage. To see the potential of this approach, suppose that the firm's profits are given by

$$\pi = f(e(W)N) - WN \tag{8-19}$$

where N are the numbers employed and W is the wage. The unusual feature is the production function which contains the term $e(W)N$; this represents employment in efficiency units. The idea is that an increase in the wage will increase worker productivity, hence it is assumed that $d(e(W))/dW > 0$. The standard textbook treatments exclude such prices from the production function. For the moment suspend judgement as to why wages should act in this way, in order to focus attention on the implications.

In the standard competitive model the firm would choose a value for N given W. Here the firm chooses both an N and W, but the latter is subject to the constraint that it must not lie below the competitive wage $\bar{W}$. It will sometimes be worth while for the firm to pay over the competitive wage because of the productivity enhancements this induces. The first-order conditions for profit maximization, assuming that the $\bar{W}$ constraint does not bind, are

$$\frac{\partial \pi}{\partial W} = f'e'(W^*)N^* - N^* = 0$$

$$\frac{\partial \pi}{\partial N} = f'e(W^*) - W^* = 0 \tag{8-20}$$

where W^* and N^* are the respective optimal values. Combining the above conditions gives the so-called Solow condition:

$$\frac{e'(W^*)W^*}{e(W^*)} = 1. \tag{8-21}$$

The Solow condition states that the wage should be set so that the elasticity of effort (where effort is synonymous with $e(W)$) with respect to the wage should be unity. Restated, this simply means, set the wage to minimize the cost of each efficiency unit, which is the only plausible result. If we let C be the cost per efficiency unit $(= W/e(W))$, then minimization requires

$$\frac{dC}{dW} = \frac{e(W^*) - e'(W^*)W^*}{[e(W^*)]^2} = 0 \tag{8-22}$$

which is easily seen to be condition (8-21) once more. Figure 8-2 illustrates the Solow condition. It plots the cost per efficiency wage against the wage. The efficiency wage W^* is shown as the minimum value of this function. Because of the $\bar{W}$ constraint, the efficiency wage W^* will not always prevail. It is perfectly possible for the efficiency wage to be less than the market-clearing wage. Thus, if $\bar{W}$ lies to the right of W^* in the region where the effort elasticity is less than 1, the firm is obliged to pay $\bar{W}$.

The interesting case is obviously when $W^* > \bar{W}$, because here there will be involuntary unemployment. There is no incentive to reduce the wage even though the unemployed would be willing to work for less. Efficiency wages lead directly to the idea of involuntary unemployment. Akerlof and Yellen concluded that, 'Without equivocation or qualification, we view efficiency wage models as providing the framework for a sensible macroeconomic model, capable of explaining the stylized facts characterizing business cycles.' Notice how the simple benchmark model can predict a constant wage as the state of demand varies; for example, if output is given by $\theta f(e(W)N)$, where θ represents the state of demand at any point in the cycle, then it is easy enough to see that the optimal wage is independent of θ with only variations in employment as θ changes. Note, however, that the constant wage prediction requires the demand parameter to appear in this particular way, so the constant wage prediction need not always prevail.

There are a large number of justifications for the efficiency wage idea. The first is a direct nutritional impact. A market-clearing wage might be well below that required for minimum physical efficiency. Such an idea may be relevant in poor third-world countries,

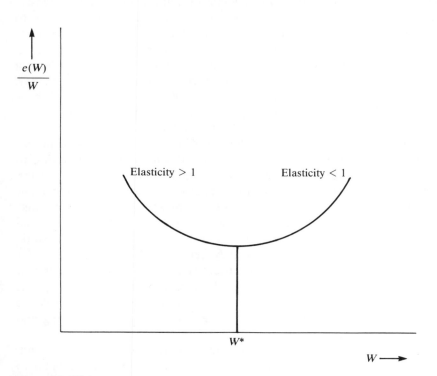

Figure 8-2 Efficiency wages

but hardly relevant to sophisticated and wealthy western economies. However, there may be a direct 'morale' effect on productivity, the idea being that, if people think they are being treated well by the employer, they will perform in excess of the minimum efficiency expected of them to retain their job. Akerlof is a firm advocate of this idea and he is also an interesting exception in that he attempts to provide some thoughtful empirical evidence to support his ideas. There surely is something in the idea that if people think they are well rewarded, they will perform rather better. Productivity is a somewhat elastic quantity and not as rigidly fixed as the textbook production function seems to imply. A second idea is to introduce transaction costs once again. Here transaction costs are related to labour turnover, giving an incentive to reduce the latter. Paying a premium over the market wage is one way of achieving this.

The final two ideas concern *moral hazard* and *adverse selection*. Both of these can involve some highly complex and technical modelling. The two concepts developed from the literature on insurance, but it was quickly realized that they have a much more general application. Suppose I do not have my car insured. I clearly have an incentive to drive carefully, because I will bear the cost of any accident. If I then insure it, I will now no longer bear the full cost of an accident and I will probably not drive as carefully as before. This is an example of moral hazard.

Adverse selection is the idea of *Gresham's law*, the bad driving out the good. An insurance company will attempt to do its best to assess individual risks and set premiums accordingly. For example, young drivers will have an insurance loading and property insurance in inner city areas will be similarly loaded. However, it is prohibitively expensive for companies to ascertain everything about individual risks, so premiums will be set to reflect the *average* risk for a particular set of characteristics. Individuals, naturally enough, might know better than the insurer what their own particular risks are. For example, although young, I may be a conscientious and safe driver, or my property might be in a particularly safe oasis even though located in the inner city. Low-risk individuals may, therefore, choose not to insure at the average premium, whereas high-risk individuals have every incentive to insure. Adverse selection is simply the idea that insurers are left with a residual of high-risk individuals by this process of self-elimination. If this process were taken to extremes, it might no longer be worth while to offer insurance at any premium.

An efficiency wage could arise in the labour market through employers trying to mitigate these two problems. Suppose the firm pays a competitive market-clearing wage. Now suppose an employee were to shirk on the job. The firm can fire the individual, but the person will then immediately be hired by another firm at the competitive wage. That is what paying the going-rate competitive wage means. The moral hazard arises because at the competitive wage the potential employee has no incentive not to shirk. Human nature being what it is, many will shirk if they feel they will not be penalized for doing so. Paying over the market wage reduces the incentive to shirk because there is now a real penalty attached to being fired for shirking. Like Insider–Outsider theory, the shirking model takes a dim view of human behaviour, requiring the employer to devise subtle strategies to motivate employees without the need for expensive monitoring and enforcement of performance.

Here is an example of adverse selection and how an efficiency wage can be the result. Suppose there are two groups, A and B. Group A's productivity does not respond to education, and because of this lack of ability it finds it more expensive to achieve any particular level of qualification compared to group B. Group B, by way of contrast, does respond to education and unit costs for any particular level of qualification are lower. All this is illustrated in Fig. 8-3. Group A's productivity is shown as the horizontal line and group B's as the upward-sloping line with diminishing returns. Costs of education are shown, with group A costs the steeper of the two lines.

Now the usual human capital model would predict the following. Group A should invest nothing in education since marginal costs are positive and marginal benefits are zero. Group A locates at O with net benefit OZ (this assumes each individual is paid a wage equal to his or her productivity). Group B will locate at F, where the marginal benefit of education equals the marginal cost. Point F maximizes the distance between the productivity and cost line. This gives a net benefit of CE.

Now introduce the complication of imperfect information and, in particular, suppose that employers have no prior knowledge of an employee's productivity when they decide to hire. All they can do is observe the individual's level of qualification and from this infer something about that person's productivity. As long as group A invests O and group B invests F, paying a wage of Z and C respectively will correctly reflect both groups' productivity. However, there is a potential adverse selection problem. Suppose group A chooses to invest to qualification level F. This is certainly more expensive for an A, but it does offer net benefits CD which *exceed* OZ. As long as employers offer C for qualification level F, group A has an incentive to mimic group B. This is the adverse selection and the standard Pareto efficient human capital equilibrium is no longer sustainable in this circumstance. With qualification level F, the average productivity of applicants will fall below C, the precise amount depending on the relative proportions of group A and

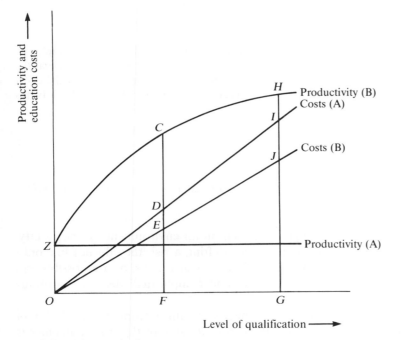

Figure 8-3 Adverse selection

group B. In this instance education fails in its role as an effective 'signalling' device, a means by which employers can accurately filter applicants into low- and high-productivity groups.

If education is to have an effective signalling role, as well as being productivity-augmenting for group B, the qualification level must be set high enough to give group A *no* incentive to mimic group B (and group B no incentive to mimic group A, for that matter). Qualification level G illustrates a signalling equilibrium where group A is better off with net benefit OZ rather than HI and group B receives net benefit JH, which is lower than CE but still higher than OZ.

Notice that the requirement for education to be effective as a signal leads to a Pareto inefficient outcome. Group B is obliged to over-invest in qualifications and this is, in a real sense, a pure waste of scarce resources. The model, therefore, casts light on the modern phenomenon of 'credentialism', the apparent requirement to be over-qualified for many types of job such as accountancy. The Pareto inefficiency also suggests that a better outcome might be to reject the signalling equilibrium. For example, if group A is very small in proportion to group B, then group B might prefer a salary that gives the expected marginal product *including* the dilution caused by including group A. With group A being a small proportion, this would only be a small reduction in wage below C, giving a higher net wage than the signalling wage.

It is quite clear how adverse selection has caused an efficiency wage. A high wage is associated with high-quality applicants, where the qualification level causes potential applicants to preselect themselves. A low wage can result in a dramatic fall in the quality of the average applicant.

PROBLEM

8-5 A firm's output is given by $Q = F(E, N)$, where E represents 'effort' and N numbers employed. Effort is related to the wage according to $E = E(W)$, where $dE/dW > 0$. By demonstrating that the optimal choices of N and W are invariant to any positive monotonic transformation of the effort index, show that the effort index in efficiency wage models need only be ordinal, not cardinal. Is this an important result?

8-5 IMPLICIT CONTRACTS

(*If unsure about expected utility maximization, readers are advised to review Chapter 6 once more.*)

Implicit Contracts are all about wage bargaining in an environment of uncertainty. Wage rigidity is justified on the basis of employees shifting a risk they do not like onto the employers. The latter are assumed to be indifferent to such risks, or are possibly less risk-averse than employees. Because it is a clever and complicated idea, an enormous literature has grown up around it.

Risk aversion means that individuals often prefer a certain outcome to the chance of one of a set of risky outcomes, even though the expected value of the risky outcomes is above the value of the certain outcome. Being prepared to accept a lower expected value in return for the avoidance of risk is what risk aversion is all about. By shifting risks, Pareto-improving outcomes can be achieved and it turns out that many contracts, which take risk into account, will exhibit wage rigidity. A risk-neutral firm could exploit the risk premium and increase its expected profits by offering contracts that give workers a reduced set of risks. These are termed 'Implicit Contracts'.

To make this more concrete, let there be T uncertain states of nature $\theta_1, \ldots, \theta_T$. One of these states will be realized, but the point is that agents do not know in advance which this will be. Attached to these states are the probabilities $p_1, \ldots, p_T$ respectively. The possible states and their associated probabilities are all common knowledge. An unsophisticated bargaining regime would be one that simply let markets clear after the state of nature has been realized. Such a regime is denoted as the 'spot' market and the Implicit Contracts idea seeks to show that Pareto-superior bargains exist compared to the spot contract.

The spot market will associate utilities $U[\bar{W}(\theta_1), L(\theta_1)], \ldots, U[W(\theta_T), L(\theta_T)]$ with each state of nature, where $W(\theta_i)$ is the wage in the ith state and $L(\theta_i)$ is the amount of leisure. Since the discussion is perfectly general, some of these states could represent unemployment, with the 'wage' representing social security payments. Although a considerable amount has been written which focuses on the effort or 'hours dimension' of the labour contract, a convenient simplification, which characterizes most of the literature, is to work with the single argument of wage, ignoring the effort or hours dimension. In effect, this assumes a fixed additive disutility of work which is subsumed within the wage.

Given this, let there be associated with each wage a von Neumann–Morgenstern utility indicator $V(W(\theta))$. With risk aversion assumed, then $V' > 0$ and $V'' < 0$. The expected utility offered by the spot contract regime is therefore

$$Z = \sum_{i=1}^{T} p_i V(W(\theta_i)). \tag{8-23}$$

The expected wage is

$$\bar{W} = \sum_{i=1}^{T} p_i W(\theta_i). \tag{8-24}$$

If agents received the expected wage with certainty, this would give utility $V(\bar{W})$. Because of risk aversion $Z < V(\bar{W})$. (This result is intuitively obvious, but Problem 6.1(d) of Chapter 6 asked for a justification.)

Implicit Contracts exploit this wedge. There is every incentive for a risk-neutral employer to offer a *constant* wage, irrespective of the state of nature, which gives an expected utility at least as high as Z. Since this certain wage can lie below $\bar{W}$, the firm can increase its expected profits. The simplest possible model, which reaches to the heart of the matter, considers a profit-maximizing firm operating in an environment of uncertainty:

$$\pi = \theta f(l) - W(\theta)l \tag{8-25}$$

where l are the numbers employed. Risk is reflected in the state of nature parameter θ, which is a random variable taking the values $\theta_1, \ldots, \theta_T$ with probabilities $p_1, \ldots, p_T$ respectively, as before. Higher values, therefore, represent better states of nature. The firm is obliged to choose l before the state of nature is revealed. The firm's goal is to maximize its expected profits. (Note that a similar problem was discussed in Sec. 6-1 of Chapter 6.)

One possibility is for the firm just to pay the spot wage that would obtain in each state of nature. However, the discussion has suggested that the firm can do rather better than that. The contract should not make workers any worse off, so the constraint on wage-setting is that workers receive a level of expected utility at least as high as Z. The firm maximizes the expected value of profits subject to the constraint

$$E\{V(W(\theta))\} \geq Z. \tag{8-26}$$

Since the spot contract has been discarded, there are now $T + 1$ choice variables. In addition to l, a wage must be specified for each of the T states of nature $\theta_1, \ldots, \theta_T$. The basic and powerful result of Implicit Contracts is that the wage offer will be *constant*, and consequently independent of the realized state of nature. The appeal to neophyte Keynesians is obvious. Here is a justification for wage rigidity in the face of varying demand, based on optimizing behaviour and Pareto optimality rather than *ad hoc* assertion. To see this, form the Lagrangian associated with the optimization problem:

$$L = E\{\theta f(l) - W(\theta)l\} + \lambda[Z - E\{V(W(\theta))\}]. \tag{8-27}$$

The first term is expected profits. Notice how the problem assumes that the firm is risk neutral, which is rather crucial for the rigid-wage result, as it turns out. The second term is the expected utility constraint and λ is the associated Lagrange multiplier. The solution will assume that the constraint holds exactly, since there is no reason for the firm to offer above the minimum level of utility required to satisfy Eq. (8-26).

Solving Eq. (8-27) is a straightforward stochastic optimization, but to see exactly what is involved write this out in full as

$$L = \sum_{i=1}^{T} p_i[\theta_i f(l) - W(\theta_i)l] + \lambda\left[Z - \sum_{i=1}^{T} p_i V(W(\theta_i))\right]. \tag{8-28}$$

An l, $W(\theta_1), \ldots, W(\theta_T)$ are chosen to maximize this. The first-order conditions for a maximum are

$$\frac{\partial L}{\partial l} = \sum_{i=1}^{T} p_i[\theta_i f'(l^*) - W^*(\theta_i)] = 0 \tag{8-29}$$

$$\frac{\partial L}{\partial W(\theta_i)} = p_i l^* + \lambda p_i V'(W^*(\theta_i)) = 0, \qquad i = 1, \ldots, T \tag{8-30}$$

where l^* is optimal employment and $W^*(\theta_i)$ is the optimal wage in the ith state of nature. Notice that Eq. (8-30) is not just one condition but T conditions which must hold for $i = 1, \ldots, T$. Equations (8-29) and (8-30) can be re-expressed as

$$l: \qquad E\{\theta f'(l^*) - W^*(\theta)\} = 0 \tag{8-31}$$

$$W(\theta): \quad l^* + \lambda V'(W^*(\theta)) = 0 \tag{8-32}$$

where, as with Eq. (8-30), Eq. (8-32) summarizes T separate conditions. This equation and its equivalent, Eq. (8-30), are crucial. Since l^* (chosen *ex ante*) and λ are independent of θ, this says that the marginal utility of the wage must be constant in every state of nature. A constant marginal utility implies a constant wage irrespective of the outcome of θ. Denote the fixed, optimal wage as W^*. From Eqs (8-23) and (8-24) it follows that W^* must be less than $\bar{W}$; in effect, the employer exploits the risk premium associated with the spot contract to increase expected profits.

Eq. (8-31) says that the expected marginal product of labour equals W^*. If $\theta_i < \bar{\theta}$ (the mean of the θ distribution) the firm will wish it had hired rather less labour, and if $\theta_i > \bar{\theta}$ it will wish it had hired rather more labour. Either way it is the firm that bears the risks, with profits linearly related to the realization of θ, since $\Delta\pi/\Delta\theta$ just equals $f(l^*)$.

The solution illustrates the important features of the Implicit Contracts approach. First, risk is shifted away from risk-averse workers to the risk-neutral firm. Secondly, a constant wage obtains, independent of the realized state of nature. Risk neutrality on the part of the firm is crucial for this; if, additionally, the firm were risk averse, the optimal wage would no longer show independence from the state of nature. In the extreme case, with risk-neutral workers and a risk-averse firm, profits would be fully insured with workers bearing all the risks (see Problem 8-7). There is, in fact, a close relationship between Implicit Contracts and profit sharing—the idea that workers' salaries should be related to company performance.

Do not think of Implicit Contracts as somehow representing yet another capitalist conspiracy whereby the workers are exploited to extract yet more surplus for the capitalist. Nothing could be further from the truth, despite the fact that the problem set-up seems to suggest that this is so. The framework is simply a means to demonstrate the potential gains from trade, or in this case the gains from trading in risk. The Implicit Contract has been shown to be Pareto superior to the spot contract, which means it is possible to make both parties better off. We have simply chosen the benchmark of keeping workers as well off as before. An entirely symmetric problem, giving exactly the same wage-rigidity result (see Problem 8-6), would be to maximize expected utility subject to the constraint that the firm receives the same level of expected profits as in the spot contract. In this case, the gains appear to accrue entirely to the workers. Of course, the whole issue is entirely artificial; all that is being done is to locate the Pareto-efficient contract, and nothing should be inferred from that about how these gains are to be shared.

A subsequent development has been the issue of incentive compatibility. This introduces less than perfect information once more, posing the question of what happens when the realized state of nature is not common knowledge to both parties in the wage bargain. Incentive compatibility asks what should happen if there is asymmetric information, with the true state of nature known only to one side, usually the employer. An incentive-compatible contract is one which gives the firm no incentive to lie about the true state of nature. The Implicit Contract described previously is obviously incentive compatible. Since W^* is independent of the state of nature, it does not matter what state of nature the firm announces since the wage bill will be unchanged. It might as well tell the truth. However, W^* was derived on the assumption that information was common to all.

In other situations, incentive compatibility may not hold. Suppose the optimal contract specifies that the wage varies with the realized state of nature. If the true state is θ_i, incentive compatibility would require

$$\theta_i f(l) - W(\theta_i)l \ge \theta_i f(l) - W(\theta_j)l \tag{8-33}$$

where θ_j is any other state of nature. Thinking of θ_j as the lie, Eq. (8-33) says that unless the inequality holds, the employer has an incentive to lie in order to increase the firm's profits. With asymmetric information, workers might reasonably specify incentive compatibility as a requirement for any contract. Equation (8-33) would have to hold for all values of i and j. Such incentive-compatibility constraints add another layer of complication.

Although interesting, Implicit Contracts are not without their problems. One difficulty is that it is hard to see how unemployment can emerge. In most reasonable models the employment level exceeds the spot market contract. Notice that, in our case, W^* lay below $\bar{W}$, so the firm recruits *more* labour, not less, under the Implicit Contract. Incentive compatibility may modify this uncomfortable finding to a limited extent but, clearly, Implicit Contracts are hardly the final word in explaining business cycles. Their greatest advantage is to give a rigorous and systematic treatment of uncertainty, which other approaches fail to do. A promising way forward would be to combine this rigour with other approaches.

PROBLEMS

8-6 Suppose that under a 'spot' contract the firm received expected profits $\bar{\pi}$. Workers have a von Neumann–Morgenstern utility function $V(W(\theta))$, where θ is a random variable representing the state of nature. Workers maximize expected utility subject to the constraint that the firm receives expected profits $\bar{\pi}$. Show that the optimal contract specifies a constant wage across all states of nature.

8-7 Suppose that the firm is risk averse with utility function $F(\pi)$ and that the workers, by way of contrast, are risk neutral. The problem is to maximize the expected utility of profits subject to the constraint that the workers receive an expected wage of $\bar{W}$. Show that this leads to risk shifting from the firm to the workers, with profits fixed over all states of nature and the wage varying over states of nature.

8-8 Suppose that both the firm and the workers are risk averse with quadratic utility functions. Show that this leads to a profit-sharing contract of the type $W(\theta_i) = a + b\pi(\theta_i)$, where $W(\theta_i)$ is the wage in the ith state and $\pi(\theta_i)$ are profits in the ith state. Both a and b are parameters.

8-6 SUMMARY

This chapter has reviewed some New Keynesian ideas. As has been said, the approach is essentially eclectic, reflecting a modelling style rather than a precise set of beliefs. The issues involved, however, are age old, reflecting a deep-seated 'gut reaction' that New Classical equilibrium-type conclusions are not entirely satisfactory. Unemployment is not always a case of 'everything for the best in this the best of all possible worlds'. At their best New Keynesians play by fundamentally the same rules as the New Classicals, which is why they are not, in the final analysis, conflicting paradigms.

ESSAY TOPICS

8-1 What are the distinguishing features of New Keynesianism? Can New Classical and New Keynesian economics ever live in harmonious company?

8-2 What is meant by the idea that the labour market is a social institution, and what are the implications for macroeconomics?

8-3 How useful are Insider–Outsider ideas to understanding the labour market? Do you believe that insiders would actually behave in the way suggested by the model?

8-4 'Yet another false dawn, with the usual exaggerated hype from its protagonists.' Is this a fair assessment of efficiency wage theory?

8-5 'Implicit Contracts are another case of economists re-discovering Pareto-efficiency and then asserting that this is how labour markets will behave.' Discuss.

READING

A comprehensive and advanced text is Tirole (1988). For a discussion of scientific management and a view of the labour process see Braverman (1977). The example of Sec. 8-1 is taken from Solow (1990). Solow is highly sceptical of rational expectations and has made several important recent contributions in this area. A useful, but quite difficult, discussion of transaction costs is to be found in Chapter 8 of Blanchard and Fischer (1989). The point about small transaction costs causing severe price rigidity is made in Akerlof and Yellen (1985). Insider–Outsider theory was developed by Lindbeck and Snower (1988) and Blanchard and Summers (1987) describe a specific hysteresis model. The literature on efficiency wages is vast and expanding. A brief but excellent survey is Yellen (1984), whereas Stiglitz (1987) offers rather more detail, in an accessible way. Akerlof and Yellen (1986) offer a comprehensive survey and collection of articles. Specific models on various aspects are: morale effects, Akerlof (1982) and (1984); moral hazard and shirking, Shapiro and Stiglitz (1984). An introduction to moral hazard and adverse selection is Chapter 20 of Gravelle and Rees (1981). There is an enormous literature on this topic, but my example is based on Spence (1973) and (1976). The two early references on Implicit Contracts are Azariadis (1975) and Baily (1974). Two useful surveys are Rosen (1985) and Manning (1990). Another classic and closely related article is McDonald and Solow (1981), which clarifies the difference between 'efficient' and 'right to manage' contracts. My advice is to read McDonald and Solow first, before delving into the Implicit Contracts literature proper. Finally, some of the antecedents to this literature should not be overlooked. The book by Doeringer and Piore (1971) is a classic. Just about one of the greatest articles in economics ever written is Oi (1962), which is rarely referenced and more or less says it all. Students who are interested in exploring the promising area of New Keynesianism more deeply would be well advised to take a course in industrial relations to develop a confident feel for the institutional detail that pervades the labour market.

RULES VERSUS DISCRETION: THE CONSTITUTIONAL PERSPECTIVE

The broad issues addressed in previous chapters of this book pose many questions about how any society should (or should not) organize itself and the relationship between a country's economy and its political institutions. Mainstream economics, which is claimed to be a technical, scientific subject, has tended to shy away from such questions. Most textbooks on macroeconomics begin and end with a model, and this is a pity. The revolution wrought by rational expectations carries with it some fairly strong policy advice just as the earlier Keynesian revolution which preceded it, and macroeconomists are bound to consider the broader political framework. They need a basic understanding of political theory and the appropriate institutional arrangements to complement the economic framework. Lucas, whose ideas have been so influential and have formed much of the subject-matter of this book, recognizes the need for this. In doing so, macroeconomists can make their subject more interesting and exciting in contrast to the dull, mechanical paradigms of purposeless detail produced by some anoetic practitioners of the subject.

Broadly speaking, there are four types of professional economist, although it should be said that the same economist might wear different hats at different times. First are the 'pure technicians' who strictly separate their professional and political lives. They see their role as advisory, using internally consistent formal models and adopting best practice empirical analysis whenever possible. They have little or no political agenda and regard themselves basically in a servicing role to the next group to be described. Like all castes, they believe their very lack of contamination with the 'polity' sets them apart from the common herd, and this group ethic sustains them. For example, rather than do empirical analysis this group might spend time refining techniques to enable others to perform these tasks better. Any academic discipline will require such people, and the fact that 'pure technicians' command high salaries in the marketplace and fill the top posts in universities is evidence of their worth.

The second group are the 'politico-technicians' and these probably constitute the majority of the mainstream. 'Politico-technicians' are in the business of *persuasion*; they do have a political agenda of varying degrees of scale. What distinguishes this group is their belief that they use a superior methodology to derive their conclusions. State-of-the-art modelling and econometric practice are central for this group and they consider that their good scientific practices and superior techniques entitle their pronouncements to carry more weight in the marketplace for ideas. An example is the extremely well-regarded book by Richard Layard, Steven Nickell and Richard Jackman, *Unemployment: Macroeconomic Performance and the Labour Market*, published in 1991. At the end of a complex model-building exercise and investigations spanning many countries, they adjudicate upon at least 13 separate policies to reduce unemployment. It must be stressed that there is absolutely nothing wrong with this; it should be recognized that inside most economists there is a 'political manifesto'—even if only on a single issue—waiting to emerge. However, the 'politics' is conducted within technical economic terms, isolated from a broader philosophical perspective.

The third group are the 'utopians'. Unlike the 'politico-technicians', who are often concerned with small-scale tinkering at the *status quo*, this group are prone to make pronouncements on the grand scale. The political manifesto is central and for many of this group there is no separation between their professional and personal lives, which is one of unrelieved political activity. Utopian economists are found across the whole political spectrum and their common feature is the lack of need to pay much attention to empirical evidence or feasibility. They simply do not accept the constraint of devising institutional structures which take account of mankind's flawed standards of decency; rather, they would claim that individual selfishness is conditioned by current political arrangements and this would disappear once the institutions were reformed. A cynical view of this group is of people inventing fantasy worlds in which they themselves would like to live, and probably be invited to run by popular acclaim.

The fourth group are the political economists and this also covers a wide spectrum. For example, most 'utopians' would describe themselves as political economists. This chapter will focus on an important subset which might be described as neo-Austrian classical political economy and, in particular, the ideas of Professor James Buchanan. This is a tradition steeped in the history of the subject and professing an avowed disgust at the false prophet Keynes, the creeping collectivization of western liberal democracies and the 'depoliticization' of the subject through its obsession with mathematical technique and formalistic models. The political agenda is to advocate arrangements that would promote and extend those activities, regulated through the free enterprise system, with a minimum of external organization. The danger of the 'Collective' is real and the eternal vigilance of argument must be there to educate others to the virtues of free markets. The proper role of the economist is the search for obtainable structures—given mankind's basic self-interested, non-altruistic nature—within which non-coerced enterprise can prosper. The collapse of the socialist order in eastern Europe is not surprising to this group of political economists because such systems were based on unreasonable expectations of the perfectibility of human nature. Modern economics is either not interested in, or is technically ill-equipped to answer, these large questions about how societies should organize themselves.

Perhaps the next great revolution in economics will be the absorption of this smaller classical political economy tradition into the mainstream and a diminution in importance of technical economics. There are two reasons for believing this will happen. First, there is the fallacy that the only legitimate questions in economics are technical ones. Thus Ivor

Pearce, writing about the ambitious Southampton model of the economy—now defunct—said, 'There is nothing impossible about one million equations except that, as has been said, "the impossible takes a little longer".' Secondly, is the realization, with the advent of the modern number-crunching computer and the explosion in 'results', that the vast majority of these are simply statistical artefacts and that the sheer quantity of human capital used up in producing anything of substance is too large. Classical political economy offers an alternative answer to the question: 'What ought economists to be talking about?' The ideas of Buchanan represent one view, which is directly relevant to the New Classical perspective of the preceding chapters.

9-1 THE LIMITS TO TECHNICAL ECONOMICS

Buchanan, who incidentally won the Nobel Prize for economics in 1986, has written that:

Economics, as a discipline, became 'scientific' over the quarter-century, but I put the word in inverted commas and I deliberately pronounce it pejoratively here. As it is practised in the 1980s, economics is a 'science' without ultimate purpose or meaning. It has allowed itself to become captive of the technical tools that it employs without keeping track of just what it is the tools are used for. In a very real sense, the economists of the 1980s are illiterate in basic principles of their own discipline.... Their motivation is not normative; they seem to be ideological eunuchs. Their interest lies in the purely intellectual properties of the models with which they work, and they seem to get their kicks from the discovery of proofs of propositions relevant only for their own fantasy lands.

(Buchanan, 1986, p. 14)

The meaning of this is quite clear and it would be an unthinking technocrat who would bombastically dismiss these strictures. Professor Buchanan follows in the Austrian tradition of classical political economy, where the basic atom of analysis is the *individual*, not aggregate concepts. This is a tradition which is also somewhat sceptical of the use of mathematics and conventional empirical economics, and for its practitioners the 'common language' of discourse is words, not formal mathematical models. Those who follow Buchanan's approach might also be sceptical of this book, which treats economics as an aggregate science.

Buchanan sees economics and political philosophy—the study of those arrangements and institutions thought appropriate and feasible for societies to organize themselves—as the same discipline. Modern economics, which pretends it can isolate itself from the polity and be scientific in the same way as, for example, inorganic chemistry, becomes a sterile and meaningless activity. Within its narrow confines it may be intellectually demanding and interesting for its own sake, but only in the same way as solving *The Times* crossword puzzle. Technical economics can achieve little if it steadfastly refuses to recognize the political dimension. Having recognized the political dimension, economics should not be about writing political manifestos of the utopian kind. Those, no matter of what political persuasion, who regard the elaboration of such fantasyland utopian schemes as a valid research agenda, are treated by Buchanan and his fellow Austrians such as Hayek and von Mises with blistering contempt. Buchanan follows in the tradition of Adam Smith, concerned with the study of mankind as it *is* rather than how we would like it to be in some designer utopian scheme.

In the absence of rules and sanctions for misbehaviour, mankind's natural state is not particularly edifying—or so the claim goes. It is one of unconstrained self-interest, where anything goes. Without rules and sanctions many individuals are prepared to lie, cheat, rob and commit acts of violence in order to achieve power for its own sake or some economic advantage. The only sanction is the countervailing brutality of others. Even if individuals have an innate moral sense (and for some this is a dubious claim), without some higher-level minimal organization of rules and sanctions, there can be no general prosperity. Not everyone need be a brute in this primordial state, the fact that 'civilization' emerged proves this; the point is that enough are prepared to be brutes to make the expectation of advantage from trade uncertain and, in consequence, to emasculate it.

Adam Smith's discovery was to understand why the free market system, above other alternatives, allows individuals to maximize their own value. (Generally speaking, writers in the Austrian tradition would avoid teleological concepts such as 'utility'.) Without constraints, mankind would quickly revert to its impoverished state of savage brutality. However, with appropriate and minimal rules to temper the worst aspects of self-interest, the free market system, without any further intervention or centralized organization, creates, in Hayek's famous phrase, a 'spontaneous order or *kosmos*' with no need for a 'made order or *taxis*', the latter being the product of deliberate design. The minimal set of rules required must be sufficient to ensure that exchange relationships are voluntary and not coercive. Individuals should trade on the assumption that agreements once freely entered into will be adhered to and enforced and that property rights will be respected. In short, individuals should be able to trade without fear. With appropriately formulated 'rules of the game', mankind's innate desire to engage in mutually advantageous trade will, when left alone, generate individual wealth, where what defines 'wealth' is something quite personal to the individual. (For example, it might include the option of behaving in an altruistic way, and if that is what particular individuals choose, then so be it.) In the words of Hayek (1973, p. 40):

We can never produce a crystal or a complex organic compound by placing the individual atoms in such a position that they will form the lattice of a crystal.... But we can create the conditions in which they will arrange themselves in such a manner.

Although Hayek expresses his greatest admiration for the common law which articulates or 'discovers' rules formed within the spontaneous order, the rules may be the product of deliberate design or legislation, but the resultant order is of a spontaneous kind. Spontaneous orders necessarily enhance personal freedom because power or coercion can more easily be exercised over made orders. Spontaneous orders are resilient to the danger of totalitarianism.

Buchanan believes that what distinguishes human beings from the animal kingdom is an innate ability to 'truck and barter' for mutual advantage. One might add the second distinguishing characteristic, which is the ability to formulate complex rules and sanctions and obey them. It is the analysis of this insight and the formulation of the appropriate rules or constraints, subject to which individuals are free to pursue their own interests, which are, for Buchanan and his fellow 'contractarian constitutionalists', the proper subject-matter of economics. The prescriptive role of economics, if it is to have any, is in the formulation of the 'best' rules or social institutions that will allow the maximization of individual values. On this level, there is no distinction between 'ought' and 'is', between 'normative' and so-called 'scientific' economics. Buchanan further claims that the analysis of individuals in their market role as traders is a useful guide for the study of political institutions, which political theorists often ignore. The insights of political economy are highly relevant for the appropriate constraints to be placed on elected politicians and their agents.

9-2 THE BUCHANAN AGENDA

Buchanan wishes to set strict limits on the range of issues with which normal political activity may be concerned. He works within a tradition where the basic irreducible datum is the individual person. Individuals cannot simply be 'added up', and notions such as 'the common good' or 'social welfare' or 'the collective view' or even 'national income' are meaningless, vacuous concepts, given this doctrine of methodological individualism. Buchanan's ideas are fairly complicated and, necessarily, the language he uses to express them is often obscure. His work is no less demanding than some of the mathematical or technical models. Some economists consider words to be an inferior form of reasoning, but the claim is a dubious one.

Buchanan is most famous for his advocacy of an 'economic constitution', with politics confined to a set of well-defined tasks, strictly regulated by a set of constitutional constraints. All western liberal democracies have constitutions, albeit unwritten in some cases. The constitution specifies 'the rules of the game' within which 'normal' political activity can take place. It is the constitution that disciplines politicians and their agents; in the words of Tom Paine, the eighteenth-century defender of the American constitution and the French revolution, a constitution says, 'Thus far canst thou go and no further.' In political philosophy, discussion of the question 'What is a constitution?' can become abstruse and highly technical, but for our limited purposes most people can understand what Buchanan has in mind. We think of a constitution as the 'bedrock' of democracy, which in practice should mean that the requirements for elected majorities to change the constitution should be much stricter than for ordinary laws. (In the UK it is not immediately clear that this is so, since, as is well known, there is no formal constitution.) Although never immutable, a constitution carries with it the notion of *permanence*; no matter what the political persuasion of the government of the day, it will stick by the constitution. At some points Buchanan (1986) suggests that constitutional rules could only be changed through unanimous agreement, though he recognizes the practical impossibility of this extreme contractarian logic. He tempers the unanimity rule with the statement, 'the decision rule for the latter [constitutional change] should be more inclusive' (p. 246).

According to Buchanan, there is only one really legitimate role for political activity, apart from the important function of conserving and protecting the constitution from attack. He writes (Buchanan 1986, p. 255)

The fundamental role for politics, inclusively defined, is that of providing the legal framework within which individuals can go about their ordinary business of seeking to further the values they choose to seek, without overt conflict.

The danger of this Hobbesian compact is well known. Once a group of individuals are granted the authority to punish 'wrong-doers' with no retribution to be exacted from themselves, it is all too easy for these agents of the state to transform themselves from protector to tyrant. It is the constitution and its acceptance by the agents of the state that protects ordinary citizens from the potential of a 'police state'. For example, periodic elections, the independence of the judiciary, the right of trial by jury, the right to call the state's agents to account for their activities, and so on, are the proper stuff of the constitution. Western liberal democracies survive because the politicians and their agents accept the constitution and that power is sufficiently diffused so that no individual or group can seriously believe that the constitution can be hijacked without dire retribution.

Buchanan's 'big idea' is to transfer many activities now commonly accepted as part of the normal political process into the realm of the constitution. This basically consists of three elements: (i) balanced budgets; (ii) strict spending limits; and (iii) monetary order. An economic constitution would limit the discretion of the government of the day in economic affairs and oblige it to follow clearly specified, well-understood rules. The affinity between this and New Classical economics is easy to see. However, it is fair to say that Buchanan's ideas come from a profound philosophical perspective and that his beliefs would not be affected one jot if incontrovertible evidence became available that rational expectations are a completely false doctrine.

Now consider the New Classical agenda in this wider political economy context. It embodies a set of beliefs or conjectures as to how the economy behaves and some general policy advice. The beliefs are, roughly speaking, the following. Expectations are formed rationally; inflation is primarily a monetary phenomenon; markets clear with the implication that full employment is a 'strong attractor' to which the free enterprise economy will spontaneously move. Associated with this equilibrium view of unemployment is the belief that the business cycle is much less costly than moderate rates of inflation. The policy prescriptions of the New Classical agenda can be comfortably absorbed by the contractarian constitutionalists. Both favour a rule-based economic policy with a strong predisposition against discretion or policy activism. Since disorder in both employment and inflation performance is primarily identified with monetary incompetence, special importance is attached to the rules within which monetary policy may be conducted. To reinforce the credibility of the monetary rule, noting the close connection between fiscal and monetary policy discussed at length in Chapter 1, a policy of fiscal rectitude is also advocated; in practice this means a balanced budget defined in some appropriate way. Finally, there is the belief that free enterprise is the best allocation mechanism and that the range of government activities should be limited. Clearly, these ideas cohere quite comfortably with the idea of an economic constitution, which would put strict limits on the economic authority of politicians and their agents. Lucas has stated that, 'We need an ... "economic constitution" and we are at last beginning to develop the economic theory that will be helpful in designing it.'

9-3 AN ASSESSMENT

One frequently advocated scheme by the New Classicals (see Chapter 7) is to divorce the conduct of monetary policy from elected politicians, instead vesting authority onto some suitably constituted independent central bank. How would a 'contractarian constitutionalist' see this? The first point to make is that an independent central bank and one strictly limited by rules are not the same thing. There is absolutely no reason why an independent central bank, unrestricted by rules, should not pursue an activist interventionist monetary regime. Indeed, Buchanan might claim that such a bank may behave far more irresponsibly than the politicians it is supposed to replace. For politicians there is the minimal check of the ballot box, and Buchanan warns that institutions without rules limiting their behaviour are potentially dangerous.

A good analogy is to compare an independent bank with the judicial system, which for good reasons has a degree of independence from elected politicians. Does this eliminate the least savoury part of the political process? Not always and the Supreme Court of the USA provides a good example of potential difficulties. Independence from both the legislature and the executive is embodied through the fact that judges to the Supreme Court, once appointed, are effectively irremovable. The Supreme Court also has considerable discretion in interpreting the constitution of the United States. For example, it interpreted the constitution as permitting the death penalty, then ruled it unconstitutional in 1972, then restored the possibility of capital punishment once again in 1976. The issue of race and discrimination is another key area where the constitution has been flexibly interpreted. Supreme Court judges are *de facto* politicians voted in for life and obviously the appointment of such judges becomes highly politicized and the question of legal competence hardly arises. Is the nominee a liberal or a conservative? What are his or her attitudes to abortion, race, the death penalty and so on? What we see in practice is not some lofty tribunal of authority commanding universal respect, but an unedifying aspect of politics where an incumbent President attempts to extend his political agenda beyond his own shelf-life. Now it may be that the diffusion of power between the three great arms of government in the USA—the executive, the legislature and the judiciary—is highly desirable, but one should not pretend that 'independence' removes all political aspects from a process and likewise for an independent central bank, however constructed.

There is no reason why an unfettered central bank should not begin to resemble the above process, and indeed go further, because at least the American constitution limits the discretion of Supreme Court justices to some degree. The naive view of an independent central bank being run by sensible bank-manager types, who are models of propriety and rectitude, is just so much wishful thinking—incidentally, given the grotesque incompetence and dishonesty with which some commercial banks have conducted their affairs in the 1980s, it would seem that bankers may not be the people one would want to entrust with the running of monetary policy.

Suppose, by way of example, a socialist government is in what it considers to be the fortunate position of nominating the next governor of an independent Bank of England. Just why would it wish to choose someone who works by the sound money precepts of New Classical macroeconomics? Independence becomes a battleground of conflicting ideologies seeking an unaccountable home for their political agendas. In short, independence and rules are not the same thing; and for 'constitutionalists' such as Buchanan it is the rules that are critical. The case for independence is that it should accompany the rules to reinforce the credibility of the latter. Thus independence is just one way of making operational one part of the economic constitution. However, it is not clear that hiving off monetary policy in this way is any better than subsuming all the requisite parts within a common constitutional framework.

A second problem with the independence argument is that it tends to be conducted within the 'politico-technical' analytical framework. For example, Alesina has ranked central banks according to their degree of independence and shown that the lowest inflation performance over the period 1973–86 is associated with the highest degree of independence. Some classic 'politico-technical' reasoning then follows. Superior scientific investigation has revealed that low inflation performance is associated with central bank independence. The policy prescription, 'Let's have independent central banks' is then vested with the authority of a hard science in the same way that adding carbon fibres to steel leads to a superior and stronger metal. It is unacceptable that fundamental questions about how society should conduct its affairs should be reduced to the level of 'It is a good thing if it makes the trains run on time.' 'Politico-technical' economists, to their credit, frequently reveal their discomfort at the constraints their own methodology imposes on them and Alesina is no exception. There is parenthetically the proviso that the issue concerns a whole set of broader political questions about how societies should organize themselves. It is the troubled footnotes tucked away from the text that should be elevated to be part of the discourse of economics. The standard 'politico-technical' seminar would devote two minutes to the issue of the troubled footnote, whereas the classical political economy approach would devote all *but* two minutes to it. Buchanan surely has a point here.

Returning to the issue of an economic constitution, of which an independent central bank might form one part, agreeing on the necessity for a constitution does not answer the question of what should be in it. Buchanan's idea is that much normal political activity, presently accepted as extra-constitutional, should fall within the ambit of a constitution. So it is a question of where to draw the line. Is politics to become a vestigial, marginalized activity, with citizens regarding it as irrelevant to their lives as long as the economic peace and 'law and order' are maintained? Buchanan would like this to be so.

The largest function of political activity, in terms of the economic resources used up, is what Buchanan refers to as 'the productive state'. This concerns the provision and maintenance of public goods defined in the broadest sense, and its associated legislation. Chapter 2 discussed these and their inexorable tendency to grow. This type of political activity is the game itself as opposed to the making of the rules of the game. For Buchanan the general watchword is to make this area as small as possible.

Why should political activity be limited to the role of 'nightwatchman' with the state merely the upholder of property rights, enforcer of contracts voluntarily entered into and punisher of transgressors? Two reasons can be detected. First, elected politicians do not seek the 'common good', such a collectivist idea being literally meaningless to Buchanan. The analogy of the marketplace is useful here. Given that individuals are motivated by self-interest, keen to pursue their own objectives, why should elected politicians and their agents be expected to behave differently? Strict rules should be used to temper this spontaneous seeking of individual advantage and, of course, restricting the range of activities further limits the potential of politicians and their agents to exploit ordinary citizens for their own ends. Buchanan (1986, p. 25) writes,

Why did economists ... take the Keynesian theory of policy seriously? Why did they fail to see the elementary point that elected politicians will seek any excuse to create budget deficits?

Two observations are in order on this first point. The assertion of persistent budget deficits in the absence of constitutional constraints—what Buchanan sees as a decline in the Victorian values of preserving one's capital—is simply not true. The discussion of the history of UK budget deficits in Chapter 1 indicates basic fiscal rectitude, despite the ascendancy of Keynesianism and no constitutional constraints. This shows the limitations and the partial arrogance of the Austrian method, which believes that progress towards the truth can be made by a process of empathizing (*verstehen*) with how an ideal type might behave when placed in a particular context. Actual hard-core empirical evidence is treated with suspicion because the absolutely correct experimental conditions are never available.

The second observation is that the universal picture of self-interested politicians is just too Machiavellian to ring true. Many politicians are motivated by 'higher ideals'. The fact of political prisoners and those prepared to give their lives for a cause militates against a general denigration of the political process. Buchanan's own account of his academic martyrdom in Virginia is further impressive testimony that human action is frequently motivated by ideals and not purely by self-interest. Of course, the counter to this is that it is the *potential* for self-interested political activity that must be guarded against, despite the frequent observation of altruistic behaviour. One person's higher ideals are another person's potential tyranny. It is wise always to lock one's doors even though the burglars call only occasionally.

The second argument for limiting political activity is that it is, by its very nature, coercive. Since coercion detracts from individual value maximization, this should, *ipso facto*, be limited insofar as it is possible. Buchanan does not have a particularly elevated view of the power and desirability of the ballot box. Issues decided through the ballot are fundamentally coercive. To non-Austrians this notion might appear strange, but not when one's standpoint is that of methodological individualism. Buchanan (1986, p. 252) writes that,

All persons equally express their preferences as between two outcomes presented; but those who are out-voted find their own desired outcome is not selected. They must acquiesce in a result that runs counter to their own interests or values. Clearly, with respect to the particular choice examined, those whose interests are submerged gain little or nothing from their participation in the electoral procedure.

Thus politics is the exercise of *power* (a bad thing) not of *choice* (a good thing), irrespective of whether or not that power derives from the ballot box or an all-powerful Hobbesian sovereign. The conclusion is that the range of political activity should be limited where possible. Clearly, there are many mutually exclusive public goods over which the exercise of individual choice is simply impractical. Thus, a referendum on the issue of whether the UK should have joined the European Community was appropriate since some individuals cannot unilaterally decide to remain in the Community and others decide to leave it. However, Buchanan's thesis is that only those activities that have a high degree of mutual exclusivity should be political. Buchanan's claim for constitutional reform is that most western liberal democracies have extended the range of issues decided upon by the political process far beyond the mutual exclusivity criterion. Much of the activity described in Chapter 2 would fail Buchanan's mutual exclusivity test.

Buchanan's philosophical position leads to a degree of ambivalence with regard to the process of democracy itself, or more accurately, Buchanan believes in democracy but thinks that the best way to achieve it is not necessarily through the exercise of the vote. He writes (Buchanan 1986, p. 250).

Effective political decision-making authority may be lodged in a committee of experts, a set of philosopher-kings, a single party's ruling clique, a military junta, or in a single monarch; any one of which structures may be held better to attain 'that which is good for all members of the community' than ordinary electoral processes with inclusive voting franchise.

Democracy for Buchanan is the objective of achieving '*ex ante* political equality'. As a practical matter he suggests that the best way to achieve this is that 'the franchise be open to all, that political agents be rotated on some regular basis and that gross bundling of separate collective choices be avoided' (Buchanan 1986, p. 246). Buchanan stresses that this is not the only way and that democracy is not synonymous with the ballot box.

Can constitutional rules be imposed on economic matters in practice? Take, as an example, one key Buchanan idea that the budget should balance. The constitution would need to be *precise* about the requirement, because a vague definition is immediately open to abuse by self-interested politicians, with *de facto* discretion the result. Is budget balance defined over one fiscal year? If not, over how long a period? How are capital items such as privatization receipts to be treated? Are there to be automatic refunds or surcharges for under- or overshoots? Is budget balance a zero nominal financial deficit or a constant debt-to-income ratio? What degree of error will be permitted before sanctions are imposed on those charged with following the rule—1, 2 or 3 per cent of GNP, or what? What is to be done if there is some large unforeseen contingency? Presumably, war might permit the suspension of the rule, but what about the 'Savings and Loan' scandal in the United States? In the United Kingdom the contingent liabilities of the Export Credit Guarantees Department is around one quarter of the National Debt and some unforeseen scandal is not unimaginable here, and on a massive scale. Are the country's citizens to be subject to a huge one-off surcharge?

In short, following 'rules' or following 'discretion' is not a separate choice, rather there is a continuum with degrees of 'ruleness' and degrees of 'discretionness'. Inevitably, no matter how well in advance the rule framer tries to plan for every contingency, there will be the claim by some that the constitution has been violated, accompanied by equally virulent denials by the state's agents. Laws that are perceived to have been violated by the rule maker bring the whole edifice of constitutional government into disrepute. The search for an economic constitution is akin to the search for a mechanical system of jurisprudence whereby judges' discretion on the identification and punishment of transgressors is entirely eliminated. Such notions appeal to the tidy-minded civil service mentality, and irrespective of whether such mechanical schemes are desirable, we might as well face up to the fact that an all-encompassing economic constitution is simply not obtainable. Because 'basic' constitutions are seen as useful devices ensuring the success of western liberal democracies, this is no way suggests a role over and beyond this basic function which the economic constitutional arguments imply.

Thus constitutional democracy, where the frontier of control is shifted to the constitution and away from politicians, may be a Faustian pact with the devil. When it works, all is fine, but when things go wrong the ability of a country's citizens to reform an all-pervasive constitution is severely restricted. The constitution becomes the new dictator, if the obvious anthropomorphism may be forgiven here. Democracy is not just about maximizing individual values, but also about the right to 'screw things up'. Unruly children become better citizens when allowed the calming effect of making their own decisions, even though the grown-ups know these are bad choices. One should not overlook the fact that democracy, through the exercise of the ballot box, might have the same cathartic effect and that the peaceful spontaneous order of the market, which economists find so appealing, may be the product of each individual feeling that he or she counts equally. The so-called experts—the grown-ups in this context—who claim to know best are well advised to grit their teeth and accept what they consider to be the foolish outcomes of the ballot box.

9-4 SUMMARY

Macroeconomics has moved on considerably from the assertion 'We are all Keynesians now', and this book has tried to cover a small part of these developments. It has also tried to capture some of the tensions between the believers in the 'spontaneous order' of the market, with their strong predilection to leave well alone and the neo-Keynesian counter-attack that the 'spontaneous order' requires a greater degree of organization from without. As always in a a lively and vibrant subject, the jury is still debating the matter. This final chapter has tried to suggest that the debate is not one that can be conducted or settled within the narrow confines of technical economics. Clearly, if the summit of one's ambition is to sit in front of a video screen looking at stock prices, exchange rates or whatever in order to make a decent living, then concentrate on technique and forget the rest. If, however, one sees the study of economics not only as instrumental in securing a living (useful and necessary as that may be) but also as giving important insights into the structures of societies, then technique alone is not sufficient.

READING

The main source of inspiration for this chapter is Buchanan (1986). Since I quote extensively from this book, page numbers to locate quotations are given in the text. For a discussion of spontaneous orders see Hayek (1973) and a useful supplement is Hayek (1944), which is a famous polemical essay in which he writes of the 'spontaneous forces' that should be harnessed in a free society in contrast to the conscious direction of a planned (socialist) society, which can lead only to disaster. A good primer to political philosophy is Barry (1989). For an influential statement of the conventional positive 'scientific' role of economics, see the introduction to Lipsey (1966). The plea for a one-million-equation econometric model is from the introduction to Pearce et al. (1976); and Section VIII of Lucas (1987) relates New Classical economics to the economic constitution debate. Alesina (1989) discusses the inflation performance of independent central banks. Goldfeld (1982) describes the practical difficulties of defining the rules that policy makers are supposed to follow. A formal proof of the impossibility of an aggregate social welfare function, other than through unanimity, is Arrow (1951).

ANSWERS TO PROBLEMS

CHAPTER 1

1-1 (a) 10 per cent. This is $(110 - 100)/100$.

(b) From Eq. (1-6), $(1 + r) = (1 + 0.02)110/100 = 1.122$. Thus $r = 12.2$ per cent and the bond is redeemed at £1.122.

(c) From Eq. (1-13) the market price is $[1.122/(1 + 0.02)](100/105) = £1.0476$. There is a 4.76 per cent capital gain.

(d) Not really. Other asset prices would have adjusted to reflect change in expectations. The bond still offers a real rate of 2 per cent. Keynesian speculative motive suggests selling the bond if you believe the market forecast of 5 per cent is too low, because of expected capital loss exceeding any interest payments. Answers ignore attitude to risk—see Chapter 6.

1-2 (a) 10 per cent—use Eq. (1-6) and $\rho^{\varepsilon}_{t-1} = 2$ per cent.

(b) $P^{\varepsilon}_t = P_t = 1.1$. Hence $G_t - T_t = 1/1.1$. From Eq. (1-17), the real value of the bonds is $1/(1.1) + (1 + 0.02)10 = 11.11$ billion.

(c) We require $B_t = B_{t-1} = 10$. From Eq. (1-17), $1/(P_t) + (1 + 0.02)(11)/P_t = 10$, noting that $G_t - T_t = 1/P_t$. Hence $P_t = 1.222$. Authorities must deliver an inflation surprise of 12.2 per cent over and above the expected 10 per cent to cause the real debt erosion.

(d) From Eq. (1-17), $1 + (1 + 0.02)(10)(1.1) = B_t = 12.22$.

1-3 $B_t/B_{t-1} = 1.02$. $Y_t/Y_{t-1} = 1.01$. Hence $B_t/Y_t = [(1.02)/(1.01)]B_{t-1}/Y_{t-1}$. This is a first-order difference equation with solution $B_t/Y_t = (1.0099)^t B_0/Y_0$. We know that $B_0/Y_0 = 1$ and $B_t/Y_t = 3$. Hence, $t = \ln 3/\ln 1.0099 = 111.5$ years. (A long time!)

1-4 (a) PV of disposable income is $1000 + (1020)/(1.02) = 2000$. This equals PV of consumption. Hence, $900 + C_{t+1}/1.02 = 2000$. $C_{t+1} = 1122$.

(b) PV of disposable income is $[500 + 1020 + 500(1.02)]/1.02 = 2000$, where $500(1.02)$ is the offsetting reduction in debt repayments in the next period. Consumption plan does not change. This is Ricardian equivalence in its purest form.

(c) The latter regime requires individual to borrow 400 in first period, unlike the first regime. Capital constraints may prevent this.

1-5 (a) From Eq. (1-18), $(G_t - T_t)/Y_t = [B_t - B_{t-1}(1.02)]/Y_t$. Furthermore, $B_{t-1} = B_t/(1 + 0.05)$. Substitute out B_{t-1}. Hence, $(G_t - T_t)/Y_t = (B_t/Y_t)(1 - 0.9714)$. Deficit in base year is 2.86 per cent. In current year 8.57 per cent. Question does not ask whether fiscal regimes are feasible.

(b) We require $(G_t - T_t)/Y_t = 3[1 - (1.02)/(1 + g)] = 0.0286$. Hence $g = 2.98$ per cent.

1-6 (a) With a constant price level, $\pi = 0$, hence, $(M_t - M_{t-1})/P_t = A[Y_{t-1}(1 + g)]^\delta \rho^\Phi - AY_{t-1}^\delta \rho^\Phi$. Divide by M_{t-1}/P_t to derive $(M_t - M_{t-1})/M_{t-1} = (1 + g)^\delta - 1$. This is the growth rate giving the maximum non-inflationary seigniorage.

(b) $\delta = 1$.

(c) Let $M_t/P_t = A_0(\rho + \pi)^{-1}$, where $A_0 = AY_t^\delta = $ constant. From Eq. (1-27), the inflation tax is $Z_t = [\pi/(1 + \pi)]M_t/P_t$. Differentiate to derive

$$dZ_t/d\pi = \frac{A_0(\rho + \pi^*)^{-1}}{(1 + \pi^*)^2} - \frac{A_0\pi^*(\rho + \pi^*)^{-2}}{(1 + \pi^*)} = 0$$

where π^* is the maximum inflation rate. Hence $\pi^* = \rho^{1/2}$.

(d) With $\Phi \neq -1$, then:

$$\frac{dZ_t}{d\pi} = \frac{(\rho + \pi^*)^\Phi}{(1 + \pi^*)} + \Phi\pi^*(\rho + \pi^*)^{\Phi-1} = 0.$$

Hence, $\rho + \pi^* + \Phi\pi^*(1 + \pi^*) = 0$. This is quadratic in π^*, so choose the positive root:

$$\pi^* = \frac{-(\Phi + 1) - \sqrt{(\Phi + 1)^2 - 4\Phi\rho}}{2\Phi}.$$

1-7 (a) Let $b_t = P_t B_t/P_t Y_t$. With $P_t B_t$ and Y_t constant then $b_t = (1 + \pi)^{-1}b_{t-1}$, where π is the inflation rate. Hence $b_t = [(1 + \pi)^{-1}]^t b_0$. If debt to income ratio is to halve, then $b_0/2 = ((1 + \pi)^{-1})^t b_0$. Hence, t has to be at least 8 years before debt is halved.

(b) From Eq. (1-15) with nominal debt unchanged $P_t G_t - P_t T_t + rP_{t-1}B_{t-1} = M_t - M_{t-1}$. Hence, $G_t - T_t = A/P_t + (M_t - M_{t-1})/P_t$, where $A = -rP_{t-1}B_{t-1}$ is a constant. Noting the following,

$$\frac{M_t - M_{t-1}}{P_t} = \frac{[(M_t - M_{t-1})/M_{t-1}]M_{t-1}}{(1 + \pi)P_{t-1}}.$$

Hence, $G_t - T_t = A/P_t + A_1(0.1/1.1)$, where A_1 is the demand for real balances and is a constant. Since P_t is increasing, $G_t - T_t$ must decline and becomes $\simeq 0.09$ times the demand for real balances in the limit.

1-8 It remains constant. The real value one period ahead was shown to be $(P_t/P_{t+1})D/(\rho + \pi + \rho\pi)$. The nominal price is P_{t+1} times this, which implies a constant value. This must be true in all future periods.

1-9 After j periods the nominal value of the index-linked perpetuity is $P_{t+j}D/\rho$. The value of the non-index-linked perpetuity is as in **1-8** above. The ratio is $[P_{t+j}/P_t](\rho + \pi + \rho\pi)/\rho$. Since $P_{t+j}/P_t = (1 + \pi)^j$, the price of the index-linked coupon grows relative to the non-indexed coupon at the underlying inflation rate π.

1-10 The PV of the non-indexed perpetuity will be:

$$PV = \frac{D}{(1 + \rho^\varepsilon)(1 + \pi_0^\varepsilon)(1 + g)} + \frac{D}{(1 + \rho^\varepsilon)^2(1 + \pi_0^\varepsilon)^2(1 + g)^2} + \cdots$$

where π_0^ε is the base period expected inflation rate. Summing the above geometric series gives: $D/[(1 + \rho^\varepsilon)(1 + \pi_0^\varepsilon)(1 + g) - 1]$. The long-term expected inflation rate must be such that this equals $D/[(1 + \rho^\varepsilon)(1 + \pi_L^\varepsilon) - 1]$. Hence the long-term expected rate is $\pi_L^\varepsilon = g + \pi_0^\varepsilon(1 + g)$.

1-11 (a) For index-linked it is always £1 billion (see text). With non-indexed the PV of tax liabilities is $(\rho + \pi_L^\varepsilon + \rho\pi_L^\varepsilon)/(\rho + \pi_L + \rho\pi_L)$ billion, where π_L^ε is the expected long-term inflation rate and π_L is the delivered long-term rate. For $\pi_L = 0$ this is £6.1 billion.

(b) £0.54 billion.

1-12 (a) Let A be the fixed nominal repayment. The following is derived from Eq. (1-38): $P_t B_t = (1 + r)P_{t-1}B_{t-1} - A$. Treating this as a first-order difference equation gives the solution (see Chapter 4 for some techniques):

$$P_t B_t = A/r + (1 + r)^t(P_0 B_0 - A/r).$$

Now $P_0 B_0 = £80\,000$ and $r = 0.1$. We also require $P_{20}B_{20} = 0$. This gives sufficient information to evaluate A, since $A/0.1 = -(1.1)^{20}(80\,000 - A/0.1)$. Hence $A = £9396.77$.

1-13 The following relationship must hold: $1 + (1 - t_0)r = [1 + \rho(1 - t)][1 + \pi]$. This is $t_0 = \rho t(1 + \pi)/r = \rho t(1 + \pi)/[\pi + \rho(1 + \pi)]$.

CHAPTER 2

2-1 The amount transferred to pensioners is $(N - P)Y_0[1 + g]^t z(t)$. This must equal the number of pensioners times γ, the take-home pay of non-pensioners. This is evaluated as $P\gamma(1 - z(t))Y_0[1 + g]^t$. Hence, after substituting for P and simplifying, $z(t)[1 - \delta(1 - b^t)] = \delta\gamma[1 - b^t][1 - z(t)]$. Thus:

$$z(t) = \frac{(1 - b^t)\delta\gamma}{1 - \delta(1 - b^t)(1 - \gamma)}.$$

As $t \to \infty$, $z(t) \to \delta\gamma/(1 - \delta + \delta\gamma)$. This is ≤ 1, so the system is feasible in the sense that $z(t)$ need never exceed 1. If $\gamma = 1$, then $z(t) \to \delta$. If $\delta = 1$, $z(t) \to 1$. Note that, although feasible, average living standards may decline despite g. Non-pensioners might object.

2-2 (a) 30 fridges.

(b) Let x be the resources required to produce one fridge, let f be productivity growth in fridge production and let h be productivity growth in hip replacement. In t years it will require $x(1 + f)^{-t}$ resources to produce one fridge and $30x(1 + h)^{-t}$ resources to produce one hip replacement. For example, if $t = 20$ and $f = 0.04$ and $h = 0.01$, then opportunity cost rises to $30(1 + 0.01)^{-20}/(1 + 0.04)^{-20} = 53.87$ fridges.

2-5 $K_m = (1 + \pi_m)B_m Y_m/B_g Y_g$ and $K_p = (1 + \pi_p)B_p Y_p/B_g Y_g$, where π_m and π_p are defined by Eqs (2-12) and (2-13). $B_m = W_0/b_1$, $B_p = W_0/b_2$ and $B_g = W_0$. Hence Eq. (2-18) converges to $1/(1 + K_m) = b_1 Y_g/[b_1 Y_g + (1 + \pi_m) Y_m]$.

2-6 First, note that unit costs will remain as in Eqs (2-9), (2-10) and (2-11) and that Eqs (2-12) and (2-13) are also true. Hence, Eq. (2-17) also holds. Substituting $A(t)$ for Y_{gt}/Y_{pt} will therefore give $z(t) = 1/[1 + K_m + K e^{(\alpha - \gamma)t}/A(t)]$, where K is a constant. Since $z(t)$ is constant by construction it follows that $A(t) = A(0)e^{(\alpha - \gamma)t}$, where $A(0)$ is again another constant. Hence the proportion of government services to manufactures must decline at the rate $\alpha - \gamma$.

CHAPTER 3

3-1   Noting that the r.h.s. contains P_t, derive an explicit expression for P_t as:

$$P_t = aM_t + b \sum_{i=1}^{\infty} \lambda^i P_{t-i}, \qquad a = \frac{1}{\alpha_1 - \alpha_2(1 - \lambda)}, \qquad b = a\alpha_2(1 - \lambda).$$

This is $P_t = aM_t + b[1 - \lambda L]^{-1} \lambda L P_t$, where L is the lag operator. Multiply by $(1 - \lambda L)$ to derive $(1 - \lambda[1 + b]L)P_t = a(1 - \lambda L)M_t$. Hence $P_t = a[1 - \lambda(1 + b)L]^{-1}(1 - \lambda L)M_t$. Not very illuminating!

3-2   *CASE 1*: Sum the geometric series to derive $\ln P_t = \ln M_t + b(\ln M_{t+1})/(1 - b)$, and where $M_{t+1} = M_t + D$, where D is the budget deficit; $\ln P_{t+1} = (\ln M_{t+1})/(1 - b)$, thus it follows that the inflation rate $\ln P_{t+1} - \ln P_t = \ln M_{t+1} - \ln M_t$.

CASE 2: $\ln P_t = \ln M_t + b \ln M_t + b^2(\ln M_{t+2})/(1 - b)$, where $M_{t+2} = M_t + D(1 + r)$ and where r is the nominal interest rate payable on the one-period bond. Similarly, note $\ln P_{t+1} = \ln M_t + b(\ln M_{t+2})/(1 - b)$. Hence, $\ln P_{t+1} - \ln P_t = b \ln M_{t+2} - b \ln M_t$. Therefore, for the second case to give a higher initial rate of inflation, despite the tightness of monetary policy, requires $b \ln M_{t+2} - b \ln M_t > \ln M_{t+1} - \ln M_t$. Now let $\gamma = D/M_t$. Substituting and simplifying, it follows that $b \ln(1 + \gamma(1 + r)) > \ln(1 + \gamma)$ is the requirement for a higher inflation rate. If γ is small, as seems reasonable, then to a very good approximation $b\gamma(1 + r) > \gamma$ is the requirement. This simplifies to $r > (1 - b)/b$.

3-3   (*a*) The natural rate occurs when $\dot{P}_t = \dot{P}_t^*$. Hence $0.04/U - 0.4 = 0$. Thus the natural rate is 10 per cent.

(*b*) With expected inflation = 20 per cent, a sudden end to inflation implies the following must be true: $0 = 0.04/U - 0.4 + 0.2$. Thus unemployment rises to 20 per cent.

(*c*) Under gradualism inflation falls by 4 per cent per annum. In the first year it follows that $0.16 = 0.04/U - 0.04 + 0.2$. Hence unemployment rises to 11.1 per cent. It is easily seen to stay at this value for the five years of the gradualist strategy. The non-linear Phillips curve implies an increasing 'sacrifice ratio' for faster rates of inflation reduction, where the 'sacrifice ratio' is the total amount of additional unemployment (in man-years) required to reduce the inflation rate by 1 percentage point.

3-4   With $\Delta^2 P = 0$, implies $(a + b)U_t = bU_{t-1} + aU^*$. Hence $U_t = (1 - d)U^* + dU_{t-1}$, where $d = b/(a + b) < 1$. This gives the steady inflation path for unemployment as $U_t = U^* + (U_0 - U^*)d^t$.

CHAPTER 4

4-1   (*a*) Direct substitution shows that $Y_t = aT + Y_{t-T} = aT$ if $Y_{t-T} = 0$.

(*b*) Rewrite the equation as $Y_t = -a + Y_{t+1}$. Direct forward iteration derives

$$Y_t = -aT + Y_{t+T} = -aT$$

if $Y_{t+T} = 0$.

4-2   (*a*) This is best seen through Eq. (4-9) which can be written in terms of Y_{t-j} as

$$Y_{t-j} = \bar{Y} + \lambda^{T-j}(Y_{t-T} - \bar{Y}).$$

Clearly, $|Y_{t-j}| \to \infty$ if $Y_{t-T} \neq \bar{Y}$. Consequently, the restriction required for a finite Y_{t-T} is $Y_{t-T} = \bar{Y}$.

(*b*) No restriction need be placed on Y_{t-T} in this case. The equation is stable in the conventional sense.

(c) The answer reverses in this case. No restriction for Y_{t-j} to be finite and $Y_{t-T} = \bar{Y}$ if Y_{t+j} is to be finite as $j \to \infty$.

(d) This makes no difference as the discussion of Eq. (4-14) makes clear.

4-3 Equation (4-17) gives the relevant information, where $T = 10$, $\rho = 0.02$ and $B_t = £1000$. Direct substitution gives $R = £111.33$. Inflation affects this because the rule asks for a constant real repayment. Thus £111.33 is the real repayment expressed in period t prices and would have to be adjusted upwards in line with inflation as life of loan proceeds. 'Surprise' inflation would add further complications.

4-4 Manipulating Eq. (4-15) gives: $B_{t+1}/B_t = 1 + \rho - R_t/B_t$. Hence, $k = 1 + \rho - R_t/B_t$ and $k = 1 + \rho - R_{t+1}/B_{t+1}$ moving one period forward. Substitute kB_t for B_{t+1} and divide the previous two equations to derive $R_{t+1} = kR_t$. Multiply both sides by P_{t+1} to derive $P_{t+1}R_{t+1} = kP_tR_t(1 + \pi)$. Constant nominal repayments obviously requires $P_{t+1}R_{t+1} = P_tR_t$. Hence $\pi = (1 - k)/k$. This is independent of the real rate of interest.

4-5 No there is not. Suppose $\lambda \neq 1$, then by setting $Y_0 = a/(1 - \lambda)$, the equilibrium value then $Y_T = Y_{-T}$. However, if $\lambda = 1$, and the question does not rule this out, then $Y_T = aT + Y_0$ and $Y_{-T} = -aT + Y_0$. Except if $a = 0$, there is no way Y_T could equal Y_{-T}.

4-6 The solution is of form Eq. (4-21) which, after substituting out X_{t-i} gives

$$Y_t = (1 + \beta)^t \sum_{i=0}^{t-1} \left(\frac{\lambda}{1 + \beta}\right)^i X_0 + \lambda^t Y_0.$$

Now apply the moves shown in Eqs (4-6), (4-7) and (4-8) to derive

$$(1 + \beta)^t \sum_{i=0}^{t-1} \left(\frac{\lambda}{1 + \beta}\right)^i X_0 = (1 + \beta)^t \bar{Y} - \lambda^t \bar{Y}$$

where $\bar{Y} = X_0/(1 - \lambda/[1 + \beta])$. Substitute back in to derive

$$Y_t = (1 + \beta)^t \bar{Y} + \lambda^t (Y_0 - \bar{Y}).$$

Clearly, this converges to the equilibrium growth rate β.

4-7 (a) Forward iteration reveals the solution:

$$Y_t = a \sum_{i=0}^{T-1} \lambda^i + \sum_{i=0}^{T-1} \lambda^i u_{t+i} + \lambda^T A$$

where A has been substituted for Y_{t+T}. Since $E_{t-1}u_{t+i} = 0$ for all i, then $E_{t-1}Y_t$ is

$$E_{t-1}Y_t = a \sum_{i=0}^{T-1} \lambda^i + \lambda^T A.$$

$E_{t-1}Y_t$ can be given a specific value at time $t - 1$, because this is based on known information. By contrast, Y_t depends on the hypothetical future realizations of the u_{t+i} terms. Unlike $E_{t-1}Y_t$, therefore, Y_t can be given no specific value at $t - 1$.

(b) $E_{t-1}Y_{t+1} = a + \lambda E_{t-1}Y_{t+2}$, since $E_t u_{t+2} = 0$. Forward iteration reveals the solution:

$$Y_t = a \sum_{i=0}^{T-1} \lambda^i + \lambda^T A + u_t.$$

The solution for $E_{t-1}Y_t$ is the same as 4-7(a). Here, unlike 4-7(a), $Y_t - E_{t-1}Y_t = u_t$.

4-8 c is given by (equivalent to Eq. (4-43)):

$$c = [Y_{t+T} + (1 - \lambda^{-1}F)^{-1}(b\lambda^{-1}FX_{t+T})]\lambda^{-(t+T)}.$$

Substitute back into Eq. (4-40) to derive

$$Y_t = -(1 - \lambda^{-1}F)^{-1}b\lambda^{-1}[FX_t - FX_{t+T}\lambda^{-T}] + \lambda^{-T}Y_{t+T}.$$

From which Eq. (4-46) follows directly.

4-9 (a) $-F\nabla Y_t = -F[Y_{t-1} - Y_t] = Y_{t+1} - Y_t = \Delta Y_t.$
(b) $-\Delta L Y_t = -\Delta Y_{t-1} = Y_{t-1} - Y_t = \nabla Y_t.$
(c) $(\Delta + 1)Y_t = Y_{t+1} - Y_t + Y_t = FY_t.$
  $(\nabla + 1)Y_t = Y_{t-1} - Y_t + Y_t = LY_t.$
  Consequently, $(\Delta + 1)(\nabla + 1) = FL = 1.$

4-10 In the current period the expected monetary return is simply profits plus the expected capital gain. Hence, $r = Z_t/P_t + (E_t P_{t+1} - P_t)/P_t$, or $P_t = aE_t P_{t+1} + aZ_t$, where $a = 1/(1 + r)$. Structurally this is exactly like the Cagan problem considered earlier and the rational expectations solution for the current price is

$$P_t = aZ_t + a\sum_{i=1}^{\infty} a^i E_t Z_{t+i} + b\left(\frac{1}{a}\right)^t.$$

The fundamentals solution sets $b = 0$, thus the current price is just the present value of expected future profits. Note that other lines of reasoning would derive the same answer and it is interesting to note that these implicitly embody rational expectations.

4-11 Suppose profits in the first equity are expected to grow at the rate g_1 and the second equity at the rate g_2. Substituting into the fundamentals price equation gives the price earnings ratio $P_t/Z_t = 1/(r - g_1)$. Hence it follows that $(r - g_1)/(r - g_2) = 3$. Thus $g_2 = \frac{2}{3}r + \frac{1}{3}g_1$. Notice that this exceeds $3g_1$ given that $r > g_1$. Answer ignores possible risk differences.

4-12 In the non-fundamentals solution with a positive bubble, $b > 0$. It can be seen that this implies a price in excess of the fundamentals. In effect, the bubble is already capitalized in the higher spot price and investors would still only receive the safe return r. Clearly, there is more to it than this since speculators presumably want an expected return better than the safe asset. This problem is discussed extensively in Blanchard and Fischer (1989 chapter 5).

4-13 The equation can be written as $(1 - 0.5L)(1 - 2L)Y_t = 10$, hence the roots are $\lambda_1 = 0.5$ and $\lambda_2 = 2$. Thus this is a saddlepoint. The general solution can be written as

$$Y_t = [(1 - 0.5L)(1 - 2L)]^{-1}10 + c_1 0.5^t + c_2 2^t.$$

Since the future path of Y_t is bounded we can apply the particularization $c_2 = 0$. The choice of c_1 is somewhat more problematical. A 'typical' economic problem might allow Y_{t-1} to be the side condition to pin down Y_t. In this case we can derive $(1 - 0.5L)Y_t = (1 - 2L)^{-1}10$. Rearranging gives $Y_t = -10 + 0.5Y_{t-1}$. Where the economic context specifies that Y_t is totally disconnected from the past, the particularization of Y_t is not achievable without further information. Any value of c_1 reflecting a 'future' side condition would make (Y_{t+j}) a bounded sequence.

4-14 The general solution is $Y_t = (1 - \frac{1}{2}F)^{-1}(1 - \frac{1}{3}F)^{-1}X_t + c_1 2^t + c_2 3^t$. Boundedness requires c_1 and c_2 to be set to zero. The problem suggests a forward representation as the solution (is this absolutely essential?). The solution for Y_t can be re-expressed as $Y_t = 3(1 - \frac{1}{2}F)^{-1}X_t - 2(1 - \frac{1}{3}F)^{-1}X_t$. Hence $Y_t = (8/5)X_t$, which can easily be checked as being consistent with the original equation in the question.

4-15 Substitute out the unobservable P_t^* to derive $P_t - 0.5P_{t-1} = 0.5aM_t + 0.5bE_tP_{t+1}$. This can be rearranged for a typical future term as $(1 - (2/b)L + (1/b)L^2)E_tP_{t+j} = -(a/b)LE_tM_{t+j}$, where L is the lag operator. Hence $(1 - \lambda_1 L)(1 - \lambda_2 L)E_tP_{t+j} = -(a/b)LE_tM_{t+j}$, where

$$\lambda_1, \lambda_2 = \frac{1}{b} \pm \sqrt{\frac{1}{b^2} - \frac{1}{b}} = \left(\frac{1}{b}\right)(1 \pm \sqrt{1 - b}).$$

Since the square root of $1 - b$ exceeds $1 - b$, it is easily seen that this implies $\lambda_1 > 1$ and $\lambda_2 < 1$. The solution is a saddlepoint and the problem structure justifies treating P_{t-1} as one side condition and a requirement for the 'fundamentals' solution as a means of tying down the other required side condition. Noting that E_tP_t is P_t, write the fundamentals solution as $(1 - \lambda_2 L)P_t = (1 - \lambda_1^{-1}F)^{-1}\lambda_1^{-1}(a/b)E_tM_t$. Thus partial adjustment leads to an eclectic view of the determination of the current price level which looks *both* backwards to history as embodied in P_{t-1} as well as to the future path of monetary policy.

4-16 The solution is $y(t) = (D - \lambda)^{-1}bt + c\,e^{\lambda t}$. The fundamentals path imposes $c = 0$. The forward solution is, therefore, $y(t) = -b\int_t^\infty e^{(t-s)\lambda}s\,ds$. Integrating by parts (see Chiang, 1984, chapter 13) gives $y(t) = b[e^{(t-s)\lambda}\lambda^{-1}(s + \lambda^{-1})]_t^\infty$. Evaluating gives $y(t) = -b\lambda^{-1}(t + \lambda^{-1})$.

4-17 Write as $(D + \lambda)P^*(t) = \lambda P(t)$. Clearly, with adaptive expectations the backward representation is appropriate. Hence $P^*(t) = \lambda\int_{-\infty}^t e^{-(t-s)\lambda}P(s)\,ds$, where in addition the fundamentals particularization has been imposed.

4-18 Substituting for $P(t)$ gives $P^*(t) = \lambda\int_{-\infty}^t e^{-(t-s)\lambda}P(0)(1 + e^{-gs})\,ds$. Thus it follows that

$$P^*(t) = P(0) + \lambda P(0)[e^{-(t-s)\lambda - gs}(\lambda - g)^{-1}]_{-\infty}^t = P(0) + \lambda P(0)(\lambda - g)^{-1}e^{-gt}.$$

Notice how this implies that $P^*(t)$ always over-predicts $P(t)$.

4-19 $y(t) = [(D - 3)(D + 4)]^{-1} - 12 + c_1 e^{-3t} + c_2 e^{4t}$. This is clearly a saddlepoint. Boundedness requires $c_2 = 0$. Hence $y(t) = 1 + c_1 e^{-3t}$. Also, $y(0) = 10 = 1 + c_1$. Consequently, $y(t) = 1 + 9 e^{-3t}$.

4-20 Setting $Dy_1 = 0$, gives the demarcation line $y_2 = 2y_1 - y_1^2 + 10$. This is a quadratic with a maximum at $(1, 11)$ and cuts the y_2 axis at $(0, 10)$. $\partial Dy_1/\partial y_1 = -2 + 2y_1$, which is >0 if $y_1 > 1$ and <0 if $y_1 < 1$. Consequently, the streamlines point away from the demarcation line when it slopes downwards and towards it when it slopes upwards. For the second equation the demarcation line is $y_2 = 2y_1 + 6$. It is clear that the streamlines point away from the demarcation line. The two demarcation lines intersect where $2y_1 + 6 - 2y_1 + y_1^2 - 10 = 0$. This occurs at $y_1 = +2$ and -2. The phase diagram confirms that the former is a saddlepoint and the latter an unstable equilibrium. A further check is to evaluate the determinant of the local partial derivatives given by

$$A = \begin{vmatrix} 2y_1 - 2 & 1 \\ -2 & 1 \end{vmatrix}.$$

This is >0 and has a positive trace when $y_1 = 2$. Hence unstable. The determinant is <0 when $y_1 = -2$, hence a saddlepoint.

4-21 The price demarcation line remains as before. With $\alpha > 0$, the exchange rate demarcation line is downward sloping with the streamlines pointing away from the line. This is a saddlepoint as the associated determinant confirms. There is still exchange rate overshooting. With $\alpha < 0$, the exchange rate demarcation line is upward sloping with the streamlines pointing towards the line. There are two cases. First, when the price demarcation line is steeper than the exchange rate demarcation line, there is a saddlepoint (confirm this by exploring the determinant once more). There is overshooting once again. Secondly, when the price demarcation line is less steep than the exchange rate demarcation line, the system is stable. This poses problems since the exchange rate can now 'jump' to any value and converge to its equilibrium value. The problem with the question is that the modified interest parity condition has not been motivated. Frenkel and Rodriguez (1982) motivate a version of Dornbusch by considering a modified interest parity equation based on imperfect capital mobility. This leads to exchange rate *undershooting* as a possibility.

CHAPTER 5

5-1 (Allen, 1959, chapter 7 provides a full discussion.) Rearranging terms gives the second-order difference equation $Y_t - [\beta + \beta(1 + k)] Y_{t-1} + \beta(1 + k) Y_{t-2} - v_0 = 0$. This has an equilibrium output level of $v_0/(1 - \beta)$, as before. The modified reduced form offers much broader possibilities as far as cyclical behaviour is concerned. The solution has the form of Eq. (5-5), where

$$\lambda_1, \lambda_2 = \frac{\beta + \beta(1 + k) \pm \sqrt{[\beta + \beta(1 + k)]^2 - 4\beta(1 + k)}}{2}.$$

If $4\beta(1 + k) > [\beta + \beta(1 + k)]^2$ then there are complex roots as before. The cycle will be damped if $\beta(1 + k) < 1$, and explosive otherwise. The roots need not always be complex, however. Noting that $\lambda_1 + \lambda_2 = \beta + \beta(1 + k)$ and that $\lambda_1\lambda_2 = \beta(1 + k)$, it follows in the real root case that both roots must be positive and that output is non-oscillatory and damped if $\beta(1 + k) < 1$ (note $(1 - \lambda_1)(1 - \lambda_2) = 1 - \beta$ implying both roots are < 1 if $\lambda_1\lambda_2 < 1$); same condition for damped cycle as the complex root case.

5-2 (*a*) $E\{Y - Y^*\}^2 = [\xi(1 - b)]^2 E\{P - \hat{P}\}^2 = [\xi(1 - b)]^2 \sigma_u^2$.

(*b*) Differentiating $E\{Y - Y^*\}^2$ w.r.t. σ_u^2 and setting to zero for a maximum gives the following: $-2\xi^2(1 - b)\sigma_u^2 \, db/d\sigma_u^2 + [\xi(1 - b)]^2 = 0$. Simplifying gives the following expression: $-2\sigma_u^2 \, db/d\sigma_u^2 + (1 - b) = 0$. Next evaluate $db/d\sigma_u^2$, which is $\sigma_\varepsilon^2/(\sigma_\varepsilon^2 + \sigma_u^2)^2$. Substituting and simplifying gives $-2\sigma_u^2/(\sigma_\varepsilon^2 + \sigma_u^2) + 1 = 0$. Hence, setting $\sigma_u^2 = \sigma_\varepsilon^2$ gives the maximum fluctuation.

5-3 (*a*) In *per capita* terms, $q = k^\alpha$. From Eq. (5-38), the golden rule path requires that $\alpha(k^*)^{(\alpha - 1)} = n$. Hence the golden rule capital stock per head $k^* = (n/\alpha)^{1/(\alpha - 1)}$.

(*b*) Since $s = vn$, then $s = \alpha k^{(\alpha - 1)} k/k^\alpha = \alpha$. The quick solution is to note that aggregate profits must equal aggregate savings on the golden rule path. With a Cobb Douglas, α is the profit share!

(*c*) The solution is $Dk = sk^\alpha - nk$, where D is the differential operator. This is clearly non-linear because of the k^α term. In fact, this is a Bernoulli equation which can be shown to have the following explicit solution (see Chiang, 1984, p. 500 for details) $k(t)^{(1 - \alpha)} = [k(0)^{(1 - \alpha)} - s/n] e^{-(1 - \alpha)nt} + s/n$.

(*d*) The parameter values are $\alpha = s = 0.4, k(0) = 200, n = 0.02$. Equilibrium k is $(0.4/0.02)^{1/(1 - 0.4)} = 147.36$. A 90 per cent adjustment requires $k(t) = 152.63$. Substituting gives $(152.6)^{0.6} = [(200)^{0.6} - 20] e^{-0.012t} + 20$. Solving for t gives $t = 187.1$ years! Obviously, if there was some capital depreciation, this process would be speeded up.

CHAPTER 6

6-1 (*a*) Risk aversion. $V(Z) = \ln Z$. Thus $V' = 1/Z > 0$ and $V'' = -1/Z^2 < 0$.

(*b*) In the first case expected utility is $\frac{1}{3} \ln 30 + \frac{1}{3} \ln 60 + \frac{1}{3} \ln 90 = 4.00$. In the second case it is $\frac{1}{3} \ln 0 + \frac{1}{3} \ln 60 + \frac{1}{3} \ln 150 = 3.03$. Hence the first is preferred, even though the second offers a higher expected value.

(c) The gamble offers expected utility $\frac{1}{2}\ln 100 + \frac{1}{2}\ln 200 = 4.95$. Hence the certain quantity ($=$ antilog(4.95)) would be indifferent to the gamble. This is 141.4. The risk premium is the expected value of the gamble minus this, which is $150 - 141.4 = 8.6$.

(d) By drawing a diagram, it can be established that if $\pi > E\{\pi\}$ then the following must hold: $V'(E\{\pi\}) > [V\{\pi\} - V(E\{\pi\})]/(\pi - E\{\pi\})$. (The slope at the mean exceeds the slope of the arc between π and $E\{\pi\}$.) Also, if $\pi < E\{\pi\}$ then it can be seen that

$$V'(E\{\pi\}) < [V(E\{\pi\}) - V(\pi)]/(E\{\pi\} - \pi).$$

It can then be seen that the following is true for all π: $V'(E\{\pi\})(\pi - E\{\pi\}) > V(\pi) - V(E\{\pi\})$. Taking expectations, note that the l.h.s. of this expression is zero since $V'E\{\pi\}$ is non-stochastic and $E\{\pi - E\{\pi\}\} = 0$. Hence, $E\{V(\pi)\} - V(E\{\pi\}) < 0$.

6-2 Let $T = [0.8\pounds 1 \text{ bil.}; 0.2\pounds 0] \text{ I} \pounds 1 \text{ mil.}$ Now consider $L_1 = [0.1T; 0.9\pounds 0]$ and $L_2 = [0.1\pounds 1 \text{ mil.}; 0.9\pounds 0]$. The independence of irrelevant alternatives assumption says that $L_1 \text{ I} L_2$. Hence the figures given. See Machina (1987) for a critique of this and other expected utility axioms.

6-3 This can be seen directly from Eqs (6-40) and (6-41), and assuming $c < 0$ to reflect risk loving. The slope is negative and the second derivative is also negative. Hence the indifference curves are *concave* to the origin. Apparently, the axioms of expected utility maximization exclude the possibility of indifference curves being *convex* to the origin, which seems slightly counter-intuitive.

6-4 The risky stream offers expected utility $-(0.95C^{-1} + 0.05(0.5C)^{-1})$. This must be indifferent to $-\hat{C}^{-1}$, where $\hat{C}$ is the certain consumption alternative. Thus $\hat{C}/C$ is 0.952. The individual is prepared to give up 4.8 per cent of employed consumption to avoid unemployment. Given that expected consumption, when facing the unemployment risk of 0.05, is 0.975 of employed consumption, then this represents a risk premium of 2.3 per cent of employed consumption.

6-5 Yes. $-E\{Y - Y^*\}^2 = -E(P_1 + P_2 + u - Y^*)^2 = -(P_1 + P_2 - Y^*)^2 - 2\hat{u}(P_1 + P_2 - Y^*) - \sigma^2 - \hat{u}^2$. Now differentiate: $\partial(-E\{Y - Y^*\}^2)/\partial P_1 = -2(P_1 + P_2 - Y^*) - 2\hat{u} = 0$. Exactly the same condition holds for P_2. It is clear that the objective function can still be maximized even if either P_1 *or* P_2 is set to zero.

6-6 Substitute out W, using the budget constraint, from the utility function to obtain the following expression: $E\{V(W)\} = E\{W_0 + A(r + g)\} - cE\{W_0 + A(r + g)\}^2$. The problem is to choose an A to maximize this. Differentiating gives the expression: $dE\{V(W)\}/dA = E\{r + g\} - 2cE\{[W_0 + A(r + g)][r + g]\} = 0$. Noting that $E\{g\} = 0$, this is $dE\{V(W)\}/dA = r - 2cW_0r - 2cA(r^2 + \sigma^2)$. Thus $A = (r - 2cW_0r)/2c(r^2 + \sigma^2)$.

CHAPTER 7

7-1 (a) If believed, this is obtainable since $X_t^\varepsilon = X_t = 0$ is consistent with rational expectations and the inflation–unemployment trade-off. $S^* = -U^{*2}$.

(b) 'First best' says max. S s.t. $U_t = -\lambda X_t + U^*$. Substituting into S, therefore, gives $-U_t^2 - [(U^* - U_t)/\lambda]^2$. Solving gives $U_t = U^*/(1 + \lambda^2)$. The implied level of welfare $S^{**} = -U^{*2}/(1 + \lambda^2)^2$. Clearly, $S^{**} > S^*$. Hence the optimal policy is time inconsistent.

(c) This requires the slope of an indifference curve dX_t/dU_t to equal $-1/\lambda$ at U^*. Hence $X_t = \lambda U^*$. Clearly, the implied level of welfare is less than S^*.

7-2 It follows directly that $Y_t - Y_{t-1} = \alpha(m_t - m_{t-1}) + u_t - u_{t-1}$. Noting that the money surprise is just $m_t - m_{t-1} = S_t$, and $Y_{t-1} - u_{t-1} = A + \alpha m_{t-1}$, it follows $Y_t = \alpha S_t + A + \alpha m_{t-1} + u_t$.

Successive iteration of $Y_t - Y_{t-2}$ and so on will derive the result given in the question. Because 'observational equivalence' between a 'traditional' model and a 'surprise' has been demonstrated, the 'Lucas Critique' works both ways! This fact of observational equivalence means considerable care is required in testing models of rational expectations involving surprises.

7-3 (*a*) Substitute out C_{t+1} in the utility function to derive the following expression for expected utility: $\ln C_t + (1 + \delta)^{-1} E\{\ln[R_{t+1} + (R_t - C_t)(1 + r)]\}$. Choose a C_t to maximize this. This gives $1/C_t - [(1 + r)/(1 + \delta)]E\{1/C_{t+1}\} = 0$.

(*b*) No. Remember that in general $E\{1/C_{t+1}\} \neq 1/E\{C_{t+1}\}$.

(*c*) In this case $C_{t+1} = (R_t - C_t)(1 + r)$. Consequently, it can be seen that the $(1 + r)$ terms will cancel in optimization (*a*). Optimal consumption is then $C_t - (1 + \delta)(R_t - C_t) = 0$. When, in addition, $\delta = 0$ then $C_t = \frac{1}{2}R_t$. C_{t+1} is not a random walk because the model is non-stochastic when $R_{t+1} = 0$.

CHAPTER 8

8-1 This follows immediately. Suppose $U(w)$ is the risk-averse utility indicator. The problem then proceeds exactly as before, with Eq. (8-6) modified to be the following:

$$[U(w) - U(w_0)][1 - ke(w)] < 0.$$

The no-wage-undercutting condition does not change.

8-2 With the addition of fixed costs, optimal output and the optimal price remain as $a/2b$ and $a/2$ exactly as before. Profits are $a^2/4b - F$. The profit penalty for not adjusting price in response to a shock is, as before, $(\Delta a)^2/4b$. The critical value of the transaction cost relative to profits (equivalent to Eq. (8-12)) is given by $\gamma/\pi = (\Delta a)^2/(a^2 - 4bF)$. Suppose $\gamma/\pi = 0.01$ as before. Manipulation shows the following to hold: $\Delta a/a = [0.01 - 0.04bF/a^2]^{1/2}$. Now $\Delta a/a = \Delta p/p$, if it is worth while to adjust prices. At the critical value of the transaction cost it follows that $\Delta p/p = [0.01 - 0.04bF/a^2]^{1/2}$. This is <10 per cent and could be any order of smallness, depending on the size of F.

8-3 With the addition of a marginal cost element, c, optimal output and the optimal price become $(a - c)/2b$ and $(a + c)/2$ respectively. Profits are easily derived as $(a - c)^2/4b$. The profit penalty for not adjusting price in response to a shock is, as before, $(\Delta a)^2/4b$. The critical value of the transaction cost relative to profits (equivalent to Eq. (8-12)) is $\gamma/\pi = (\Delta a)^2/(a - c)^2$. Now $(\Delta a)/(a + c) = (\Delta p)/p$, if it is worth while to adjust prices, noting the new optimal price. Thus, at the critical value it follows that $\Delta p/p = (\gamma/\pi)^{1/2}(a - c)/(a + c) < (\gamma/\pi)^{1/2}$. This is like case **8-2** above, because a 1 per cent critical transaction to profits ratio would mean less than a 10 per cent price change.

8-4 Nothing substantive happens, except to reinforce insider 'advantage' over outsiders. The modified problem, equivalent to Eq. (8-17) and with the same constraints as Eq. (8-18), becomes:

$$\text{Max: } \pi = \theta f(AL_{\text{I}} + BL_{\text{E}}) - W_{\text{I}}L_{\text{I}} - R_{\text{E}}L_{\text{E}} - C(m - L_{\text{I}})$$

where m is the incumbent force of insiders. Figure 8-1 would then be modified as follows. Instead of employment on the horizontal axis, plot 'efficiency' units $Z = AL_{\text{I}} + BL_{\text{E}}$, with the demand schedule now plotted in efficiency units. Insiders will now only be fired if the efficiency marginal product is below $W_{\text{I}} - C$. (Think carefully of the intuition as to why this is so.) Alternatively, the modified problem can be solved as an elementary non-linear programme, as, indeed, can the simpler problem considered in the text. Maximizing π in the above equation, subject to the constraints given by Eq. (8-17), requires the following to hold:

$$\frac{\partial \pi}{\partial L_I} = \theta A f' - (W_I - C) \geq 0$$

$$\frac{\partial \pi}{\partial L_E} = \theta B f' - W_E \leq 0.$$

(See Chiang, 1984, chapter 21 for methods.) The first equation reflects the $L_I \leq m$ constraint. Since the constraints assume $L_I > 0$, the other non-negativity condition can be ignored. The second equation reflects the $L_E \geq 0$ constraint. If $L_I < m$, then the first equation holds as an equality, otherwise the inequality must hold. Similarly, with the second equation, if $L_E > 0$ then it must hold as an equality, otherwise the inequality must hold. These conditions are equivalent to the diagrammatic solution. Suppose $L_I < m$, then because $W_I - C < W_E$, the second equation becomes a strong inequality and L_E must be zero. This is equivalent to the m_c case in the simple problem. Now suppose the optimum has $L_E > 0$. In this case a strong inequality must hold in the first equation, given that the equality holds in the second. Hence $L_I = m$. This is equivalent to the m_a case in the simple problem. The final possibility is that the inequality holds in both equations and, clearly, the larger the 'wedge' the more likely this is. In this case, $L_I = m$ and $L_E = 0$. This is equivalent to the m_b case in the simple problem.

8-5 Note that the question refers to a more general problem $F(E, N)$ and not the case involving E *times* N as arguments of the production function. Thus anything true for the more general case must also be true for more specific cases, which impose more structure. Letting $G(W, N) = F(e(W), N)$, the problem is to choose an N and a W to maximize $G(W, N) - WN$. The two first-order conditions are $G_W - N = 0$ and $G_N - W = 0$, where G_W is the partial of G w.r.t. W, etc. The second-order conditions require $G_{WW} < 0$ and $G_{WW}G_{NN} - [G_{WN} - 1]^2 > 0$. The task is to show that the optimal values of W and N are exactly the same as these if the original effort index $E = e(W)$ is made the subject of a positive monotonic transformation. Let $\hat{E} = h(E)$ be such a positive monotonic transformation where $h' > 0$. Inverting functions, we have $W = e^{-1}(E) = e^{-1}(h^{-1}(\hat{E}))$, which can be written more simply as $k(\hat{E})$, where k' must be positive. The problem is now to choose an $\hat{E}$ and N to maximize $G(k(\hat{E}), N) - k(\hat{E})N$. The first-order conditions are $G_W k' - k'N = 0$ and $G_N - k(\hat{E}) = 0$. Notice that these are easily simplified into exactly the original conditions, so exactly the same optimal values of W and N must prevail. The only difference, not surprisingly, is that the optimal $\hat{E} = h(E)$. The final thing to check, and no less important, is that the second-order conditions remain unaltered. These are the two conditions: $(k')^2 G_{WW} < 0$ and $(k')^2[G_{WW}G_{NN} - [G_{WN} - 1]^2] > 0$. Again these are (qualitatively) exactly as before. Ordinality is sufficient for efficiency wage theory. This is a very important conclusion. Since 'effort' is a somewhat nebulous concept, it is highly dubious whether it can, except in very specific instances, be measured cardinally. Our result shows that ordinality of the effort index is sufficient to locate optimal values. We simply do not require cardinality. This strengthens the efficiency wage approach. It is analogous to the famous result in consumer demand theory showing that a utility indicator need only be ordinal because optimal consumption choices are invariant to positive monotonic transformations of the utility indicator.

8-6 The associated Lagrangian is

$$L = E\{V(W(\theta))\} + \lambda[\bar{\pi} - E\{\theta f(l) - W(\theta)l\}]$$

and the relevant first-order conditions are

$$l: \qquad E\{\theta f'(l^*) - W^*(\theta)\} = 0$$
$$W(\theta): \quad V'(W^*(\theta)) + \lambda l^* = 0.$$

This is exactly the same as Eqs (8-31) and (8-32). Both locate an efficient bargain, but, as is well known, there is a locus of such bargains. An alternative framework which takes explicit account of how potential gains might be shared is the generalized Nash Bargain. This also locates an efficient bargain and maximizes the function $A^\alpha B^{1-\alpha}$, where α is a parameter $(0 < \alpha < 1)$ reflecting bargaining strength. A represents expected profit gains over a fallback position if no bargain is struck, hence $A = E\{\theta f(l) - W(\theta)l\} - \bar{\pi}$. B represents the expected utility gain to the union, in this case $B = E\{V(W(\theta))\} - Z$. The closer α to unity the more the bargain favours the firm, and the closer to zero the more the bargain favours the union.

8-7 The associated Lagrangian is

$$L = E\{F(\theta f(l) - W(\theta)l)\} + \lambda[Z - E\{W(\theta)\}]$$

and the relevant first-order conditions are

$$l: \qquad E\{F'[\theta f'(l^*) - W^*(\theta)]\} = 0$$
$$W(\theta): \quad l^*F' + \lambda = 0.$$

The final equation says that the marginal utility of profits is constant across all states of nature. Consequently, profits are fully insured with wages varying over the states of nature. Workers bear all the risks.

8-8 The associated Lagrangian is

$$L = E\{F(\theta f(l) - W(\theta)l)\} + \lambda[Z - E\{V(W(\theta)\}]$$

and the relevant first-order conditions are

$$l: \qquad E\{F'[\theta f'(l^*) - W^*(\theta)]\} = 0$$
$$W(\theta): \quad l^*F' + \lambda V'(W^*(\theta)) = 0.$$

The final equation is the critical one. If preferences are quadratic then F' is linear in profits $(=d + c\pi(\theta_i)$, with d and c both parameters). V' is similarly linear in wages. It follows immediately that the resultant profit-sharing scheme is a linear one. Interestingly, most actual profit-sharing schemes resemble this structure. Implicit Contracts are, therefore, of more general interest than might be first thought since they are the obvious vehicle to analyse the whole issue of profit-sharing, which is only properly analysed as a problem in risk-sharing.

REFERENCES

Akerlof, G. (1982) 'Labour contracts as a partial gift exchange', *Quarterly Journal of Economics*, **97** (November), 543–69.

Akerlof, G. (1984) 'Gift exchange and efficiency wages: four views', *American Economic Review (Proc.)*, **74** (May), 79–83.

Akerlof, G. and Yellen, J. L. (1985) 'Can small deviations from rationality make significant differences to economic equilibria?', *American Economic Review*, **75** (September), 708–21.

Akerlof, G. and Yellen, J. L. (1986) *Efficiency Wage Models of the Labour Market*, Cambridge University Press, Cambridge.

Alesina, A. (1989) 'Politics and business cycles in industrial democracies', *Economic Policy*, **8** (April), 57–98.

Allen, R. D. G. (1959) *Mathematical Economics*, Macmillan, London.

Allen, R. D. G. (1967) *Macro-Economic Theory: A Mathematical Treatment*, Macmillan, London.

Arrow, K. J. (1951) *Social Choice and Individual Values*, Wiley, New York.

Artis, M. J. (1984) *Macroeconomics*, Clarendon Press, Oxford.

Attfield, C. L. F., Demery, D. and Duck, N. W. (1985) *Rational Expectations in Macroeconomics* (2nd edn), Blackwell, Oxford.

Azariadis, C. (1975) 'Implicit contracts and underemployment equilibria', *Journal of Political Economy*, **83** (December), 115–25.

Bacon, R. and Eltis, W. (1976) *Britain's Economic Problem: Too Few Producers*, Macmillan, London.

Bain, A. D. (1980) *The Control of the Money Supply* (3rd edn), Penguin Books, Middlesex.

Bailey, M. J. (1956) 'The welfare costs of inflationary finance', *Journal of Political Economy*, **64** (April), 93–110.

Baily, M. N. (1974) 'Wages and employment under uncertain demand', *Review of Economic Studies*, **41** (January), 37–50.

Barro, R. J. (1974) 'Are government bonds net wealth?', *Journal of Political Economy*, **59** (April), 93–116.

Barro, R. J. (1986) 'Latest developments in the theory of Rules vs. Discretion', *Economic Journal (Supplement)*, **96**, 23–37.

Barro, R. J. and Gordon, D. (1983) 'Rules, discretion, and reputation in a model of monetary policy', *Journal of Monetary Economics*, **94** (August), 589–610.

Barry, N. P. (1989) *An Introduction to Modern Political Theory*, (2nd edn), Macmillan, London.

Baumol, W. J. (1965) *Economic Theory and Operations Analysis*, (2nd edn), Prentice-Hall, New Jersey.

Baumol, W. J. (1967) 'Macroeconomics of unbalanced growth', *American Economic Review*, **57** (June), 415–26.

Begg, D. K. H. (1982) *The Rational Expectations Revolution in Macroeconomics*, Allan, Oxford.

Blanchard, O. J. and Fischer, S. (1989) *Lectures on Macroeconomics*, MIT Press, Cambridge, Massachusetts.

Blanchard, O. J. and Summers, L. H. (1987) 'Hysteresis in unemployment', *European Economic Review*, **31** (March), 288–95.

Blinder, A. S. and Solow, R. M. (1973) 'Does fiscal policy matter?', *Journal of Public Economics*, **2** (November), 319–37.

Brainard, W. (1967) 'Uncertainty and the effectiveness of policy', *American Economic Review (Proc.)*, **57** (May), 411–25.

Braverman, H. (1977) *Labor and Monopoly Capital: The Degradation of Work in the Twentieth Century*, Monthly Review Press, New York.

Brunner, K. S. (1971) 'The Monetarist view of Keynesian ideas', *Lloyds Bank Review*, **102** (October), 35–49.

Buchanan, J. M. (1986) *Liberty, Market and State: Political Economy in the 1980s*, Harvester Press, Brighton.

Cagan, P. (1956) 'The monetary dynamics of hyperinflation', in M. Friedman (ed.), *Studies in the Quantity Theory of Money*, University of Chicago Press, Chicago.

Chiang, A. C. (1984) *Fundamental Methods of Mathematical Economics*, McGraw-Hill, New York.

Christ, C. (1968) 'A simple macroeconomic model with a government budget constraint', *Journal of Political Economy*, **76** (February), 53–67.

Doeringer, P. B. and Piore, M. J. (1971) *Internal Labor Markets and Manpower Analysis*, Heath, Lexington, Massachusetts.

Dornbusch, R. (1976) 'Expectations and exchange rate dynamics', *Journal of Political Economy*, **84** (December), 1161–76.

Dornbusch, R. (1980) *Open Economy Macroeconomics*, Basic Books, New York.

Eastwood, R. K. and Venables, A. J. (1982) 'The macroeconomic implications of a resource discovery in an open economy', *Economic Journal*, **92** (June), 285–99.

Eltis, W. (1979) 'How rapid public sector growth can undermine the growth of the national product', in W. Beckerman (ed.), *Slow Growth in Britain*, Clarendon Press, Oxford.

Fischer, S. (1977) 'Long-term contracts, rational expectations, and the optimal money supply rule', *Journal of Political Economy*, **85** (February), 191–206.

Flemming, J. (1976) *Inflation*, Oxford University Press, Oxford.

Forsyth, P. J. and Kay, J. (1980) 'Oil revenues and manufacturing output', *Fiscal Studies*, **1** (July), 9–17.

Foster, J. (1976) 'The redistributive effects of inflation—questions and answers', *Scottish Journal of Political Economy*, **23** (February), 73–97.

Frenkel, J. A. (1981) 'Flexible exchange rates, prices, and the role of "News": Lessons from the 1970s', *Journal of Political Economy*, **89** (August), 665–705.

Frenkel, J. A. and Rodriguez, C. A. (1982) 'Exchange rate dynamics and the overshooting hypothesis', *IMF Staff Papers*, **29** (March), 1–30.

Friedman, M. (1957) *A Theory of the Consumption Function*, Princeton University Press, Princeton, New Jersey.

Friedman, M. (1968) 'The role of monetary policy', *American Economic Review (Proc.)*, **58** (March), 1–17.

Friedman, M. (1975) *Unemployment versus Inflation*, Institute of Economic Affairs, London.

Friedman, M. and Schwarz, A. J. (1963) *A Monetary History of the United States*, Princeton University Press, Princeton, New Jersey.

Geary, P. T. and Kennan, J. (1982) 'The employment–real wage relationship: an international study', *Journal of Political Economy*, **90** (August), 854–71.

Goldfeld, S. M. (1982) 'Rules, discretion and reality', *American Economic Review (Proc.)*, **72** (May), 361–66.

Goodhart, C. A. E. (1984) *Monetary Theory and Practice*, Macmillan, London.

Gravelle, H. and Rees, R. (1981) *Microeconomics*, Longman, London.

Hall, R. E. (1978) 'Stochastic implications of the life cycle–permanent income hypothesis: theory and evidence', *Journal of Political Economy*, **86** (December), 971–87.

Hall, R. and Taylor, J. B. (1986) *Macroeconomics: Theory, Performance and Policy*, Norton, New York.

Hayek, F. A. (1933) *Monetary Theory and the Business Cycle*, Jonathan Cape, London.

Hayek, F. A. (1944) *The Road to Serfdom*, Routledge, London.

Hayek, F. A. (1973) *Law, Legislation and Liberty*, Routledge & Kegan Paul, London.

Hey, J. (1979) *Uncertainty in Microeconomics*, Robertson, Oxford.

Hicks, J. R. (1950) *A Contribution to the Theory of the Trade Cycle*, Clarendon Press, Oxford.

Holden, K., Peel, D. A. and Thompson, J. L. (1985) *Expectations: Theory and Evidence*, Macmillan, London.

Hoover, K. D. (1988) *The New Classical Macroeconomics*, Blackwell, Oxford.

Inman, R. P. (1985) *Managing the Service Economy*, Cambridge University Press, Cambridge.

Johnston, J. and Timbrell, M. (1973) 'Empirical tests of a wage bargaining theory of wage determination', *Manchester School*, **41** (June), 141–68.

Kaldor, N. (1966) 'Causes of the slow rate of economic growth in the United Kingdom', Inaugural Lecture, Cambridge University Press, Cambridge.

Kaldor, N. (1970) 'The new Monetarism', *Lloyds Bank Review*, **97** (July), 13–27.

Kaldor, N. (1986) *The Scourge of Monetarism* (2nd edn), Oxford University Press, Oxford.

Klamer, A. (1984) *The New Classical Macroeconomics*, Wheatsheaf, Brighton.

Kydland, F. E. and Prescott, E. C. (1977) 'Rules rather than discretion: the inconsistency of optimal plans', *Journal of Political Economy*, **85** (June), 473–92.

Kydland, F. and Prescott, E. C. (1982) 'Time to build and aggregate fluctuations', *Econometrica*, **70** (November), 1345–70.

Laidler, D. E. W. (1968) 'The permanent income concept in a macroeconomic model', *Oxford Economic Papers*, **20** (March), 11–23.

Laidler, D. E. W. (1973) 'Expectations, adjustment and the dynamic response of income to policy changes', *Journal of Money, Credit and Banking*, **5** (February), 60–72. Reprinted in *Essays on Money and Inflation* (same author), Manchester University Press, Manchester.

Laidler, D. E. W. (1982) *Monetarist Perspectives*, Allan, Oxford.

Laidler, D. E. W. (1985) *The Demand for Money: Theory, Evidence, and Problems* (3rd edn), Harper & Row, New York.

Layard, R., Nickell, S. and Jackman, R. (1991), *Unemployment: Macroeconomic Performance and the Labour Market*, Oxford University Press, Oxford.

Leslie, D. G. (1987) 'Real wages and real labour cost growth: a disaggregated study', *Applied Economics*, **19** (May), 635–50.

Leslie, D. G. (1990) 'A disequilibrium model under bilateral monopoly', *Bulletin of Economic Research*, **42** (July), 155–74.

Leslie, D. G. and Laing, C. (1978) 'The theory and measurement of labour hoarding', *Scottish Journal of Political Economy*, **25** (February), 41–56.

Lindbeck, A. and Snower, D. J. (1988) *The Insider–Outsider Theory of Employment and Unemployment*, MIT Press, Cambridge, Massachusetts.

Lipsey, R. G. (1966) *An Introduction to Positive Economics* (2nd edn), Weidenfeld and Nicolson, London.

Lucas, R. E. (1973) 'Some international evidence on output–inflation tradeoffs', *American Economic Review*, **63** (June), 326–34.

Lucas, R. E. (1976) 'Econometric policy evaluation: a critique', in K. S. Brunner and A. H. Meltzer (eds), *Carnegie–Rochester Conference on Public Policy*, **1**, pp. 19–46.

Lucas, R. E. (1977) 'Understanding business cycles', in K. S. Brunner and A. H. Meltzer (eds), *Carnegie–Rochester Conference on Public Policy*, **5**, pp. 7–30.

Lucas, R. E. (1987) *Models of Business Cycles*, Blackwell, Oxford.

Luce, R. D. and Raiffa, H. (1957) *Games and Decisions*, Wiley, New York.

McDonald, I. M. and Solow, R. M. (1981) 'Wage bargaining and employment', *American Economic Review*, **71** (December), 896–908.

MacDonald, R. and Taylor, M. P. (1989) 'Economic analysis of foreign exchange markets: an expository survey', in R. MacDonald and M. P. Taylor (eds), *Exchange Rates and Open Economy Macroeconomics*, Blackwell, Oxford, pp. 4–107.

Machina, M. J. (1987) 'Choice under uncertainty: problems solved and unsolved', *Journal of Economic Perspectives*, **1** (Summer), 121–54.

Malinvaud, E. (1977) *The Theory of Unemployment Reconsidered*, Blackwell, Oxford.

Malinvaud, E. (1984) *Mass Unemployment*, Blackwell, Oxford.

Manning, A. (1990) 'Implicit contract theory', in D. Sapsford and Z. Tzannatos (eds), *Current Issues in Labour Economics*, Macmillan, London.

Metzler, L. A. (1941) 'The nature and stability of inventory cycles', *Review of Economics and Statistics*, **23** (August), 113–29.

Modigliani, F. and Brumberg, R. (1954) 'Utility analysis and the consumption function: an interpretation of cross-section data', in K. K. Kurihara (ed.), *Post-Keynesian Economics*, Rutgers University Press, New Jersey, pp. 388–436.

Morris, D. (ed.) (1985) *The Economic System in the UK*, Oxford University Press, Oxford.

Muellbauer, J. (1983) 'Surprises in the consumption function', *Economic Journal (Supplement)*, **93**, 34–50.

Mussa, M. (1979) 'Empirical regularities in the behaviour of exchange rates and theories of the foreign exchange market', in K. S. Brunner and A. Meltzer (eds), *Carnegie–Rochester Conference on Public Policy*, **11**, pp. 9–58.

Muth, J. F. (1961) 'Rational expectations and the theory of price movements', *Econometrica*, **29** (July), 315–35; reprinted in R. E. Lucas and T. J. Sargent (eds) (1981) *Rational Expectations and Econometric Practice*, Allen & Unwin, London.

Nickell, S. (1990) 'Unemployment: a survey', *Economic Journal*, **100** (June), 391–439.

Oi, W. (1962) 'Labor as a quasi-fixed factor', *Journal of Political Economy*, **70** (December), 538–55.

Pearce, I. F., Trivedi, P. K., Stromback, C. T. and Anderson, G. J. (1976) *A Model of Output, Employment, Wages and Prices in the UK*, Cambridge University Press, Cambridge.

Phelps, E. S. (1990) *Seven Schools of Macroeconomic Thought*, Oxford University Press, Oxford.

Poole, W. (1970) 'The optimal choice of monetary policy instruments in a simple stochastic monetary model', *Quarterly Journal of Economics*, **84** (May), 197–216.

Prescott, E. C. (1986) 'Theory ahead of business cycle measurement', in K. S. Brunner and A. Meltzer (eds), *Carnegie–Rochester Conference on Public Policy*, **23**, pp. 11–44.

Rosen, S. (1985) 'Implicit contracts: a survey', *Journal of Economic Literature*, **23** (September), 1144–75.

Rowthorn, R. E. and Wells, J. R. (1987) *De-Industrialization and Foreign Trade*, Cambridge University Press, Cambridge.

Ryan, T. M. (1978) *Theory of Portfolio Selection*, Macmillan, London.

Sachinides, P. (1991) 'On inflation tax', *Mimeo*, University of Manchester.

Salter, W. E. G. (1960) *Productivity and Technical Change*, Dept of Applied Economics, Monograph No. 6, Cambridge University Press, Cambridge.

Samuelson, P. A. (1939) 'Interactions between the multiplier analysis and the principle of acceleration', *Review of Economics and Statistics*, **21** (May), 75–8.

Sandmo, A. (1971) 'On the theory of the competitive firm under price uncertainty', *American Economic Review*, **61** (March), 65–73.

Sargent, T. J. (1986) *Rational Expectations and Inflation*, Harper & Row, New York.

Sargent, T. J. (1987a) *Macroeconomic Theory* (2nd edn), Academic Press, New York.

Sargent, T. J. (1987b) *Dynamic Macroeconomic Theory*, Harvard University Press, Massachusetts.

Sargent, T. J. and Wallace, N. (1976) 'Rational expectations and the theory of economic policy', *Journal of Monetary Economics*, **2** (April), 169–83.

Shapiro, C. and Stiglitz, J. E. (1984) 'Equilibrium unemployment as a discipline device', *American Economic Review*, **74** (June), 433–44.

Schoemaker, P. J. H. (1982) 'The expected utility model: its variants, purposes, evidence and limitations', *Journal of Economic Literature*, **20** (June), 529–63.

Skidelsky, R. (1983) *John Maynard Keynes: Hopes Betrayed 1883–1920*, Macmillan, London.

Solow, R. M. (1956) 'A contribution to the theory of economic growth', *Quarterly Journal of Economics*, **70** (February), 65–94.

Solow, R. M. (1990) *The Labour Market as a Social Institution*, Blackwell, Oxford.

Spence, M. (1973) 'Job Market Signalling', *Quarterly Journal of Economics*, **87** (August), 355–74.

Spence, M. (1976) 'Competition in salaries, credentials and signalling pre-requisites for jobs', *Quarterly Journal of Economics*, **90** (February), 51–74.

Stevenson, A., Muscatelli, V. and Gregory, M. (1988) *Macroeconomic Theory and Stabilisation Theory*, Allan Oxford.

Stiglitz, J. E. (1987) 'The causes and consequences of the dependence of quality on price', *Journal of Economic Literature*, **25** (March), 1–48.

Swan, T. W. (1956) 'Economic growth and capital accumulation', *Economic Record*, **32** (November), 334–61.

Taylor, J. (1974) *Unemployment and Wage Inflation*, Longman, London.

Taylor, J. B. (1979) 'Staggered wage setting in a macro model', *American Economic Review (Proc.)*, **69** (May), 108–112.

Theil, H. (1968) *Optimal Decision Rules for Government and Industry*, North-Holland, Amsterdam.

Tirole, J. (1988) *The Theory of Industrial Organisation*, MIT Press, Cambridge, Massachusetts.

Tobin, J. (1958) 'Liquidity preference as behaviour towards risk', *Review of Economic Studies*, **25** (February), 65–86.

Walters, A. A. (1971) 'Consistent expectations, distributed lags, and the quantity theory', *Economic Journal*, **81** (June), 273–81.

Winters, A. L. (1985) *International Economics*, Allen & Unwin, London.

Wood, G. H. (1909) 'Real wages and the standard of comfort since 1850', *Journal of the Royal Statistical Society*, **72** (March), 91–103.

Yellen, J. L. (1984) 'Efficiency wage models of unemployment', *American Economic Review (Proc.)*, **74** (May), 200–5.

INDEX